EX·LIBRIS·SUNE·GREGERSEN

CROSS-DISCIPLINARY ISSUES IN COMPOUNDING

AMSTERDAM STUDIES IN THE THEORY AND HISTORY OF LINGUISTIC SCIENCE

General Editor

E.F.K. KOERNER

Zentrum für Allgemeine Sprachwissenschaft, Typologie
und Universalienforschung, Berlin
efk.koerner@rz.hu-berlin.de

Series IV – CURRENT ISSUES IN LINGUISTIC THEORY

Advisory Editorial Board

Lyle Campbell (Salt Lake City)
Sheila Embleton (Toronto)
Elly van Gelderen (Tempe, Ariz.)
Brian D. Joseph (Columbus, Ohio)
John E. Joseph (Edinburgh)
Manfred Krifka (Berlin)
Martin Maiden (Oxford)
E. Wyn Roberts (Vancouver, B.C.)
Joseph C. Salmons (Madison, Wis.)

Volume 311

Edited by Sergio Scalise and Irene Vogel (eds.)

Cross-Disciplinary Issues in Compounding

CROSS-DISCIPLINARY ISSUES IN COMPOUNDING

Edited by

SERGIO SCALISE
University of Bologna

IRENE VOGEL
University of Delaware

JOHN BENJAMINS PUBLISHING COMPANY
AMSTERDAM/PHILADELPHIA

The paper used in this publication meets the minimum requirements of American National Standard for Information Sciences – Permanence of Paper for Printed Library Materials, ANSI z39.48-1984.

Library of Congress Cataloging-in-Publication Data

Cross-disciplinary issues in compounding / edited by Sergio Scalise, Irene Vogel.
      p.   cm. (Amsterdam studies in the theory and history of linguistic science. Series IV, Current Issues in Linguistic Theory, ISSN 0304-0763 ; v. 311)
Includes bibliographical references and index.
  1. Grammar, Comparative and general--Compound words. I. Scalise, Sergio. II. Vogel, Irene, 1952-
P245.C76   2010
415--dc22   2009051898
ISBN 978 90 272 4827 5   (Hb ; alk. paper)
ISBN 978 90 272 9089 2   (Eb)

© 2010 – John Benjamins B.V.
No part of this book may be reproduced in any form, by print, photoprint, microfilm, or any other means, without written permission from the publisher.

John Benjamins Publishing Co. · P.O. Box 36224 · 1020 ME Amsterdam · The Netherlands
John Benjamins North America · P.O. Box 27519 · Philadelphia PA 19118-0519 · USA

Table of contents

Acknowledgments	VII
Why compounding? *Sergio Scalise and Irene Vogel*	1

PART I. Delimiting the field

The role of syntax and morphology in compounding *Peter Ackema and Ad Neeleman*	21
Constraints on compounds and incorporation *Marianne Mithun*	37
Compounding versus derivation *Angela Ralli*	57

PART II. At the core of compounding

Units in compounding *Fabio Montermini*	77
Compound construction: Schemas or analogy? A construction morphology perspective *Geert Booij*	93
The head in compounding *Sergio Scalise and Antonio Fábregas*	109
On the lexical semantics of compounds: Non-affixal (de)verbal compounds *Rochelle Lieber*	127
The phonology of compounds *Irene Vogel*	145

PART III. Typology and types of compounds

The typology of exocentric compounding　　　167
　Laurie Bauer

Coordination in compounding　　　177
　Giorgio F. Arcodia, Nicola Grandi and Bernhard Wälchli

Parasynthetic compounds: Data and theory　　　199
　Chiara Melloni and Antonietta Bisetto

Synthetic compounds: With special reference to German　　　219
　Livio Gaeta

Corpus data and theoretical implications: With special reference
to Italian V-N compounds　　　237
　Davide Ricca

PART IV. Quantitative and psycholinguistic aspects of compounding

Frequency effects in compound processing　　　257
　R. Harald Baayen, Victor Kuperman and Raymond Bertram

Computational issues in compound processing　　　271
　Vito Pirrelli, Emiliano Guevara and Marco Baroni

Relational competition during compound interpretation　　　287
　Christina L. Gagné and Thomas L. Spalding

Sign languages and compounding　　　301
　Irit Meir, Mark Aronoff, Wendy Sandler and Carol A. Padden

First language acquisition of compounds: With special emphasis
on early German child language　　　323
　Wolfgang U. Dressler, Laura E. Lettner and Katharina Korecky-Kröll

List of abbreviations　　　345
Master list of references　　　349
Language index　　　377
Subject index　　　379

Acknowledgments

Cross-Disciplinary Issues in Compounding comes as a response to the strong interest in compounds and issues related to compounds that have been developing in the last few years. At the core of this interest is the question of where and how compounds fit into the grammar, and in this respect, the ways in which compounds challenge our view of the organization and architecture of the language capacity more generally.

To address such issues, a conference was organized in Bologna, Italy in June 2008, representing the conjunction of two large research projects: Componet and ENLM. The Componet project (http://componet.sslmit.unibo.it/), with its center at the University of Bologna, has offered a home to a very fruitful research effort dedicated to compounds, in particular their description across a wide range of languages. A database consisting of information on approximately 30 languages is in the process of being developed with the intention of making access available to the entire linguistics community. The European Network for Linguistic Morphology, whose center is also in Bologna, is a project that has brought together major European research centers with the goal of addressing issues of morphology in a broader sense, including psycholinguistics, language acquisition and computational approaches. It was in the context of the activities of these two projects that the idea for the 2008 Bologna conference was developed, and ultimately brought to fruition. In keeping with the broad interests of the projects, speakers were invited to participate in diverse areas with respect to languages studied as well as to areas of research- theoretical linguistics as well as issues in sign language and language acquisition, and quantitative and typological analytical approaches.

The present volume, thus, has its origins in relation to the Bologna conference. It has aimed at retaining the cross-linguistic and inter-disciplinary approach to compounds, however, it represents a significantly revised and restructured contribution to the field. A selection of the topics covered at the conference was made so as to yield a well-rounded book, not simply a series of conference papers. To this end, too, the authors of the chapters of this book substantially revised their contributions so that they were more generally authoritative with respect to their topic, providing both a strong background and interesting original research.

The Master list of references collects the references of all of the individual contributions, and thus serves as a unified, up-to-date and quite complete list of literature on compounds, from the wide variety of perspectives present in the book. This, in itself, will serve as a valuable resource for researchers interested in issues related to compounding.

In order to make the Bologna conference, as well as this volume a success, scholars came from around the world — from New Zealand to the USA and Canada, among others. We extend our thanks to all the participants.

We would like to especially thank the Magnifico Rettore of the University of Bologna, Pierugo Calzolari, for establishing our research office, and the staff of this office for all of their assistance

Last but not least, we would also like to thank all the people who served as anonymous reviewers of the chapters of this book — spending part of their summer vacation to help make this volume as successful and complete as possible. In addition, we are grateful to Francesca Forza, Emiliano Guevara and Hillary Schepps for their outstanding help with the editing of individual papers. Finally, we extend our thanks to Prof. E.F.K. Koerner for his insightful and invaluable help and patience during the process of editing this book, and to the various staff members at John Benjamins, in particular Anke de Looper, who have helped with technical matters.

Bologna & Newark, Delaware, 12 September 2009   Sergio Scalise & Irene Vogel

Why compounding?

Sergio Scalise and Irene Vogel
University of Bologna and University of Delaware

1. Introduction

The study of compounds is currently at the center of attention in all areas of linguistics – both theoretical and applied. In our introduction to this book, we discuss the reasons compounds have been considered so important, and why it is interesting to advance hypotheses not only regarding the construction of compounds, but also where they fit into the model of grammar, and what aspects of compounds still present the most challenges within different areas and frameworks.

The importance of compounding to our understanding of language was very clear to Greenberg (1963: 92), who stated

(1) "There are probably no languages without either compounding, affixing, or both. In other words, there are probably no purely isolating languages. There are a considerable number of languages without inflection, perhaps none without compounding and derivation."

Although it has recently been claimed that there are languages without compounds,[1] it remains true that compounding is a fundamental process of word formation. Indeed, in some languages, it is the only one.

In what follows we will discuss the following issues with regard to compounds: (a) why they have been attracting so much attention in theoretical linguistics, (b) where they are formed in the grammar, (c) their definition, (d) their classification, (e) headedness and exocentricity and (f) the lexical categories involved.

---

1. Stekauer, Valera & Körtvélyessy (2008), for example, have recently claimed that in their corpus of 55 languages 'only' 50 languages have compounds. Languages that these authors claim lack compounds include East Dangla, Karao, West Greenlandic, Diola Fogny, and Kwak'wala.

2. The interest of compounds

Compounds are particularly interesting linguistic constructions for a number of reasons. First, they constitute an anomaly among grammatical constructions because they are 'words', but at the same time exhibit a type of 'internal syntax'. This syntax, furthermore, is somewhat 'invisible'. This can be seen in the following three compounds:

(2) a. taxi driver
    b. hard ball
    c. poet painter

In order to interpret these compounds one must 'add' a syntactic relation between the two constituents (i.e. driver <u>of a</u> taxi, a ball <u>which is</u> hard, poet <u>and</u> painter); the 'internal syntax' is not overtly present.[2]

Compounds, furthermore, represent a contact point between several crucial linguistic and non-linguistic notions such as those in (3):

(3) a. syntagmatic and paradigmatic relationships
    b. syntax and morphology
    c. linguistic knowledge and pragmatic knowledge

As for (3a), observe that in a compound such as *taxi driver* there is not only a 'relation' between the two constituents, but a special one: *taxi* is the internal argument of the verb *drive*. The verb in effect 'selects' its own argument[3] (i.e. a form like **appledriver* would be ungrammatical), and this selection is a syntagmatic relationship.

In addition to syntagmatic relations observed in compounds, we also find the situation in which a number of compounds appear to present a type of paradigmatic class (or compound family). That is to say, the head appears to constitute a source of 'attraction' for elements leading to the construction of many other compounds. This can be seen with the Italian word *capo* 'chief', in the series of items listed in (4):

(4) capostazione   'station master'
    capoclasse   'head of the class'
    capogruppo   'head of the group'
    caposcuola   'head of school'
    capofila   'head of the line'

With regard to (3b), it has often been observed that compounds are the morphological constructions that are closest to syntactic constructions. Consequently, there is no general agreement on which component of the grammar is responsible for their formation (see Ackema & Neeleman, this volume). In relation to (3c), a simple example

---

2. Jackendoff (2009) observed that "Compounds can show evidence of a little internal syntactic structure," e.g. a conjunction in *[health and welfare] fund*.

3. See Scalise, Bisetto & Guevara (2005).

will suffice. As pointed out by Jackendoff (2009), in order to understand that *bike girl* refers to 'a girl who left the bike in the vestibule', we not only need linguistic information but also contextual information so as to exclude other possible interpretations such as 'a girl who habitually goes to work by bike'.

Compounds are additionally interesting because they exhibit what Pirrelli (2002) has called "weak compositionality." That is to say, the meaning of a compound may have a range of possible meanings, as well as a range of meanings that are not possible, as observed earlier by Allen (1978).[4] Examples of such ranges of meaning with respect to *water mill* are shown in (5a) and (5b). Crucially, the range of acceptable interpretations is most often dictated by paradigmatic relations holding between members of the same compound family, rather than by combinatorial principles of syntactic composition:

(5) a. mill powered by water
    mill located by water
    mill for producing water
  b. mill which grinds water
    mill which drinks water
    mill made out of water

Moreover, the study of compounds is of interest in psycholinguistics, in particular in relation to the mental lexicon (see Gagné & Spalding, this volume). Libben (2006: IX) formulates some of the questions in this area as follows:

(6) "What are the psychological mechanisms that allow such free creation? Are the production and comprehension processes involved the same for both existing lexicalized words and novel combinations? How are these processes related to other lexical and non-lexical processes? When are they acquired? How are they compromised by damage to the brain? How might they differ across languages? What shape might compound processing take among bilinguals?"

Finally, it has recently been proposed that compounds provide insight into the early stages of language evolution, being relics of a protolanguage as Jackendoff (2009: 113) points out:

(7) "This view of modern language as 'laid over' a protolinguistic substrate leads to the intriguing possibility that the coverage is not complete: that there exist pockets of modern language that are relics of earlier stages of the language capacity. Such relics would be areas where there is only rudimentary

---

4. The range of possible meanings is much greater in some languages than in others. Delfitto & Melloni (2009: 80) for example observe that Germanic languages, as opposed to Romance languages, have a relatively large range of interpretative freedom, "whereby the semantics of compounds only depends on context-related encyclopedic information." Thus, *tree man* could refer to 'a man who is standing beside a tree'; 'a man who is sitting in a tree'; 'a man who usually sits in trees'; 'a man who defends trees or forests'; 'a man who resembles a tree', and so on.

grammatical structure, and in which such grammatical structure as there is does not do much to shape semantic interpretation. Rather, we would expect semantic interpretation to be highly dependent on the pragmatics of the words being combined and on the contextual specifics of use. I suggest that compounding fills the bill completely."

One might also maintain, however, that compound formation fulfills a communicative strategy that is intrinsically different from that of syntactic expressions and, therefore, their existence could be motivated by human communication purposes.[5] That is, compounding is a manifestation of the tendency towards multiword constructions such as idioms, collocations, binomial constructions, or the so-called prefabs.

3. Where are compounds formed?

The question of which component of grammar is responsible for the formation of compounds is complex, and the answers that have been proposed are quite varied. This can be seen in the following, most likely not exhaustive, list:

(8) Compounds are formed through transformations and deletion of lexical material
(Lees 1960)
Compounds are formed by Morphological Rules in a specific morphological component (Lexicalist Morphology, Scalise 1984).
Compounds are formed by syntactic rules 'all the way down'
(Harley & Noyer 1999)
Complex words are generated in an independent morphological submodule
(Ackema & Neeleman 2004)
Compounding is a type of incorporation into an acategorial root, in a framework in which word-formation is treated purely syntactically
(Distributed Morphology, Harley 2009).
Compounds are formed by filling available slots in lexical templates
(Construction Morphology, Booij 2009)

We will not discuss all of these positions, but we would like to point out that there is evidence in favor of a basic framework in which morphological facts are handled by a morphological module, or submodule, of the grammar. The relevant evidence comes from a variety of sources: psycholinguistics (experiments show that compounds are stored in the lexicon and storage cannot be a property of the syntactic component[6]), neurolinguistics (aphasic studies provide evidence for the application of compound

---

5. An attempt to answer the question 'Why are compounds part of human language?' is found in Di Sciullo (2009).
6. See Gagné & Spalding (2009); Plag, Kunter & Lappe (2007).

formation rules[7]), and theoretical linguistics (compounding shares many properties with derivation such as allomorphy, linking elements and furthermore stress patterns of compounds may differ systematically from those of phrases).

4. Definition of compound

In spite of the growing interest in compounds, there is no satisfactory definition for 'compound', as in fact there is no uncontroversial definition of other basic units such as 'word' or 'sentence'. Although we cannot review all of the literature on this topic,[8] some examples of attempts to define 'compound' elucidate the difficulties we face:

(9) a. A word-sized unit containing two or more **roots** (Harley 2009: 130)
 b. A lexical unit made up of two or more **elements**, each of which can function as a **lexeme** independent of the other(s) in other contexts, and which shows some phonological and/or grammatical isolation from normal syntactic usage (Bauer 2001: 695)
 c. [...] a compound word contains at least two bases which are both **words**, or at any rate, **root morphemes** (Katamba 1993: 54)
 d. A complex lexeme that can be thought of as consisting of two or more **lexemes** (Haspelmath 2202: 85)
 e. Its defining property is that it consists of the combination of **lexeme**s into larger words. In simple cases, compounding consists of the combination of two **words**, in which one word modifies the meaning of the other, the head (Booij 2005: 75)
 f. Composition [...] denotes the combining of two **free forms** or **stems** to form a new complex word referred to as compound (Olsen 2000: 280)
 g. [...] root compounds consist of two **stems** combined as one, with the compound as a whole bearing the category and morphosyntactic features of the right-hand stem (Lieber 2004: 47)
 h. When two or more **words** are combined into a morphological unit, we speak of a compound (Marchand 1960: 11)

The following general observation can be drawn from the above definitions: in the majority of the proposals, the definition of 'compound' coincides with the definition of the units that form a compound (see Montermini, this volume). However, this fact raises new problems. First, there is no agreement about which units are the basic ones in compounding, since different authors propose different units such as stems, roots, lexemes, and words. Moreover 'stem' must be identified differently in different languages (e.g. in English stems are typically free forms; in Greek they are bound forms

---

7. See Mondini, Jarema, Luzzatti, Burani, & Semenza (2002).
8. See most recently a comprehensive discussion in Lieber & Stekauer (2009: 4 ff.).

(Ralli 2007)). Furthermore, words can be typically monomophemic in some languages but bi-or plurimorphemic in others, etc.

Donalies (2004: 76)[9] attempts to define compounds by combining a number of criteria. Specifically, compounds are (a) complex, (b) formed without word-formation affixes, (c) spelled together, (d) right headed, (e) inflected as a whole, (f) syntactically inseparable, (g) syntacto-semantic islands, and (h) conceptual units. In addition, they may have specific stress patterns and include linking elements.

Lieber & Stekauer (2009) show, however, that even such a long list of properties fails to define compounds unequivocally. In addition to their criticism, we might add the observation that there are counter-examples to some of the proposed defining properties of compounds. With regard to (b), we observe that compounds may contain affixes (e.g. *blue eyed*). Contrary to (d), compounds are not always right headed (e.g. in Romance languages they are left headed); and contrary to e) compounds may exhibit plural inflection on one of the constituents yet still be singular (e.g. It. *portalettere* 'carry letters, mailman').

From a different perspective, a recent definition of compounds has been proposed by Guevara and Scalise (2009), according to which a compound is defined in categorial terms as in (10), where X, Y and Z are lexical categories and 'r' is the (hidden) grammatical relation between the two constituents.

(10) $[\text{X r Y}]_Z$

This definition assumes that the constituents of a compound - roots, stems, lexemes or words - have a lexical category. Z may be the same as X or Y or different from both, which gives rise to the following three patterns:

(11)   a. $[\text{X r Y}]_Y$ is a compound with the head to the right
       b. $[\text{X r Y}]_X$ is a compound with the head to the left
       c. $[\text{X r Y}]_Z$ is an exocentric compound[10]

For completeness, this definition must in addition be coupled with certain prototypical features of compounding. Based on current theories, the relevant assumptions include the following: (a) that compounds observe syntactic atomicity and lexical integrity, (b) that the constituents are members of major lexical categories, and (c) that the head is lexical (while the non-head may be lexical or phrasal).

---

9.   Cited in Lieber & Stekauer (2009: 6).

10.   There can be also $[\text{X r Y}]_Y$ or $[\text{X r Y}]_X$ structures that are exocentric such as $[[\text{red}]_A [\text{skin}]_N]_N$, or the Italian form $[[\text{pelle}]_N [\text{rossa}]_A]_N$ 'red skin'.

5. Classification of compounds

Classifying compounds also presents a number of challenges. In fact, every textbook of morphology seems to propose its own classification. Let us consider here a recent proposal by Scalise & Bisetto (2009) represented as follows:

(12)

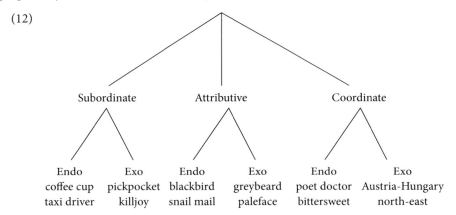

The first classificatory level in this proposal is based only on the grammatical relation between the two constituents (the 'r' seen above in (10)). The types of relations found in compounds are comparable to those in syntax:

a. **Subordinate:** the two constituents have a relation of "*complementation*," which is particularly evident in deverbal compounds (*taxi driver*), but also in N+N compounds (*apron string*)
b. **Attributive:** the grammatical relation is of *attribution*, typically A+N or N+A structures (e.g. *high school, ice cold*). N+N structures may also be attributive. In *snail mail*, for example, the only information carried by the non head *snail* relevant for the interpretation of the compound is 'slow'. The non-head noun has thus an attributive value.
c. **Coordinate:** the relation between the two constituents is one of *coordination*, typically conjunctive coordination (*poet painter*). Within this classification, two other types of compounds can be accommodated: phrasal compounds and the so-called neoclassical compounds shown in (13a) and (13b), respectively.

(13) a. Af. [lach of ik schiet] humor 'smile or I shoot mood'
　　　　 Eng. [floor of a birdcage] taste
　　 b. Eng. anthropology
　　　　 It. odontotecnico 'lit. tooth technician'
　　　　 It. colorificio 'lit. color factory'

The compounds in (13a) can be paraphrased as 'aggressive mood' and 'terrible taste' so their semantic interpretation is akin to what we have called 'attributive compounds'. The compounds in (13b), on the other hand, can be paraphrased as 'the study of man', 'a technician of teeth' and 'factory of colors', and can be considered subordinate compounds according to the definition given above.

6. Headedness

There are numerous questions concerning the head of a compound, which include, but are not limited to, the following: Are morphological heads similar to syntactic heads? How can we identify the morphological head? What properties percolate from the head? We will not address these questions here since they are discussed in specific chapters of this book (e.g. Scalise & Fábregas, this volume), but instead we will comment here only on the issue of identifying the position of the head. As can be seen in (14), a number of different proposals have been advanced in this regard.

(14) the head is on the right (the 'Right Hand Head Rule' of Williams 1981)
the head can be a *relativized* head (Di Sciullo & Williams 1987)
languages can have the head either on the right or on the left (Scalise 1992)
there are languages where the head can be either on the right or on the left according to the compound structure (Packard 2000; Ceccagno & Basciano 2007)

The complexity of even this one question demonstrates that understanding the linguistic facts relating to the head of compounds will not result from a simple or sudden discovery, but instead requires continuous refinement of hypotheses, contingent on analyses of an increasing body of data.

7. Exocentricity

At first glance it might seem that exocentricity is a marginal pattern in compounding, and may thus be relegated to the so-called 'periphery' of the language. It turns out instead, that it is not uncommon across languages, and must be considered a core component of compounding (see Bauer, this volume). The MorboComp database[11] gives the following figures regarding the position of the head, and the absence of a head - the exocentric compounds - based on a sample of 23 languages (Table 1 below).

Although right-headed compounds are by far the most prevalent type of compound, exocentric compounds are the second most frequent type. Interestingly, different languages or linguistic groups exhibit different percentages of exocentric compounds, however, the general tendency for them to follow right-headed compounds in frequency is observed across the groups in the sample, as shown in Table 2.

---

11. This is the morphological database developed at the University of Bologna. For details, see Footnote 1 in Scalise & Fabregas, this volume.

Table 1. Frequency of compound types with different head positions

	General %
Right	66.7
No head	16.3
Left	6.8
Both	5.9

Table 2. Frequency of compound types with different head positions in different language groups

	General %	Rom %	Germ %	Slav %	East A. %
Right	66.7	40,7	87,0	61,9	57,5
No head	16.3	31,4	8,9	12,2	17,7
Left	6.8	20,3	1,9	6,0	6,8
Both	5.9	6,8	1,3	3,1	15,0

As can be seen, the Slavic group follows the general pattern more closely than the other groups. The Romance languages exhibit a relatively high percentage of exocentric constructions, while Germanic languages are more consistently right-headed. The East Asian languages are different in allowing a relatively high percentage of compounds with two heads, most of which are coordinate compounds.

In languages such as Italian, the exocentric pattern V+N is one of the most productive processes in compound formation. In some languages we also find a pattern that has been called 'absolute exocentricity' (Scalise, Fabregas & Forza 2009), from both a categorial and semantic point of view. In such compounds, the output category is entirely different from the categories of the constituents, as illustrated in (15) for Chinese, Turkish and Italian.

(15) A+A = N   Ch.   大小 dàxiǎor   'large small = size'
     A+A = Adv Tu.   aptal aptal   'stupid stupid = in a stupid way'
     V+V = N   It.   sali scendi   'go up, go down = elevator'

Despite their relative frequency, exocentric compounds have generally been viewed as a problem for morphological theory, since it is necessary to account for information present in the whole structure that is not present in the constituents. In fact, this has led to a number of analyses in which endocentric readings have been proposed for such compounds. For example, Bisetto (1999) claims that the Romance V+N compounds such as the Italian *portalettere,* seen above, is endocentric on the assumption that there is a null nominalizing suffix after the verb expressing the meaning of *portatore di lettere* 'carrier of letters'. Booij (2005) claims that a different type of exocentric compound, exemplified by *redskin*, can also be considered endocentric. In this case, the explanation offered is that there is a metonymic relation between the whole compound and the constituent in the head position. Even if such accounts work in certain cases, exocentricity has been found to be relatively common across languages, and not a marginal phenomenon.

8. Lexical categories

Traditional work on compounds has focused primarily on two structures: N+N compounds, the so-called root compounds, and N+V+Suf compounds, the so-called synthetic (or verbal nexus) compounds. This has left numerous other types of compounds relatively understudied. Based on the sample of 23 languages, we find a total of 110 compound types, shown in Table 3. In fact, there are many additional types of compounds in the languages of the world.

While N+N is the most frequent compound structure (20% of the sample),[12] it is nevertheless the case that 80% of the corpus consists of different types of compounds, including complex words that are compounded and derived, compounds formed with pronouns, adverbs and numerals, many types of compounds formed with so-called semiwords[13] (sN, sA), and compounds containing phrases, usually as non-heads. Ultimately, all attested types of compounds must be thoroughly investigated.

9. Input, output and combination of categories

Looking more closely at the lexical categories involved in compounds (as either the first or the second constituent), we find the distribution shown in Table 4.

As can be seen, there is a clear hierarchy with respect to the relative frequency of the different categories of compounds:

(16) N > A > V > Adv > P

With regard to the output categories, we find the distribution shown in Table 5.

Interestingly, the order of preference of the output categories is exactly the same as that of the input categories seen in (16). It should be noted, however, that Noun is substantially lower as an input category than it is as an output category. Adjectives and verbs are also fairly frequent as outputs, although it turns out that their distribution varies somewhat across languages.

---

12. For these and subsequent figures, cf. Guevara & Scalise (2009).

13. Semiwords (often called 'affixoids') are items from Greek or Latin origin such as *logo-*, *anemo-*, etc. (Scalise 1984).

Table 3. Types of compound structures

MorboComp - All structures (110 different combinations) - ordered by incidence

[N+N]	[Num+N]	[sN+sA]	[P+N+SufN]	[N+N+SufA]	[A+PP]	[Num+Num+N]
[A+N]	[N+Ple]	[P+N+SufA]	[Num+V]	[N+N+A]	[A+A+SufN]?	[N+sP]
[N+A]	[A+N+SufA]	[Adv+P]	[Num+N+SufN]	[Adv+V+SufA]	[sW+A]	[N+sA]
[A+A]	[Pro+N]	[A+N+SufN]	[N+sW]	[Adv+Ple]	[sA+A]	[N+Adv]
[V+N]	[NP+N]	[Pro+V]	[sA+sN]	[A+[N+N]]	[[[Neg+V]+N]+SufN]	[Conj+Adv]
[N+V]	[sN+N]	[PP+N]	[XP+N]	[A+Ple]	[V+N+SufA]	[Adv+extN]
[V+V]	[Adv+Adv]	[N+V+SufN]	[V+V+SufN]	[V+Conj+V]	[Prt+Pro]	[Adv+Pro]
[Adv+A]	[sW+sW]	[CP+N]	[V+Prt]	[P+Adv]	[Prt+Adv]	[Adv+PP]
[sN+sN]	[P+A]	[P+V]	[V+Pro]	[A+sW]	[Pro+V+SufN]	[Adv+Conj+Adv]
[Adv+N]	[Pro+A]	[Num+N+SufA]	[V+N+SufAdv]	[A+Wh]	[Pro+V+SufA]	[A+V/N]
[N+PP]	[Num+A]	[N+sA/sN]	[V+DP]	[sA+N]	[Pro+Prt]	[A+N/V]
[A+V]	[sW+N]	[VP+N]	[Prt+Ple]	[[A+N]+N]	[Pro+Pro]	[A+Adv]
[V+A]	[Prt+V]	[N+N+SufN]	[Prefixlike+A]	[Num+Num]	[Pro+N+SufA]	[A+A+SufN]
[P+N]	[sN+A]	[V+N+SufN]	[Ple+N]	[N+N+N]	[Pro+Adv]	[A+A+N]
[N+sN]	[V+Adv]	[N+Conj+N]	[Num+V+SufA]	[Adv+N+SufAdv]	[PP+V]	
[Adv+V]	[P+P]	[A+A+A]	[N+V+SufA]	[AP+N]	[P+A+N]	

Table 4. Input categories of compounds

Input category	Percent
N	42.12
A	22.39
V	14.00
Adv	5.84
P	2.45

Table 5. Output categories of compounds

Output category	Percent
N	52.91
A	26.79
V	10.97
Adv	5.40
P	0.41

Table 6. Category combinations in compounds

Combination	Percent	Combination	Percent
[N+N]	20.02	[N+V]	4.08
[A+N]	8.79	[V+V]	3.51
[A+A]	7.75	[Adv+N]	2.37
[N+A]	7.58	[A+V]	2.21
[V+N]	6.22	[Adv+A]	1.85

Finally, if we consider the combinations of categories, we find that the ten most frequent patterns are those shown in Table 6.

As can be seen, the combination N+N is more than twice as frequent as the next combination, A+N. In fact, among the ten types of compound in Table 6, we might identify three levels of preference, shown in (17).

(17) a. [N+N] >
b. [A+N] > [N+A] > [A+A] > [V+N] >
c. [N+V] > [V+V] > (…)

Thus, while there are many different types of compounds, there are only a few types that can be said to be fairly common.

10. Conclusion

This brief examination of the core issues related to compounding shows the richness and complexity of the topic – and thus why we believe it is important to publish this book on compounding. As was pointed out, there are challenges relating to compounds at all levels (i.e. phonological (see Vogel, this volume), morphological (see Booij, Ralli, this volume), syntactic (see Ackema & Neeleman, this volume), semantics (see Lieber, this volume)) and across a variety of sub-fields (e.g. typology (see Arcodia, Grandi & Wälchli, this volume), psycholinguistics (see Gagné & Spalding, this volume), acquisition of language (see Dressler et al., this volume) and Sign Language (see Meir et al. this volume) computational linguistics (see Pirrelli et al. this volume)). Compounds, moreover, present challenges with regard to demarcation in relation to incorporation (see Mithun, this volume), and to derivation (see Ralli, this volume). Finally, compounds exhibit an impressive range of different constructions (see Booij, Melloni & Bisetto, Gaeta, Ricca, this volume). The papers in this volume address many of these challenges, and begin to fill in lacunae in their respective areas.

11. Summary of book chapters

The chapters of this book are organized into four parts. The first part, *Delimiting the Field*, addresses issues that relate to the basic nature of compounding – and in particular, precisely which phenomena should be included in this category and why, and which phenomena should not be included. In the second part, *At the Core of Compounding*, the papers address the fundamental theoretical issues associated with compounding from the perspectives of different areas of grammar. The third part of the book, *Typology and Types of Compounds*, introduces more specific issues relating to the classification and specific types of compounds in a variety of languages. Finally, in the last section, *Quantitative and Psycholinguistic Aspects of Compounding*, the contributions show extensions of the main theoretical and typological issues that have been previously presented to more applied realms involving quantitative analyses as well as sign language and language acquisition. Given the inter-relatedness of many of the contributions, unified subject and language indexes, and a single list of abbreviations and list of references can be found at the end of the book.

11.1 Delimiting the field

This first part of the book opens with a paper by **Peter Ackema and Ad Neeleman** on "The role of syntax and morphology in compounding." In this paper, the controversy of whether compound formation is a syntactic or a morphological operation is addressed, and the position is advanced that there is a crucial competition between the two components of grammar. Ackema and Neeleman support their position on the basis of data from the development of Saramaccan and other creole languages.

The next paper, "Compounding and incorporation," by **Marianne Mithun**, also concerns itself with issues related to the morphological vs. syntactic nature of compounding, in particular with relation to the phenomenon of noun incorporation. Data from Kapampangan, Mohawk, and Central Alaskan Yup'ik Eskimo are analyzed and it is shown that all of the structures under investigation share a number of fundamental formal and functional features, including (a) the combining of a verbal and a nominal element to form a new verb headed by the verbal element, (b) their classification as endocentric and synthetic structures, and (c) the expression of a range of semantic relationships between the incorporated noun and the verb. Crucially, however, the three languages show differences with regard to two core morphological principles, the No Phrase Constraint and the Lexical Integrity Hypothesis. It is proposed that observation of these principles in the different languages in question allows us to identify different stages in diachronic development. At one end, representing an early stage, we find the Kapampangan constructions with their more syntactic and less integrated formations. At the other end, we find the Yup'ik derivational construction in which certain verb roots that recurred frequently as heads of noun-verb compounds have eventually become more general and abstract in meaning, and less phonologically transparent. The constructions in Mohawk fall at an intermediate stage between these two end points.

Another challenge in delimiting the phenomenon of compounding, more specifically within the field of morphology, is addressed in the paper by **Angela Ralli**, "Compounding versus derivation." As the title suggests, the challenge discussed here is that of drawing the line between phenomena involving affixation, in particular derivation, and those that belong to the realm of compound formation. The data that serve as the basis for the present paper come from Standard Modern Greek and its dialects. Examination of such issues as the application and ordering of compounding and derivational processes, and the status of certain items as words or affixes in different dialects, leads Ralli to conclude that the only way the observed patterns can be accounted for is if the phenomena in question are interspersed. The only way this can be done is if both types of word formation phenomena are considered morphological.

11.2 At the core of compounding

This part of the book focuses on theoretical issues relating to compounding that arise within the different components of the grammar. The first paper of this section, **Fabio Montermini**'s "Units in compounding," to some extent continues the discussion about the fine line, or perhaps fuzzy line, between morphological and syntactic aspects of compounds. Specifically, Montermini raises the questions of what structures constitute compounds, and what the linguistic units are that make up the compounds. A word-based approach is adopted, and based on a cross-linguistic sample of data, it is proposed that compounding results in constructions that are lexical units, like those of derivation, but it also constructs items that cannot be considered lexical. We are thus led to the conclusion that compounding must be viewed as a case of mismatch between morphology and syntax.

Another theoretical concern regarding compounds is raised in the chapter by **Geert Booij**, "Compound construction: Schemas or analogy? A construction morphology perspective," The issue investigated here is the relationship between analogy and abstract schemas in the formation of compounds. It is argued that, in fact, there is no clear boundary between the two phenomena, but rather that they represent endpoints on a scale of schematicity. Between these points, we find a series of subschemas based on such properties as semantic specialization, variation in headedness, diachrony and the selection of allomorphs.

Scalise & Fábregas, in their chapter "The head in compounding", analyze the concept of head and provide a review of the conceptual and empirical problems that have been raised in this regard in recent years. Several such issues are semantic exocentricity (e.g. *pale face*), categorial exocentricity (i.e. where lexemes belonging to a particular grammatical category give rise to a word belonging to a different category), and what the authors call 'morphological exocentricity' (i.e. where morphological properties of a compound such as gender or conjugation class are distinct from those of its internal components). A proposal advanced here on the basis of a sample of compounds taken from the MorBoComp database suggests that morphological operations cannot take place in the phonological component of the grammar, in contrast with Distributed Morphology. Instead, different constituents inside a compound itself must contain the features responsible for the different properties of the word. This leads to the generalization with regard to the architecture of morphological theories that morphologically exocentric compounds are cross-linguistically also semantically exocentric.

The issue of the semantics of compounds is examined in **Rochelle Lieber's** paper "On the lexical semantics of compounds: Non-affixal (de)verbal compounds." This paper focuses on a particular, relatively understudied, type of English construction referred to as "Non-affixal (de)verbal compounds". These compounds consist of a noun and a verb, or noun derived from a verb, a combination also associated with synthetic compounds. It is argued, however, that Non-affixal (de)verbal compounds are crucially different from synthetic compounds in that they tend to exhibit a subject oriented interpretation.

The last chapter of this part of the book is **Irene Vogel's** "The phonology of compounds". It is shown that while the usual view of compounds is that the components, Phonological Words, tend to exhibit their own properties, there are in fact a number of phonological phenomena that can be seen as characteristic of compounds as a whole. These include rules that apply at the juncture of the member of compounds as well as phenomena such as stress and tone that apply throughout entire compounds. In addition, problems associated with the nature of the prosodic structure of the components of compounds as well as that of compounds as a whole are addressed. Data are examined in a wide range of languages including Dagbani, Dutch, English, Fijian, Hausa, Italian, and Portuguese.

11.3 Typology and types of compounds

The third part of the book looks more in detail at different types as well as the distribution of compound formations. The first chapter, "The typology of exocentric compounding" by **Laurie Bauer** explores what types of exocentric compounds can be discerned in linguistic descriptions currently available and whether exocentric compounds can be seen as marginal types. Based on a sample of over 50 languages, the author reports that there were surprisingly few recurrent major patterns of exocentric compounds. He discusses each of these types, but also cautions, however, that there may be additional, less common types, that are not reported in basic grammars. In-depth work with linguistic informants would be required to probe such possibilities in future work.

"Coordination in compounding," by **Giorgio Francesco Arcodia, Nicola Grandi and Bernhard Wälchli** is concerned with the expression of coordination relations in compounds. Two general types of compounds are identified with this regard, hyperonymic coordinating compounds (co-compounds), and hyponymic coordinate compounds, and their areal distribution is examined and found to be rather skewed. While the former are common in the Eastern part of Eurasia, New Guinea and Mesoamerica, they seem to be absent in Standard Average European languages, where hyponymic coordinate compounds are found instead. The two types of compounds appear to be in a complementary distribution: languages seem to choose either one or the other kind to be expressed by means of compounding, leaving the other type of coordination for syntax.

Chiara Melloni and Antonietta Bisetto address a different type of compound formation in "Parasynthetic compounds: Data and theory." Specifically, they examine the formation of parasynthetic compounds, constructed via the addition of a derivational suffix to a combination of two lexical stems, though this combination itself is a non-attested form. They present data from a number of Slavic, Romance and Germanic languages, as well as several other languages, and use these data as the basis for the comparison between a Construction Morphology account and a configurational analysis. The authors conclude that for their data, and for Indo-European languages in general, a configurational analysis is to be preferred, as the Construction Morphology analysis cannot adequately account for the observed compound formation patterns.

The chapter by **Livio Gaeta**, "Synthetic compounds: With special reference to German," also makes use of a large corpus as the basis of its analysis. The analysis is based on a large text corpus, which offers the possibility of examining in depth a highly productive word formation process of German, synthetic compounding, from several perspectives. It is argued that while a syntactic approach to these formations falls short, the lexical approach of Construction Morphology is able to account for fine-grained distributional patterns and complex relationships exhibited between the deverbal head and nominal modifier in these constructions.

Davide Ricca's chapter, "Corpus data and theoretical implications: With special reference to Italian VN compounds," demonstrates the usefulness of a quantitative approach to the analysis of compounding. The focus is Italian verb+noun compounds, taken from a large newspaper corpus. It is shown that the use of a particularly large corpus is important in evaluating the proposed morphological and phonological constraints on the compounds in question. Moreover, it provides the opportunity of observing a word formation process at work in a language, and the distinction between production and lexicalization or lexical storage of compounds, which, it is suggested, could be relevant for other types of morphological processes as well.

11.4 Quantitative and psycholinguistic aspects of compounding

Harald Baayen, Victor Kuperman and Raymond Bertram, in "Frequency effects in compound processing," present evidence from a number of different types of studies that the processing and understanding of compounds is more complex than originally assumed. Specifically, data are considered from large-scale visual lexical decision and visual word naming studies carried out with English compounds, as well as a reanalysis of an eye-tracking study of compound processing in Dutch. Generalized additive regression modeling, using a number of different frequency measures (compound token frequency, head and modifier token frequency, and head and modifier compound family type counts), indicates that staged models of compound interpretation are inadequate, and that a more complex and dynamic system of processing is involved.

In "Computational issues in compound processing", **Vito Pirrelli, Emiliano Guevara and Marco Baroni** point out that from the computational perspective, understanding compounds is a particularly challenging area of investigation. In fact, it falls at the intersection of issues relating to their representation, the architecture of grammar and algorithmic processing, and involves such matters as (a) the identification of compounds within a text, (b) the syntactic analysis of structurally ambiguous compounds, (c) the assignment of prosodic features to compounds, (d) the translation of compounds into phrases of other languages, and (e) the interpretation of the semantic relations implicit in compounds. The authors present major findings from the last twenty years of computational research on these issues, and evaluate this research on the basis of both theoretical and cognitive considerations.

In "Relational competition during compound interpretation," **Christina Gagné and Thomas Spalding** extend the study of compounds into the domain of psycholinguistic investigation. The focus here is on the process of interpretation of compounds, in particular with regard to the relation between their components. A theoretical framework is presented for compound interpretation that is derived from three types of empirical findings: the fact that the availability of relational structures influences ease of processing, inhibition from competing relations, and the observation that relation availability is specific to a constituent's use in a particular morphosyntactic role.

The next paper, **Irit Meir, Mark Aronoff, Wendy Sandler and Carol Padden**'s "Sign languages and compounding," further extends the field to the visual language mode. It investigates compounds in a variety of sign languages, from the well known American Sign Language to lesser known ones including Al-Sayyid Bedouin Sign Language. The latter has only been in existence for about 75 years, and thus provides the opportunity to observe how compounds arise and develop structure in sign languages. Through this investigation, a pattern is shown whereby the conventionalization of a compound within a community leads to the emergence of both morphological and phonological structures.

The final paper in this volume, "First language acquisition of compounds: With special emphasis on early German child language," by **Wolfgang U. Dressler, Laura E.**

Lettner and Katharina Korecky-Kröll, examines the process of the acquisition of compounds by two Austrian children, and compares these findings with what is known about compound acquisition in other languages. A clear order of acquisition is observed, in which two-member subordinate and endocentric Noun + Noun compounds emerge first, with the presence of verb inflection and diminutive formations. The presence of linking elements is not observed until somewhat later, followed by left-headed and exocentric compounds, the last two, in fact, being still absent in the corpus under consideration. It is proposed that the pattern of compound emergence follows from a variety of linguistic properties, including productivity, morphotactic and morphosemantic transparency, and is compatible with major principles of the theory of Natural Morphology.

PART 1

Delimiting the field

The role of syntax and morphology in compounding

Peter Ackema and Ad Neeleman
University of Edinburgh and UCL

In this chapter it is argued that, although syntax is not directly involved in the formation of compounds themselves, competition between the syntactic and morphological modules of grammar (Ackema and Neeleman 2001, 2004) has a decisive influence on compounding. This is because this type of competition has the effect that certain, grammatically possible, compounds will not surface in a language. This is why synthetic compounds can be based on root compounds that do not themselves surface. We argue that, if the morphology of a language really does not allow for the relevant type of root compound to be formed, then the associated synthetic compounds are ruled out just as well. The fate of synthetic compounds during the development of Saramaccan (and some other creole languages) is shown to provide clear evidence for this hypothesis.

1. Is syntax involved in compounding?

Roughly speaking, there are two contrasting views on how morphologically complex words are formed. Either there is a designated morphological module with generative capacities that is responsible for this,[1] or syntax, the module responsible for deriving syntactically complex phrases, is responsible for deriving morphologically complex items as well. The latter is usually achieved by assuming that a syntactic mechanism such as head movement (or an equivalent operation) raises the head Y in a syntactic structure like (1) to the higher head X and that the resulting X-Y complex can be a complex word.

---

1. This module should not be confused with the lexicon (which contains the list of those properties of simplexes, morphologically complex items, and syntactically complex items that are not predictable from grammatical principles); see Di Sciullo and Williams 1987, Jackendoff 1997, Williams 2007 for discussion.

(1)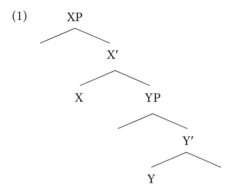

In the specific case of compounds at least, adopting this idea would lead to various problems. The main problem is that, without further modifications of the theory, it is predicted that, whenever a compound Y-X occurs, we should find evidence for the presence of a syntactic YP phrase in the complement position to this compound, in the form of modifiers or complements to the head Y that are stranded by the head movement of Y to X. In contrast, if Y and X are directly put together in a morphological module to form a compound Y-X, no such material should occur. The evidence clearly shows that the latter situation holds:[2,3]

(2) a.   a fan of loud music
    a'. *a music-fan of loud
    b.   to bake in a very hot oven
    b'. *to oven-bake in a very hot

---

2. As argued by Baker (1988, 1995), the situation might be different in cases of so-called 'noun incorporation' in polysynthetic languages, though see Rosen 1989, Ackema 1999, Mithun (this volume) for alternative interpretations of the relevant data.

3. A reviewer suggests that, if 'cartographic' approaches to syntactic structure are correct, head movement of Y to X is expected to be blocked by the silent heads that introduce adverbs and other modifiers of YP (see for example Alexiadou 1997 and Cinque 1999): the head movement constraint would block movement of Y to X across these heads. This suggestion is insufficiently general, as it would still allow stranding of complements of Y, something that is not empirically attested. Moreover, there is no reason why movement of Y could not take place in a head-to-head roll-up fashion, taking the various silent heads along. Finally note that the reviewer's suggestion would require that all cases that do involve syntactic head movement would have to be re-analysed somehow, as these can all involve movement of a head past one or more of its dependents (if the head movement is to the left; why rightward head movement cannot do so is explained by Ackema and Neeleman 2002 as a processing effect). What this would probably lead to is a theory that assumes two different types of apparent head movement, one involved in compounding and the other involved in uncontroversially syntactic processes such as verb clustering, N-to-D movement or Verb Second. But this would again undermine the idea that compounding is dealt with by independently motivated syntactic processes.

Another argument put forward by Ackema and Neeleman (2004) against the idea that syntax is involved in compounding in this way (or in the actual formation of any morphological complexes, for that matter) is based on the observation that syntax does have the means to make complex heads by head-to-head movement. The point is that the resultant complexes in cases which arguably involve such movement consistently have very different properties from compounds in the same language. A case in point are the verb clusters that arise as the result of V-to-V raising in the Germanic OV languages (cf. Evers 1975). These systematically differ from V-V compounds, which also occur in these languages, with respect to such things as the position of the head (always on the right in compounds, sometimes on the left in verb clusters) or the possible inflection on the non-head (must be a bare stem in the case of compounds, must carry non-finite morphology in verb clusters).

Although we cannot go into this in any more detail here, we assume that for reasons like these there is no reason to think syntax is directly involved in compounding.[4] A reviewer suggests that perhaps a syntactic approach can be validated by assuming that, instead of head movement (or an equivalent operation) being involved, noun-verb compounds could be analysed as having the following base-generated structure, with X some unspecified functional head (an analogous analysis can be given for compounds involving other categories):

(3)

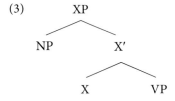

Although ostensibly syntactic in nature because of the phrasal nature of the categories involved, this analysis in fact does not conform to the idea that, as we put it above, "syntax, the module responsible for deriving syntactically complex phrases, is responsible for deriving morphologically complex items as well". This is because the structure in (3) in many languages does not comply with the independently motivated phrasal syntax of that language. In particular, in VO languages with right-headed morphology (such as English), the order between N(P) and V(P) in the compound in (3) is the wrong way around for the syntax of the language in case N is the internal argument of V (as in synthetic compounds). If the order in (3) is to be regarded as the result of movement of the NP to spec-X, rather than base-generation (or 'external merge' in current terms), the problem would be that this movement should happen in compounds

---

4. A different matter is that syntactic phrases can occur inside compounds (see for example Lieber 1992, Booij 2002). This does not mean either that syntax is directly involved with the formation of the compound itself, see Ackema and Neeleman (2004) for discussion.

but not in phrasal syntax. Either way, the compound is subject to rules or principles that differ from those motivated for phrasal syntax, which is our contention.[5,6]

Although it is not the means of deriving compounds, we have argued elsewhere (Ackema and Neeleman 2001, 2004) that syntax does have an important indirect effect on compounding. In particular, the idea that the syntactic module and the morphological module can be in competition when it comes to the privilege of combining a head and its dependents can explain certain data regarding synthetic compounds. In particular, it explains that the root compounds that they are based on, at least according to one analysis of synthetic compounds, do not occur independently. In this paper, we will provide more evidence for this theory, based on what happened to synthetic compounds during the development of some creole languages. But first, we will explain the issues regarding the proper analysis of synthetic compounds, and the idea of competition between syntax and morphology, in more detail.

2. The structure of synthetic compounds

There are various analyses of synthetic compounds, but, under the assumption of binary branching structure, the two most straightforward ones are those in (4a) and (4b).

---

5. Apart from this main point, the structure in (3) is not unproblematic in itself. It is not quite clear to us on what basis the categories in a simple N-V compound like *breastfeed* can be regarded as phrases rather than heads. Also, the reviewer's suggestion that there may be evidence for the presence of the functional head X in compounds in the form of the linking element that can show up in many languages between the head and the non-head is not very helpful in an account of the relevant data, it seems to us. At least in the language we are most intimately familiar with (Dutch), it is notoriously unpredictable whether or not a linking element shows up in a compound. They are often fossilized left-overs from historic case morphology on the left-hand part of (what is now) the compound, and, more to the point, attempts at a synchronic account of their present status seem to involve prosodic and semantic notions (having to do with the avoidance of stress clashes and whether or not the left-hand part is easily seen as a plural or not); the linking element does not seem to have any syntactic function. For discussion of the issues involved see for instance Neijt et al. 2002. Josefsson (1998) provides an analysis of Swedish compounds in which the presence or absence of a functional head in a compound that is expressed by a linking element is claimed to follow from certain syntactic considerations, but it appears quite problematic to extend this account to other languages, see Ackema 2000.

6. A similar remark could be made, though for somewhat different reasons, about the interesting account of compounding in the framework of Distributed Morphology in Harley 2009. Here, too, it seems to us that the part of the 'syntactic' representation/derivation that is involved in the formation of a compound is not motivated independently by the processes taking place in the phrasal syntax of the same language and has some properties that cannot readily be explained by an appeal to the phrasal syntax. We do not have space here, though, for a discussion of Harley's analysis.

(4) a. [$_N$ N [$_N$ V affix $_N$]]
    b. [$_N$ [$_V$ N V] affix $_N$]

The major problem with (4b) appears to be that the N-V compound on which it is based is systematically absent. English has plenty of N-V compounds (Bauer 1983 and others), but not ones in which N is an argument of V.[7] However, the analysis in (4a) is, if anything, even more problematic. The structure is based on the observation that a deverbal derived noun can inherit the arguments of its verbal base (cf. *love music – lover of music*).Adopting this structure for synthetic compounds gives rise to at least the following issues (from Ackema & Neeleman 2004).

First, the analysis rules out synthetic compounds based on verbal idioms, given that idiomatic arguments can *not* be inherited:

(5) a.   John always makes trouble
    a'. #John is a maker of trouble
    b.   Someone I met wants to blow the whistle
    b'. #But then, he is known to be a blower of whistles
    c.   This game usually breaks the ice at parties
    c'. #This game is a great breaker of the ice

In fact, however, synthetic compounds based on verbal idioms are fine, as the following illustrate:

(6) a. John is a real troublemaker
    b. The company didn't know who the whistleblower was
    c. This game is a great icebreaker at Christmas parties

Second, the analysis is insufficiently general, because there are compounds, such as those in (7), that must have the structure [$_N$ [$_V$ N V] N]. The alternative structure [$_N$ N [$_N$ V N] is not viable in this case, because there is no inheritance from the left in compounds (cf. Di Sciullo and Williams 1987), as (8) shows. Therefore, a structure as in (9), based on inheritance, is not viable for these cases. Yet, just as in the case of synthetic compounds, the N-V unit on which these larger compounds must be based then does not exist separately, as shown in (10).

(7) a. [$_N$ [$_V$ appel pluk] machine]
       apple pick machine
       'machine for picking apples'

    b. [$_N$ [$_V$ hout snij] kunst]
       wood cut art
       'woodcutting'

---

7. Apparent counterexamples, such as *to brain-wash*, are, indeed, only apparent, as the verb in such cases is not de-transitivised (*they brainwashed the victim*), meaning it is problematic to see the left-hand noun in the compound as the internal argument of the verb.

c. [$_N$ [$_V$ aardappel schil] mesje]
potato peel knife
'potato peeler'

(8) a. *[$_{NP}$ [$_N$ pluk machine] van appels]
pick machine of apples
b. *[$_{NP}$ [$_N$ snij kunst] van hout]
cut art of wood
c. *[$_{NP}$ [$_N$ schil mesje] van aardappels]
peel knife of potatoes

(9) a. *[$_N$ appel [$_N$ pluk machine]]
apple pick machine
b. *[$_N$ hout [$_N$ snij kunst]]
wood cut art
c. *[$_N$ aardappel [$_N$ schil mesje]]
potato peel knife

(10) a. *De boerenknecht [$_V$ appel plukt] de hele dag
the farmhand apple picks the entire day
'The farmhand picks apples all day long.'
b. *Deze ambachtsman [$_V$ hout snijdt] heel wat af
this artisan wood cuts quite a lot
'This artisan does quite a lot of wood cutting.'
c. *De dienstplichtige soldaten [$_V$ aardappel schilden] de ganse dag
the drafted soldiers potato peeled the whole day
'The conscripts were peeling potatoes all day long.'

Third, the analysis offers no insight as to *why* root compounds where N is an argument of V are impossible. This is striking as soon as cases dubbed to be 'backformations' are taken into consideration:

(11) a. [$_N$ baby [$_N$ sit er]] →
b. [$_N$ [$_V$ baby sit] er] →
c. to [$_V$ baby sit]

After all, why would 'backformation' suddenly be blocked in a case like the following?

(12) a. [$_N$ truck [$_N$ drive er]] →
b. [$_N$ [$_V$ truck drive] er] →
c. *to [$_V$ truck drive]

Ackema and Neeleman (2004) conclude from these considerations that in fact (4b) is the correct structure for synthetic compounds. (4a) is a possible structure as well, but it cannot receive an interpretation in which N is an argument of V. This follows from a theory of competition sketched in the next section, as does the fact that N-V compounds in which N is an argument of V do not occur independently (even though they serve as the base for synthetic compounds).

3. The effects of competition

We assume that syntax and morphology are separate structure-building modules (see Section 1). However, syntax and morphology *compete* for the privilege of combining categories into larger hierarchical structures (see also Melloni and Bisetto, this volume). We further assume that (in non-polysynthetic languages at least) syntax beats morphology when all else is equal. "All else is equal" means, first, that projections of the same categories merge, and, second, that the semantic relationship between these projections is identical. The relevant assumptions and definitions are given in (13) and (14). (Note that the principle regulating competition, as formulated in (14), compares complete structural representations. As such this does not imply anything about how these structures are built, that is, whether syntax and morphology themselves should be modelled as in a derivational grammar or as in a representational grammar.)

(13) a. Syntax and morphology are independent generative systems.
 b. The lexicon is a list of syntactic, morphological and phonological irregularities.
 c. Syntactic generation of structures is unmarked with respect to morphological generation.
 d. Complex lexical items can be underspecified in various ways; one type of underspecification concerns their locus of realisation (that is, syntax or morphology).

(14) Let α_1 and α_2 be syntactic representations headed by α. α_1 blocks α_2 iff
 (i) In α_1 (a projection of) α is merged with (a projection of) β in syntax, while in α_2 (a projection of) α is merged with (a projection of) β in morphology, and
 (ii) the semantic relation between α and β is identical in α_1 and α_2.

Because of competition as defined in (14), a morphological structure like (15b) will be blocked by the syntactic structure in (15a) in case the semantic relationship between α and its complement β is the same in both.

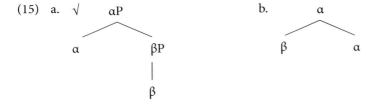

(√ marks the winner)

No blocking is expected to occur between (16a) and (16b), however, because different categories merge.

(16) a.

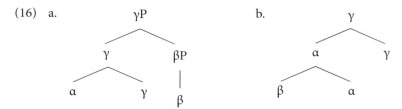

It may seem that competition entails that (16b) will be blocked by (17). But notice that according to (14) competition only obtains between syntactic structures headed by the same category α. Whereas in (17) there is a syntactic category headed by α (namely αP), this is not the case in (16b): the node that results from merger of α and β occupies a morphological nonhead position and hence it will never be able to project into the syntax. Thus, competition is suspended in morphological nonhead positions, with the consequence that these may in principle contain both heads and phrases as in (17).

(17)

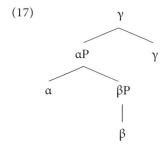

There is an issue with the linearization of (17) to which we turn in Section 4.

If (4b) is correct, synthetic compounds are derivatives of root compounds that do not occur independently. Competition explains how this situation can arise. In one instantiation of the structures in (15), α is a verb and β a nominal category functioning as its internal argument. Since (15a) blocks (15b), VPs like *drive a truck* block compounds like *truck-drive*. But, as noted, (16a) (the structure for e.g. *driver of a truck*) does *not* block (16b) (the structure for *truck driver*), because different categories are merged in the two structures: in (16a) γ (the suffix) merges with a projection of β (the noun), while in (16b) γ merges with a projection of α (the verb). Hence, the synthetic compound *truck driver* can co-occur with the syntactic phrase *driver of trucks*.

In sum, N-V compounds with an argumental noun do not occur independently, because they are blocked by syntactic phrasal counterparts. (In general, this theory predicts that existing root compounds must have a noncompositional meaning which is not available under syntactic merger of the same categories; this appears to be correct on the whole, though see Padrosa Trias 2007 for some discussion of potential counterexamples). The synthetic compound is not blocked, because it does not compete with a syntactic phrase (as a consequence of a different order of merger).[8]

4. The effects of mapping

If synthetic compounds such as *truck driver* in English are derivations of N-V root compounds, as argued above, the question arises as to how an agentive nominalisation of an X-V combination can be generated in a language that has no X-V compounding? The answer is that, in that case, the derivation takes as its base a syntactic phrase combining V and X(P), resulting in a structure like (18).

(18) $[_N [_{VP} \text{ V XP}] \text{ affix}_N]$

We will argue that this structure is ruled out in languages that do have X-V compounding, as a consequence of restrictions on the mapping between morpho-syntax and morpho-phonology.

We assume a form of the *separation hypothesis* according to which morpho-syntax does not contain any phonological material. Rather, phonological forms are mapped onto morpho-syntax (see Anderson 1992, Beard 1995, Jackendoff 1997, Halle and Marantz 1993, Sproat 1985, and many others). An example like (18) (from Jackendoff 1997) shows that morpho-syntactic structures need not be isomorphic to phonological structure; moreover, the types of constituent occurring in both are of an entirely different nature. Hence, we need some principles that determine what are possible correspondences between the two types of structure and what are not.

(19) a. $[_{DP} \text{ a } [_{NP} [_{AP} \text{ big}] \text{ house}]]$
    b. $[_\phi [_\omega \text{ a big}] [_\omega \text{ house}]]$

The following mapping principles define well-formed correspondences between morpho-syntactic and morpho-phonological representations. (We represent morpho-syntactic affixes as AFFIX and morpho-phonological affixes as /affix/. The former occupy a position in the morpho-syntactic tree and carry features like lexical category; the latter are corresponding forms in morpho-phonology).

(20) *Linear Correspondence*   (compare Sproat 1985)
       If   X is structurally external to Y,
                 X is phonologically realised as /x/, and
                 Y is phonologically realised as /y/
       then   /x/ is linearly external to /y/.

---

8. It should be noted that the idea of competition between syntax and morphology is not designed just to account for these data regarding synthetic compounds; see Ackema and Neeleman 2001, 2004 for other applications.

(21) *Input Correspondence* (compare Sadock 1991)
 If an AFFIX selects (a category headed by) X,
  the AFFIX is phonologically realised as /affix/, and
  X is phonologically realised as /x/,
 then /affix/ takes /x/ as its host.

(22) *Quantitative correspondence* (compare Noyer 1993)
 No element in the morpho-syntax is spelled out more than once.

We can illustrate the effects of the mapping principles by considering agentive nominalisations based on verb-particle constructions in Swedish. In isolation, particle and verb can be combined syntactically (as in (23)) or morphologically (as in (24)), resulting in different orders between verb and particle, with the syntactic order reflecting the general syntactic head-complement order of Swedish, and the morphological order reflecting the general right-headedness of Swedish morphology (data from Gunlög Josefsson, personal communication). (Note that morphological combinations of V and P are not blocked by their syntactic counterparts in this case because they must be listed as belonging to a more formal register, and often also having an idiosyncratic meaning; see Holmes and Hinchliffe 1994. If something needs to be listed anyway because of some unpredictable property, it can be listed with the additional idiosyncratic information that it is a morphological complex, thereby in effect suspending competition. This is also the rationale in our model for why root compounds can exist and why, in contrast to synthetic compounds, these must all have an unpredictable meaning, as otherwise there would be no reason to list them; for discussion see Ackema and Neeleman 2004: 80–85).

(23) stiga upp resa av   låna ut   somna in
  rise up   travel off lend out   sleep in
  'to rise' 'to depart' 'to lend out' 'to fall asleep'

(24) uppstiga avresa   utlåna   insomna
  up-rise   off-travel out-lend   in-sleep
  'to rise' 'to depart' 'to lend out' 'to fall asleep'

The mapping principles given above predict that only the morphological particle-verb combinations can be derived. A derivation (with the suffix *-are*) of a particle-verb compound has a morpho-syntactic structure as in (25a) and a phonological structure as in (25b). These two structures can be related to each other without violating the mapping principles. In contrast, any attempt at making an *-are* derivation on the basis of syntactic verb-particle combinations leads to a violation of one of the mapping principles, see (26). This prediction holds true, as the data in (27) show.

(25) a. [[PRT V] ER]
   b. [[$_\omega$ /prt/] [$_\omega$ /v/ /are/]]

(26) a. [[V PRT] ER]
     b. *[[$_\omega$ /v/ /are/] [$_\omega$ /prt/]]   (violates Input Correspondence)
     c. *[[$_\omega$ /v/] [$_\omega$ /prt/ /are/]]   (violates Linear Correspondence)
     d. *[[$_\omega$ /v/ /are/] [$_\omega$ /prt/ /are/]]   (violates Quantitative Correspondence)

(27) a. angripare   utgivare
         on-clutch-er   out-give-er
         'attacker'   'publisher'
     b. *gripanare   *givutare
         clutch-on-er   give-out-er
     c. *gripare an   *givare ut
         clutch-er on   give-er out
     d. *gripare anare   *givare utare
         clutch-er on-er   give-er out-er

We assume that the grammar of a language can specify for specific affixes that the mapping principles can be violated, but crucially only when there is no alternative that satisfies the mapping principles, and even then violations are minimised (see Ackema and Neeleman 2004). Evidence for this from English comes from two areas.

To begin with, English, as opposed to Swedish, does not have P-V compounds (see (28)). This means that agentive nominalisations based on a particle-verb combination cannot be based on a head-final structure. As a consequence, various forms are produced, each of which in violation of one of the mapping principles:

(28) a.   to throw away
     a'. *to away-throw
     b.   to stand in
     b'. *to in-stand
     c.   to let down
     c'. *to down-let

(29) a. [[$_V$ CUT UP] ER]
     b. [[$_\omega$ /cut/ /er/] [$_\omega$ /up/]]
     c. [[$_\omega$ /cut/] [$_\omega$ /up/ /er/]]
     d. [[$_\omega$ /cut/ /er/] [$_\omega$ /up/ /er/]]

(30) a. passer by   (cf. Yip 1978, Sproat 1985, 1988)
     b. come outer
     c. cleaner upper

A further piece of evidence that phrasal derivations become possible when a particular type of root compound is not available as the base for nominalisation comes from

English L1 acquisition. In the acquisitional process, children start out without N-V compounding and without overt affixation (Clark et al. 1986):

(31) a. [$_N$ [$_{VP}$ KICK$_V$ [$_{NP}$ BALL]] ER]
    b. [[$_\omega$ /kick/] [$_\omega$ /ball/]]

(32) *Stage I (around age 3): VO order, no overt affix*
    a. a kick-ball   (someone who kicks a ball)
    b. a build-wall   (someone who builds a wall)
    c. a bounce-ball   (someone who bounces a ball)

The overt form of the affix is acquired before N-V compounding becomes available. This is the crucial stage, in which we see that *-er* derivations can take syntactic VPs as base. Again, the position in which we see the /affix/ /er/ showing up varies, as all possibilities violate one of the mapping principles:

(33) a. [$_N$ [$_{VP}$ KICK$_V$ [$_{NP}$ BALL]] ER]
    b. [[$_\omega$ /kick/ /er/] [$_\omega$ /ball/]]
    c. [[$_\omega$ /kick/] [$_\omega$ /ball/ /er/]]
    d. [[$_\omega$ /kick/ /er/] [$_\omega$ /ball/ /er/]]

(34) *Stage II (around age 4): VO order, overt affix on either V, N or both (in order of decreasing frequency)*   (Clark et al. 1986)
    a. a giver-present   (someone who gives a present)
    b. a dry-hairer   (someone who dries hair)
    c. a mover-boxer   (someone who moves boxes)

Once N-V root compounding is acquired in addition to the agentive affix, we find the synthetic compounds of the adult stage, which are (on our analysis) derivations of such root compounds (on a par with derivations of particle-verb compounds in Swedish). As noted, no mapping principle needs to be violated to make these (cf. (35)), and as a consequence phrasal derivations cease to be produced.

(35) a. [$_N$ [$_V$ BALL$_N$ KICK$_V$]] ER]
    b. [[$_\omega$ /ball/] [$_\omega$ /kick/ /er/]]

We conclude that phrasal derivation is blocked if there is the option of generating a base for agentive nominalisation through X-V compounding. This allows a mapping that satisfies all mapping principles. (Note that Input Correspondence is satisfied if in synthetic compounds /er/ is attached to /v/, as in (35b). The syntactic structure in (35a) corresponds to a phonological structure in which there are two phonological words, /ball/ and /kicker/).

5. Synthetic compounds in Saramaccan

We now turn to some evidence from creolisation which strongly supports the proposal outlined above (except where indicated, all data below and all empirical generalisations are based on work by Tonjes Veenstra; see Veenstra 2006 and references mentioned there). The language we will consider is Saramaccan. This is a creole language, whose main lexifier is English. The main substrate language is Fon (or a closely related Gbe language). Saramaccan has an agentive suffix, -*ma*:

(36) hondi-ma sabi-ma   (from Bakker et al. 1995)
　　 hunt-MA　know- MA
　　 'hunter'　'expert'

The affix -*ma* derives from English *man*, and was still a free morpheme in the earliest stages of creolisation. However, in the current language, it has been reanalyzed as an affix. As evidence for this, Veenstra (2006) notes that in the realisation of its tone, it is phonologically dependent on the category to which it attaches in a way that sets it apart from free morphemes. Moreover, it allows argument inheritance, as opposed to free morphemes:

(37) a.　[hondi-fou-ma]
　　　　 hunt-bird-MA
　　　　 'birdhunter'

　　 b.　[hondi-ma] u　　di　 fou
　　　　 hunt-MA　 for　DET　bird

Saramaccan also has N-N compounding, as illustrated by the following examples from Good 2004:

(38) honi　wata beei gaasi　　hedi uwii
　　 bee　 water eyeglass shield　head hair
　　 'honey'　'eyeglass lens'　　'hair'

In contrast, Saramaccan, unlike English, does not appear to have N-V compounds. Veenstra (personal communication) notes that: "there is no shred of evidence to the contrary [i.e. that Saramaccan would have N-V compounding] and all circumstantial evidence points in a different direction".

To summarise:

(39)　i.　 Saramaccan has an agentive affix –*ma*.
　　　ii.　Saramaccan has N-N compounding.
　　　iii. Saramaccan lacks N-V compounding

Moreover, the languages in the contact situation out of which Saramaccan developed had synthetic compounds (probably with the exception of the secondary lexifier,

Portuguese). An example from Fon is given in (39). (English examples have been given above, of course).

(40) nàkí-sá-tó
firewood-sell-AFF

Given this state of affairs, the analyses of synthetic compounds in (4a) and (4b) make radically different predictions. If the analysis in (4a) is correct, Saramaccan should have synthetic compounds. All the ingredients required to generate the relevant structure are present: there is an agentive affix, and there are N-N compounds (and, moreover, both the mother languages had them). If the analysis in (4b) is correct, Saramaccan should not have synthetic compounds, as a crucial ingredient to generate these, namely N-V compounding, is absent. At best, the language may resort to agentive nominalisations of VP, on a par with what is found in stage II of English L1 acquisition (see Section 4).

The data support our proposal: Saramaccan does *not* have synthetic compounds. Instead, it has V-N-affix combinations plausibly analyzed as nominalised VPs:

(41) a. [_N [_VP V [_NP N]] ER]
b. [[_ω /v/] [_ω /n/ /ma/]]

(42) a. ondosúku-tóngo-ma
research-language-MA
'linguist'

b. tjá-búka-ma
carry-mouth-MA
'messenger'

c. nái-koósu-ma
sew-clothes-MA
'tailor'

It can easily be shown that the base of the derivations in (42) is indeed phrasal. First, the word order V-N is consistent with the head-initial syntax of the language, but inconsistent with its morphology, which is generally right-headed (compare the N-N compounds in (38) above). Second, the following data from Bakker et al. 1995 show that there can be other material in the base for affixation, indicating that we are dealing with a full-fledged syntactic structure. Note that in the final two examples the internal argument of the verb is an embedded clause rather than a noun:

(43) tja-boto-go-a-wosu-ma   subi-kununu-go-a-liba-ma
carry boat go LOC house MA   climb mountain go LOC top MA
'pilot'   'mountain climber'

seti-u-kanda-ma   bigi-u-wooko-ma
start to sing MA   begin to work MA
'precentor'   'first worker'

In sum, phrasal derivation is used, rather than synthetic compounding, because the base for the synthetic compound (the N-V root compound) is not available. The forms that surface violate Input Correspondence, since the /affix/ /ma/ does not show up on the phonological realisation of the verb (the head of the VP). But as there is no form that does satisfy all mapping principles, this is consistent with the generalisations outlined in Section 4.

There is one remaining issue: why does Saramaccan choose to violate Input Correspondence, rather than display the variations observed with English derived particle verbs and agentive derivations in English child language? Our suggestion is that this has to do with the fact that –*ma* was originally a free morpheme. Therefore, when it was reanalyzed as an affix, there were already V-N-*ma* forms in the input for L1 learners. This is because compounds with a phrasal left-hand part (such as [$_N$ [$_{VP}$ V NP] N]) pose no problem with respect to the mapping principles, given that a free morpheme N is not subject to Input Correspondence (see Ackema and Neeleman 2004 for data and discussion). When –*ma* was reanalyzed as affix, this evidence in the input could not be ignored by the L1 learners. They hence opted to specify –*ma* as being not subject to Input Correspondence (rather than any of the other mapping principles).[9]

6. Conclusion

There is every reason to think that syntax is not involved in the formation of compounds themselves. However, given the idea of syntax-morphology competition, syntax can have a decisive influence on compounding, in the sense that it can rule out that certain, grammatically possible, compounds will surface. This is why synthetic compounds can be based on root compounds that do not themselves surface. More evidence for this view comes from the observation that, if the morphology of a language really does not allow for the relevant type of root compound to be formed, then the associated synthetic compounds are ruled out just as well. Instead, the language has to take recourse to an otherwise dispreferred strategy, namely deriving full syntactic phrases. The fate of synthetic compounds during the development of Saramaccan (and some other creole languages) is a clear illustration of this.

---

9. Veenstra (2006) proposes a different analysis, based on the assumption that, before –*ma* affixation, first a process of zero derivation of the VP takes place. As Veenstra notes, the order of operations in that case leads to a structure that satisfies Input Correspondence (see Ackema and Neeleman 2004 for discussion). Our main objection to this analysis is the lack of independent evidence for zero derivation in this case.

Acknowledgments

We have benefited from helpful comments and discussion by Tonjes Veenstra, an anonymous reviewer, and the audience at the Componet Congress on Compounding, University of Bologna (June 2008).

Constraints on compounds and incorporation*

Marianne Mithun
University of California, Santa Barbara

This chapter examines the status of a type of compounding often cited as a construction that straddles the boundary between morphology and syntax. Noun incorporation constructions in Kapampangan, Mohawk, and Central Alaskan Yup'ik Eskimo are evaluated with respect to the No Phrase Constraint and the Lexical Integrity Hypothesis. Though they share certain fundamental properties, the constructions differ in crucial ways, reflecting differing stages of diachronic development.

1. Introduction

A central issue within morphological theory has been the delimitation of the domain and its relation to syntax. Two hypotheses have been central to the discussion, traced in detail in Lieber and Scalise 2006. The No Phrase Constraint, described by Botha (1981: 18), denies morphological operations access to the output of syntax: words cannot be formed from syntactic phrases. The Lexical Integrity Hypothesis, first proposed by Lapointe (1981: 22), denies syntactic operations access to the internal structure of words. Compounding has played a prominent role in these discussions, in part because of its position at the border between the two domains. On one side, it produces lexical items, a classic morphological function. On the other, it can take words as its input, and, in some languages, phrases which are the products of syntactic operations.

---

* All examples are cited in the practical orthographies in use in the communities, but the phonetic values of the symbols are generally not far from standard IPA conventions. Kapampangan writers usually spell clitics as separate words. The digraph <ng> represents the velar nasal <ŋ>. For Mohawk, the letter <i> represents a palatal glide before a vowel, and a high front unrounded vowel otherwise. The digraphs <en> and <on> represent nasalized vowels, caret and high back rounded u respectively. The colon <:> indicates vowel length, the acute accent <á> stress with high or rising tone, and the grave accent <à> stress with falling tone. The apostrophe <'> represents glottal stop. For Yup'ik, the symbols <g> and <r> represent velar and uvular fricatives respectively, and the digraphs <gg> and <rr> their voiceless counterparts, except before a voiceless consonant where they automatically assimilate the voicelessness. The letter <e> represents a schwa.

One type of compounding that seems particularly syntactic is noun incorporation, the combination of a noun and a verb to form a larger verb. A typical example is the Mohawk verb stem *-itsi-ienta'-* 'fish-get' = 'to catch fish'. In work on the morphology-syntax interface, Li has proposed that parts of words 'are invisible to syntax *unless there is a thematic relation expressed sublexically*' (2005: 4). If any kind of compounding constitutes such a case, noun incorporation should be a prime candidate, since it consists of a verb and a noun that bears some relation to it.

Here it is shown that noun incorporation can be characterized by certain basic properties, but it is not homogeneous cross-linguistically, nor is it necessarily static through time. Examples are drawn from three genetically and areally unrelated languages: (1) Kapampangan, an Austronesian language of the Philippines; (2) Mohawk, an Iroquoian language of northeastern North American, and (3) Central Alaskan Yup'ik, an Eskimo-Aleut language of Alaska. The constructions are first described, then evaluated with respect to the No Phrase Constraint (the prohibition against syntactically complex non-heads, here incorporated nouns) and the Lexical Integrity Hypothesis, specifically the claim that parts of words (here incorporated nouns), cannot serve as antecedents of pronominals). Differences among the constructions in the three languages are related to properties associated with different stages of diachronic development.

2. The constructions

Incorporating constructions in the three languages share certain properties. All consist of a noun and a verb which constitute a larger verb or verb phrase. Each is formally intransitive. The fish are not syntactic arguments, nor are they distinguished for number, definiteness, or case.

(1) 'They caught fish.'*
    Kapampangan   *Ikualang asan.*
    Mohawk   *Wahatitsiaién:ta'ne'.*
    Yup'ik   *Neqetut.*

In what follows, all examples attributed to speakers are from spontaneous speech.

2.1 Kapampangan

Argument structure is indicated in Kapampangan in three ways: (i) by the verbal morphology, (ii) by case-marked pronominal enclitics, and (iii) by case-marked determiners.

Verbs are inflected for transitivity, voice, and tense/aspect/modality with combinations of prefixes, infixes, and suffixes. The verb *labas* 'pass by' has the intransitive (INTR) form *lumabas* in (2a), but the transitive (TR) form *labasnan* in (2b). Pronominal enclitics identify the core arguments of the clause, whether or not they are further identified by lexical nominals. Some of the clitics are fused forms. The clitic *ku* in the intransitive clause 'I'll pass by' refers to just one argument: absolutive 'I'. The clitic *ke* (*ku*+*ya*) in 'I'll pass their house' refers to two: ergative 'I' and absolutive 'it' (the house). The determiner *ing* before 'their house' identifies this constituent as the absolutive argument.

(2) Kapampangan clause structure: Bernadette Mangasar, speaker p.c.
    a. *Lumabas=ku.*
        pass.INTR=1SG.ABS
        'I'll pass by.'
    b. *Labasnan= **ke**   ing   bale   da.*
        pass.TR=**1SG.ERG/3SG.ABS** ABS.SG.LK house 3PL.POSS
        'I'll pass their house.'

The pronominal clitics identify only core or syntactic arguments: ergatives and absolutives. The determiners on noun phrases distinguish three cases: ergative, absolutive, and oblique. In addition to case, the determiners also mark singular/plural and common/proper distinctions.

(3) Kapampangan clause structure: Clemente Roman, speaker p.c.
     *Ing   Bataan, sinuk=ya,   **karing**   Apones.*
     ABS.SG Bataan surrendered.INTR=3SG.ABS **OBL.PL.PROP.LK** Japanese
     'Bataan surrendered to the Japanese.'

Constituents of a phrase may be linked by the enclitic =*ng* (velar nasal =*ŋ*). In (4) the linker (LK) relates the constituents of 'the old woman.'

(4) Kapampangan linker =*ng*: Clemente Roman, speaker p.c.
     *Migtakaya   **ing**   matuang   babai.*
     Migtaka=ya   [i=**ng**   matua=**ng** babai.]
     surprised.INTR =3SG.ABS   ABS.SG=LK old=LK   woman
     '[The old woman] was surprised.'

The structure of the Kapampangan 'they caught fish' in (1) can now be appreciated. The form of the verb *ikua* 'got' is intransitive. The only argument of the clause is the absolutive =*la* 'they'. The fish have no syntactic status: they are not represented by a pronominal clitic, and there is no determiner before the noun. The noun is linked directly to the verb.

(5) Kapampangan incorporation: Clemente Roman, speaker p.c.
     Ikualang   asan.
     ikua=la=ng   asan
     got.INTR=3PL.ABS=LK **fish**
     'They caught fish.'

2.2 Mohawk

Mohawk verbs consist minimally of a pronominal prefix and a verb root. The pronominal prefix identifies the arguments of the clause: one for intransitives and two for transitives (provided both are animate). The verb in (6) contains the pronominal prefix *-hi-* 'I/him'.

(6) Mohawk clause: Kahentoréhtha Marie Cross, speaker p.c.
    Wahí:iehte'   *ne*   *riièn:'a.*
    wa-hi-ie-ht-e'   ne   ri-ien'=a
    FACTUAL-1SG/M.SG-awake-CAUS-PRF   the   1SG/MSG-have.as.offspring=DIM
    I awakened **him**   the   my son
    'I woke my son up.'

Nouns are unmarked for number or case.

Verbs may also contain various other prefixes and suffixes, as well as an incorporated noun stem. The incorporated noun occurs after the pronominal prefix and immediately before the verb root. If the noun stem ends in a consonant, and the following verb root begins in a consonant, a linker vowel *-a-* is inserted between the two.

(7) Mohawk incorporation: Sonny Edwards, speaker p.c.
    Wahatitsiaién:ta'ne'.
    wa-hati-**itsi**-a-**ient**-a'n-e'
    FACTUAL-M.PL.AGT-**fish**-LK-**have**-INCHOATIVE-PRF
    'They caught fish'

2.3 Central Alaskan Yup'ik

All Yup'ik verbs begin with a root, potentially followed by one or more derivational suffixes. They end with a mood and pronominal suffixes. Most of the mood suffixes, including the indicative, distinguish transitivity. The pronominal suffix refers to the core or syntactic arguments of the clause: one for intransitives and two for transitives.

(8) Yup'ik clause: Elena Charles, speaker p.c
    *Tangerruryartullrua**qa**.*
    tangerr-ur-yartur-llru-ar-qa
    see-purposely-go.in.order.to-PAST-TR.INDIC-1SG/3SG
    'I went to see **him**.'

Noun suffixes specify number, possessor, and case: ergative, absolutive, allative, ablative, locative, vialis ('through'), and aequalis ('like').

Some Yup'ik verbs are based on a noun root followed by a derivational verbalizing suffix with relatively concrete meaning, such as 'hunt', 'gather', 'eat', 'say', 'buy', 'smell or taste like', 'encounter', 'acquire', 'lack', 'hit', 'cook', 'make', and more (Mithun 1998a,b). The Yup'ik 'they caught fish' consists of an initial noun root *neqe-* 'fish, food' followed by a verbalizing suffix -*te*- 'catch'. It is clear from both the intransitive mood suffix -*u*- and the third person plural absolutive pronominal -*t* that the clause is grammatically intransitive.

(9) Yup'ik
Neqtut.
neqe-te-u-t
fish-catch-INTR.INDIC-3PL.ABS
'They caught fish.'

3. Internal structure

The 'catch fish' constructions in all three languages are endocentric. All consist of a nominal element and a verbal element. The verbal element functions as the head: structurally, its lexical category is passed on to the construction as a whole; semantically, it is a hyponym of the whole: its meaning is modified or narrowed by the non-head: catching fish is a kind of catching. The constructions might qualify as synthetic compounds according to classical definitions: their nominal constituents seem to 'bear a thematic role in relation to that verb stem identical or very similar to the role it has in a corresponding verb phrase' (Carstairs-McCarthy 1992: 109) or 'in a sentence, could function as an argument of that verb' (Bauer 2003: 44).

In all of the languages, the incorporating constructions have analytic counterparts. (The two structural alternatives are not always equally idiomatic with specific noun-verb combinations, but the two structures co-exist). Often the noun in the analytic counterpart is a syntactic argument. In (10), for example, the fish is the absolutive of a transitive.

(10) Kapampangan alternatives: Bernadette Mangaser, speaker p.c.
Selakatne   ing   asan.
selakat=na=ya   i=ng   asan.
trapped.TR=3SG.ERG=3SG.ABS   3SG.ABS=LK   fish
'He trapped **the fish**.'

Only definite nominals can function as syntactic arguments in Kapampangan. Indefinites appear either in incorporating constructions or as obliques.

The roles of incorporated nouns are not limited, however, to those which could be interpreted as syntactic arguments. They are, furthermore, semantically heterogeneous: often semantic patients or goals, but also instruments, locations, and others more difficult to specify.

(11) Kapampangan
   a. *Pota midinanlang sabun.*
      later they get splattered soap
      'They might be splattered **with soap**.'
   b. *Mitambunanta nang basura.*
      we will be buried already garbage
      'We'll just be buried **in garbage**.'

(12) Mohawk
   a. *kahseriie'táneren'*
      'It is **string**-tied' = 'It is tied up **with string**'
   b. *onke'nionhsókha'*
      'I **nose**-leak' = I have a runny nose'
   c. *thiwakate'nonión:ni*
      'I've just **knot**-made myself' = 'I'm all hunched up'

(13) Yup'ik: Jacobson 1984
   imarpigkuartua
   'I'll **sea**-go.by.way.of = I'll go **by sea**.'

It is well known that the semantic relationships between the constituents of noun-noun compounds are not generally predictable. The non-heads of English endocentric noun-noun compounds, for example, need only be 'appropriately classificatory' in the sense of Downing (1977). Relationships between members of synthetic compounds are generally thought to be more constrained: the verbal element 'usually determines unequivocally the meaning of the compound, thus ruling out other readings' (Scalise 1984: 90). The interpretation of the incorporating constructions described here is not specified by either the grammar or the verbal head. Incorporated nouns with different semantic roles can appear with the same verb root.

(14) Mohawk verb root *-itahkhe-*
   ratiia'titáhkhe'   'they were **body**-moving' = 'they were riding'
   ka'nerohkwitáhkhe'   'it is **box**-moving' =
                                  'there's a box inside carried along'
   tahonathahítahkhe   'they were **road**-moving hither' =
                                  'they came walking down the road'

4. Transitivity and argument structure

The constructions seen so far have all been intransitive, and in some languages this is the only possible product of noun incorporation. In the three languages under discussion here, noun incorporation can produce both intransitive and transitive verbs.

The majority of Kapampangan verb roots have both intransitive and transitive forms, often multiple forms of each. The same is true of incorporating constructions. The sentence in (15) is transitive.

(15) Kapampangan transitive: Bernadette Mangaser, speaker p.c.
Sekedakaming gebara.
they put us   barge
'They put us on a barge.'

Some Mohawk verb roots are inherently intransitive, some transitive, and some are used both ways. The same is true of verb stems containing incorporated nouns. The transitivity is a lexical feature of the whole. The incorporated noun may or may not have any relation to a core argument of the clause. In (16), the incorporated *-iar-* 'bag' narrows the meaning of the verb 'turn' to actions appropriate for mattresses. The clause is transitive.

(16) Mohawk transitive: Kahentoréhtha' Marie Cross, speaker p.c.
Enstiarakarhathóhseron   kaiarahrónnion.
again I will bag-turn them   **bag**s sitting here and there
'I was going to flip the mattresses.'

The verb in (17) contains an incorporated noun *-na'tsi-* 'pot', and the clause is transitive, but that noun has no relation to the clausal argument 'white beans'. It is just an element of the stem *-na'tsi-a-niiont-* 'pot-suspend' = 'cook (in an iron pot over a fire)'.

(17) Mohawk transitive: Sonny Edwards, speaker p.c.
Tanon' kará:ken nikasahe'tò:ten   ensewana'tsianiión:ten'.
and   white   so it is a kind of bean you will **pot**-hang
'And you'll cook the white beans (in a big, iron pot).'

The transitivity of the Yup'ik constructions is also a lexical matter. Some verb roots are used only intransitively, some only transitively, but most both ways. The constructions under discussion here show the same variation. A number of derived N-*ir*- stems exist: *kavc-ir-* hailstone-*ir*- 'hail', *puy-ir-* smoke-*ir*- 'be smoky', *neg-ir-* 'snare-*ir*- 'set a snare', *ken-ir-* fire-*ir*- 'build a fire under something' or 'cook something', *ac-ir-* name-*ir*- 'name something' *mur-ir-* wood-*ir*- 'stoke something', and more (Jacobson 1984: 457–8). The semantic roles of the nouns vary. Some of the derived stems are intransitive, some transitive, and some either, as in (18).

(18) Yup'ik *-ir-* 'occur', 'set', 'provide': Jacobson 1984: 457–8
   a. *atsirtuq*
      atsa-ir-tu-q
      berry-provided-INTR.INDIC-3SG
      'it is well provided with berries'

b. *atsiraa*
atsa-ir-a-a
berry-provide-TR.INDIC-3SG/3SG
'she added berries to it'

Because incorporation can alter the argument structure of a verb, in all three languages it can provide alternatives that speakers exploit for discourse purposes. The Kapampangan speaker cited in (19) could have said 'Remove the leaves from the trees', casting the leaves as a core argument and the trees as oblique. Instead, he said 'Strip (leaf-remove) the trees', casting the trees as the core argument. The trees, important to the discussion at hand, continued as a core argument of the following clause.

(19) Kapampangan: Clemente Roman, speaker p.c.
Gisandalang   *piglako*   *bulung*
Gisan=da=**la**=ng   piglako   bulung
finished=3PL.ERG=**3PL.ABS**=LK   removed   leaf
'They stripped **the trees** of their leaves

at   *balát*   ***di*=ng**   *taná:man.*
and   killed   COMMON.PL.ABS=LK   tree
and killed them.'

Kapampangan constructions with this effect generally lack the linker =*ng*.

Incorporation in Mohawk provides speakers with similar options. Asked whether she knew a certain person, the speaker in (20) replied 'I've name-heard him' = 'I've heard of him' rather than 'I've heard his name'. The topic of conversation was the person, not his name.

(20) Mohawk topical person as argument: K. Jacobs, speaker p.c.
Rihsennahrónkha'.
ri-hsenn-ahronk-ha'
M.SG/1SG-name-hear-HABITUAL
I used to name-hear **him** =   'I've heard of **him**.'

Similar alternations are available to Yup'ik speakers. Discussing a hunting trip, the speaker in (21) reported that a hunter 'wing-hit the bird' rather than 'he hit its wing'. The bird, cast as a core argument (absolutive), was of more interest to the hungry hunters at that point than the wing.

(21) Yup'ik topical argument: George Charles, speaker p.c.
Yaqulek   *yaqurartaa*
yaqu-lek   yaqur-arte-a-a.
wing-thing.with   wing-hit-TR.INDIC-3SG/**3SG**
bird   he wing-hit **it**
'He hit **the bird** right in the wing.'

In all three languages, both intransitive and transitive verbs can enter into the construction, and the incorporating constructions can be intransitive or transitive.

5. The no phrase constraint and syntactically complex constituents

The No Phrase Constraint states that morphological operations should have no access to the output of syntactic operations. If compounding is a morphological process, it should not be possible to form compounds from syntactic phrases. Yet compounds with syntactically complex constituents are well documented, such as the English *pipe and slipper husband* and *God is dead theology* (Botha 1985, Lieber 1992, Lieber and Scalise 2006). The constructions under discussion here vary with respect to this property.

In the Kapampangan construction, syntactically complex nominals are in fact quite common. A typical example is (22).

(22) Kapampangan syntactically complex nominal: C. Roman, speaker
Gawa=la=ng   tahada=ng mani   at   letsi plan.
will.make=3PL.ABS=LK brittle=LK peanut and milk flan
'They'll make **peanut brittle and milk flan**.'

In Mohawk, incorporated nouns are never complex syntactically. Some are complex morphologically, but these are already well-established lexical items. The verb in (23) contains the incorporated stem 'table'. This stem is a nominalized verb with an incorporated noun of its own: *ate-khw-a-hra*-MIDDLE-*food*-LINKER-*set*.

(23) Mohawk complex nominal: Kaia'titáhkhe' Jacobs, speaker p.c.
katekhwahra'tsheria'ákhons
k-**atekhwahra-'tsher**-ia'ak-hon-s
1SG.AGT-**table**-NOMINALIZER-hit-DISTRIBUTIVE-HABITUAL
'I'm **table** pounding' = 'I'm pounding on the table.'

Some Mohawk incorporation might appear to involve syntactically complex nominals as input. On the basis of the English translation, the example in (24) might be interpreted as the result of incorporating just the head of a phrase 'other story', leaving the remainder 'stranded' outside.

(24) Mohawk stranded modifier?: Watshenní:ne Sawyer, speaker p.c.
Shé:kon   ò:ia'   wakká:raien'
shekon   ohia'   wak-kar-a-ien-'
still   other   1SG.PAT-story-LK-have-STATIVE
still   **other**   I **story** have
'I have another story.'

But ò:ia' 'other' also appears with verbs without an incorporated noun, such as 'wear' in (25). It is a referring expression on its own: 'other ones'.

(25) Mohawk independent nominal: Margaret Edwards, speaker p.c.
Enwá:ton'   *ò:ia'*   *entsítewatste'*
en-w-aton-'   ohia'   en-tsi-tewa-at-st-e'
FUTURE-N.AGT-be.possible   other   FUTURE-REP-1.INCL.AGT-MIDDLE-use-PRF
it will be possible   **other** we will wear
'We can change clothes.'

Quantifiers and numerals occur with verbs containing incorporated nouns.

(26) Mohawk quantifier *é:so'* 'much': Watshenní:ne Sawyer, speaker p.c.
Iah   *é:so'*   *teionkwa**hwíst**aien'.*
iah   eso'   te-ionkwa-hwist-a-ien-'
not   much   NEG-1PL.PAT-money-LK-have-STATIVE
not   **much** did we **money** have
'We didn't have much money.'

But the same quantifiers also occur without an incorporated noun.

(27) Mohawk quantifier *é:so'* 'much': Watshenní:ne Sawyer, speaker p.c.
Iah   *é:so'*   *tekaién:tahkwe'*
iah   eso'   te-ka-ient-ahkwe'
not   **much** NEG-NEUTER.AGT-lie-FORMER.PAST
'There wasn't much.'

It is possible in Mohawk to evoke a whole event or fact, normally expressed in a clause, within a verb, but this is accomplished by a simple incorporated noun root like -*rihw*- 'fact, matter, affair, idea, etc.'

(28) Mohawk incorporated stand-in for a clause: Lazarus Jacob, speaker
*Io**rihw**anónhste'*   *tsi*   *nihatí:iere'*
io-**rihw**-anon-hst-e'   tsi   ni-hati-ier-e'
N.PAT-**matter**-confidential-CAUS-STATIVE so   PRT-M.PL.AGT-do-STATIVE
it is **matter**-confidential   so   they did

ne   onhwentsakaiòn:ne   ne   ratitsihénhstatsi.
the old world place   the priests
'What the priests did in Europe has been kept confidential.'

In Yup'ik, syntactic phrases do not serve as stems for verbal derivation. The nominal base can be complex morphologically.

(29) Yup'ik morphologically complex noun stem: E. Charles, speaker p.c.
Enecuarirluki.
ene-cuar-ir-lu-ki
house-small-build-SUBORD-3PL/3PL
'They would build them **small houses**.'

Yup'ik does exhibit constructions which might appear to be derived from syntactically complex NPs by head movement, stranding a modifier.

(30) Yup'ik stranded modifiers? Elena Charles, speaker p.c.
Qantangqerrlallriit	*angelrianek.*
qanta-ngqerr-lar-llrii-t	ange-lria-nek
bowl-have-customarily-INTR.PARTICIPIAL-3PL	be.large-NMZ-ABL.PL
they **bowl**-have	**large**

'They have **large bowls**.'

The word *angelrianek* 'large', however, is a nominal in its own right. It is a nominalized verb, best translated 'large ones'. Similar nominalized forms appear in construction with verbs containing no noun root at all.

(31) Yup'ik similar 'modifiers' without no noun base: E. Ali, speaker
Assitelriamek-gguq	*tunellinikiit.*
assite-lria-mek=gguq	tune-llini-kii-t
be.bad-NMZ-ABL.PL=HEARSAY	sell-apparently-TR.PARTICIPIAL-3PL
bad one	they apparently sold him

'They sold him **a bad one**.'

As in Mohawk, numerals can appear in sentences with verbs based on a noun stem. Here, too, however, the same numerals also appear with verbs containing no noun stem.

(32) Yup'ik stranded numeral?: Elena Charles, speaker p.c.
Tutgarangqerrsaaqua,	*Seattleami*	*malrugnek.*
tutgar-ngqerr-yaaqe-u-a	Seattle-ami	malrug-nek
grandchild-have-actually-INTR.INDIC-1SG	Seattle-LOC	two-ABL.DU
I actually **grandchild**-have	in Seattle	**two**

'I actually have **two grandchildren** in Seattle.'

(33) Yup'ik numeral without noun base: Elena Charles, speaker p.c.
Malrugnek	*qavarluta.*
malrug-nek	qavar-lu-ta
two-ABL.DU	sleep-SUBORD-1PL.ABS
two	we slept

'We stayed **two** nights.'

6. The lexical integrity hypothesis and sublexical reference

Lieber and Scalise 2006 provide a useful survey of the literature on the Lexical Integrity Hypothesis. As characterized by Anderson (1992: 84) this says that "The syntax neither manipulates nor has access to the internal structure of words". More recently, Ackema and Neeleman (2005: 109) have proposed that "The structure of complex words is invisible to syntax because syntax builds up the 'host structure' and morphologically complex words are inserted into this structure". Booij (2009) argues, on the other hand, that morphological and syntactic structure are built up in parallel, so 'that the possibility of syntax and semantics having access to word-internal structure is to be expected'. An indication that syntactic processes have access to the internal structure of words would be sublexical reference, in our case, reference to incorporated nouns.

In some incorporating constructions in Kapampangan, the constituents are linked by the enclitic =*ng*. In others, they are simply juxtaposed. When the linker is present, the noun is not an argument, but subsequent pronominal reference to the entity it introduces is very common.

(34) Kapampangan linked nominal as antecedent: C. Roman, speaker
*Kumalang   mitsa, sindian=**de**.*
kuma=la=ng   mitsa, sindian=**de**.
get=3PL.ABS=LK wick   ignite=3PL/**3SG**
'They will get a wick and ignite **it**.'

In constructions without the linker, the noun is again not an argument, and there is no evidence that the incorporated nominal ever serves as an antecedent for subsequent reference. When speakers wish to refer to an entity evoked in this construction, the noun is repeated.

(35) Kapampangan repetition of noun: Clemente Roman, speaker p.c.
['They will start tinkering with the pig's ears.']

*Paglakoro   **dinat**.*
Paglako=ro   **dinat**
remove=3PL/3PL   **dirt**
they will **dirt**-remove them

Ampo itang pambuk na kini,
and then its snout,

*paglakore   **dinat**.*
paglako=re   **dinat**
remove=3PL/3SG   **dirt**
they will **dirt**-remove it

'They'll clean the **dirt** off of its ears and clean the **dirt** off its snout.'

In Mohawk, incorporated nouns also do not establish reference for subsequent pronominal reference in spontaneous speech. To establish an antecedent for subsequent reference, an independent nominal is supplied.

(36) Mohawk subsequent reference, lexical nominal: S. Edwards speaker
Shaià:ta   ronkwe'tarákwen
one **male person** he **person**-chose him
'He picked one man

ne nen ówera' enhaten'nikòn:raren.'
the that wind **he** will his mind-set on it
who would guard the wind.'

Incorporated nouns are not themselves referential, though they may evoke an identifiable referent, like 'mind' in the verb 'guard' ('mind-set') in (36). If a given incorporated noun occurs repeatedly within a short span of discourse, each instance does not necessarily evoke the same referent. In (37), speakers were discussing a book they were translating. The same book was being translated into other languages, but the Mohawk version was scheduled to be published first. The root *-wenn-* is not coreferential.

(37) Mohawk lack of coreference: C. Bush and J. Horne, speakers p.c.
CB *Ohén:ton í:kate'   onkwawén:na'.*
    in front   it is standing our **language**
    'Our language is the first in line.'

JH [...] *ni: ónhka' entionkhiiatewennátahse'*   [...]
    also who   one will put one's **voice** in to us hither
    '[Yes, it will be for sale], and whoever calls us on the telephone,
    [we'll have it in stock for them to purchase it.]'

CB [...] *ahatiwennahnotónnion'*
    they could **word** stand variously
    '[That's right, isn't it, and they can really] read it.'

The noun bases in the Yup'ik constructions are also not usually picked up referentially by pronominals. In order to establish a referent, speakers usually supply an independent noun, often the same as the base.

(38) Yup'ik lexical nominal for subsequent reference: E. Charles, speaker
Iciugg',   Frankiq angyangqellrul'.
remember Frank   he **boat**-had
'Remember Frank had **a boat**.

Angyaq-llu camek imainani.
boat-and   things it contents-lacked
And **the boat** was empty.'

Yup'ik constructions like that in (38), with light verbs like 'have', 'exist', 'arrive', 'make', etc., are often used to introduce the idea of an entity into the discourse, normally followed by establishment of the referent in an independent lexical nominal. On relatively rare occasions, speakers skip the nominal.

(39) Yup'ik rare antecedent in light presentative: E. Charles, speaker p.c.
Ucilirluteng,   avegluku.
they **load**-made they halved **it**
'They made **a load**, dividing **it** in half.'

The constructions in the three languages thus differ in the possibility of sublexical reference. Nominals in the Kapampangan =*ng* construction can and often do serve as antecedents for subsequent pronominal reference. Those in which the nominals are simply juxtaposed to verbs do not. Mohawk incorporated nouns do not normally establish reference. Yup'ik noun bases rarely establish reference.

7. Wordhood

The incorporating constructions in the three languages thus differ with respect to both the No Phrase Constraint and the Lexical Integrity Constraint. The variation is not random. A major function of morphology is word formation. The processes described here vary in the degree to which they create words.

The Kapampangan construction consists of the juxtaposition of full words, each recognizable and pronounceable in isolation. There are no phonological processes that apply specifically to these constructions, such as a compound stress rule. Speakers may pause between the verbal and nominal constituents. In the transcription of (40), three dots [...] represent a substantial pause, and two dots [..] a shorter pause. The verb and noun in the second line were separated by a substantial pause, and those in the third line by another, briefer pause.

(40) Kapampangan pauses: Clemente Roman, speaker p.c.
Magdalalang sabun,
'They will bring soap,

magdalalang	...	*pintura,*
they will bring	...	paint,
magdalalang	..	*miyaliwang gamit*
they will bring	..	other things [to clean the graves of their relatives].'

The verbal and nominal constituents in such constructions are sometimes even separated by additional words, such as the particle *pa* 'also' in (41).

(41) Kapampangan intervening word: Clemente Roman, speaker p.c.
At   biasaya   **pa**=ng   manese.
and   she knew also=LK cook.rice
'And she **also** knew how to cook rice.'

Mohawk noun incorporation is a process of stem compounding. Neither the incorporated noun stem nor the incorporating verb stem can stand alone as a word, and speakers would not normally recognize either in isolation. Independent nouns generally contain a prefix indicating gender or a possessor, and a noun suffix. The noun root for 'fish' is *-itsi-*, but the noun word for 'fish' is *kéntsion'*. Verbs must contain, minimally, a pronominal prefix identifying their core arguments, as in 'they caught it'.

(42)   Mohawk noun
       kéntsion'   *wahatiién:ta'ne'*.
       ka-itsi-on'   wa-hati-ienta'n-e'
       NEUTER-fish-NOUN.SUFFIX   FACTUAL-M.PL.AGT-catch-PRF
       'fish'   'they caught it'

There is no question that verbs with incorporated nouns, like *wahatitsiaién:ta'ne'* 'they caught fish', are single words both phonologically and morphologically. Stress is consistently penultimate (with certain epenthetic vowels not counted, including the linker *-a-*). Numerous phonological processes occur word-internally but not between words. Within words, apart from the insertion of the linker *-a-*, the same kinds of phonological processes operate between incorporated noun stems and incorporating verb stems as elsewhere. Morphologically, both nouns and verbs show strict templatic ordering of morphemes. Asked to repeat sentences word-by word, speakers always pronounce verbs with incorporated nouns as single units. They never pause inside of words, and words are never inserted inside of words.

The Yup'ik constructions are also clearly single phonological and morphological words. The word constitutes a phonological domain for stress and numerous other word-internal sandhi phenomena. Words also have strict word-internal morphological structure. All verbs begin with a root. Speakers never pause within words then continue, and they never insert other words inside of them.

8. Frequency and productivity

A difference often observed between morphological and syntactic processes is productivity. Degree of productivity is sometimes assessed in terms of frequency: highly productive processes are assumed to result in greater frequency of occurrence. The constructions in the three languages do vary in their frequency, though perhaps not in the way that might be expected. The figures in (43) contrast the densities of incorporating constructions in comparable 3000-word samples of spontaneous speech in the three languages, primarily conversation. Incorporation is significantly more frequent in Mohawk than in the other two languages.

(43) Frequency: percentages of clauses with the construction
Kapampangan 7.5%
Mohawk 38.3%
Yup'ik 7.3%

But comparisons of actual productivity reveal a different pattern.

The Kapampangan construction shows full productivity: any noun phrase can be combined with any verb so long as it makes sense. Loanwords are easily and spontaneously accommodated.

(44) Kapampangan loan: Bernadette Mangaser
Ibalutmeng aluminum foil.
'Wrap it in aluminum foil.'

Mohawk differs substantially. Noun incorporation is productive, as can be seen in (45), with the incorporated loan *job* plus nominalizer *-tsher*.

(45) Mohawk incorporated loan
*Ronwati**jobtsher**awíhne.*
they had **job**-given them
'They had given them jobs.'

But innovation is relatively rare. Speakers generally notice neologisms and comment on them. This particular combination 'job-give' has now found a place in the language as a lexical item.

The productivity of Mohawk noun incorporation is actually not a feature of the construction as a whole, but of individual noun and verb stems: some stems occur exclusively in such constructions, some often, some occasionally, some rarely, and some never. The situation is similar to that of derivation: productivity is not a feature of derivation as a whole in a language, but rather of individual derivational processes.

Yup'ik shows a similar pattern. The productivity of the verbalizing derivation can be seen in its application to loanwords, a process that occurs more frequently in Yup'ik than in Mohawk. The noun *potlatch* (a kind of feast), for example, came into the language from Chinook Jargon, which adopted it from Nuuchahnulth *patlač* 'gift'.

(46) Yup'ik productivity: loanword base: Elena Charles, speaker p.c.
Potlatch-*aliyalriit.*
they **potlatch**-participate in
'They come to the potlatch.'

The productivity of the Yup'ik construction is also a property of individual morphemes rather than the process as a whole. Some suffixes are highly productive, such as *-u-* 'be' and *-li-* 'make'. Some are marginally productive, such as *-ir-* 'deprive'. Some are unproductive, such as *-llite-* 'encounter'. Much is of course domain-specific, such as *-virte-* 'go to', which occurs only with demonstrative bases that have allative forms, like *kia-ni* 'upriver, inside, inland', *kiavirtuq* 'he is going upriver, inside, inland'; (Jacobson 1984: 458, 461).

9. Lexicalization and institutionalization

Word-formation processes function to create lexical items, which can be learned and accessed as units. The property of being stored in memory is often termed *lexicalization*. Bauer proposes a finer distinction between those stored items which are semantically regular and those which are not.

> It might in addition be useful to have a label for those established words which, despite their being established, still form part of a synchronically productive series, differing only from potential words in that, by being used, they have come to have a specific reference. Following Bauer 1983, I shall term such words *institutionalized*. *Institutionalized* and *lexicalized* are thus, by definition, complementary terms, co-hyponyms of *established*. Bakken (1998: 72) prefers the term *conventionalization* here, defining a conventionalized word as one which can be recognized and understood out of context, while a coinage requires its context to be comprehensible. She also notes that conventionalization is a scale, sliding into lexicalization.
>
> (Bauer 2001: 46).

The Kapampangan constructions show little evidence of either lexicalization or institutionalization, no more than other syntactic verb-complement constructions. They are generally transparent semantically. The language contains other word-formation devices that serve some of the functions of the incorporating constructions in Mohawk and Yup'ik. There are highly productive derivational verbalizing processes which operate not only on native roots but on borrowed forms as well.

(47) Kapampangan word formation: Clemente Roman, speaker p.c.
Mig-apartmentya.
mig-apartment=ya
VERBALIZER-apartment=3SG.ABS
'She rented her own apartment.'

Mohawk noun incorporation, though much more frequent in speech than its Kapampangan counterpart, shows comparatively strong institutionalization and lexicalization. Speakers are generally aware of which combinations exist in the language and which do not but could, even where all formations are perfectly regular. Awareness of innovations varies to some degree with the individual productivity of the constituents.

There is good evidence that most compound stems are established, stored in memory rather than formed online during speech. The passage in (48) contains

4 clauses, each with an incorporated noun. Each pertains to fish. But the noun root *-itsi-* 'fish' was incorporated in only two of the verbs. The noun root *-ia't-* 'body' was incorporated in the other two.

(48) Mohawk *-itsi-* 'fish' and *-ia't-* 'body': Sonny Edwards, speaker p.c.
Tanon' ní: kon'tákie'   ionwan**itsi**atorá:ton
and   we all day long we were **fish**-hunting
'And we were fishing all day long

kwah iah ne   skaià:ta teionkw**entsi**aiontà:'on.
even not that one   did we **fish**-get
and we didn't even get one fish.

wahshe**ia**'tatshén:ri'   karón:takon kont**iià**:ti   kéntsion'.
you **body** found them log inside   they're **body** in it fish
[How could it be that] you found the fish inside a log?'

The speaker was not assembling the verbs with incorporated nouns as he spoke. He was accessing known compound verb stems as units: 'fish-hunt', 'fish-get', 'body-find', and 'body-be.in'.

Yup'ik shows similar patterns of lexicalization and institutionalization. The same derived forms tend to recur in speech. Speakers know that *neqe-te-* 'fish-catch' exists, but that the combination **luqruuyar-te-* 'pike-catch' does not, even though it would be perfectly regular. Catching pike can be expressed only in separate words: *Luqruuyanek pitnaurtukut*.

As is typical of compounds, the meanings of the Yup'ik derivational constructions are not necessarily semantically compositional. The derived stems are usually formed for a specific purpose and learned and stored as units. They are free to shift in meaning through use, independently of their parts. The suffix *-te-* does not always contribute the precise meaning 'catch': *mallu* 'beached carcass', *mallutuq* 'he **found** a beached carcass'; *yuk* 'person', *yugtuq* 'he committed murder'; *kass'aq* 'white person', *kass'artuq* 'he went to the city on a shopping trip' (Jacobson 1984: 586).

In Yup'ik, as in Mohawk, speaker awareness of innovations varies with the productivity of individual morphemes. New formations with highly productive suffixes may be noticed barely if at all, but others are recognized as neologisms even when regular in form and meaning.

10. Conclusion

The Kapampangan, Mohawk, and Yup'ik constructions share some fundamental formal and functional features. All involve the combination of a verbal element and a nominal element to form a new verb headed by the verbal element. All could be classified as endocentric and synthetic. All show a range of semantic relationships between the incorporated noun and the verb. All provide speakers with choices: verbs with alternative argument structures that can be selected to shape coherent discourse.

The constructions in the three languages show different behaviors with respect to the No Phrase Constraint and the Lexical Integrity Hypothesis, however. The Kapampangan =*ng* construction often violates the No Phrase Constraint: the nominal elements in these constructions can be syntactically complex. The same construction is also frequently out of line with the Lexical Integrity Hypothesis: the nominal elements in these constructions are apparently visible to the syntax, in that they often serve as antecedents of subsequent pronouns. When the nominal constituent is more tightly bound, however, simply juxtaposed, subsequent reference is not possible. Noun incorporation in Mohawk, by contrast, shows no exceptions to either hypothesis. The incorporated noun is never syntactically complex, and it does not serve on its own as an antecedent for subsequent reference in spontaneous speech. The Yup'ik construction is much like Mohawk noun incorporation. The nominal element may be a noun root or stem, but it is never syntactically complex. It does not normally serve as the antecedent of subsequent pronominals, though in constructions with certain light verbalizing suffixes, it may. The differences among the constructions in the three languages are not random. They correlate with the degree of formal integration of the constituents and the status of the output.

The Kapampangan constructions are the most syntactic: they involve the combination of whole words and phrases. They are not distinguished phonologically from other syntactic constructions. Speakers may pause between the constituents and even insert certain particles. They are fully productive. They do not generally form new lexical items, at least no more often than basic predicate-argument combinations. They are semantically compositional. They can be fully described in terms of general principles: any nominal phrase may be expressed as a non-argument by means of the linker =*ng* or simple juxtaposition in place of a determiner.

The Mohawk and Yup'ik constructions, by contrast, are solidly word-formation devices. They create single phonological and grammatical words. They generally produce lexical items that are stored and retrieved as units. Their productivity is variable, a characteristic not of the constructions but of the individual morphemes that enter into them. The constructions also vary in their semantic transparency. As institutionalized lexical items, they are free to evolve in meaning with use, independently of the meanings of their constituents. It is important to note that there is no clear line between fully productive incorporating or derivational processes on the one hand, with fully transparent semantics and regular syntactic consequences, and an irregular residue on the other. As word-formation processes, they are exploited to form lexical items corresponding to specific concepts. Productivity of a word-formation process does not necessarily entail full regularity of form and meaning.

Incorporation is thus not a homogenous process, nor is it static over time. The constructions examined here appear to reflect different stages of development. The Kapampangan constructions are typical of early stages: more syntactic and less integrated. They operate over full words and syntactic phrases, and their constituents are still accessible to speakers. Though they are not core arguments, the nominal elements in =*ng* constructions can still be referential in their own right and serve as antecedents of subsequent pronouns. The nominal elements of constructions without the linker =*ng*, more tightly bound to their verbal heads by simple juxtaposition, do not serve as antecedents. It is likely that Mohawk noun incorporation developed from a similar structure, in which uninflected nouns were juxtaposed to verbs as qualifiers rather than syntactic arguments. As the constructions evolved over time, recurring combinations came to be processed as chunks, the formal and semantic bonds grew stronger, and the process became increasingly morphological. The Yup'ik derivational construction is likely to have developed from a stem compounding construction much like that in Mohawk (Mithun 1997, 1998a,b). Certain verb roots that recurred frequently as heads of noun-verb compounds became more general and abstract in meaning over time and began to erode phonologically. The result is a continuum, as formal and functional properties emerge and fade.

Compounding versus derivation

Angela Ralli
University of Patras

This chapter examines the demarcation of compounds and derivative items. It is argued that the two types of constructions belong to word-formation, and intermingle in such a way that only the same grammatical domain could handle them properly. This domain is considered to be morphology, and claims and proposals are exemplified with data drawn from Standard Modern Greek and its dialects.
The following issues are tackled:
a. The order of application of the two processes. It is shown that there are cases which advocate a non-linear order between the two.
b. The existence of a specific constraint, which demonstrates the close interaction of the two processes, since the structure of derivative items seems to be accessible to compounding and affected by its application.
c. A peculiar borderline case, according to which a free lexical item in Standard Modern Greek has acquired a fuzzy categorial status in one dialect, but has become a pure prefix into another. To this end, the chapter focuses on the crucial role of dialectal evidence.

1. The issue – previous literature

It is generally known that compounding denotes the combining of words or stems to form a new complex item, while most derivative items imply the presence of an affix, unless derivative words are formed by conversion (considered also as zero affixation, see Marchand 1969), or stem-internal modification.[1] Traditionally, both processes are considered to belong to word formation, but there are also proposals, such as that put forward by Anderson (1992), who considers compounding to be a fundamentally different mechanism from derivation. More specifically, he argues that word-internal structure does not exist in derivative items but only in compounds.

In more recent literature, the strongest reaction to these views has come from Probal, Ford & Singh (2000), who claim that there is no difference between derivation

---

1. See Sapir (1921: 61) for the notion of stem- or root-internal modification, and Don, Trommelen & Zonneveld (2000) for the issue of conversion.

and compounding, and that both processes are instances of word formation and should be accounted for by the same rule pattern.[2] A weaker position is expressed by other authors, such as Naumann & Vogel (2000), ten Hacken (2000), and Booij (2005), who have argued that, although different, derivation and compounding are not sharply distinguished, and that their borderline can be permeable in both ways. Their main arguments are based on the existence of certain categories of an unclear status, which can be classified as categorially marginal affixes or categorially marginal lexemes, showing properties that can be shared by both affixes and lexemes. In the past, most of these categories had been considered to belong to a different class, situated between lexemes and affixes. They had been called affixoids, pseudo-affixes (cf. Fleischer 1969, Schmidt 1987), semi-affixes (Marchand 1967, 1969), or semi-words (Scalise 1984). To take an example, *–ware* in *hardware* or *–like* in *Godlike* could be classified as suffixoids, since, according to Marchand (1969: 326), they are used as second members of morphologically-complex items, although they are still recognizable as words. Crucially, Booij (2005: 117) has observed that the postulation of affixoids is a convenient description of the fact that the boundary between derivation and compounding is blurred, independently of whether affixoids could form a separate class. This piece of evidence has driven him to propose that derivation and compounding should receive the same treatment within morphology, along the lines of the *Construction Morphology* framework.[3] Bauer (2005) has put the problem in another way by arguing that it is not the distinction between the two processes which is questionable, but the fact that diachronically, items do not always maintain their independent status. On the basis of certain borderline cases, he raises an important question, as to whether derivation and compounding are two distinct processes or prototypes at each end of a single dimension (2005: 97). Although he does not provide an explicit answer to this question, his position seems to be towards the direction that compounding should not be assigned to a different grammatical domain from that of derivation.

Another criterion for distinguishing compounding from derivation relates to the kind of units which participate in a morphologically-complex item, and the position which they occupy within a word.[4] It is usually assumed that compounding involves free items (Fabb 1998), which may appear either as left-hand or right-hand constituents. On

---

2. In previous literature, a unified treatment of compounding and derivation within the same grammatical domain is implicitly assumed by Lieber (1980), who claims that both affixes and stems are part of the lexical entries of the permanent lexicon, but also by Kiparsky (1982) and Mohanan (1986), who assign compounding and derivation to different levels of a stratified lexicon.

3. Among the recent linguistic studies which have dealt with the same issue see, for instance, Beard (2000), Naumann & Vogel (2000), Stekauer (2005), Scalise, Bisetto & Guevara (2005), Fradin (2005), and Amiot (2005).

4. Ten Hacken (2000: 352–353) provides an overview of the different semantic criteria, which have been proposed for the determination of the semantic differences between derivation and compounding.

the contrary, affixes participating in derivation are bound elements, which obey strict positional restrictions: prefixes precede the base, while suffixes follow. The criterion of the position seems to be more or less valid, although in the so-called 'neoclassical compounds', there are elements, which may appear either as left or right-hand constituents. *Phil-* is such an element in English words like *philharmonic* and *Francophile*. In fact, the categorial status of these items is not very clear in that they share properties of both affixes and lexemes, and Martinet (1979) has called them 'confixes'. Boundness, however, cannot be a safe criterion. For instance, bound forms can participate as basic components in compound structures, as is the case of Modern Greek (hereafter Greek) compounds, where the first constituent is most of the times a stem, which cannot be used as an autonomous word without the appropriate inflectional ending.

Historically, the fuzzy border between the two processes is reflected in the traditional grammatical descriptions of classical languages, such as Ancient Greek and Latin, where there is a tendency to group together prefixation and compounding, as opposed to suffixation, which is considered to belong to derivation (see, for instance, the work by Grimm 1826 and the neo-grammarian Wilmanns 1896). This tendency is based on the idea that while suffixes are capable of deriving further notions from basic roots, prefixes do not have this capacity. The same idea has led Marchand (1967) to view suffixation as being part of *transposition*, while he classifies prefixation and compounding under the category of *expansion*, that is as processes where the determinatun (head) is situated at the right side of a morphologically complex word, and the determinant (modifier) at the left side.

Today, it is a common practice to put together prefixation and suffixation under the process of derivation. However, the fact that prefixes behave differently from suffixes, in many respects, is questionable, and the demarcation of prefixation and compounding seems to be a challenging task. For instance, in many languages, prefixes are category neutral, while suffixes can change the category of the base. Since this particular property of prefixes is usually shared by left components of right-headed compounds, it could serve as an argument for incorporating prefixation into compounding, and consequently, as an argument for compounding being not clearly distinct from derivation.

Finally, a possible overlap between compounding and derivation can also be diachronically motivated, since many prefixes and suffixes originate from first or second components of compounds (see Wilmanns 1896 and Paul 1920). For instance, as reported by Olsen (2000: 901), this is true for a number of German suffixes, such as *–heit* (e.g. *manheit*), and their English counterparts (e.g. *–hood* in *manhood*).

In this chapter, derivation and compounding are considered to constitute instances of word formation, and as such, they are accounted for within morphology. However, there is no explicit position on whether they are generated by rule (cf. Probal, Ford & Singh 2000), or are analogically created according to certain basic schemas (cf. Booij 2005). Although their occurrences rely on the presence of different units (for instance, in some languages compounds involve stems, and derivation affixes), it is shown that they intermingle in several ways. The main arguments are based on the following issues:

a. The order of application of the two processes. Within a level/strata-based model, it has been claimed that the level of compounding follows that of derivation (see, for example, Mohanan 1986). This claim could be used as an argument for postulating the different character of compounding, and assign it to syntax. In the next section, it is demonstrated that there is no linear ordering between the two processes, since, on the one hand, there are cases where derivation precedes compounding, and on the other hand, there are several instances of derivational affixes, which are added to productive compound formations.

b. The existence of morphological constraints, which refer to one process, but may have an impact on the other. Specific reference is made to a constraint, which affects the internal form of Greek compounds by prohibiting derivational suffixes to appear as parts of the first stem components.

c. The well-known issue of affixoids, which are tackled from a different perspective from that which appears in recent literature, as for instance, in the work by Naumann & Vogel (2000), Olsen (2000), ten Hacken (2000), Bauer (2005), and Booij (2005). Most of these studies point out the crucial role of affixoids in showing the non distinct boundaries between derivation and compounding, since the border of the two processes can be crossed several times in the history of a language. Although new data can always lead to insightful observations, the purpose of this chapter is not to add another piece of evidence to the already long list of these elements, across languages. Instead, it demonstrates the important contribution of dialectal evidence to the discussion about the limits of the two processes because dialects can provide significant testimony to changes, which have occurred in the past, but cannot be detected in the actual form of the Standard Language. To this end, according to an ongoing cross-dialectal change in Greek an adverbial lexical item in Standard Modern Greek (hereafter SMG) has acquired a blurry categorial status in one dialect, while it has become a pure prefix in another.[5]

As already mentioned, this paper takes a position in favor of compounding being a word-formation process, together with derivation. If there is no clear demarcation between the two processes, and they intermingle and constraint each other, there is no reason why they should be treated separately in different grammatical components. The obvious question that arises though is whether an approach of classifying

---

5. As stated in Ralli (2009b), dialectal evidence is of significant importance for the study of various linguistic phenomena, since dialects may make visible a phenomenon, which can be masked by the Standard language for various reasons. This is the case for Greek. SMG has been developed in the last two centuries, following the constitution of the Modern Greek State, while the dialects are direct descendants of Hellenistic Koine (ca 3rd c. BC – 3rd c. AD). Whereas SMG reflects a conservative linguistic policy to preserve certain structures, dialects constitute a real and rich source of information concerning innovations.

compounding among the word-formation processes could apply across languages, or depends on the particular language one deals with. A plausible answer to this question goes beyond the limits of this paper. However, a study, which draws conclusions on a possible interaction between derivation and compounding, as well as on their domain of application, should rely on data from languages with particularly developed derivational and compounding systems. Moreover, suggestions and proposals are sufficiently motivated if they can be tested against a wealth of possible phenomena. Therefore, the argumentation is based on Greek, which abounds in derivational affixes, suffixes and prefixes, and is extremely rich in compounding. With respect to the latter, it should be noticed that Greek seems to have a bigger variety of compound structures than any other language of the Indo-European family, since it builds productively not only nominal and adjectival compounds, but also verbal ones, of all types and patterns, even V V dvandva compounds (e.g. *anigoklino* 'open-close' < *anig(o)* 'open' *klino* 'close'), which are unknown, or rare, in the other Indo-European languages.[6]

2. Order of application between derivation and compounding

A simple answer to the question whether compounding is related to derivation can be given by the fact that derivational affixes can appear within compounds. As noticed by Beard (1998: 53) and Fabb (1998: 67), this is the case for synthetic compounds. Another issue with respect to the same question concerns the order according to which the two processes occur.

Within a strata-ordered framework (see Kiparsky 1982, Mohanan 1986), Ralli (1988) has claimed that in Greek, most derivational processes occur before compounding, and that the stratum of derivation precedes that of compounding. As a corollary of this order, one could predict that derived items should generally appear as constituents of compound words.[7] This prediction seems to be borne out as far as the second

---

6. Crucially Greek abounds in borderline cases too. Numerous examples can be found either as right-hand constituents, for instance, in the so-called 'neoclassical compounds' or as left-hand components, where preverbs originate from Ancient Greek prepositions or adverbs. For more information on Greek preverbs see Ralli (2004), Dimela & Melissaropoulou (2007), and on neoclassical compounds Ralli (2008b, in preparation).

7. With respect to derivation, we restrict our attention only to suffixation, since, as already mentioned, the derivational status of several prefixes is not a clear-cut case, and that in many respects several prefixes behave like the left-hand constituents of compounds. For instance, in English prefixation, suffice to mention the properties of stress subordination and categorial neutrality that are shared by the so-called Class II prefixes (e.g. *pro-* and *en-* as in the words *proclitics* and *enclitics*) and the left-hand constituents of compounds (see, among others, Stekauer 2005).

compound constituent is concerned, which, in several instances, constitutes a derived item. Consider the following examples:[8]

(1) a. AN-compound   Structure
        mikrovarkada   [[mikr]-o-[vark-ad-a]]   vs.   ?mikrovarka
        little boating   little-Cm-boat-Daff-Infl   little boat

    b. NN-compound
        nixokoptis   [[nix]-o-[kop-ti-s]]   vs.   *nixokovo
        nail clipper   nail-Cm-cut-Daff-Infl   cut nails

    where Cm=compound marker/linking element,[9] Daff=derivational suffix, and Infl=inflection.

On the basis of these examples, one could safely claim that the second constituent has been derived before compounding, since formations like ?*mikrovarka*, and **nixokovo* are either not possible or sound peculiar.

Significant support to the suggestion that the derivation of the second constituent occurs before compounding is provided by the position of stress. As shown by Nespor & Ralli (1996), a compound which is built on a [Stem Stem] pattern is subject to a compound-specific stress rule, which places stress on the antepenultimate syllable of the word, independently of where stress falls when the two constituents are taken in isolation (after being supplied with the appropriate inflectional ending):

(2) a. [[Stem-Cm-Stem]$_{stem}$-Infl]$_{word}$ <   [Stem-Infl]$_{word}$ [Stem-Infl]$_{word}$
        nixt-o-lúlud-o   <   níxt-a   lulúd-i
        night flower   <   night   flower
        vs.
    b. *nixtolulúdo

In (2a), compounding builds the complex stem *nixtolulud-* by combining two stems, *nixt-* 'night' and *lulud-* 'flower'.[10] An inflectional ending -*o* is added to this formation, and the compound word *nixtolúludo* 'night flower' gets its stress on the antepenultimate syllable by the compound-specific stress rule. Significant proof to the hypothesis that *nixtolúludo* is a [Stem Stem] compound comes from the fact that it bears a different inflectional ending (i.e. -*o*) from the ending shown by the second constituent (-*i*), when used as an independent word.

Crucially, when the right-hand slot of the compound is filled by a derived item, the application of the antepenultimate-stress rule is blocked, and the formation displays the stress of the derived item. Consider the example in (3), where *thalasodarménos* 'sea beaten' is stressed in the same way as its second component *darménos* 'beaten',

---

8. Greek examples are given a broad phonological transcription, and stress is noted only if it is relevant for the argumentation.
9. About compound markers/linking elements in Greek and other languages, see Ralli (2008a).
10. See Mithun (this volume) for stem-based compounds in Mohawk.

while an occurrence such as *thalasodármenos, bearing a compound-specific stress on the antepenultimate syllable, is not acceptable:

(3) [[Stem-Cm-[Stem-Daff-Infl]$_{word}$]$_{word}$ < [Stem-Infl]$_{word}$ [Stem-Daff-Infl]$_{word}$
    thalas-o-dar-mén-os   < thálas-a   dar-mén-os[11]
    sea beaten   sea   beaten
    vs.
    *thalasodármenos

Following work by Nespor & Ralli (1996) and Ralli (2007, 2009a, in preparation), the vast majority of compounds with derived items at their right-hand side have a different structure from those illustrated by the example in (2). They belong to a [Stem Word] pattern, where the second constituent is built as an inflected derived word before entering compounding.[12] As such, it preserves its stress, structure, and its inflectional ending, which are inherited by the compound as a whole.

2.1 The bare-stem constraint

The prediction that derivation occurs before compounding does not seem to be confirmed as far as the first constituent is concerned, because derivational suffixes do not usually appear within compounds, the first member of which has the form of a bare stem.[13] However, as noticed by Ralli & Karasimos (2009), derived material does not

---

11. For simplicity reasons, I give a flat structure to the item darménos, although I should have provided a binary representation: [[dar$_V$-men]$_A$-os]$_A$.

12. The only examples of compounds bearing a derived right-hand constituent, which are of a [Stem Stem] structure, and thus subject to the compound-specific stress rule, are those whose derived component is a deverbal adjective in –t(os):

   (i) Compound   Stem 1   Stem 2
       efkolomajíreft-os < [efkol]-$_{ADV}$ [[majirev]$_V$ –t]$_A$
       easily cooked   easily   cooked
                              vs.
       Adjectival phrase Adverbial word   Adjectival word
       éfkola majireftós éfkola   majireftós
       easily cooked
       See Ralli (2007, in preparation) for more details on these constructions.

13. In Modern Greek, there is no structural difference between a stem and a root, on synchronic grounds, since stems can be morphologically simple (in this sense, they may coincide with roots), or morphologically complex, which may contain derivational affixes (derived stems) or more than one stem (compound stems). This position is also diachronically justified because the Ancient Greek thematic vowels have lost their function to form stems by combining with roots:

   (ii) Ancient Greek   Modern Greek
        [anthro:p-o]-s   anthrop-os
        [root-thematic vowel]$_{STEM}$-Infl   stem-Infl

surface inside compounds only as far as its overt form is concerned. Semantically, the first constituent may have the meaning of a derived item. For example, in the compound verb *krifomilo* lit. secretly speak, 'speak in secret' (4), the first constituent *krif-* 'secretly' does not surface with its derivational affix *–a* (*krif-a*), which is responsible for giving to the constituent the category and the adverbial meaning.

(4)   Compound Structure   Constituent 1   Constituent 2
       [[Stem]-Cm-[Stem-INFL]$_{word}$]$_{word}$ <   [Stem-Daff]$_{word}$ [Stem-Infl]$_{word}$
       krif-o-mil-o   <   *krif-a*   *mil-o*
       speak in secret   secret-ly   speak

Ralli & Karasimos have argued that the non-appearance of derivational suffixes inside compounds, more specifically those attached to the first component, does not depend on the particular order according to which the processes of compounding and derivation occur, but is due to the so-called 'Bare-stem constraint', which requires the two basic constituents of a compound to be tied by a strong structural bond. This requirement follows from the general structure of Greek compounds, where the left-hand position is generally filled by a stem, that is by a bound item deprived of its inflectional ending. According to Ralli & Karasimos the bond between the two compound components is better guaranteed if the first stem is as bare as possible, that is a stem without any affixal material. A question that may be raised is as to whether the Bare-stem constraint is also responsible for the absence of inflectional affixes within compounds, since, as an anonymous reviewer has suggested, the boundness of the two compound constituents is more impaired by internal inflection than by internal derivation. However, this is not the case, because inflectional material seems to be entirely absent from the first constituent, in that there is no trace of either a form or the appropriate morphosyntactic features. On the contrary, derivational affixes may not be overtly realized, but their semantics play a crucial role for the semantic composition of the compound. As already said, in a compound like *krifoxorevo* 'dance in secret' the meaning of the first constituent (*krif-*) is that of an adverb, while the form resembles an adjectival stem. Therefore, while derivational affixes participate in compounding and the Bare-stem constraint masks their overt realization, inflectional affixes can only follow the compounding process.

Interestingly, the application of the Bare-stem constraint presupposes that
a.   the process of compounding has access to the internal structure of the derived items, which participate in it, and
b.   compounding affects structures produced by derivation, since it masks the appearance of derivational material, which may be part of the first compound component.

In other words, the Bare-stem constraint provides proof for the interaction between compounding and derivation.

Significant support to the postulation of the *Bare-stem constraint* comes from the domain of verbal dvandva compounds, as shown by Ralli (2009c).[14] Consider the examples below, from both SMG and its dialects (Andriotis 1960), where the derivational suffix of the first constituent is separated from its base by a hyphen:

(5) a. *alonotherizo*   < *alon-iz-*   *therizo* (Crete)[15]
       thresh and reap   thresh   reap

    b. *klidabarono*   < *klid-on-*   *abarono* (SMG)
       padlock   lock   bar

    c. *ksimerovradiazome*   < *ksimer-on-*   *vradiazome* (SMG)
       be found by dawn-   be found by dawn   be overtaken by evening
       be overtaken by evening   'stay up all night'
       'stay up all day and night'

    d. *kuklustsipazumi*   < *kukl-on-*   *stsipazumi* (Lesbos)
       wrap up and cover   wrap up   cover

    e. *majirukinonu*   < *majir-ev-*   *kinonu* (Imbros)
       cook and pour   cook   pour

    f. *kseromarenome*   < *kser-en-*   *marenome* (Skiros)
       dry and wither   dry   wither

Like in other typical dvandva compounds (see Ralli 2007, 2009a, in preparation), in these examples, constituents like *aloniz(o)* 'thresh', *klidon(o)*, 'lock', *etc.* are juxtaposed to items of the same grammatical category, that is to verbs, and express a parallel or opposite meaning. For instance, *klidon(o)* 'lock' has a parallel meaning to *abaron(o)* 'bar', and *ksimeron(ome)* 'be found by dawn, stay up all night' has an opposite meaning to *vradiaz(ome)* 'be overtaken by evening'. It is important to note that cases, such as the ones described in (5), do not constitute blends, and should be distinguished from them; in these examples, the element which is not overtly realized is only the derivational suffix of the first constituent (the suffix which is responsible for its category and semantics), while in blends, various portions of the two constituents may be subtracted, and subtraction may involve segments of the root. For instance, in Hatzidakis (1905–1907) and Koutita & Fliatouras (2001), there are blends of coordinative verbs, such as *malafo* 'massage and touch' (< *malas(o)* 'massage' + *psilafo* ' touch'), and *korojelao* 'mock and laugh' (< *korojdev(o)* 'mock' + *jela(o)* ' laugh'), which illustrate that both root components may be affected by segment subtraction.

To conclude this section, the non-overt realization of derivational material inside Greek compounds may cast doubt on the validity of the hypothesis that derivation occurs before compounding. However, as argued above, this absence is not related to the

---

14. These compounds have appeared during the late medieval period (14th c. AD), and belong to the most productive categories of dialectal Greek compounds (see Ralli 2009c for more details).
15. The geographic area where the examples come from is given in parenthesis.

order according to which the two processes occur, but is due to independent reasons, namely to the existence of the Bare-stem constraint, which makes derived stems to look deprived from any suffixal material. In fact, the semantics, the category and the general structure of compounds prove that derived stems are possible as first components of compound words, but the derivational affixes are not overtly realized because this constraint masks them in order to maximize the bond between the two constituents. More importantly though, this constraint is crucial for proving the close interaction between derivation and compounding, since the structure of derivative items seems to be accessible to compounding, and is affected by its application.

2.2　Order of application revisited

As shown in Section 2.1, the non-existence of derived stems as first constituents of compounds is misleading if, on the basis of this absence, we conclude that derivation follows compounding. It is suggested that derivative structures may precede compounds, and the operation of the Bare-stem constraint adds proof to this order. As argued in Section 2, this order is also advocated by the position of stress in compounds with a derivative item at their right-hand side, as well as by the examples given in (1), where items such as ?*mikrovarka* 'little boat' and *nixokovo 'cut nails' are not actual words. For convenience, the same examples are repeated below:

(6)　a.　AN-compound　　　　Structure
　　　　mikrovarkada　　　　< *mikr-o-vark-ad-a*　　　vs.　　?*mikrovarka*
　　　　little boating　　　　little-Cm-boat-Daff-Infl　　　　　　little boat

　　　b.　NN-compound
　　　　nixokoptis　　　　< *nix-o-kop-ti-s*　　　vs.　　*nixokovo
　　　　nail clipper　　　　nail-Cm-cut-Daff-Infl　　　　　　cut nails

However, a closer examination of these words reveals that the absence of ?*mikrovarka* and *nixokovo may not be due to an extrinsic order between derivation and compounding but to independent reasons. As far as ?*mikrovarka* (6a) is concerned, a plausible solution would be to suggest that its creation is blocked by the presence of the most frequent diminutive formations *varkaki* (neuter) and *varkula* (feminine), which also mean 'little boat', and are built with the attachment of the suffixes –*aki* and –*ula* to the stem *vark*- 'boat'.[16] In other words, one could assume that a Blocking constraint (see Aronoff 1976) may apply to compound structures in order to prohibit formations expressing the same meaning with certain derivative ones, which are based on the same root. With respect to *nixokovo (6b), it is also possible that its non-occurrence is due to the fact that compounds consisting of a noun and a verb are not particularly

---

16.　–*aki* selects all kinds of nominal bases and produces neuter diminutives, while –*ula* attaches only to feminine bases without changing their gender value. See Melissaropoulou & Ralli (2008) for more information about Greek diminutives.

productive formations because of the difficulties which are posed by an internal theta-role saturation.¹⁷ Thus, items, such as the ones provided in (1) (repeated in (6)), do not constitute strong evidence in favor of a derivation > compounding order. Nevertheless, the operation of a Blocking constraint, which affects compound structures by appealing to derivative ones is another instance of interaction of the two processes.

Crucially, the language provides a considerable number of counter-examples to this particular order. Consider, for instance, the verb *ladoksidono* 'pour oil and vinegar', the adjective *xartopektikos* 'card-playing, gambling' and the noun *pederastia* 'pederasty'. They are built on the basis of compound nouns, as depicted in (7), where segments in parentheses denote the inflectional endings of the compound nouns, which do not participate in compounding:

(7) Compound verb   Compound noun   Daff   Derived item
  a. *ladoksidono*   < *ladoksid(o)*   -on-   vs. **ksidono*
     pour oil and vinegar   oil-vinegar   pour vinegar
  b. *xartopektikos*   < *xartopekti(s)*   -ik   vs. **pektikos*
     gambling   card player   playing
  c. *pederastia*   < *pederasti(s)*   -ia   vs. **erastia*
     pederasty   child lover, pederast   love

In (7), there are no actual derived words **ksidono*, **pektikos* and **erastia*, which would have justified a possible order according to which derivation occurs before compounding. On the contrary, the existence of compounds, like *ladoksido* 'oil (and) vinegar' (< *lad-* 'oil' + *ksid(i)* 'vinegar'), *xartopektis* 'card player, gambler (< *xart-* 'cards' + *pektis* 'player') and *pederastis* (< *ped-* 'child' + -*erastis* 'lover'), indicate that in these cases, compound formation precedes derivation.

The same order seems to be advocated by certain verbs produced by conversion, since they imply a nominal compound converted into a verb without the presence of an overtly realized derivational suffix:

(8) [stem-Cm-stem-Infl]_verb [stem-Cm-stem-Infl]_noun Original verb [stem-Infl]
  a. *anth-o-for-ó*   < *anth-o-fór-os*   *fer-o*
     carry flowers   flower-carrier   carry
  b. *vivli-o-det-ó*   < *vivli-o-déti-s*   *den-o*
     bind books   book binder   tie/bind

---

17. It should be noticed though that verbal compounds are structurally possible in Greek, as for example, *xartopezo* 'play cards', and *thalasodernome* 'be beaten by the sea':

(ii) a. *xartopezo*   < *xart-*   *pezo*
        play cards   card   play
     b. *thalasodernome*   < *thalas-*   *dernome*
        be beaten by the sea   sea   be beaten

See Di Sciullo & Ralli (1999) for an examination of compound-internal theta-role saturation in Greek.

c. *dani-o-dot-ó*   < *dani-o-dóti-s*   *din-o*
   give a loan   loan giver   give

As shown by Ralli (2008b, in preparation), verbs like the ones of the first column of (8) are not primary compound formations, since they derive by conversion, on the basis of those of the second column, which are nominal compounds. The composition of the latter is based on the combination of two stems, the second of which is a deverbal item (in this case, *-for-*, *-det-*, and *-dot-*, which are derived from the verbs *fer-(o)* 'carry', *den-(o)* 'tie/bind', and *din-(o)* 'give', respectively). The same stems appear in other derived formations as well, such as *for-a* 'course, direction', *de-ti(s)* 'binder' and *do-ti(s)* 'giver'. Corroborating evidence for the suggestion that items, like those of the first column, constitute derivative structures, which are based on nominal compounds, comes from diachrony, since the examples of the second column are attested before those of the first. This order is also justified in pure morphological terms, because the conversion process of forming verbal stems out of compound nominal ones is well known in Greek morphology throughout its long history, and is still productive today. For instance, it can also be shown in a number of verbal constructions, which are built on the basis of exocentric (bahuvrihi) nominal compounds, like the example given in (9):

(9) [stem-Cm-stem-Infl]$_{verb}$ [stem-Cm-stem-Infl]$_{adjective}$ Constituent stems
   kak-o-glos-ó   < *kak-o-glos-os*   < *kak- glos-*
   talk badly   who has a bad tongue   bad tongue

In this example, **glos-o* is not an actual verb. Therefore, a construction like *kakogloso* is a secondary formation, created on the basis of the primary nominal exocentric compound, *kakoglosos*, consisting of two stem constituents, *kak-* 'bad' and *glos-* 'tongue'.

Additional proof to the claim that the items of the left column are not primary compound formations, but derive from nominal compounds without the presence of an overtly realized suffix, is also provided by the fact that they display a different inflectional paradigm from that which would have been shown if their second constituent was a non-derived verb. In fact, they belong to the second inflection class, while the original verbs, *fero* 'carry', *deno* 'bind' and *dino* 'give' (see (8)), are conjugated according to the first inflection class.

To sum up, there is no clear-cut proof about an extrinsic order of application of the two processes, since derived items can be created before or after compounds. Nevertheless, constraints such as the Bare-stem constraint and the Blocking constraint, which refer to both processes, show the intermingling of derivation and compounding, and add a serious argument against their separation in different domains of application. I believe that if derivation is accounted for by morphology, compounding should receive a morphological treatment as well.[18]

3. Prefixization and the role of dialectal evidence

As already stated in Section 1, most authors who have stressed the non-radical distinction between derivation and compounding have drawn their main arguments from certain categorially unclear items, which are situated at the border between the two processes. The blurry status of these items is generally accepted as the product of historical evolution. For instance, Wilmanns (1896) and Paul (1920) have provided several examples of affixes which originate from stems, and the actual derived structures into which they participate were once compounds.

In this section, it is shown that there is a way to have a synchronic look at the diachronic fact that the boundary of the two processes with respect to their units can be crossed. Corroborating evidence is given from the comparison of certain contemporaneous dialectal systems of the same language, in this case Greek, where a clear-cut lexeme in one system, may behave as an affixoid in a second, while it may have acquired the status of an affix in a third. In this respect, dialectal evidence is precious in providing a synchronic confirmation to the development of borderline cases between compounding and derivation.

More particularly, the case to be examined refers to an item, which is an autonomous word in SMG and a number of dialectal varieties (e.g. Corfiot and the Peloponnesian dialects), a prefix in Cretan (the dialect of the island of Crete), and an affixoid in Lesbian (the dialect of the island of Lesbos), Aivaliot and Moschonisiot (LAM).[19]

SMG has a directional adverb *isja* 'straight', which can be used as a modifier in verbal phrases (10a) as well as in locative adverbial ones, where it bears an intensifying function (10b):

(10) SMG
    a. *vale to isja*
       put it straight

---

18. However, the long debated issue of the delimitation of word formation (in this case, derivation and compounding) with respect to syntax still requires much work, which goes beyond the limits of this paper. The same issue is also tackled by Ackema and Neelemans (in this volume), on the basis of synthetic compounds. For these authors, syntax competes with morphology for the privilege of combining equal categories in compound structures, and whether syntax 'beats' morphology depends on the particular language we deal with.

19. Aivaliot and Moschonisiot are two dialectal varieties which belong to the same dialectal group as Lesbian. They were spoken once in Northwest Asia Minor (areas of Kydonies and Moschonisia), and today are still in use by second and third generation refugees, who settled on the island of Lesbos after the exchange of populations between Greece and Turkey (Lausanne treaty in 1923).

b. ela   isja   pano
come straight up.there

As shown by Dimela (2005), this adverb has been reduced into a prefix in the Cretan dialect, where it functions as a pure intensifier, and has the form of *sjo-* in Western Crete and *so-* in the eastern part of the island. Being a prefix, it can be combined with several categories, i.e. with verbs (11a), adjectives (11b), and adverbs (11c):

(11) Cretan
    a. sojerno   < so-   jerno
       become very old   become old
    b. soaspros   < so-   aspros
       very white   white
    c. sodreta   < so-   dreta
       very straight   straight

The Cretan *s(j)o* is extremely frequent, and participates in the creation of everyday neologisms, some of which cannot be detected in the most updated Cretan dictionaries (e.g. Idomeneas 2006 and Ksanthinakis 2000). For instance, Dimela (2005) reports the verb *sjoksejivedizo* 'highly humiliate', which has been produced by native speakers during her field work. The prefixal status of *s(j)o-* is further shown by the fact that, on synchronic grounds, native speakers make no link between its initial lexical meaning of 'straight' and the actual intensifying function. For instance, they often mix up *s(j)o-* originating from *is(j)a* 'straight', with *so-*, which comes from the preposition *sin* 'with, plus'.[20] Interestingly, in the files of the *Centre of Research of Modern Greek Dialects of the Academy of Athens,* the verb *sofiliazo* (< *filiazo*[21] 'apply') is given two different interpretations: in certain files, *so-* is attributed to the word 'straight', while in others, an anonymous lexicographer claims that *s(j)o-* comes from the preposition *sin*.

It is important to notice that *isja* behaves differently in LAM. Consider the following examples, which are taken from Ralli & Dimela (to appear), and Ralli (2009b):

(12) *sapera* 'far away'   < *sa- pera* 'away'[22]
     sadju 'over here'   < *sa- edju* 'here'
     saki 'over there'   < *sa- iki* 'there'

---

20. The final vowel /o/ of *s(j)o-* is nothing else but the linking element which appears inside Greek compounds. The presence of this vowel constitutes a piece of evidence that *so-* has its origin in compounding.

21. The verb either comes from *thiliazo* (< *thilia* 'noose, eyelet') or is of an unknown etymology.

22. Like all Greek words, these formations bear only one stress, which is that of the head, i.e. the locative adverb, while the stress of the original directional adverb *isja* has disappeared.

sakatu 'straight down there'   < sa- katu 'down'
sapanu 'straight up there'   < sa- apanu 'above'
samesa 'more inside'   < sa- mesa 'inside'

(12) exhibits a number of spatial adverbs containing a locative adverb and a bound element *sa*, which also acts as an intensifier of the locative adverbial meaning. As opposed to Cretan speakers though, all native speakers of LAM are aware of the relationship that *sa* bears with the original directional adverb *isja* 'straight', which, under the form of *isa*, still exists as an autonomous word, and can also act as a verbal modifier, in the same way as in SMG:

(13) a. SMG
        vale to isja
        put it straight

   b. LAM
        val tu isa

However, when *isa* modifies a locative adverb, it always appears with the short bound form *sa*.

(14) a. SMG
        ela   isja   epano
        come straight up there

   b. LAM
        ela   sapanu
        come straight. up.there

Compared to the original *isja*, *sa* has undergone a phonological attrition with an initial /i/ deletion and the internal loss of the semi-vowel /j/. As argued by Ralli & Dimela (to appear) though, this phonological attrition cannot constitute a safe criterion for assigning to *sa* a prefixal status, since both phonological changes are due to general phonological laws, which apply to several Modern Greek dialects, independently of the particular morphological environment of *sa* formations: as shown by Newton (1972), unstressed /i/ is deleted at the beginning of words, and /j/ is deleted in word-internal contexts between a /s/ and a vowel. More importantly, the appearance of *sa* in morphologically complex adverbs is of limited productivity, since it is restricted to a handful of examples containing a locative adverb, and does not combine with all locative adverbs, as illustrated by the unattested and unacceptable example of *saksu in (15):

(15) *saksu 'more outside'   < sa-   oksu 'outside'

The fact that *sa* in LAM is still semantically transparent with respect to *isja* casts doubt on the hypothesis that *sa* is a prefix. If it is a lexeme, its combination with the locative adverbs could be analyzed as an instance of compounding. In fact, *sa*, under its full adverbial form *isa*, also appears at the right-hand position of adverbial compounds, as for instance, in the following formation:

(16) *uloisa* 'all straight'   < *ulu* 'all' *isa* 'straight'[23]

However, the 'compounding' hypothesis runs against the fact that *sa* in (12) combines only with locative adverbs, since categorial restrictions do not usually characterize compounds. Moreover, the meaning of *isa* as a second member of compounds, like in the example of (16), is not reduced into the general intensifying function displayed by *sa*.

Given the fact that there is no sufficient semantic or formal justification for the hypothesis that *sa* is a lexeme, or that it has been morphologized into a prefix, one may suppose that it is in the process of losing its word independence, and thus, can be considered as a kind of prefixoid (see Ralli 2009b, Ralli & Dimela to appear). In other words, although *sa* does not have all the properties of a real prefix, and there is no guarantee that it will result into being one, there are certain indications (e.g. form reduction and reduced meaning), which could suggest a morphologization (or grammaticalization) in progress.[24]

Items, the structural status of which is unclear, have always been a problem for morphological theory in synchronic terms: they cannot be classified into one particular category and the processes into which they participate cannot be adequately delimited. *sa* seems to be an instance of these problematic cases, since no synchronic morphological analysis could decide whether it should be registered as a prefix or a lexeme, and whether its combination with locative adverbs should be treated as prefixation or compounding. In accordance with Ralli (2009b), the existence of problematic cases, such as the Greek adverb *isja*, which may also appear under the form of *so* or *sa*, depending on the dialect, adds support to Bauer's (1983, 2005) idea that items involved in derivation and compounding can be placed on a cline (see Bybee 1985 for the general notion of cline). In this cline, the SMG adverb *isja* (or *isja* in Corfiot and the Peloponnesian dialects) is situated in one of the poles, together with the other lexemes. The Cretan *s(j)o*, which has a prefixal character, appears with other affixes on the other pole, and *sa* in LAM, whose status is unclear, is situated between the two poles.

4. Conclusions

This chapter has shown that derivation and compounding interact in several ways, and not only as far as the units which they involve are concerned. More specifically, crucial evidence has demonstrated that there is no extrinsic ordering between the two processes, since derivation may occur before or after compounding, and that there are

---

23. In this case, there is no need for /i/ deletion, since /i/ is not in the initial position.

24. For details about morphologization, and its difference from grammaticalization, see Joseph (2003).

constraints which apply to compounds but affect derivational material within their structure. On the basis of this close interaction, it has been argued that derivation and compounding should not be treated as separate processes of different grammatical domains, but as processes of the same domain, i.e. morphology. Finally, with the help of data drawn from Modern Greek Dialects, the important role of dialectal evidence is stressed, since it provides synchronic testimony to the view that the border of the two processes is not clearly distinct and that it can be easily crossed.

PART II

At the core of compounding

Units in compounding

Fabio Montermini
CLLE-ERSS, CNRS & Université de Toulouse

This chapter addresses such questions as 'what kind of linguistic units are compounds?' and 'what kind of linguistic units are they made of?' In order to answer these questions a strictly word-based approach is adopted, in which words (lexemes) are considered as the basic units of morphological and lexical organization cross-linguistically. Several examples in which canonical and non-canonical words appear as inputs and outputs of compounding are analyzed. It is claimed that, unlike derivation, compounding constructs both typical lexical units, and units which are not made to be lexicalized. This conclusion is consistent with the common assumption that compounding constitutes a case of mismatch between morphology and syntax.

1. Introduction

This chapter addresses the question of the units found in compounding from the point of view of both the input and the output. It aims, thus, to give an answer to such questions as 'what kind of linguistic unit is a compound?' and 'what kind of linguistic units is it made of?' As for many other questions, the answers that linguists have given are of various kinds, and have greatly changed over the years. I will thus start with a brief excursus of the treatments which have been proposed for compounding in the history of linguistics, and in particular after the renewal of interest in morphological studies in the last quarter of the 20th century (§ 2). Then, I will address the question of the linguistic nature of compounds from the point of view of the output. In particular, I will consider to what extent compounds can be considered 'words', like all the units produced by derivational morphology (§ 3). In the third part of this chapter, instead, I will address the question of the input units of compounds (§ 4). Once again, their nature will be investigated in relation with the notion of word. Finally, § 5 presents some concluding remarks.

One of the main assumptions of this chapter is that morphology should be viewed as strictly word-based (or lexeme-based[1]). It is assumed that, while other kinds of units (morphemes, roots, etc.) may have a descriptive value in some particular languages, the psychological and typological value of words makes them a good candidate for being a universal unit of morphological and lexical organization. In other words, although lexemes are not assumed to be the only units of morphology, they are considered the most important ones on a large typological scale (cf. Dixon & Aikhenvald 2002). Moreover, I assume that morphological operations emerge primarily as schemes originating from generalizations which speakers make on the basis of the existing lexicon, even if they are subjected to the influence of more universal constraints. Such assumptions are consistent, at least in their basic inspiration, with the role assigned to schematization and analogy by recent morphological frameworks such as Construction Morphology (cf. Booij 2005; 2009; this volume). A terminological point is necessary: labels such as 'compounding operation' or 'compound construction' do not suggest a 'dynamic' view of morphology, considered as a set of oriented operations from an input to an output. Rather, they are shorthand labels for 'morphological scheme', i.e. an abstract pattern which speakers use to analyse existing complex lexemes and to build up new ones.

2. Units in compounding: An overview

It is customary in articles on compounding to start with one or more quotations containing descriptive definitions of compounding. Probably the most basic of these definitions is the one given by Fabb (1999: 66): "a compound is a word which consists of two or more words". Other definitions make reference to more specific terms, such as 'lexeme', 'stem', etc. In general, it is also pointed out that giving a correct definition of compounding is not a simple task, since one is obliged to make reference to terms (such as 'word', 'root', 'stem') that need to be precisely defined themselves. If there is one thing on which most definitions of compounding agree, it is that a compound is a word (whatever meaning one gives to this term). This too, however, cannot be taken as an absolutely uncontroversial truth. First, it is well known that the notion of 'word' is a relative one, and that what is a word for morphology is not necessarily identical to what is a word for phonology, for syntax, etc. Consequently, a compound might happen to be a word for morphology, but not for phonology and syntax, and *vice-versa*. We will see that there are compounds that are not 'words' in the canonical sense for any of the widely recognized components of language. Moreover, if we take the division between morphology and syntax as a division between units which are primarily

---

[1]   Unless otherwise specified, in what follows 'word' and 'lexeme' will be used as synonyms. The notion of lexeme adopted here is fairly similar to the definition given by Matthews (1974), and subsequently adopted by several morphologists (see Aronoff 2007 for a recent survey).

memorized and units which are primarily built on-line, we will see that there are various compounds that not only are not memorized, but do not even possess the characteristics of linguistic objects which are normally memorized. In other words, some compounds do not seem to be made to be included into the lexicon. In this sense, many of the definitions that are proposed for compounding are too strict: a compound may not be a word. We will come back to this issue in § 3.

Often, the definitions which are given for compounding are also too loose: there are linguistic sequences consisting of two or more independent units, with no grammatical element intervening to link them, which can hardly be considered compounds (and to my knowledge have never been considered as such); cf. such expressions as *sister Mary* in *This is my sister Mary* or *President Obama*. A discussion of this issue, which involves semantic and syntactic criteria, goes beyond the scope of the present chapter. The point here is to underline that, although everyone, linguists and non linguists, seems to possess a naïve, pre-theoretical conception of what a compound is, this conception is hard to formalize, without a previous definition of the type of units involved.

An interesting approach is the one adopted by Guevara & Scalise (2008: 104). In their view, "[t]here are [...] many fundamental notions in linguistics that are ill-defined but, nevertheless, constantly used in the literature in an intuitive way (cf. *sentence*, *phrase*, *word*, etc.), and compounding may very well be one of them". Instead of searching for a universally valid definition of compounding, Guevara and Scalise suggest that there is a prototype of compound words in the world's languages, whose "essence" can be captured with the schema:

(1) [X ℜ Y]Z
"where X,Y and Z represent major lexical categories, and ℜ represents an implicit relationship between the constituents (a relationship not spelled out by any lexical item)"

Guevara and Scalise's proposal represents a real advance in the definition of compounding, for two reasons: first, it stresses the fact that the elements involved in compounding must be members of major lexical categories (and *a fortiori* words); second, it makes explicit that the two elements of a compound must be linked by some (grammatical or semantic) relationship. These properties, they claim, allow us to delimit 'canonical' instances of compounding in the world's languages. In this introduction I push their proposal a little further, and suggest another feature of canonical compounds. The fundamental point is that, at least prototypically, a compound is a unit that may potentially acquire lexical status, and in most cases it does. In other words, the simple juxtaposition of two units occurring independently in the language may not be sufficient count as composition, at least in the sense of a morphologically driven process. Thus, the adoption of the above mentioned constraint is a necessary step in determining whether composition, as is often stated, is really a universal feature of all languages.² This step, however, will not be addressed here. Psycholinguistic and acquisition studies show that the ability of semantically linking two units by simply juxtaposing them may be considered as a universal ability of all speaking humans.³ If this ability is sufficient *per se* to consider that a language has compounding is a question that I leave open (cf. also Bauer 2006: 721). Compounding, on the other hand, is first of all a grammatical concept. In its most prototypical sense, it constitutes a lexical enrichment procedure presupposing a morphological competence, probably rooted in the most general cognitive ability referred to above. Large-scale typological studies on compounding are quite recent (cf. Bauer 2001; Wälchli 2005; Scalise & Guevara 2006; Guevara & Scalise 2008). Further work in this direction will certainly contribute to determining whether compounding, as a grammatical means of lexical enrichment, is really a universal feature of all languages. For the moment, we can reasonably consider it to be the most widespread of such means.

In the introduction it was said that in this chapter I consider the lexeme as the fundamental unit of morphology: it is the main unit of lexical organization (i.e. the lexicon consists primarily of lexemes), and it is the main base unit of morphological operations (i.e. derivational morphology has lexemes as inputs and outputs). This statement is coherent with the characterization of compounding given above. Prototypically, compounding (as other derivational operations) produces lexemes, although they may be non-canonical instances of words according to one or more levels of linguistic analysis, as we will se below.⁴ This fact has perhaps not been adequately stressed in works on compounding but it appears to be quite uncontroversial. On the contrary, questions arise concerning the characterization of the inputs of compounding.

Intuitively, it is commonly admitted that a prototypical instance of compounding is the product of the combination of more than one word. However, it is also commonly stated that a compound may contain elements that are either larger or smaller than a word. The first is the case of the so-called phrasal compounds, i.e. compounds containing units constructed by syntax, phrases (2a), or even sentences (2b) (often in non-head position):

(2)   a.   over the fence gossip
      b.   God-is-dead theology   [Lieber & Scalise (2006: 10)]

Many authors writing on compounding also stress that the inputs of compound words may be units smaller than words, namely roots or stems. While we may have an at least intuitive understanding of what a word is, the definition of such objects as roots or

---

2.   The first formulation of this idea probably dates back to Greenberg (1963: 92). See also Dressler (2006: 23); Guevara & Scalise (2008).

3.   For acquisitional and psycholinguistic perspectives on compounding, see Clark (2003); Libben & Jarema (eds) (2006); see also Gagné & Spalding, Dressler *et al.* (this volume).

4.   See also Dressler (2006) for an analysis of compounding in terms of prototypes. Of course, it is frequent for non-prototypical compounding to form non-lexicalized or even nonce words (see below).

stems crucially depends on the theoretical framework adopted. In general, such sub-lexical items are defined as units that cannot stand alone in syntactic constructions. In this respect, the kind of compounds involving units smaller than words can be divided in two categories, with, of course, several overlapping and borderline cases.

The first category includes several types of compounds for which one or both members are identified as roots or stems because, although they are clearly forms of particular lexemes of the language, the form they have within the compound is never found independently in syntax. This non-coincidence between a word's form in syntax and in compounds basically has three possible explanations:

(i) historical, partially unpredictable, reasons as in the following examples:

(3) Danish: jom-fru   'young + lady, virgin'
               (vs. ung 'young')
               [Bauer (2005: 103)]
    French: col-porter   'neck + carry, peddle'
               (vs. cou 'neck')
    Armenian: jeŕ-a-tetr[5]   'hand + notebook, small notebook'
               (vs. jeŕk' 'hand')   [Donabédian (2004: 17)]

(ii) a form found in compounds does not correspond to one of the forms of the lexeme as an independent unit. In most cases, it corresponds to the common segment underlying inflected forms, what we would traditionally call a 'stem' or a 'root':

(4) German: Schwimm-bad   'swim + bath, swimming pool'
               (vs. schwimmen$_{INF}$)
    Russian: pyle-sos   'dust + suck, vacuum cleaner'
               (vs. sosat'$_{INF}$)
    Persian: soxan-gu   'word + say, spokesperson'
               (vs. guftan$_{INF}$)   [Perry (2007: 1014)]

(iii) the lexemes, when they are included in compounds, undergo modifications deriving from the application of regular morphological or phonological rules, specific to compounding operations. These modifications are in most cases predictable, as in Greek (Ralli 2007, 2008; see also Ralli this volume), where the first element systematically ends in -o-, independently of the form it has as an autonomous lexeme:

(5) psaro-kaiko   'fish + boat, fishing boat'
    (vs. psari)
    kuklo-spito   'doll + house'
    (vs. kukla)

---

5. -a- is a segment frequently used in Armenian to link the two members of a compound.

A similar phenomenon is observed in bases of Chinese origin when they appear as the first element of a compound in Japanese. Here a series of phonological operations of vowel deletion and consonant assimilation applies:

(6)   gaku + koo →   gakoo   'learning + school, school'
       hatu + kaku →   hakkaku   'come + light, detection'   [Kurisu (2000)]

We will see later that all these cases can, in fact, be considered as particular cases of word-based compounds. If we consider a lexeme as an abstract unit of lexical organization, it is clear that it cannot *per se* stand alone in syntactic constructions. A lexeme may appear in phrases and sentences only in the form of a concrete word form. The same is true for compounds: in most cases these concrete forms are identical to forms appearing independently in syntax; sometimes (as in the cases (3)-(6)) they are not. This does not imply that there is a substantial difference between word-, root- and stem-based compounds (cf. also Bauer 2006: 719).

The second category of non-word-based compounds identified in the literature includes compounds whose elements never appear as independent syntactic elements. These can be semantically linked to existing lexemes, but cannot immediately be identified as a special forms of a particular lexeme. It is the case, for instance, of the so-called neoclassical compounds found in several Indo-European languages (cf. Fr. *ludothèque* 'toy library', It. *cardiologo* 'cardiologist'), and of other special types of compounds (such as *cranberry* compounds in English or compounds derived by clipping, like It. *palazzo + ghiaccio* → *palaghiaccio* 'palace + ice, skating arena'). These special kinds of compounding are sometimes based on rules which differ from those of 'native' compounds in the languages in which they appear.[6] Nevertheless, if we consider just the components, the most reasonable conclusion seems to be the one given by Guevara & Scalise (2008): "neoclassical compounds need not be classified separately from 'normal' compounds". In fact, such elements as those exemplified above may receive the same treatment as all other, canonical, words. Whether forms like *ludo-* and *cardio-* should be considered as suppletive forms of the autonomous lexemes JEU ('game, toy') and CUORE ('heart'), respectively, or whether they should be considered separate, bound, lexemes partially depends on the framework adopted, and it is likely that the best solution would be a case-by-case decision. But in any case, they can be considered as particular (forms of) lexemes bearing some sort of [+bound] feature in their lexical representation (cf. Corbin 1992). Units of this kind are frequent in Western Indo-European languages of culture, but they are not limited to them, and to elements of neoclassical origin.[7] If we consider words as units of mental lexical

---

6.   Numerous articles have been devoted to neoclassical compounds in recent years, especially on French (cf. e.g. Fradin 2000; Amiot & Dal 2007; Namer 2007 and, for Italian, Iacobini 2004).

7.   In most cases, for instance, the clipped forms found in compounds as It. *palaghiaccio* or Rus. *texničeskij + otdel* → *texotdel* ('technical department') do not behave differently from genuinely neoclassical forms.

organization, there is no reason for treating these cases and the neoclassical compounds cited above differently.

3. Are compounds words?

The first question posed in the introduction concerns the linguistic nature of compounds, and in particular whether they should be considered words or not. In languages where compounding is an available and productive means of lexical enrichment, there are many words that speakers can partially analyse as being compounds, but which display all the characteristics of memorised lexical items. The examples of *jomfru* and *colporter* cited in (3) are of this kind. The effects of this lexicalisation are the ones usually observed for morphologically complex words: loss of semantic transparency, phonological coagulation, etc. However, it is well known that in many cases even structures built by syntax may be memorised as lexical items. Conversely, in many cases morphology builds nonce formations which do not enter the lexicon. This may not be taken, therefore, as a single criterion for distinguishing morphological from syntactic structures. The substantial difference between the two is that memorisation of syntactic objects is the exception (i.e. it is random and unregulated), while derivational morphology builds objects for which lexicalisation is the typical outcome. As in many other respects, compounding lies in between syntax and morphology.

3.1 Are compounds phonological words?

From a phonological point of view, in many languages compounds either behave like simple or derived words, or they display special characteristics that distinguish them from syntactic objects (in general, making them more 'cohesive'). These may include sandhi phenomena, observed in compounds, but not in syntactic constructions, as shown in (7):

(7) Gr: ksilo + anγuri → ksilanγuro
   'wood + cucumber, hard cucumber'
   vs.
   meγalo anγuri (*meγalanγuri)
   'big cucumber'   [Nespor (1999: 130)]

   It.: clerical-conservatore
   'clerical-conservative'
   vs.
   *sia clerical che conservatore
   'both clerical and conservative'   [Gaeta & Ricca 2009]

They may also involve the definition of specific prosodic domains. Thus, in some languages, compounds may exhibit a stress pattern that differs from that of the component words when produced individually:

(8) Gr.[8]:   kúkla + spíti   →   kuklóspito   'doll + house'   [Nespor 1999: 129]
     Jap.:   ákita + inú   →   akitáinu   'Akita + dog'   [Kubozono 2002: 45]

The same holds for domains of tone-assignment in tone languages:

(9) Bambara: sàga + sògo → sàgasogo   'sheep + meat, mutton'
                                                              [Creissels 2004: 29–30]
     Muinane[9]:   gíísi + ʔíiba → gíísiʔiibà   'stone + hole, rapids'

More often, however, compounds display a phonological behaviour more typical of syntactic structures than of words (cf. also Vogel this volume). That is, the two members of a compound may behave like two distinct prosodic words, as in (10):

(10) a. It.:   p[ɔ]rta-f[ɔ]glio   'carry + sheet, wallet'
     b. Cat.: c[ɔ]bre-llit   'cover + bed, bed spreads'
     c. Rus.: g[o]ro[t] geroj   'city + hero, hero city'
     d. Tu.:   yemek odası   'eat + room, dining room' [Nespor 1999: 138]

Example (10a) has two low-mid vowels, which are normally found only under primary word stress in Italian. Examples (10b-c) show the underapplication of vowel reduction (/ɔ/ → [u] in Catalan and /o/ → [a] in Russian), which normally applies word-internally in unstressed position in these languages. In (10c), the observed final consonant devoicing is typically only found in relation to a word boundary. Finally, example (10d) shows the non-application of vowel harmony between the members of a compound.

3.2 Are compounds morphological words?

From a morphological point of view, compounds (especially the lexicalized ones) may occasionally carry inflectional markers in the canonical position (e.g. suffixal inflection on Italian nouns, cf. *posacenere / posaceneri* 'pose + ash, ashtray$_{SG/PL}$'). In many cases, however, inflection occupies a non-canonical position, for example in many

---

8. The difference in the ending between *spiti* and *kuklospito* is due to a difference in gender (*spiti* is feminine while *kuklospito* is neuter).

9. I thank Consuelo de Vengoechea for this example.

Indo-European languages, where it appears word-internally (including cases of allomorphic variation, cf. (11b-c)):

(11) a. Gr.: πεδi-θαυμα / πεδju-θαυμα
'boy + wonder$_{\text{NOM/GEN}}$'
[Drachman & Malikouti-Drachman 1999: 929]

b. Welsh: maes chwarae / meysydd chwarae
'field + play, sports field$_{\text{SG/PL}}$' [Awbery 2004: 325]

c. It.: uomo rana / uomini rana
'man + frog, frogman$_{\text{SG/PL}}$'

3.3 Are compounds lexical objects?

As seen, compounding may form canonical lexical items, which may acquire idiosyncratic meanings. More often than not, however, they produce non-canonical lexemes, which do not constitute single phonological or morphological words. To account for the lexical status of compounds, Gaeta & Ricca (2009) propose a four-way distinction based on the parameters [±morphological] and [±lexical]. The first parameter refers to the fact that a unit may or may not be formed by morphology; the second refers to the fact that it may or may not be stored in the lexicon, as shown in Table 1.

Cases (a) and (d) correspond, respectively, to canonical derived / compound words and to canonical syntactic constructions. Case (c) corresponds to lexicalized syntactic constructions (e.g. It. *luna di miele* 'moon + PREP + honey, honeymoon'). The real innovation of Gaeta and Ricca's proposal, however, is the identification of a fourth class of objects (i.e. (b) in Table 1), which corresponds to the cross of the [+morphological] and [−lexical] parameters, and represents what is referred to as "non-lexeme-forming derivation" (see Gaeta & Ricca 2009 for several examples). The identification of this class appears particularly useful when one deals with compounds, that in many languages tend not to be lexicalized. Moreover, compounds are different from typical lexical units in that their interpretation crucially depends on the context. It is true that these observations are also valid for other morphological processes, but there is a substantial difference. On the one hand, other derived words may – exceptionally – be formed on-line and depend on context for their interpretation, and may not exhibit the typical form of lexicalized objects. Compounds, on the other hand, typically

Table 1. Typology of linguistic objects (adapted from Gaeta & Ricca 2009)

		lexical	
		+	−
morph.	+	(a)	(b)
	−	(c)	(d)

exhibit such properties. Although the dependency of compounds on context for their interpretation is often neglected or, at best, considered as marginal, it has been noted for a long time.[10] As for the second characteristic, Ricca and Gaeta provide examples of morphologically complex words that are not typical lexical objects (e.g., words derived from proper names, as It. *gheddafiano* 'Qadafi+SUF, relating to Qadafi'). These are compared to VN compounds frequently found in newspapers and to phrasal compounds, illustrated in (12a) and (12b), respectively:

(12) a. astensione salva-Prodi
'abstention save + Prodi, Prodi-saving abstention'
b. copri-borsa dell'acqua calda
'cover + hot water bag, hot water bag cover'

On the basis of such examples, I propose a corollary to Gaeta and Ricca's analysis. It may be true that neither *gheddafiano* nor *copri-borsa dell'acqua calda* is lexicalized. There is, however, an important difference between the two. *Gheddafiano* (a derived word) is, at least potentially, a lexeme, with the structure of any other item ending with the suffix *-iano*, including a paradigm, which any speaker of Italian is able to reconstruct when it encounters this nonce word. By contrast, apart from having been formed by morphology, *copri-borsa dell'acqua calda* is not a typical lexeme. Far from being a secondary issue, this appears to be the crucial aspect of the question: units such as those in (12), which correspond to the types of objects typically constructed by syntax, are exceptional in derivation,[11] but represent a programmed and 'normal' output for compounding. I return to this mismatch between compounding and syntax in Section 4.2.

4. Are compounds made of words?

Let us now turn to the second question raised in the introduction, namely 'what are compounds made of?' The answer that follows from what has been seen thus far is that a compound is made of (at least) two words, i.e. two lexemes. At this point, it is thus necessary to define clearly what a lexeme is. In most word-based theories of morphology the lexeme defines as an elementary sign combining at least three sets of properties, corresponding to three types of linguistic information: a phonological representation, a semantic representation, and morphosyntactic information (e.g. grammatical

---

10. For instance, Lyons (1977: 538–539), in commenting on the ambiguity of *London bus* in the sentences *Has the London bus* [the bus to London] *left yet?* and *Has the London bus* [the bus from London] *arrived yet?* states that "compounds are no different from very many sentences, whose ambiguity usually goes unnoticed because they are interpreted within a framework of shared ontological or contextual assumptions". Cf. also Lieber (this volume).
11. See, however, Montermini (2008b: 47–48, 114–116) for some examples.

category).¹² This chapter mainly deals with structural and phonological properties of compounds, so I leave aside the semantic and morphosyntactic properties. The identification and definition of morphological objects, such as 'roots', 'stems', etc. crucially depends on the theoretical framework adopted, and on the language observed. In this work, I adopt a Word-and-Paradigm model of morphology (cf. Stump 2001: 1–30). In such a model, it can be assumed that the phonological properties of a lexeme (even of the most regular ones) cannot be reduced to a single form from which all the others can be derived. Rather, a lexeme is a structured set of connected forms, each of which is connected to a particular cell of the lexeme's paradigm. According to this view, each word form as a whole expresses the set of morphosyntactic properties which correspond to one particular cell in the paradigm. Its segmentation into smaller pieces (a root / stem and one or more inflectional morphemes) may be a useful descriptive tool, but ceases to be a crucial theoretical matter. Such a view is particularly useful when one deals with inflecting languages, in which the segmentation of word forms is not straightforward and cumulation of exponence is the norm. It is not inadequate, however, for more agglutinating, and even with isolating languages. Whether such a model should be extended to these types of languages is mainly an empirical choice. The important point is that there is no theoretical obstacle to doing this. Specifically, we may consider that the feature [+plural] is conveyed by the whole word form *books*, rather than by the suffix *-s* attached to the root *book*. This does not mean that it is not possible to identify a function for plural noun formation in English. Rather, it means that: i) this function is reversible; that is, $X_{SG} \rightarrow Xs_{PL}$ corresponds to $Xs_{PL} \rightarrow X_{SG}$ and ii) *book* and *books* are both forms of the lexeme BOOK, having equal status. This might seem trivial, but the usefulness of such an approach becomes clear when we deal, for instance, with the approximately fifty forms that constitute the paradigm of a verb in Romance languages.

4.1 Word forms as compound inputs

It is clear now that the distinction between root-, stem- and word-based compounds is relatively unimportant in the approach adopted here. Instead, roots and stems are simply concrete manifestation of a lexeme in a subset of its syntactic and morphological functions. Morphological operations, in fact, select one particular form of a lexeme as their base, independently of its semantic, and sometimes phonological, properties (i.e., a morpheme in Aronoff's 1994 sense). Considering a basic example, in most cases adverbs formed by means of the suffix *-ment* in French select the form of an adjective which we encounter in the feminine. Thus, the adverb derived from FORT ('strong', [fɔr]$_{MASC}$ ~ [fɔrt]$_{FEM}$) is *fortement* ([fɔrt(ə)mɑ̃]). Clearly, this has no semantic justification (there is no feminine, nor masculine, value in an adverb), and it is also rather odd

---

12. See, e.g., Lyons (1977: 512–520); Aronoff (1994: 1–59); Beard (1995: 44–50); Fradin (2003: 80–106) for an outline.

phonologically (the clash between two consonant leads in many cases to the insertion of an epenthetic [ə]). Synchronically, it is a purely morphological rule.

The same kind of explanation may be invoked for compounding. The form observed in a compound may simply be one of the forms of the paradigm, arbitrarily selected by a morphological operation. This allows us to resolve some problems often discussed in the literature on compounding such as the presence or absence of inflectional markers within compounds from the same base, without any apparent difference in meaning. This phenomenon is particularly frequent in Germanic languages, where the appearance of 'linking elements', homophonous to inflectional endings, is systematic; but it can be also observed occasionally in other language families (cf. 13c):

(13) a. Germ.: Kind-bett   'child+bed, childbed'
              Kinder-garten   'child+garden, nursery school'
              Kindes-annahme   'child+assumption, adoption'
     b. Dutch: boek-handel   'book+commerce, bookshop'
              boeken-kast   'book+case, bookcase'
                                   [Don (2009: 381)]
     c. It.: portafoglio / portafogli   'carry+sheet, wallet'
              marciapiede / marciapiedi[13]   'march+foot, sidewalk'

Another problem that can be resolved by adopting the lexematic view of morphology sketched above is the nature of the first element of Romance VN compounds (cf. Bisetto 1999; Villoing 2009; Ricca this volume, among others). It has often been observed that the first element of these compounds is homophonous to a second person imperative, although a paraphrase containing an imperative is rather odd. In fact, at least as far as Italian is concerned, the second person imperative is the only form in the paradigm that is systematically identical to the first element of a VN compound (cf. Thornton 2005: 158). The scheme for Italian VN compounds may thus be informally represented as in (14):

(14) $[X_{S3}]_V + [Y]_N \rightarrow [XY]_{N/A}$

where S3 is an arbitrary label assigned to the form also used in the 2nd person imperative cell.[14]

Both VN compounds in the Romance languages and the cases cited in (13) contain forms that are identical to one or more inflected forms of the lexeme. The same treatment, however, may be proposed for elements that clearly correspond to a word, although they do not correspond to any inflected form of the lexeme. In one sense, we might consider them as suppletive stems that are only used in compounding. Exactly as for inflected forms, these suppletive stems may come from historical changes or be

---

13. Although *portafoglio* / *marciapiede* on the one hand, and *portafogli* / *marciapiedi* on the other hand are more common as the singular and the plural forms of the whole compound, respectively, the latter may also function as singulars.

14. For the output category of Italian VN compounds cf. Ricca (2005; this volume).

regularly derived via some morphological scheme. The examples of *jomfru* and *colporter* cited in (3) would be of the first type, as well as several *cranberry* and neoclassic compounds, at least in Western European languages. As noted in 2, deciding whether a compound element is a specific form of a lexeme or a distinct (bound) lexeme is mainly an empirical question, and should probably be dealt with in terms of a continuum. Thus, it is almost certain that the first elements in compound ethnic terms (*Anglo-American*, *Hispano-Portuguese*, etc.) can be considered suppletive forms of the corresponding independent lexemes, while highly technical compound forms of neoclassical origin (e.g. *dermo* for 'skin' or *hem(at)o* for 'blood') might be considered separate lexemes. A compound form may also be derived from one of the autonomous forms of the lexeme via a rule that is specific to compounding. This may be the case of the first elements of Greek compounds ending in -*o* cited in (5). In this case, the compounding scheme would contain not only a rule for combining two lexeme forms, but also a specification of the phonological functions that apply, exactly as for derivational schemes. Thus, the schemes in (15b) may be proposed for the Dutch examples given in Booij (2007: 89), (cf. also Booij 2008; Don 2009: 381):

(15) a. schaap-herder   'sheep+shepherd, shepherd'
        schaaps-kop   'sheep+head'
        schapen-vlees   'sheep+meat, mutton'
    b. $[X]_N + [Y]_N \rightarrow [XY]_N$
        $[X]_N + [Y]_N \rightarrow [XsY]_N$
        $[X]_N + [Y]_N \rightarrow [XenY]_N$

Moreover, exactly as with derivational morphology, (15) illustrates a case of alternation between different concurrent schemes. Speakers choose a scheme on the basis of generalizations made on the existing lexicon (in other words, of analogy, cf. Booij 2007: 248–249). The schemes in (15b) illustrate a relatively straightforward case of agglutinating morphology. Phonological rules of the same type, however, may apply to more complex cases, as those in (5) or (6) above. If rules of the type in (15) apply, there is no need to postulate that root- or word-based compounds are substantially different. In fact, being root- or word-based is no longer an issue in the perspective adopted here.

Finally, a further element indicating that compounds are non canonical lexemes, is that, exactly as an inflected form, the internal element of compounds conform to the phonotactics of the language in question. As observed by Ralli (2007), compound-markers such as those illustrated in (15) are common in particular in languages displaying overt inflection.

4.2 Inflected forms and syntactic structures as compound inputs

In the examples seen so far we have illustrated the case of forms appearing in compounds which are simply homophonous to inflected forms of lexemes, without bearing any particular morphosyntactic meaning. The presence of real inflected forms inside compounds is, however, a fact commonly observed in a large number of unrelated languages. Some examples are given in (16):

(16) a. Eng.: suggestions box
 b. Finnish: auton-ikkuna 'car$_{GEN}$ + window' [Bauer (2006: 720)]
 c. Jap.: hi-no-de 'sun + GEN + rise, sunrise'
 [Kageyama (2009: 518)]

With respect to examples such as those in (16), I would like to note two facts. First, the observation of compounds in inflectional languages suggests that even apparently unmarked cases may be considered as inflected. Thus, it can be maintained, in the perspective adopted here, that in the Italian examples in (17a) the second member is inflected as singular, exactly as those in (17b) are inflected as plural:

(17) a. segnalibro *segnalibri
 'mark + book$_{SG}$, bookmark'
 pausa pranzo *pausa pranzi
 'break + lunch$_{SG}$, lunch break'
 b. tagliacarte *tagliacarta
 'cut + paper$_{PL}$, letter opener'
 raccolta rifiuti *raccolta rifiuto
 'collection + garbage$_{PL}$, waste collection'

Second, it does not seem justified to draw a clear demarcation line between the cases in (16) and the cases of compounds containing a more complex syntactic structure, like a phrase (often, a noun phrase) or a sentence, such as those cited in (2) and in (12) above. Exactly as a phrase or a sentence may contain just one lexeme in syntax, there seems to be no theoretical obstacle to considering that the compounds in (17) also contain a phrase without complements. It would not be justifiable to establish a distinction in nature between *raccolta rifiuti*, cited in (17b), and the following compounds:

(18)[15] raccolta rifiuti di tipo individuale
 'collection of waste of individual type'
 raccolta rifiuti di provenienza agricola
 'collection of waste of agricultural origin'

An important, and underestimated, fact about compounds that contain complex structures, like the ones exemplified above, is that compound-internal phrases, like structures constructed in syntax, and unlike typical bases of derivational morphology, may

---

15. Both examples were collected on the Web (Google search, April 2009).

be referential units. For example, in some cases, in the appropriate context the internal element of this type of compound may be coreferent with an anaphoric expression:

(19) a. Eng.:   Although *cocaine*$_i$ use is down, the number of people using *it*$_i$ routinely has increased
      b. It.[16]: Era disponibile a diventare capo*gruppo*$_i$ di *quello*$_i$ da noi appena costituito
                  'He was available for being the group$_i$ leader of the one$_i$ we just costituted' [Montermini (2006: 139)]
      c. Jap.:   *Kenkyuu*$_i$-shitara, *sore*$_i$ ga hyooka sareta
                  'After I had research$_i$ed, it$_i$ received appreciation'
                  [Lombardi Vallauri (2005: 323)]

As already observed, the possibility of having syntactic structures as bases is not completely excluded in derivational morphology, but it is exceptional. What is crucial about compounding, by contrast, is that it is normal to have a referential unit as a base (i.e. a unit clearly constructed by syntax). Such mismatches between syntax and morphology, and in particular the possibility for morphological operations to take fully compositional syntactic units as inputs, are nowadays commonly accepted by several models of morphology (cf. Lieber & Scalise 2006 for an overview; cf. also several works by Booij 2005; 2009; this volume).

4.3 Lexemes as compound inputs

In the previous analysis of the input units of compounding, an aspect was kept implicit. All the units analysed so far are units that can appear in compounding in non-head position. However, as exemplified in (11) above, it is the norm for a compound (when it is endocentric cf. Scalise & Fábregas this volume) to be inflected on the head element. In this respect, it is also possible to identify an important feature, crucially distinguishing compounding from most canonical derivational operations. What we encounter in head position, in fact, is not just one phonological form corresponding to a lexeme, but a full lexeme, bearing all its phonological and morphological specifications, including, for instance, information about inflectional class, unpredictable allomorphy, etc. This is also true for some types of prefixation (cf. Eng. *bind – bound / unbind – unbound*), but in general not for suffixation.

---

16. An anonymous reviewer correctly pointed out that a compound like **capogruppo numeroso* ('leader + group + numerous'), meaning 'leader of a numerous group' would be unacceptable. It seems, however, that this depends primarily on the properties of compounds having *capo* in head position (a type of compounding which is clearly on the way to lexicalisation in Italian). A form like *accoglienza gruppi numerosi* ('acceptance + group + numerous, large groups acceptance') is perfectly normal in Italian.

5. Conclusion

In the present chapter I have analysed the nature of the linguistic units that appear in compounding. In particular, I have tried to determine whether compounds can be considered words (in the sense of lexemes). This question has received only a partially positive answer, thus confirming that the notion of lexeme is a relative one, as observed by several scholars (cf. Dixon & Aikhenvald 2002, among others). I have also addressed the nature of the elements that form compounds, and I have shown that, in a strictly lexeme-based approach, such distinctions as root- vs. word-based compounds are not justified: if we consider lexemes as the primary unit of lexical organization, it can be maintained that what we find in compounds are forms of lexemes of various kinds. They may be homophonous to autonomously existing inflected word forms or specific forms only encountered in compounds. We also observed two crucial features that distinguish compounds from other morphological operations: first, unlike derivational processes, compounds take syntactic units as input systematically, and not just occasionally, thus representing the most relevant area of overlap between morphology and syntax; second, unlike canonical derivational processes, which only pick one form of a lexeme as input, compounding may take, in head position, full lexemes, from which they inherit all inflectional properties, including information about inflectional classes and allomorphy. Further research should allow us to define more precisely the way in which lexemes appear in compounding, in particular those forms that are only encountered in compounding. It would be also interesting to establish a connection between compound types, according to the classification into coordinating, attributive and subordinating compounds proposed by Bisetto & Scalise (2009), and the type of units they take as input (see Montermini 2008a; Arcodia *et al.* 2009 for some suggestions).

Compound construction: Schemas or analogy?
A construction morphology perspective

Geert Booij
University of Leiden

This chapter argues that there is no absolute boundary between analogy and abstract schemas in word formation. Patterns of compounding are captured by constructional schemas of various degrees of abstraction. The necessity of such subschemas is argued for on the basis of observations on semantic specialization, headedness variation, diachrony, and allomorphy selection. Analogy and abstract schemas are opposite endpoints on a scale of schematicity.

1. Introduction: Rule or analogy?

Compounding is the best type of evidence for the claim that word formation should at least partially be accounted for in terms of abstract symbolic rules or schemas. In many languages the formation of new compounds is by far the most productive type of word formation (cf. Gagné & Spalding, this volume). The formation of new compounds is not necessarily based on the model of existing compounds. Hence, compounding is often used to illustrate rule-governed creativity in the domain of word formation, and seems to be the best case for the theoretical position that word formation cannot be fully accounted for in terms of analogy.[1]

It is obvious that analogical word formation does exist, as illustrated here by some examples from Dutch:

(1) moeder-taal 'lit. mother language, native language' vader-taal 'lit. father-language, native language of father'

---

[1] For discussion of the notion 'analogy' with respect to word formation, see Becker (1990, 1994), Hüning (1999).

hand-vaardig 'lit. hand-able, with manual skills' muis-vaardig 'lit. mouse-able, with mouse-handling skills'

nieuw-komer 'lit. new-comer, recent immigrant' oud-komer 'lit. old-comer, immigrant who has arrived a long time ago'

For these words we can indeed point to one particular compound as the model word for the formation of the new compound, and the meaning of this new compound is not retrievable without knowing the (idiomatic) meaning of the model compound.

Analogical word formation may develop into a pattern that abstracts from specific model words. In English, the word *Watergate* functioned as the model of a number of compounds in -*gate* that all denote a particular political scandal, and hence this looks like a clear case of analogical word formation. However, since a set of such words has been formed in the meantime, it is no longer obvious that it is always the word *Watergate* itself that functioned as the model word. Once a set of words in -*gate* has been formed, languages users may discover the commonality of such words in -*gate*, and hence this kind of productive compound formation is now better characterized by the schema:

(2) $[[x]_{Ni} [gate]_N]_{Nj} \leftrightarrow [\text{political scandal pertaining to SEM}_i]_j$

(where SEM stands for the meaning of the co-indexed word constituent). That is, the word *gate* has acquired the meaning 'political scandal' when embedded in compounds. The assumption of such a schema expresses that it is no longer necessarily the case that language users model their new *gate*-compounds after the word *Watergate*. Dutch speakers have extended this use of -*gate* to Dutch, as illustrated by the following examples (Hüning 2000):

(3) kippen-gate 'chicken-gate, scandal concerning chickens'
Stadion-gate 'financial problems concerning renovation of the Olympic Stadium'
Zuid-Holland-gate 'financial scandal concerning the province of Zuid-Holland'

Hüning concluded that the set of -*gate* words gave rise to a new morphological process in Dutch. This use of -*gate* is comparable to that of endings like -*burger*, -*holic*, -*tainment*, and -*zine* in English: a new type of compound constituent with a specific meaning is created, with the structural reinterpretation of an existing complex word being the first step. In the case of *hamburger*, the rise of -*burger* presupposed a morphological reanalysis: *hamburg-er* > *ham-burger*, whereas in the case of -*gate*, the compound structure of *Water-gate* is maintained, but with a different interpretation of *gate*. A similar example from Italian is the emergence of -*poli* 'scandal' (Ramat 2001). This use of -*poli* emerged from the word *tangento-poli* 'rake-of town, town where the rake-of system is dominant'. New coinages are *sanito-poli* 'the affair of the health ministry' and *banco-poli* 'bank scandal'.

In this chapter I will provide evidence that language users are able to discover compound schemas of various degrees of abstraction. At one end of the scale of abstractness we find analogical word formation based on a concrete model word, as illustrated above in (1). At the other end of the scale of abstractness, we have the following schema for Dutch compounds (and those in other Germanic languages) which expresses the generalization that Dutch compounds are right-headed:

(4) $[X_i\ Y_j]_{Yk} \leftrightarrow [\text{SEM}_j$ with some relation R to $\text{SEM}_i]_k$

(where X and Y are variables for lexical categories). Between these two extremes, there are many generalizations about subsets of compounds that need to be expressed as part of the linguistic knowledge of the language user. This knowledge can be modeled in a hierarchical lexicon (Booij 2005a, 2007). In a hierarchical lexicon the set of established words is listed together with generalizations over subsets of words that share certain properties. Sets of words that share a particular form and corresponding meaning form the basis for discovering morphological regularities. In this chapter, arguments for such a model of the lexicon are provided by four different kinds of phenomena: the bound meanings of compound constituents (Section 2), headedness variation (Section 3), the emergence of derivation out of compounding (Section 4), and allomorphy patterns (Section 5). In Section 6, I summarize my findings, and their implications for analogical models of morphology.

2. Semantic subpatterns in compounding

It is well known that many, if not all, derivational affixes derive historically from lexemes used as the first or second constituent of compounds. "Diachronically, the transmutation of a "blurred" compound into an affixal derivative is an almost trivial phenomenon" (Malkiel 1978: 128). Lots of examples have been discussed in the literature on Germanic languages like Dutch, English, German, and Swedish (Ascoop 2005; Ascoop & Leuschner 2006; Booij 2005a, 2007; Dalton-Puffer & Plag 2000; Leuschner & Decroos 2008). The relation between compounding and derivation in Modern Greek is discussed in Ralli (this volume).The phenomenon is not so trivial as Malkiel suggested, since it reveals how the lexicon is organized: compound words beginning with or ending in the same constituent may form word families that can be characterized in terms of schemas for complex words in which one of the constituents is lexically specified.[2] When such a specified constituent lost its status as independent word, it could

---

2. The existence of constituent families is confirmed by psycholinguistic evidence, in particular through the family size effect: the larger the size of a constituent family of a word, the faster it will be retrieved (Baayen 2003; Schreuder & Baayen 1997).

become an affix since it survived as part of a compound schema, with sometimes less lexical and semantically more abstract meanings (Booij 2005a, 2007).

In other cases, the compound constituent still corresponds to a word that also occurs independently, but has acquired a specific meaning when part of a compound. In that case, one might speak of affixoids, but this is just a convenient descriptive term, not a new morphological category. In some cases, the meaning of the lexeme becomes more abstract, and may lose lexical content. An example of this phenomenon is the set of words with intensifying meaning that occur as the left constituents of Dutch XA compounds. Some examples are listed in (5).

(5) | noun: | | example |
|---|---|---|
| ber-e | 'bear' | bere-sterk 'very strong', bere-aardig 'very kind' |
| bloed | 'blood' | bloed-serieus 'very serious', bloed-link 'very risky' |
| dood | 'death' | dood-eng 'very scary', dood-gewoon 'very ordinary' |
| poep | 'shit' | poep-heet 'very hot', poep-lekker 'very pleasant' |
| ret-e | 'ass' | rete-leuk 'very nice', rete-spannend 'very exciting' |
| reuz-e | 'giant' | reuze-leuk 'very nice', reuze-tof 'very good' |
| *adjective* | | |
| dol | 'mad' | dol-blij 'very happy', dol-gelukkig 'very happy' |
| stom | 'stupid' | stom-toevallig 'completely coincidental', stom-verbaasd 'very surprised' |
| *verb* | | |
| kots 'vomit' | | kots-misselijk 'very sick', kots-beu 'very tired of' |
| snoei 'prune' | | snoei-hard 'very hard', snoei-heet 'very hot' |

These are clear cases of semantic reanalysis: the first constituent is reanalyzed as a morpheme with intensifier meaning. This reanalysis is made overt by the fact that these morphemes are attached to new semantic types of words. A noteworthy point concerning *bere-*, *rete-*, and *reuze-* is that they consist of a consonant-final stem followed by a linking element *-e* [ə]. This linking element is a necessary part of these nouns when used as intensifier prefixoids.

We can represent the affixoid nature of these compound-initial lexemes by specifying them in constructional idioms of the following form:

(6) $[[\text{bere}]_N [x]_{Ai}]_{Aj} \leftrightarrow [\text{very SEM}_i]_j$
$[[\text{dol}]_A [x]_{Ai}]_{Aj} \leftrightarrow [\text{very SEM}_i]_j$
$[[\text{loei}]_V [x]_{Ai}]_{Aj} \leftrightarrow [\text{very SEM}_i]_j$
$[[\text{wereld}]_N [x]_{Ni}]_{Nj} \leftrightarrow [\text{excellent SEM}_i]_j$

Constructional idioms are morphological or syntactic schemas in which one or more positions are lexically fixed, whereas other positions are open slots, represented by variables (Jackendoff 2002). Being embedded in constructional schemas makes these words similar to prefixes. The only difference is that prefixes do not carry a lexical category label, and hence cannot be related to independent lexemes in the lexicon.

The specific meaning of intensification as illustrated in (5) is a precondition for these affixoids to be used in repetitive coordination that carries an emphatic meaning. This appears to be a systematic option for all prefixoids with intensifier meaning, as a Google search (13 May 2008) reveals:

(7) a. bere- en bere-goed 'very, very good'
bloed- en bloed-mooi 'very, very beautiful'
dood- en dood-ziek 'very, very ill'
poep- en poepheet 'very, very hot'
rete- en rete-stabiel 'very, very stable'
reuze- en reuze-tevreden 'very, very pleased'

b. dol- en dol-komisch 'very, very comical'
stom- en stom-dronken 'very, very drunken'

c. kots- en kots-beu 'very, very tired of'
snoei- en snoei-lelijk 'very, very ugly'

The same kind of repetitive coordination is possible with Dutch intensifying prefixes such as *door-* and *in-*:

(8) a. door- en door-nat
through-and through-wet
'wet through'

b. in- en in-triest
in- and in-sad
'very, very sad'

If we want to make a generalization as to which elements can occur in such repetitive coordination, we need to be able to refer to the class of compound-initial words with intensifier meaning. This is possible thanks to schemas like those in (6).[3]

The reality of the generalizations expressed in (6) is confirmed by the observation that in Dutch some of these prefixoids have developed into adjectives. This is the case for *reuze* and *kut*:

(9) [reuze-]$_N$ 'giant-' > reuze (A) 'fantastic'
[kut-]$_N$ 'cunt-'   > kut (A)   'bad, worthless'

---

3. Phrases such as *dol- en dolblij* may be derived from *dolblij and dolblij* through the rule of prosodic gapping that deletes one of two identical prosodic words (Booij 1985). However, prosodic gapping is normally optional, whereas omission of the first of two identical constituent is obligatory in these cases of emphatic repetitive coordination. This implies that this instantiation of gapping is to be considered as a subconstruction of gapping; the obligatoriness of the gapping and the formal identity of the coordinated adjectives correspond with an emphatic meaning.

The following sentences illustrate this adjectival use of these two words:

(10) a. Ik vind dat helemaal kut
I find that completely cunt
'I consider this completely worthless'
b. Het uitstapje was reuze
The outing was giant
'The outing has been great'

One also finds the superlative of *kut*, as in *Het kut-st-e van alles* 'The worst of all'. The nominal origin of *reuze* 'fantastic' is reflected by its final schwa which is a linking element, the noun itself being *reus*. Such a development can only be understood if we assume a subpattern $[[reuze]_N A]_A$ in the hierarchical lexicon of Dutch. This means that there is a productive class of adjectival compounds, with an adjectival head, and the noun *reuze* as modifier. The meaning of intensification of these nouns is a type of meaning expressed prototypically by adjectives, and hence the categorial reinterpretation of these nouns as adjectives in this context is a natural development.

Similar productive patterns have been observed for German and Swedish. In Swedish, for instance, we find *skit-bra* 'shit-good, very good' and *jätte-vinst* 'giant-profit, very high profit'. The word *jätte* can also be used as an adjective, parallel to the Dutch word *reuze*. German examples are *Klasse-* in *Klasse-film* 'class-film' and *Spitzen-* in *Spitzen-film* 'top-film' both meaning 'excellent film' (Ascoop 2005; Ascoop & Leuschner 2006).

An example of semantic concentration, a specific type of semantic development within compounds, is the use of the verb *scharrel* 'to scratch' in the word *scharrel-kip* 'lit. scratch chicken, free range chicken'. This word refers to chickens that can freely scratch the ground, and potter around. This use has been extended to other compounds:

(11) a. scharrel-vlees
scratch-meat
'free range meat'
b. scharrel-ei
scratch-egg
'free range egg'
c. scharrel-melk
scratch-milk
'free range milk'
d. scharrel-wijn
scratch-wine
'eco-wine'

This use of the word *scharrel* is a case of semantic concentration, the presence of the meaning of a word that is not a formal constituent, in this case 'free range *animal'*

(Meesters 2004: 52). As the last example *scharrelwijn* shows, even the notion of animal has disappeared as a necessary part of its meaning. That is, we have to assume an intermediate schema:

(12) $[[\text{scharrel}]_V[x]_{Ni}]_{Nj} \leftrightarrow [\text{ECO}[\text{SEM}_i]]_j$

which expresses this lexicalized yet productive ecological meaning of *scharrel* when embedded in a compound.

This type of productive lexicalization can be found in many languages. A nice example comes from Maale, a North Omotic language spoken in Southern Ethiopia. The noun *nayi* 'child' has developed the general meaning 'agent', as illustrated by the following complex words (Amha 2001: 78):

(13) a. bayi nayi
cattle child
'one who brings cattle to the grazing area'
b. waari nayi
goat child
'one who takes care of goats'
c. móótsi naya
cattle.camp child
'one who lives in a cattle camp and takes care of cattle there'

Because cattle herding is historically a task of children in the Maale-speaking society, the word for child has acquired an agent meaning, at least in the domain of cattle herding.

In sum, we need a model of compounding in which the knowledge of individual compounds, of abstract lexical patterns, and of intermediate patterns with specific properties can be accounted for. Hence, we need a hierarchical lexicon, with constructional idioms expressing intermediate generalizations.[4]

3. Headedness variation

It is clear that Williams' Right Hand Head Rule (Williams 1981) cannot be a rule in the sense of a universal since many languages have left-headed compounds, apart from the fact that languages may also have exocentric, that is, headless compounds (Bauer, this volume). Hence, one might consider the position of the head as a morphological parameter. For instance, Germanic languages may be qualified as right-headed, and Romance languages such as Italian as left-headed (Scalise 1984, 1992). Another example

---

4. Lieber suggests a constructional idiom for a subset of compounds for semantic reasons as well: compounds of the form [*media Xion*] tend to be subject-oriented, with *media* playing the role of subject, as in *media competition*, whereas in most synthetic compounds the first constituent functions as an object (Lieber 2009: fn 7).

of a left-headed language is Maori (Bauer 1993). The problem for such a parameter approach is that languages may have both left-headed and right-headed compounds. This is the case for Romance languages, and for Chinese and Japanese. Vietnamese has left-headed native compounds, and right-headed compounds borrowed from Chinese. In Javanese, compounds are left-headed except for some right-headed compounds of Sanskrit origin (Bauer 2009: 349).

Italian and Spanish also have sets of right-headed compounds, even though the default position of compound heads is the left position. Examples of such compounds in Spanish are the following, with neo-classical words or morphemes as modifiers:

(14) auto-escuela, 'car school', cine-club 'cinema club', eco-sonda 'echo sounder', tele-novela 'television novel', video-arte 'video art'

In the framework of construction morphology we can analyse these words as compounds. We then assume constructional idioms such as

(15) $[auto_i[x]_{Nj}]_{Nk} \leftrightarrow [SEM_j \text{ with relation R to } SEM_i]_k$
$[tele_i [x]_{Ni}]_{Nk} \leftrightarrow [SEM_i \text{ with relation R to } SEM_i]_k$

instead of a general abstract template for right-headed compounds. By lexically specifying the left constituent of these compound schemas we express that the class of right-headed compounds in Spanish is restricted to compounds that begin with a word of a closed set. It is possible to generalize over these schemas and assume a dominating general schema for right-headed compounds with a neo-classical element as modifier. However, this does not make the various subschemas with lexically specified modifiers superfluous because we have to somehow specify the restricted set of constituents that can function as modifier. Moreover, some of these neo-classical elements are not words by themselves, as is the case for *cine-* and *eco-*. Hence, like affixes, they only exist as parts of schemas.

Mandarin Chinese is reported to have both left-headed and right-headed compounds (Ceccagno & Basciano 2009; Packard 2000). Right-headed compounds have either a noun or a verb in head position. In the case of verbal compounds, the non-head functions as a modifier of the verb. Verbal compounds are left-headed, however, if the non-head functions as an argument of the verb. The following examples illustrate these patterns (Ceccagno & Basciano 2009: 485):

(16) right-headed $[[dú]_N[fàn]_N]_N$ drug-criminal 'drug criminal'
$[[hán]_N[shòu]_V]_V$ letter-sell 'order by mail'
left-headed $[[jìn]_V[dú]_N]_V$ prohibit-poison 'ban the sale and abuse of drugs'

In other words, generalizations about the position of the head must be made in terms of the corresponding semantic structure. In attributive compounds the head is on the right, whereas in compounds with a verb-argument structure the head is on the left.

Such generalizations can be expressed by morphological schemas, which by definition express the correlation between the form and meaning of complex words.

There are more languages whose compounds can be either right- or left-headed. The language Biak, an Austronesian language spoken on New Guinea, has left-headed NN compounds, in which the head position is filled by nouns like *man* 'man, bird-like entity' or *in* 'female person, fish-like entity'. There are also right-headed NN compounds, however. In that case, the compound expresses a specific semantic pattern, either 'N_2 is part of N_1', or 'N_2 is a product of N_1' (van den Heuvel 2006: 91–93):

(17) a. randip-vukór
pig-head
'head of a pig'

b. ai-snáw
tree-branch
'branch of a tree'

Thus, besides an abstract schema for Biak left-headed NN compounds, we need an additional one for specific semantic types of right-headed compounds. In this respect, Biak is similar to Chinese for which language we also observed a correlation between semantics and position of the head. Once more, we see that the idea of a hierarchical lexicon with subschemas expressing intermediate generalizations is essential for a proper account of patterns of word formation.

4. From compounding to derivation

When a constituent of a compound acquires a 'bound' meaning, this does not necessarily lead to that meaning being an abstract, grammatical one, as we saw above. This conclusion is supported by the existence of lexical affixes in some Amerindian languages (Gerdts 1998; Mithun 1997, 1999). Salishan and Wakashan languages have lexical suffixes, that is, suffixes with a specific, non-grammatical meaning (Gerdts 1998). Mithun reports that Spokane, a Salishan language, has about 100 lexical suffixes that are similar to noun roots except that they do not occur as independent words. Yup'ik has more than 450 verb-like derivational suffixes. Most of the Yup'ik verbal suffixes have verbal roots as counterparts, with differences in form correlating with differences in meaning (Mithun 1999: 48–56, 2009a). The Amerindian language Bella Coola also has a set of lexical suffixes (Saunders and Davis 1975).

For the Athapaskan language Slave, Rice reports that some nouns only appear as parts of compounds, not independently. Yet, such nouns can be used productively for coining new compounds. This applies, for instance, to the bound noun *teh* 'water' (Rice 2009: 544). This suggests a compound schema with its head position filled lexically with the root *teh*. Similar facts obtain for Mohawk (Mithun 2009b: 580).

Mithun points out that "a historical origin in compounding accounts well for the special properties of lexical affixes" (Mithun 1999: 55), a position also defended by Carlson: "productive compounding, particularly of nominal objects and locatives led to the set of bound morphemes referred to as lexical affixes" (Carlson 1990: 69). Lexical suffixes in Spokane developed from right members of compounds, and lexical prefixes from left members (Carlson 1990: 78). The compound origin of some of these Spokane suffixes can also be concluded from the fact that the suffix begins with a linking element [ł] or a nominalizing element [s] that does not occur at the beginning of the corresponding independent root.

Lexical prefixes also occur in Japanese. As observed by Kageyama "Japanese has a far richer stock of prefixes than English" (Kageyama 1982: 226). For instance, there is a substantial set of prefixes with an adjectival meaning such as:

(18) dai- 'big', oo- 'big', tyuu- 'middle', syoo- 'small', ko- 'small', koo- 'high', tei- 'low', sin- 'new', ko- 'old', huru- 'old', zyuu- 'haevy', kei- 'light', tyoo- 'long', tan- 'short', kyuu- 'sudden', bi- beautiful', aku- 'bad', koo- 'good'

The existence of 'bound' compound constituents or lexical affixes receives a straightforward interpretation in a lexicon with morphological schemas that express generalizations about subsets of compounds that share one of the constituents, that is constructional idioms (schemas with some slots lexically specified) at the compound level. The bound nature of a constituent is expressed by this constituent not being co-indexed with an independent lexeme in the lexicon. Hence, the meaning of such constituents has to be specified in the corresponding constructional idiom. The origin of such lexical suffixes can thus be explained by the assumption that particular lexemes can 'survive' in compound schemas in which they occupy a slot, even though the corresponding lexeme got lost. Again, as in the case of Spanish right-headed compounds discussed in Section 3, we may assume a general schema for these 'prefixoids', but since they are not words, they have to be specified in subschemas as well.

A related problem concerns the status of the morpheme *out* in English verbs such as:

(19) out-bid, out-perform, out-play, out-rank, out-stay

The morpheme *out* when combined with a verb has acquired (as one of its meanings) the meaning of excess, or more precisely 'to exceed someone else in V-ing', where V denotes the base verb. The morpheme *out-* might be considered a prefix here because of this specific meaning of *out* when combined with verbs. Indeed it is often referred to as a prefix. The same holds for a morpheme like *over* that has three meanings when combined with verbs among which the meaning of excess (Lieber 2004: 130):

(20) locational: over-lap, over-fly, over-turn
      completive: ove-rride, over-run
      excess: over-bid, over-burden, over-indulge

Lieber observes that such prefixes that correspond to a lexeme exhibit much more polysemy than derivational affixes, which do not have such a counterpart and tend to have one abstract meaning. Therefore, Lieber proposes the hypothesis that "prefixal *over-* is nothing more than a bound version of prepositional *over*" (Lieber 2004: 129). This implies that such verbs are verbal compounds but that a specific subschema is necessary to express the specific meaning of *out* and *over* in combination with verbs.

In sum, what we see here, is on the one hand a form of lexicalization, words receiving specific interpretations when embedded in complex words, and on the other hand the recurrence of such lexicalized bound meanings in new words of the same type.[5] This combination of lexicalization and productivity can therefore be interpreted as signaling the existence of constructional idioms, schemas with partially pre-specified constituents and corresponding meanings. Thus, we may assume the following constructional idiom for verbs like *outbid*:

(21) $[[\text{out}]_{\text{Adv}} [x]_{V_i}]_{V_j} \leftrightarrow [\text{to exceed someone/thing in SEM}_i]_j$

In this schema, I assign the label Adv(erb) to *out*, not the label Preposition because precisely those prepositions that allow for being used adverbially can be used in compounding. For instance, prepositions such as *at* and *between* are not used adverbially, and do not appear in verbal compounds.

The advantage of assuming subschemas is that we do not have to introduce a special category like semi-affix or affixoid for these phenomena. Subschemas suffice to express that speakers are able to make subgeneralizations about subsets of compound words, and thus create new words in which the lexicalized meaning of a subconstituent of a complex word can be used productively.

Such subpatterns are a potential source of new derivational suffixes when the relation with the corresponding independent lexeme is no longer felt, due to semantic change, and when the lexeme gets lost. For instance, the English suffixes *-ful*, as in *beautiful*, and *-able*, as in *washable*, are no longer felt to be related to the lexemes *full* and *able*. A suffix like *-hood* derives historically from a lexeme with the meaning 'quality'. The Dutch suffix *-lijk* and its English counterpart *-ly* derive from the noun *leik* 'body', and the suffix *-dom* (a suffix in both Dutch and English) derives from a lexeme for 'dominion'. The best known case for Romance languages is the adverbializing suffix *-mente* (French form *-ment*) which derives from the Latin noun *mens* 'mind' in its ablative form, as in *clara-mente* 'with a clear mind, in a clear way'.

This rise of derivational morphemes is often qualified as grammaticalization (Aikhenvald 2007: 58), since these morphemes have become affixes. Yet, if situated at the endpoint of grammaticalization, we expect these morphemes to have abstract grammatical properties, whereas a morpheme like *-dom* still has a rather specific meaning. Hence, it seems that there is a cline for such bound morphemes ranging from a more lexical to a more grammatical meaning.

---

5. This point of view is also defended in Brinton & Traugott (2005: 129).

Thus, the rise of bound meanings for lexemes embedded in complex words, and the change of lexemes into affixes shows the necessity of assuming morphological subschemas that account for the bound interpretations of lexemes, and for the possibility of such changes.

5. Allomorphy

Lexemes may exhibit systematic stem allomorphy when embedded in compounds. Such systematic stem allomorphy can be captured by means of schemas that express the relevant generalizations. In this section I discuss a number of these regularities for Dutch compounds.

A first example is the allomorphy of the lexeme MEDE 'with, together'. This word is used as preposition, postposition, and particle, and as part of a compound, with different shapes:

(22) preposition: met [mɛt]
postposition and particle: mee [me:]
first part of a compound: mede [me:də]

Historically the three forms are related as follows: the long and original form is *mede*. The short form *mee* is the effect of a historical phonological process of *de*-deletion. The form *met* is the effect of schwa apocope followed by word-final devoicing of obstruents, and vowel shortening,

The long form *mede* occurs in a few (archaic) particle verbs: *mede-dingen* (but also *mee-dingen*) 'to compete', and *mededelen / meedelen* 'to inform'. Otherwise, the particle form is identical to that of the postposition, *mee*. That is, *mede* is only productively used within compounds, and has the specific meaning 'shared with, co-, fellow-':

(23) a. [[mede]$_{ADV}$ N$_i$]$_{Nj}$ ↔ [SEM$_i$ shared with others]$_j$
b. mede-beslissing 'co-decision'
mede-bewoner 'fellow occupant'
mede-broeder 'fellow brother'

The use of *mee* as a particle is illustrated by the following particle verbs; it is a productive category:

(24) mee-bidden 'to join in praying'
mee-denken 'to join in thinking'
mee-drinken 'to join in drinking'
mee-eten 'to join in eating'

We might qualify *mede* as a prefix, but there is a clear lexical relation with the adverbial particle *mee*, both in form and meaning. A schema as given in (23a) is therefore to be preferred to a prefixal interpretation: *mede* is a form of a lexeme, but a specific allomorph selected by nominal compounds, with a correlating compound-determined meaning.

The existence of schema (23a) will block the formation of [Adv N] compounds of the form *mee* + N. Such compounds are indeed avoided in Dutch, even though the compound schema [Adv N]$_N$ is productive in Dutch; this blocking effect is illustrated by the examples in (25):

(25) mede-bewoner / *mee-bewoner 'co-occupant'
mede-gelovige / *mee-gelovige 'fellow believer'
mede-klinker / *mee-klinker 'consonant'

A noun like *mee-eter* 'one who joins in eating' is possible, however, since it is derived from the established particle verb *mee-eten* 'to join in eating', but it has a meaning different from that of the compound *mede-eter* 'fellow diner'. Therefore, the two forms are not synonymous, and hence do not compete, and blocking is not involved.

The required blocking of the incorrect forms in (25) follows from Panini's principle: the schema for Adv N compounds with *mede* specified as the Adverb position is more specific than the general schema [Adv N]$_N$. Hence, it will override the general schema, and block its application to the adverb *mee*.

In some cases we find semantic differences between the allomorphs of a noun. The word *eer* [e:r] 'honour' has a long allomorph *ere* [e:rə] that has an archaic flavour when used as an independent word. As the first constituent of a compound, we find both *eer-* and *ere-*. However, if the meaning to be expressed is 'honorary', one must always use the long form *ere-*:

(26) a. eer-wraak 'honour-revenge, revenge for the protection of family honour'
eer-betoon 'honour-show, tribute'
b. ere-lid 'honour-member, honorary member' /*eer-lid
ere-voorzitter 'honour-chairman, honorary chairman' / *eer-voorzitter
ere-doctor 'honour-doctor, honorary doctor'/ *eer-doctor

This implies that the following schema has to be assumed:

(27) $[[ere]_N[x]_{Ni}]_{Nj} \leftrightarrow [honorary\ \text{SEM}_i]_j$

This schema will block the insertion of the short noun allomorph *eer* 'honour' in a general [NN]$_N$ schema with the specific 'honorary' meaning of the lexeme *eer* since schema (27) is more specific than the general schema for NN compounds.

Allomorphy patterns thus provide additional evidence for the necessity of subschemas for the coinage of complex words.

6. Analogy or schema?

An old debate in the analysis of newly coined complex words is whether this has to be considered as a matter of analogy, or as the result of using symbolic schemas that generalize across sets of existing complex words. The implication of assuming a hierarchical lexicon with different levels of abstraction is that this is not a matter of 'either/or'; there is analogical word formation, based on an individual model word, but there is also word formation based on schemas. These schemas may, however, differ in their degrees of abstractness. Hence, specific sets of existing complex words may play a role. Moreover, it is not the case that all language users make the same subgeneralizations. Schemas are based on lexical knowledge, and this type of knowledge varies from speaker to speaker (Langacker 1991; Taylor 2002; Tuggy 2007).

The use of schemas for word formation patterns implies a symbolic approach to representing linguistic knowledge. I am fully aware of the fact that there are models of morphology that try to do away with symbolic representation of morphological knowledge, models in which analogy to existing words and memory-based learning play a central role (Daelemans 2002; Keuleers & Daelemans 2007; Keuleers et al. 2007). In such models the notion 'analogy' has received an elaborate sophistication. They have been developed for inflectional processes in which a choice has to be made between different inflectional endings, as in the case of Dutch plural nouns. The correct inflectional endings are computed by measuring the degree of similarity between the input word and the set of words in the lexicon, and selecting the inflectional form that corresponds to that of the most similar word(s) found.

Similar selection problems must be faced when selecting the proper linking element in a newly coined Dutch compound. The linking element to be selected is that of those existing compounds to which the new compound is most similar. In a study of Dutch compounding, Krott showed that analogical modeling is able to cover the selection of linking elements in an adequate way (Krott 2001). Similarly, Plag argued that analogy plays a role in computing the correct stress pattern of English compounds (Plag 2006).

In my opinion, these findings are not in conflict with the kind of word formation schemas that I proposed above. The creation of a new compound involves two stages. In the first stage of language production, it has to be decided how a particular semantic content is going to be expressed (Levelt 1989). One of the options is to select a particular word for that content. The range of possible morphological forms for the expression of semantic content is specified by a set of hierarchically ordered schemas in the lexicon. One of these schemas might be selected, and open positions filled in with lexemes. For instance, if we want to express the concept 'main' in Dutch, speakers of Dutch know that they can use the schema $[[hoofd]_N N]_N$ 'lit. head-N' with the meaning 'main N' for this purpose. This kind of knowledge must therefore be assumed to exist in addition to a set of existing compounds of that form.

In the second stage of language production, the exact form of the compound constituents must be computed. If a lexeme has more than one form – for instance since it may combine with different linking elements – the selection of a particular form may well be modeled properly by the analogical models referred to above since it is clear that the language user has access to existing compounds that share properties such as the initial constituent lexeme with the new compound. The language user who wants to speak about the food that a sheep is provided with may first decide to use an NN compound that begins with the lexeme SCHAAP 'sheep' as its modifier noun, and the lexeme VOER as the head lexeme. At this stage, use is made of the abstract schema for NN compounds that specifies that the right N is the head, or a relevant subschema thereof. Then the question arises whether the correct form of the lexeme SCHAAP is *schaap, schapen-,* or *schaaps-*. It is at that stage that analogical modeling can make predictions as to which allomorph is preferably chosen (the form *schapenvoer* should be predicted as being the most probable one since *schapen* is the most frequently used allomorph). Similarly, the choice of the correct stress pattern for a new English compound at stage 2 may be modeled analogically, after the selection of a particular compounding scheme for coining a new compound has taken place.

As pointed out by Baayen, "the symbolic approach in which paradigmatic structure provides a similarity space over which probabilities are defined provides an excellent level of granularity for understanding the role of probability in language production" (Baayen 2003: 63). A hierarchical lexicon with different levels of abstractness and generalization, as outlined in this paper, expresses this paradigmatic structure, and thus the relevant similarity space.

In sum, a hierarchical lexicon with constructional idioms for subsets of compounds is an essential tool in modeling the regularities in the semantic interpretation and formal make-up of compounds.

The head in compounding*

Sergio Scalise and Antonio Fábregas
University of Bologna and University of Tromsø

This chapter deals with the notion of head inside compounds. We will first focus on the unproblematic cases which have led researchers to determine that compounds contain a head (Section 1). Then we will analyse more problematic cases, showing that some of the properties of heads (such as their position inside the word) are not completely understood (Section 2). Problematic cases of exocentricity or multiple headedness inside compounds will be considered in Section 3, while Section 4 briefly explores the possibility that compounds contain more than one head. The main conclusion of this paper is that there are empirical grounds to propose the existence of heads inside compounds, but the determination of their properties and the identification of the units that play this role for a given feature require detailed language-particular and typological research yet to be done, although some generalizations can already be made.

1. Preliminary notions: Introducing heads of compounds

One of the main areas of interest in the study of compounds is which one of the different constituents of a word resulting from a compounding process counts as its head. However, before we start discussing the notion of head, which has been central in the modern study of grammar since American Structuralism, it is necessary to make explicit some assumptions that this concept presupposes and without which it cannot be properly understood. If the concept 'word' is not used as a merely descriptive label, talking about the head of a word presupposes i) that this word can have an internal structure, that is, that its constituents are linguistic units arranged in a particular way and not only series of phonological segments (as a-morphous morphology theories, such as Anderson 1992 would propose) and ii) that the internal arrangement of the units is asymmetrical, in such a way that one of the units –to put it roughly- has more weight or is more important than the others. In this sense, it is customary to say that

---

* The authors would like to thank Joseph Emonds, Heidi Harley, Nicola Grandi, Ad Neeleman, Edwin Williams, Carlos Piera, Gillian Ramchand and Francesca Forza for useful comments and remarks to previous versions. All disclaimers apply.

the underlined constituents in the compounds in (1) are heads of the compound in which they are embedded: this means that we have identified them as the most important unit inside the internal structure of the word.

(1) a. It. cassa forte   'box + strong, safe box'
    b. Sp. camposanto   'field + holly, graveyard'
    c. Eng. green card

The underlined constituent is identified as the head of the (compound) word in these examples because, as a unit, it has several properties that are imposed on the whole compound. During the eighties, especially since the work of Lieber (1981) and Williams (1981), the criterion that was considered most relevant in identifying the head of a compound is the definition of the grammatical category: the (morphological) head is the constituent that in a complex word determines the lexical category of that word. In the Italian example in (1a), for instance, the compound behaves as a noun, the same grammatical category of its head, *cassa*, and different from the grammatical category of the non-head, *forte*. We may call this way of identifying a head the category test.

(2) [cassa]$_N$ [forte]$_A$ -> [cassaforte]$_N$ 'box + strong, safe'

The definition of the grammatical category, however, has not always been the preferred test to identify compound heads among morphologists. Jespersen (1924) generally relies on the meaning contribution of each constituent to define heads in grammar –and, by implication, also in compounds. From this semantic perspective, the underlined constituents in (1) are the heads of the compounds because they determine, with their meaning, the kind of objects that the compound denotes: in their respective languages, (1a) refers to a class of box, (1b) to a type of field and (1c) to a particular card. We may refer to this criterion to identify the head as the semantic test. Notice that in the examples in (1), the results of the category test coincide with those of the semantic test, and nothing, in principle, makes us expect a different situation.

Sometimes morphological analysis requires in practice that both tests are combined in order to identify the compound head. Consider the case in (3), from Italian.

(3) [capo]$_N$ [stazione]$_N$ -> [capostazione]$_N$ 'chief + station, station master'

If we rely only on the lexical category, we would not be able to identify the head of the compound, since it is composed by two units which are nouns. We must thus combine this test with the semantic test. Following this test we will see that in (3) *capo* is a [+animate] noun, while *stazione* is [−animate]. The whole compound, though, is also a [+animate] noun, which leads us to the conclusion that it is *capo*, and not *stazione*, which works as the head of the whole construction.

It is important to notice that the way in which the semantic criterion is applied nowadays strongly differs from the intuitive way in which Jespersen applied it during the 1920's. The semantic criterion relies on the existence of certain grammatical properties with clear implications for the semantic component of the grammar – we can call them semantic features. These semantic features are properties that define the head as a unit and are transmitted to the whole compound. The surface manifestation of this transmission of features is that the whole compound refers 'to the same kind of entity' as its head. In an attempt to be more precise than Jespersen's intuitive approach about the nature of this semantic relationship, Allen (1978: 11) proposed the 'IS A' condition (4).

(4) In a compound [[ ]$_X$ [ ]$_Y$]$_Z$, Z "IS A" Y

This principle dictates that, whatever concept the whole compound (Z) expresses, it is a subclass of the concept that its head (Y) denotes. In other words, this principle states that the whole compound must be a hyponym of its head. Notice, also, that Allen's formulation does not specify the lexical category of the elements involved in the compound. This relationship is illustrated in (5) for some English compounds.

(5) blackboard IS A board
     mailman IS A man
     field mouse IS A mouse

Four questions immediately arise at this point: (i) what is the mechanism that guarantees that the head will transfer its properties – or features – to the whole compound; (ii) which properties are transmitted? (iii) do the category test and the semantic test always identify the same unit? and (iv) in addition to the semantics and the grammatical category, what other properties of the head are transmitted to the compound? In the following sections these questions will be considered.

1.1   Transmission of features from the head to the compound: Percolation

The mechanism which guarantees that the properties of the head – in the form of features – are transmitted to the whole word has been called percolation (Lieber 1981). Percolation can be presented as a statement that determines that, inside a tree structure, each one of the non-terminal nodes must have the same features as one – and only one – node of the immediately lower level. Consider (6).

(6)

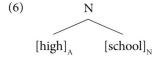

Here, percolation states that the non terminal node N – which is, by the Generalized Lexicalist Hypothesis (Lapointe 1980), the only node that syntax can access – must be identical in features to one of the units of the immediately lowel level. The two candidates are the terminal nodes *high* and *school*, and of these, it is *school* that percolates its features. It imposes its category feature N, as well as its semantic features (among them, [–animate]).

We have seen that the lexical category percolates from the head, as do the semantic features, but these two are not the only types of features that are subject to percolation. Strictly morphological features also percolate from the head to the whole compound. Although controversial for some authors, we will assume that the property of belonging to a particular gender class is a strictly morphological property, and not a syntactic or semantic one – see, for example, Harris 1991.[1] Consider (7); this case shows that purely morphological information must also be allowed to percolate.

(7) [capo]$_{masculine}$ [stazione]$_{feminine}$ -> [capostazione]$_{masculine}$

As seen in (7), *capostazione* is a masculine noun, just as *capo*, its head, is masculine. Other purely morphological properties also frequently percolate. For example, whether a particular word is morphologically regular or irregular may be represented as a diacritic feature that indicates that its paradigm is, in some sense, special. One case of such a word would be the noun *mouse*, whose plural is *mice*, not **mouses*. Notice that the same irregularity is seen in the number inflection of the compound *field mouse*, which is *field mice*, not *field mouses*.

We have seen, then, that there are three kinds of features – category features, semantic features and morphological features – that are normally transmitted from the head of the compound to the whole word. More controversial in the present state of linguistic research is whether a fourth type of feature can be identified, namely selectional features. A selectional feature would determine how many and which type of arguments a particular word must combine with. In the framework where percolation was defined, it was widely believed that this type of feature existed. Notice, however, that, when two words are combined in order to form a compound, not all the selectional features can percolate to the whole compound. Consider (8), for example; although the verb *eat* normally requires a theme argument –the thing that is eaten-, the compound *cookie eating* cannot select such an argument.

(8) a. cookie eating monster
    b. *cookie eating of pasta monster

One solution to this problem is for the head of a compound to satisfy some of its selectional features in the word-internal structure; an additional property of heads inside compounds, then, would be that they can select the non-heads as their arguments (Lieber 1983; DiSciullo & Williams 1987). Interestingly, the head and of the non-head

---

1. By 'strictly morphological property' we mean that, even though gender interacts with syntax in agreement processes, the particular choice of desinence that a noun uses to mark gender is unpredictable, specially in non-animates. For example, in the Spanish noun *man-o*, 'hand', the choice of *–o* as a word marker is not predictable on syntactic, semantic or phonological grounds.

contrast on the way their selection features act. According to Selkirk (1982), in fact, the following generalizations can be formulated:

(9) a. Arguments of the non-head are never part of the argumental structure of the compound. They do not percolate.
b. The non-head may be an argument of the head.
c. The non-head cannot be the external argument of the head.
d. Only the external argument of the head may be part of the argument structure of the compound.

These generalizations can be illustrated by the following examples. In (10a), we see that, even though the noun *destruction* allows for a patient argument –*the city*-, the whole compound cannot combine with this constituent if *destruction* is the non-head. In (10b), it can be seenthat the non-head of the compound can be interpreted as one of the arguments of the head – typically the theme or patient –, although never as the agent, explaining why (10c) – where *kid* is to be interpreted the entity that performs the action of eating – is ungrammatical. Finally, in (10d), the agent *by Vonnegut* can only denote the entity responsible for the account, not for the destruction, showing that the agent of the non-head cannot be part of the argument structure of the whole compound.

(10) a. destruction story vs. *destruction story of the city
b. truck driver
c. *kid eating makes such a mess
d. destruction account by Vonnegut

1.2 Relationship between semantic, morphological and categorial features

The percolation account states that one, and only one node, imposes its features on the node at the next level. This predicts that, *ceteris paribus*, the same unit will transmit at the same time its semantics, its grammatical category and its morphological properties. In other words, the percolation account makes a clear prediction, specifically that the semantic test will identify as a head the same constituent as the category test. We can present this generalization as in (11).

(11) In a compound the category head and the semantic head are the same unit.

The cases that we have seen thus far confirm the generalization in (11), but this is not always the case. In fact, cases where the semantic head cannot be the categorial head are not infrequent in the languages of the world. Consider, for example, the cases in (12).

(12) a. It. porta-lettere 'to carry + letters, postman'
b. It. testa rasata 'head + shaven, skin head'

The compound in (12a) is a noun, suggesting that the constituent *lettere*, a noun, is the head, and that *porta*, a verb, cannot be the head. However, the semantics of the compound are closer to the semantics of *porta,* since the compound refers to someone who carries something, and not to a type of letters. In (12b), the category test would say that the head of the compound is *testa,* but its semantics do not correctly describe the semantics of the whole compound, since the noun *testa* is [–animate], while the whole compound is [+animate]. These mismatches between the constituent identified as the head according to the grammatical category and that identified by the semantics constitute, in principle, counterexamples to the percolation account of headedness inside compounds. They show that the identification of the head is, by no means, a simple task and, also, that other factors beyond those that have already been presented are required. The problems will be considered in section three, while in the next section we consider the properties of compound heads in more detail.

2. The properties of compound heads

We have already seen that, in a perfect world, the head of a compound imposes three types of information on the whole compound: its grammatical category, its semantics and its morphological properties (such as gender or whether it is an irregular word). These are not, however, the only properties that compound heads have.

The head of a compound has also been identified as the constituent where the inflectional properties of the whole word are manifested – the head is the 'locus inflectionis' of the compound. Take for instance the compound *strawberry field*. When in the plural form, the morpheme *–s* combines with the constituent *field,* the head, giving as a result the form *strawberry fields* – not **strawberries field*.

Several problems have been identified with respect to this notion. The first one is that, when the compound shows a high degree of lexicalization, the inflectional morphemes tend to show up at one of the edges of the word – in Indoeuropean languages, the right edge-, independently of whether this edge belongs to the head or not. Thus, in Italian, the compound *pomodoro,* 'tomato', originally comes from the phrasal structure *pomo d'oro,* 'apple of gold', its plural form was originally *pomi d'oro,* but in nowadays Italian it is more frequently rendered as *pomodori,* where the segment *–i,* responsible for plural marking in masculine nouns, attaches to the segment *oro,* 'gold', which is not the head of the compound (Scalise 1984).

More problematic perhaps for the view that compound heads are *loci inflectionis* are cases, proposed in Bauer (1978), where the non-head of the compound still exhibits some inflectional morphemes. For example, in Spanish, the compound *niña prodigio,* 'girl + wonder, (female) wunderkind', shows a gender marking both in the head (*niñ-a*) and in the non-head (*prodigi-o*), and some speakers even allow both constituents to be inflected for plural (*niñ-a-s prodigi-o-s*). It is worth noting, though, as Bauer (1983) noted, that only the gender marking of the head is transmitted to the whole compound: the compound *niña prodigio* is a feminine noun, like *niña,* and not masculine, as *prodigio.*

In syntax, heads are said to impose certain formal conditions on their non-heads. Compound heads have also been claimed to have this property – sometimes described as government (Zwicky 1985)- and, thus, may impose formal conditions on their non-heads. In some languages the non-heads of compounds exhibit linking elements which mark them differently from the head (13). It has been suggested that the presence of the linking element is explained if the head of the compound imposes it as a dependency marker on the non-head.

(13) a. craft-s-man
     b. Du. regiering-s-vorm   'government-LE-form, 'form of government'
     c. Nor. barn-e-hagen   'child-LE-garden, 'kindergarten'
     d. Sp. pel-i-rrojo   'hair-LE-red, 'red haired'

Compound heads are also considered to be the most prominent element of the compound in discourse semantics. Prominence is defined, in this context, as being the only element inside the word that cannot be eliminated in second mention without giving rise to ungrammaticality or to a sharp meaning difference. The non-head, by contrast, can be removed in some second mention contexts. Consider, for example, the two sequences in (14). Only (14a) would be a plausible continuation of the sentence *I found a pig tail in the soup*. The reason is that (14a) eliminates the non-head and keeps the head of the compound, which is the most prominent element in the discourse; (14b), by contrast, is odd because the head – which is more prominent in the discourse than the non-head – has been eliminated.

(14) a. … Then, I removed the tail and continued eating.
     b. …#Then, I removed the pig and continued eating.

One of the most discussed properties of compound heads has been its position inside the word, namely whether it appears to the right or to the left of the units that it selects. We shall discuss this in detail in the next section.

2.1 The position of the head

Williams (1981) – and then DiSciullo & Williams (1987) – proposed that a pervasive property of morphological structures is that the head of a word is always the rightmost constituent of that word. By implication, then, also the head of compounds should be identifiable by the property of being to the right. Consider the cases in (15).

(15) compounding $[high]_A + [school]_N \rightarrow [high\ school]_N$
     prefixation $[re+[write]_V] \rightarrow [rewrite]_V$
     suffixation $[\,[lonely]_A + ness]_N \rightarrow [loneliness]_N$

Inside all these complex words, the head is always to the right. This generalization has been captured by proposing a principle, the Right Hand Head Rule (RHHR, Williams 1981). While the RHHR has been generally unchallenged for derived words, several crucial problems have been identified in the case of compounds. Although in Germanic languages it is generally true that compounds have their head consistently to the right, as in 16) (but see (16g) from English), Romance languages generally have their head to the left, as in (17).

(16) German   a. Herz<u>krank</u> 'heart sick'
              b. Butter<u>broot</u> 'butter bred, sandwich'
              c. Haus<u>hoch</u> 'house high, high as a house'
     Norwegian d. Kjærlighets<u>dikt</u> 'love poem, love poem'
              e. Kniv<u>drepe</u> 'knife+(to)kill, (to) knife-kill'
              f. Konge<u>tiger</u> 'king tiger, Bengala tiger'
     English g. <u>pick</u> pocket
(17) French   a. <u>bateau</u> mouche 'boat fly, excursion streamer'
              b. <u>arc</u>-en-ciel 'arch in sky, rainbow'
              c. <u>canne</u> épée 'sword stick'
     Spanish d. <u>empresa</u> fantasma 'firm ghost, cover-up-company'
              e. <u>diente</u> de leche 'tooth of milk, deciduous tooth'
              f. <u>papel</u> moneda 'paper money, money paper'

It could still be the case, though, that the RHHR applies by default to structures unless some other property interacts with it (Emonds 2008). In any case, the data in (16) and (17) show that the RHHR is not unproblematic and it is necessary to consider the data in more detail.

2.1.1   A parameter for the position of the head?

Sic stantibus rebus, one could be tempted to propose that the position of the head in the languages of the world is a binary parameter which is fixed quite consistently in a given language: Germanic languages fix it to the right – with very few exceptions – and Romance languages fix it to the left – with a somewhat higher number of exceptions. This particular analysis would reproduce in morphology the Branching Direction Theory (Dryer 1992), proposed in syntax to differentiate languages whose phrases are head-initial (such as English) from those that are head-final (such as Japanese). Before trying to verify this possibility, let us consider a wider sample of languages from the MorBoComp project.[2] The figures we report are not based on tokens but on the notion

---

2. The Morbo/Comp Project has been developed at the University of Bologna and it consists of approximately 80.000 compounds from the following languages: Bulgarian, Catalan, Chinese, Dutch, English, Finnish, French, German, Modern Greek, Hungarian, Italian, Japanese, Korean, Latin, Norwegian, Polish, Portuguese, Russian, Serbo-Croatian, Spanish, Swedish, Turkish. The sample used in this paper consists of approximately 3000 compounds, each analyzed in 18 searchable fields: Language, Compound, Output category, Internal structure, Classification, Categorial head, Semantic head, 1st constituent, Category of 1st constituent, Linking element 1,

of Compound Type. A Compound Type is defined as the intersection of the following database fields for each language considered:

(18) Output Category (Z): $[\,[\,]_X\,[\,]_Y\,]_Z$
Structure: $[\,[\,]\,[\,]\,],\,[[\,]\,[\,]\,+\text{Suf}]\ldots$
Combination of categories (X and Y): $[\,[\,X\,]\,[\,Y\,]\,]$
Relationship between the components: $[\,[\,]\,r\,[\,]\,]^3$
Position of the head: $[\,[\_\!\_]\,[\,]\,]$ or $[\,[\,]\,[\_\!\_]]$

When only compound types are computed, the MorBo database gives the following results:

(19)
Headedness	General %
Right	66.7
No Head	16.3
Left	6.8
Both	5.9

It is undoubtedly true that the majority of languages in the database are right-headed in compounding. This is also true if we consider each linguistic group separately, specifically Romance, Germanic, Slavic and East Asia languages, as in (20).

(20)
	General %	Rom. %	Germ. %	Slav. %	E.Asia %
Right	66.7	40.7	87.0	61.9	57.5
No head	16.3	31.4	8.9	12.2	17.7
Left	6.8	20.3	1.9	6.0	6.8
Both	5.9	6.8	1.3	3.1	15.0

These figures suggest that, in a surface analysis, inside compounds, the head is by default the rightmost element; however, left-headed compounds are, by no means, unattested, nor are compounds where no head can be identified or where the two constituents seem to be heads. If right-headedness is truly the default manifestation of heads inside compounds, it is necessary to determine which factors trigger left-headedness.

Other data show that it is not possible to consider the position of the head a parameter, at least in the sense it is generally interpreted in linguistics – that is, as an inviolable principle that determines the particular value of a universal well-formedness condition in a particular language. These data come from Chinese. Taking into account

---

2nd constituent, Category of 2nd constituent, Linking element 2, 3rd constituent, Category of 3rd constituent, Plural, Gender, Gloss / Translation and Observations.

3. The symbol 'r' stands for the grammatical and semantic relation that holds between the two constituents of a compound. Compounds can be classified either as subordinate or coordinate or attributive/appositive (see Scalise & Bisetto 2009).

the table in (21),[4] Huang (1984) suggests that the combination of V and N in Chinese shows that "[...] Chinese is a headless language in its morphology since neither the rightmost nor the leftmost member of a compound uniquely determines the category type of a compound."

(21)

	N	V	A
NN	6910	21	90
VN	1581	2940	378
AA	163	?	1609

We will consider the possibility that compounds without a head exist in Section 3. Leaving this question aside for the time being, Ceccagno & Scalise (2006) in fact observe that Chinese VN compounds are of two types, illustrated in (22a) and (22b).

(22) a. shípǐn 'eat + product, food'
     b. kāidāo 'open + knife, operate'

While in (22b) the verb selects the noun as one of its arguments, in (22a) it has an attributive function, where it can be translated as 'edible' inside the compound (food = 'edible product'). When the verb selects for the noun, the whole compound is a verb; if the verb has an attributive function, the whole compound is a noun. It seems, then, that in Chinese, depending on the grammatical function of each constituent, VN compounds are sometimes left-headed and sometimes right-headed. This is consistent with Packard (2001) and Ceccagno & Scalise (2006), who propose that in Chinese nominal compounds are right headed and verbal compounds are left-headed.

Similar data can be found in Japanese compounds, as pointed out by Kageyama (2009)

(23) a. yude-tamago 'boil + egg, boiled egg'
     b. soo-kin 'send + money, remit'

In (23b), the verb is argumental, the whole compound is a verb and the head is to the left, while in (23a) the verb has an attributive function, the whole compound is a noun and the head is to the right. These data from Japanese and Chinese show that the head cannot be considered to be an independent parameter, since within each language, the combination of the same two units gives different results depending on the grammatical relationship established between them.

We conclude, then, that the position of the head inside a compound can be considered neither a universal principle nor a parameter – at least, in the usual senses of these words. It rather seems that there is a canonical position for the head in each compound type in a given language. To illustrate this point, we list in (24) and (25) the

---

4. In this table, the first column indicates the internal structure of the compound –stating both the categories involved and the order in which they appear–, while the first row indicates the category of the compound as a whole.

different compound types in Italian. (24) contains the compound types that exhibit right-headedness, while (25) presents the compound types which are left-headed.[5]

(24) Right-headed compounds in Italian
    a. A+N   gentildonna   'lit. gentle woman'
    b. Adv+A   benvenuto   'welcome'
    c. N+N   gasdinamica   'lit. gas dynamics'
    d. N+sN   insettivoro   'insectivorous'
    e. sN+N   logoterapeuta   'speech therapist'
    f. sN+sN   grafomania   'graphomania'
    g. N+N   terremoto   'earthquake'
    h. N+N   scuola bus   'school bus'

(25) Left-headed compounds in Italian
    a. A+N   rosso mattone   'brick red'[6]
    b. N+A   acqua santa   'holy water'
    c. N+N   ufficio viaggi   'travel agency'
    d. N+N   uomo rana   'frog man'
    e. N+N   stud. lavoratore   'lit. student worker'
    g. [V+Suf]N + N   trasporto latte   'milk transportation

There are some differences, though, between (24) and (25). In (24) the types d., e. and f. have been called 'neoclassical compounds', because they are constructed – at least partially – with Latin or Greek lexemes, and follow the typical pattern in these languages. The compound type in (24g) is, again, of Latin origin (as evidenced by the residual ending –*e* of *terr-e*), and is generally unproductive. (24h) is normally considered a calque from English and, therefore, not constructed by the normal Italian pattern. Notice that Greek, Latin and English are generally right-headed languages in compounding. As for (24a, b) these patterns are not productive in contemporary Italian. We are therefore left with only one case of an 'Italian' right-headed compound, (24c), which, furthermore, belongs to a specific lexical domain and also has equivalents in English. To the contrary, the cases listed in (25) are all productive patterns in contemporary Italian and all are left-headed.[7]

---

5. The notation s- in front of the category-label indicates that the unit is a neoclassical stem and, thus, that it cannot constitute a word by itself, although it productively enters into compounding.

6. Compounds formed with colour terms and nouns or adjectives display an ambiguous behaviour in Italian and Spanish. Although they are more frequently used as nouns, agreement shows that some speakers are able to treat them as adjectives.

7. From a different perspective, many of the right-headed compounds in Italian show specific bound morphemes in the head. This pattern has recently been noticed by Emonds (2008) for French, as well as Ackema and Neeleman (2004) for English. All these authors relate both properties through phonological constraints.

3. Problems in the identification of heads: Multiple heads and exocentricity

The cases that we have considered thus far have shown that the category of the compound comes from the same constituent that imposes its semantic and its morphological properties. This situation is the one expected from the percolation account, however it is not always found in natural languages. Different situations may also arise. The first one is that no element seems to explain the semantics of the compound, or more than one element is necessary for this (3.1.); the second one is that the element that imposes its grammatical category does not impose its morphological properties (3.2.); the third one is that none of the elements is sufficent to explain the grammatical category of the compound or more than one could explain it (3.3.). All these situations have been considered in traditional studies of compounding as 'absence of head' – technically called 'exocentricity'- because they seem to suggest that none of the constituents of the compound percolates all its features to the whole word, or both of them are required to do so. Let us review these cases.

3.1   Problems with semantic features

The traditional view presented in Section 1 is that the head of a compound imposes its semantic type in such a way that the whole word is a hyponym of the class of objects denoted by the head. Heads in compounds, thus, follow the IS A rule.

Three different situations have been identified where the compound does not follow the IS A rule. The first case refers to so-called co-compounds (Waelchli 2005). Co-compounds, normally not attested in the major European languages, are compounds where two words – usually of the same grammatical category – which share substantial parts of their lexical semantics are combined together to denote their hyperonym. For example, in Indian English *wife-children*[8] can be used as a compound which denotes, roughly, 'family'. A family is not a type of *wife* or a type of *children*; rather, families can be defined by adding together *wives* and *children*. In Tok Pisin (Mühlhäusler 1979), the compound *brata-susa*, 'brother + sister', denotes 'siblings', which, again, cannot be considered a subclass of brothers or sisters – it is the opposite. In this same Creole language, *su-soken*, 'shoe-sock', is used to denote the whole class of pieces of clothing used for the feet. It is clear that in these cases the IS A rule cannot apply, as the hyponymy relations are reversed with respect to the usual case in European languages. The question is whether we must take these compounds to be exocentric on

---

8.   Joseph Emonds reports to us that in American English, in order to obtain the relevant reading, a linking element reminiscent of the copulative conjunction *and* must be inserted, as in *wife-n-children* (cfr. *ham-n-eggs*). Given the fact that in Germanic languages coordinative compounds normally do not have linking elements, this property would suggest either that co-compounds can be interpreted as subordinate compounds or, more plausibly, that in English they keep significant traces of an original phrasal structure and, therefore, are not prototypical cases of compounding.

semantic grounds or whether we need to give up the IS A rule and define semantic headedness in a way that also covers the co-compounds attested in the languages of the world. Intuitively, it does not seem right to say that the meaning 'sibling' cannot be easily derived from the combination of the word referring to *sister* and that referring to *brother*; each of the two constituents makes a clear and unambiguous semantic contribution to the whole word. It seems, then, that semantic headedness should be reconsidered. We propose the definition in (26).

(26) The semantic head of a compound is the constituent whose semantic contribution allows us to determine the class of objects denoted by the compound.

This covers the case of co-compounds, but notice that in these compounds the semantic contribution of both constituents is equally important in determining the semantic class denoted by the whole. In co-compounds, then, the two elements transmit semantic features, and, in this sense, co-determine the semantics of the word. Co-compounds are thus semantically close to coordinative compounds in the major European languages. For example, in the Spanish compound *poeta pintor*, 'poet painter', both constituents contribute their meaning to the whole, which refers to "a person who is at the same time a poet and a painter". Coordinative compounds have two constituents which contribute their meaning to the word and, in this sense, they may be said to have two semantic heads – that is, two heads responsible for the semantic interpretation –, which puts them close to what traditionally has been described as dvandva compounds. Notice, however, that not all coordinative compounds are clearly dvandva. In the Italian *prete-operaio* 'priest worker', the semantic head seems to be solely the first constituent, since the usual interpretation of the word is a priest who, in addition to being a priest, has another occupation.

Another case where it may be difficult to identify a semantic head arises in compounds where adjectives and nouns are combined together, such as *pale face, skin head, pretty face*, etc. It is clear, for example, that a *pale face* is not a type of face, but a class of human beings. These compounds, then, do not follow the IS A rule, and semantic features such as [±animate] are not shared by the head and the whole word. Booij (2002, 2005) and, after him, other authors (Benczes 2006) have called this class of compounds 'metonymical compounds'. As all human beings have faces and faces are part of what we define as a human being, the noun 'face' can be used to denote, by metonymy, a human being described by a particularly salient property of his/her face. If the metonymy analysis works, the *pale face* type of compound has a semantic head which, perhaps not accidentally, is also the constituent that defines the grammatical category of the word, only that this semantic head is interpreted via a metonymical relationship.

Some semantically exocentric compounds seem to exist, though. This situation is expected in a lexicalist perspective, for a crucial property of words and, in general, all units stored in the lexicon, is that they may develop demotivated meanings which are not derivable from the meaning of their parts. Such examples normally are compounds which belong to old stages of the language. For instance, in Spanish, the compound *pati-difuso*, 'leg distributed', has a meaning, 'puzzled', which does not seem easily derivable by metonymy or any other semantic operation from its internal parts. It can thus safely be said that *pati-difuso* lacks a semantic head.

3.2 Problems with morphological features

Sometimes it seems that the constituent that defines the category of a compound, as well as its semantics, does not transmit its morphological features. If we consider the *pale face* class in Romance languages, where gender is lexically defined for each noun, we see that the compounds typically allow mismatches between the gender of the head and the gender of the whole compound. Thus, the equivalent of *skin head* in Italian, *testa rasata*, has a constituent, *testa,* which defines the grammatical category of the compound as a noun. However, this constituent is feminine, as shown by feminine agreement on the adjective *rasata*, but the whole compound can be masculine and combine with the masculine singular determiner *il* (*il testa rasata*). The same situation arises in Spanish with the same class of compounds, only in this language the mismatches between the morphological properties are worsened by the fact that not only gender, but also number, can be different. The compound *relaciones públicas,*[9] 'relationships + public = public relations officer', contains a noun, *relaciones*, in feminine plural form. Still, the whole compound can be masculine singular, as seen by the choice of the determiner *el* in the phrase *el relaciones públicas*. It can thus be saidthat this class of compounds is morphologically exocentric in the languages discussed.

This situation is, of course, a reflection of the problematic nature of this class of compounds, which some authors would classify as idioms. As such, they would be characterised as syntactic structures which correspond to single lexical entries. The role of the lexical entry from this perspective would be to give an equivalence between the internal syntactic structure of the idiom and the syntactic structure to which it corresponds as a whole, i.e., where it can be inserted. Similar considerations, but with different terminology, would be in order in a Construction Grammar analysis. In any case, in this second view, the constructions are still exocentric in the relevant sense, since there is no immediate conection between the internal head of the idiom and the external properties of the structure.

Another case where morphological mismatches seem to be the rule and not the exception is co-compounds. As reported by Waelchli (2005), co-compounds typically exhibit neuter gender in languages where nouns can be neuter, independently of the gender of the nouns that are combined inside the compound. It is suggested that this may be due to the fact that co-compounds typically denote collections of things, collectivities and group entities, which are frequently characterized by the neuter gender,

---

9. We are, again, grateful to Joseph Emonds for pointing this out to us.

but the problem remains that the gender of both constituents is not transmitted to the whole. Reference to morphological exocentricity seems justified also in these cases.

3.3   Problems with categorial features

Finally, there have also been cases reported where it seems that none of the constituents percolates its grammatical category to the head. Many such cases have been identified in isolating languages, such as Chinese or Vietnamese. For illustration, consider the Chinese cases in (27).

(27)   a.   cai-feng   'cut + sew, tailor'
         b.   guang-gao   'wide + announce, advertisement'

In (27a), the combination of two verbs gives a noun as a result; in (27b), the combination of an adjective and a verb also gives a noun as a result. The noun label cannot, however, come from either of the two constituents of the compound.. It could be argued, though since Chinese has a somewhat impoverished (derivational and inflectional) morphology, we do not have direct morphological evidence of the grammatical category of the units in a particular compound. However, similar situations are also found in languages where morphological marking is richer and, therefore, where it is possible to judge the grammatical category of the units from their morphological composition.

The first relevant case is found in a variety of Romance languages, and involves nominal compounds with a (typically) agentive or instrumental meaning, composed by a verbal stem and a noun (singular or plural) which is interpreted as the semantic patient of the verb, as in (28).

(28)   a.   It. asciuga-capelli   'dry + hairs, hair dryer'
         b.   Sp. limpia-botas   'polish + boots, boot polisher'

As seen in the translations, these compounds semantically correspond to English synthetic compounds with an explicit agentive suffix. No agentive suffix is found in (28), though so the noun in the internal structure of the compound cannot be considered the head on semantic grounds. Furthermore, it does not impose its morphological properties to the whole word. The verbal stem cannot be responsible for the category of the word, although its semantic contribution is closer to being the semantic head of the word. Neither of the two units, therefore, seems to be responsible for the grammatical category of the compound. Unless zero morphemes (Varela 1990) or other operations (Scalise, Fábregas & Forza 2009) are proposed to explain this mismatch, VN compounds in Romance languages seem to be plausible candidates to illustrate categorial exocentricity.

Another relevant case refers to compounds where two verbs with an antonymic meaning are combined inside a compound which seems to belong to the noun category. (29) illustrates this class of compounds for Spanish and Italian, although such forms have been reported in other languages as well (cfr. English *see-saw*).

(29) a. bagna-asciuga,   'soak + dry, strand'
     b. subi-baja   'ascend + descend, lift'

Here the combination of the verbs results in a noun, although neither of the verbs seems to have undergone any nominalization judging from their morphological shapes, and when used in isolation, they do not allow for conversion into nouns. It seems in these cases, too, it is possible to claim that there is no head responsible for the grammatical category of the compound.

Other problems arise when both members of the compound could equally be claimed to provide the grammatical category of the entire compound. Such a situation arises in coordinative compounds, which are systematically composed of units belonging to the same lexical category. In the compound *singer-actor*, a noun composed of two nouns, it is difficult to determine which of the two constituents is responsible for the grammatical category of the whole, unless other principles,such as the canonical position of the head,are invoked.

A different problem is presented by cases where both units co-define the grammatical category of the compound. Kageyama (2008) reports that in Japanese some compounds constructed by combination of a noun and an adjective belong to the lexical class of adjectival nouns,with properties both of adjectives and nouns. In his analysis, each of the two constituents provides part of the category label to the whole word, and in this sense, neither of them alone is sufficent to define the grammatical category of the compound.

4. Different kinds of heads?

Some of the cases reviewed in the previous section suggest that the notion of head inside a compound may not be unitary. Some compounds are clearly semantically exocentric, while there is no reason to think that they are also exocentric with respect to their grammatical category. It could well be the case that inside a compound different elements can be identified as heads, depending on which feature we are considering. Indeed, a similar organization was proposed in DiSciullo & Williams (1987) as the Relativized Head hypothesis: the notion of head must be relativized to each feature, even if the usual situation is that all features come from the same head.

We have seen that the problems presented by semantic, morphological and categorial features are not identical. This could lead us to identify three distinct types of head. The semantic head would be the unit (or units, as in co-compounds or in dvandva compounds) that defines the semantic class of the whole word. The categorial head would be the unit that defines the lexical category of the word. Finally, the morphological head would be unit that defines the formal properties of the compound as a lexical item (e.g., its gender and its inflectional class). From this perspective, the cases discussed in the previous section are cases where these different notions of head are not identical. Let us briefly consider the relationship between them.

Taking into account again the data available in the MorBoComp project, several generalizations seem to be possible, at least provisionally and awaiting confirmation on the basis of a wider typological study.

1. First, whenever a unit defines the semantic type of the compound, it also defines its grammatical category. In the MorBoComp database we have not identified any semantically endocentric compounds that are categorially exocentric. Notice also that in coordinative compounds, as in co-compounds, where arguably both units co-define the semantics of the word, the units must belong to the same lexical category, identical to the grammatical category of the whole word. This effect shows how strong the correlation between being a semantic head and being a category head is. The opposite, however, does not hold, at least superficially: there are numerou categorially endocentric compounds that are semantically exocentric (e.g. *California beauty*, a type of plant).

2. Second, whenever a compound is morphologically exocentric, it is also true that its semantic type cannot be derived from the denotation of any constituent, at least without any additional meaning operation such as metaphor or metonymy. This was seen in the discussion of the *testa rasata* cases in Romance languages. Morphological unpredictability is, thus, connected with semantic unpredictability. We would like to highlight the potential significance of this generalization, which suggests a close relationship between morphological information such as the inflectional class or gender and semantic information. If this connection is confirmed, it would make it unlikely that formal morphological markers belong to the phonological component of the grammar (the PF branch), as proposed in the Distributed Morphology framework (Embick & Noyer 2001).

5. Conclusions and final remarks

We began this chapter with a discussion of cases where the identification of a unit inside the compound as its head is relatively unproblematic, and we examined the mechanism proposed to explain headedness inside a compound. From there we moved to more problematic cases where it has been argued either that there is no head or that more than one unit is playing the role of head. This has led us to relativize the definition of head inside a compound and divide it into three components: semantic head, categorial head and morphological head. We have briefly considered the possible and impossible matches among these three concepts; although our findings in this area must be considered provisional, due to the relatively small sample of languages. We believe, however, that the initial results are encouraging and deserve further attention to confirm, modify or reject them.

On the lexical semantics of compounds
Non-affixal (de)verbal compounds

Rochelle Lieber
University of New Hampshire

In this chapter I identify a type of compounding in English which I call *non-affixal (de)verbal compounds* in which one element of the compound is a noun and the other either a verb (*attack dog*) or a noun derived from a verb (*dog attack*). Unlike synthetic and root compounds in English, this type of compound has received very little attention, although it exhibits interesting properties. I illustrate that unlike typical synthetic compounds, non-affixal (de) verbal compounds show a propensity for subject-oriented interpretations, and I argue that this propensity follows from an analysis based within the framework of Lieber (2004, 2006, 2009).[1]

1. Introduction

The semantic interpretation of English compounds is a subject that certainly has not been neglected by linguists over the last forty years. Marchand (1969) devotes a lengthy chapter to the subject, and issues of compound interpretation have figured prominently in works by Lees (1960), Roeper and Siegel (1978), Levi (1978), Selkirk (1982), Lieber (1983, 2004, 2009), Ryder (1994), Jackendoff (2009), among many others. All of these analyses have something to say about so-called synthetic (also called verbal or deverbal) compounds (1a) and most also discuss the interpretation of root compounds (1b):

(1) a. synthetic compounds: fire fighter, home baked, animal training, cost containment, food production
    b. root compounds: dog bed, hand lotion, red hot, hard hat, ice cold

---

1. Many thanks to Laurie Bauer who read an earlier draft of this paper and provided useful comments.

Curiously, however, there is a sort of compound that occurs with some productivity in English, but which has escaped detailed analysis:

(2) a. dog attack, bee sting, landslide, snowdrift, birth control, haircut, bloodshed, boat ride, moon walk, pub crawl
b. attack dog, slide rule, scrubwoman, drawbridge, rowboat, drawstring, bake house

In (2a) we have compounds in which the first element is a noun, and the second element is a noun formed by conversion from a verb. (2b) contains compounds in which the second element is a simple noun, but the first element might be analyzed either as a verb, or again as a noun formed by conversion from a verb. In both sets of compounds, one element is interpreted as an argument – subject, object, or prepositional object – of the other (subject: *dog attack, attack dog*, object: *ball kick, kick ball*; prepositional object: *moon walk, bake house*). Such compounds have been noted at least by Jespersen (1943), Marchand (1969), Bauer and Renouf (2001), Huddleston and Pullum (2005), and Jackendoff (2009), but to my knowledge, they have received no systematic or detailed analysis. Also lacking is a convenient way of referring to them: as we will see, they exhibit characteristics distinct from both synthetic and root compounds, and therefore deserve a separate designation. For lack of a better term, I propose to call them *non-affixal (de)verbal compounds* (henceforth NDVCs), fully admitting that this term is somewhat awkward. I have chosen this term, however, because it is neutral, it distinguishes them from synthetic compounds, and it does not immediately bias us towards one sort of analysis or another.

What is most interesting for us is that NDVCs exhibit a characteristic that is absent from synthetic compounds. It is relatively difficult to find synthetic compounds in which the first element is interpreted as the subject argument of the deverbal second element (e.g., *caribou migration, court ruling, livestock encroachment*); the vast majority of synthetic compounds receive an interpretation in which the first element is interpreted as the object (*grapefruit appreciation, bicycle riding*) or prepositional object (*drug education, vole experiment*) of the deverbal noun. In the compounds of the type in (2), on the other hand, it is not at all unusual to find a subject interpretation, as I will show in detail below. Indeed, in the brief paragraph that Marchand (1969: 77) devotes to compounds of this sort, he notes in passing that the object-oriented type of what we are calling NDVCs is 'weak', although he does not speculate on why this should be the case. The question I raise in this chapter is why such a difference between NDVCs and synthetic compounds should exist. I will argue that the difference follows from the structure of the compounds and the nature of conversion, and that the analysis that they are given in the framework of Lieber (2004) predicts the somewhat surprising pattern that we find.

Section 2 will set out the relevant data, illustrate the characteristics of these compounds, and discuss the theoretical questions that they raise. Section 3 will digress briefly on the analysis of verb to noun conversion in the framework of Lieber (2004).

In Section 4 I will provide a detailed analysis of these compounds and show how the pattern of interpretation that they exhibit follows from my lexical semantic analysis. In Section 5 I consider the issue these compounds raise for the classification of English compounds.

2. Non-affixal (de)verbal compounds

It might be thought that NDVCs are an oddity – an unproductive type of compound that we find only occasionally. This seems not to be the case, however, as the examples in (3) and (4) suggest.[2]

(3) NDVCs, Type 1: [N][conversion noun]
Subject-oriented: dog attack, bee sting, earthquake, heartbeat, rainfall, bus stop, flea bite, land slide, cloud burst, foot step, nightfall, sunset, daybreak, frostbite, sunshine, dogfight, headache, plane crash, waterfall, troop advance, government claim, nosebleed, mouse squeak, brain bleed, sunburn, groundswell, oil spill, government collapse, heartburn, eyewink, heartbreak, footfall, moonrise, sunrise, bellyache, thunderclap

Object-oriented: ball kick, birth control, haircut, bloodshed, handshake, car park, dress design, wind break, age limit, heart attack, clambake, fishfry, robot repair, ballkick, cost control, court reform, energy audit, fare increase, fee hike, tax hike, rate hike, gun control, spending cut, sun worship, manslaughter, bodyguard, blood test, air traffic control, funding increase

Prepositional object-oriented: boat ride, home work, day dream, moon walk, field work, pub crawl, gunfight, table talk, hand stand, construction work, age limit, traffic alert, car ride, advertising battle, nanny work, tax vote, sabre cut, baby care, Harvard study

(4) NDVCs, Type 2: [V][N]
Subject-oriented: attack dog, cover letter, slide rule, clamp screw, finish coat, punch press, rip saw, spark plug, tow truck, watch dog, cry baby, go cart, call bird, drag man, jump jet, scrub woman, tugboat, rattle snake, blow torch, stopwatch, driftwood, flashlight, screechowl (possibly: cook top, fry pan, cook

---

2. These examples have been gathered from a number of sources: Jespersen (1943), Marchand (1969), Huddleston and Pullum (2005), Jackendoff (2009), Plag et al (2008), Bauer and Renouf (2001), the Morbocomp corpus, and my own collection (mostly from American newspapers). Many thanks to Sergio Scalise for permission to use the Morbocomp corpus. Ideally it would have been preferable to extract NDVCs from COCA, as the synthetic compounds were, but coding in this corpus (or indeed in any other one that I know of) is not fine-tuned enough to allow such a search.

stove, drain board, scrub brush, grind stone, whetstone, draghook, hushmoney, washcloth)[3]

Object-oriented: kick ball, row boat, draw string, rip cord, jump rope, tow net, drawbridge, show bread, throw stick, call girl, kick stand, mince meat, skim milk, bore hole, punch card, pushboat, pushcart, showplace, dropcloth

Prepositional object-oriented: bake house, washday, dial tone, wishbone, print shop, blow tube, launch pad, tow path, waitlist, assault rifle, checkpoint, search warrant, workhouse, battlefield, wash basin, washboard, washhouse, washstand, pay day, work day, play thing, swim suit, bakeshop, dancehall, dropzone, escape drain

NDVCs display a combination of characteristics that make them distinct from both root and synthetic compounds in English:

- Like synthetic compounds, NDVCs have an interpretation in which one element of the compound is construed as an argument[4] of the other.
- Like synthetic compounds one element of the compound is or is derived from a verb, but unlike synthetic compounds, there is no overt derivational affix on that element. For this reason, NDVCs at first appear formally more like root than synthetic compounds as they appear to be comprised of two bare roots.
- For Type 1 NDVCs, it is clear that the second element is a deverbal noun: compounds like *dog attack* or *ball kick* inflect as nouns. As syntactic category is determined in English by the righthand member of a compound, its head, we must conclude that the second element is a noun.
- For Type 2 NDVCs, it is not clear whether the first element is purely verbal, or a noun formed by conversion from a verb, as the second element is in Type 1 compounds. Since the first elements of compounds in English do not inflect, there is no overt evidence of their categorial status. I will assume the simpler analysis here – that the first elements of Type 2 compounds are verbs, but nothing in the analysis would change if we were to treat them as conversion nouns.
- NDVCs are endocentric. That is, a *dog attack* is a kind of *attack* and an *attack dog* is a kind of *dog*. They are thus to be distinguished from compounds like *pickpocket* or *scare crow* that are exocentric (a *pick pocket* is a kind of person, rather

---

3. I count the items in parentheses as possibly subject-oriented, although they are not as clearly subject-oriented as the other cases, since instruments make less good subjects than more agentive nouns. Strictly speaking, of course, stoves don't cook without a human agent using them. Also, for some speakers forms like *fry pan* may seem odd, *frying pan* being the prevalent term. See Stephensen (1969) for a discussion of such variant forms.

4. I include not only subject and object here, but also semantic arguments (or participants) including locations, paths, and instruments.

than a kind of pocket). *Pick pocket*-type compounds are unproductive in contemporary English and we will therefore not consider their analysis here.[5]

The final observation that I will make here is the most important one for our purposes. With regard to synthetic compounds, it has frequently been observed that object-interpretation is the norm, although interpretation of the first element as a prepositional object is also found:

(5) Synthetic compounds

Object orientation: truck driver, cat carrier, cake baking, dish washing, cost containment, food production, school closure, inventory clearance

Prepositional object interpretation: sales information, fish affection, ground feeding, home delivery

Indeed, Selkirk (1982) claims that a subject-oriented interpretation is completely ruled out for synthetic compounds; according to her items like *girl swimming* should be impossible. It has been pointed out several times, however, that although the subject-oriented interpretation is difficult to obtain, it is not absolutely impossible: in their corpus based study, for example, Bauer and Renouf (2001: 119) cite examples like *blood-pooling, schrapnel-flying*, and *director buying*, the latter clearly in context intended to mean that directors are buying, not bought. In Lieber (2004, 2009), I also discuss examples like *city employee*, where the second element itself has a object/patient interpretation, and the first element can therefore be given a subject interpretation.

When corpus data is taken into account, however, it appears that there are a non-negligible number of synthetic compounds with subject-oriented interpretations (see Appendices). However, it is far more difficult to find ordinary synthetic compounds with a subject-oriented reading than it is with NDVCs. In 112 synthetic compounds taken from Plag et al. (2008), the MorboComp corpus, and my own collection, only 13 can plausibly be interpreted as subject-oriented (*US-China cooperation, board meetings, class meeting, class participation, court ruling, EPA warnings, fish communication, Helms amendment, HIV infection, party infighting, retailers association, state decision, wind erosion*). Of 352 compounds from the Corpus of Contemporary American English in which the second noun was a derivation in *-ation*, fewer than a quarter of them (80) could plausibly be interpreted as subject-oriented in interpretation (see Appendix 1).[6,7]

---

5. They are, of course, highly productive in Romance languages. See, for example, Fradin (2009) and Kornfeld (2009).

6. This figure probably represents about half of the *-ation* compounds that might be found in COCA, as I only looked at *-ation* words beginning alphabetically with the letters *a* through *m*.

7. Of the subject-oriented compounds, one first element occurred with great frequency: the word *media* was the first element in 38 of them (e.g., *media competition, media attention, media anticipation*), suggesting that for synthetic compounds in *-ation* at least [media Xation] has become or is on the way to becoming a construction in the sense of Booij (2009).

Similarly, of the 146 synthetic compounds in which the second element ends in *–ment* in COCA, only 27 occur with a subject interpretation (see Appendix 2).

For NDVCs, on the other hand, it seems equally easy to find examples with subject, object, or prepositional object readings. Of the 164 NDVCs in my current collection (i.e., (3) and (4) above), 70 have subject-oriented interpretation, 48 object-oriented interpretation, and 46 prepositional object-oriented interpretation. This would seem to corroborate Marchand's claim above that the object variety is 'weak'.

We should note that quite a few NDVCs can be ambiguous out of context. Some NDVCs admit easily of either subject or object interpretations: consider the compound *computer design*, in which it is possible to construe the computer as either the designer or the thing designed. Indeed, the idea for this paper came from a skit called "Robot Repair" on the American TV show *Saturday Night Live*. In this skit, a robot hosts a TV show in which he demonstrates how to repair, for example, grandfather clocks. The joke, however, is that he is bombarded with complaints from disappointed viewers expecting to learn how to repair robots.[8] Even a compound like *dog attack*, which is preferentially interpreted with subject orientation, can be given the object-oriented interpretation if enough context is provided, for example, when my tiny poodle is set upon by a crazed gunman who hates yappy little dogs.

The most interesting theoretical question that we can raise, then, is why the two types of compounds – synthetic and NDVC – behave differently with respect to the availability of the subject-oriented interpretation. One possible answer is that we just haven't looked hard enough for subject-oriented synthetics or for object-oriented NDVCs. The other possibility is that this is a systematic difference between the two types of compounds, and that it follows from their semantic structure. It is this latter possibility that I intend to pursue here.

3. A digression on the analysis of verb to noun conversion

Before we proceed to the question that I raised above, it will be necessary to think about how nouns derived by conversion from verbs (which I will henceforth refer to as *conversion nouns*) should be analyzed in the lexical semantic framework of Lieber (2004, 2006, 2009).[9] In Lieber (2004) I proposed an analysis of verbs formed by conversion from nouns (henceforth *conversion verbs*), arguing that items like *to saddle, to puree, to jet*, and the like are formed by relisting; nouns are converted to verbs by virtue of being re-entered in the mental lexicon with any kind of available verbal skeleton. The evidence for this is that conversion verbs can be found in virtually any semantic class in which we find underived verbs. In other words, the hallmark of relisting is the

---

8. Thanks to Tricia Irwin for bringing this bit to my attention, and thus inadvertently pushing me to look at NDVCs in more detail.

9. I refer the reader to Lieber (2004) for an introduction to that framework.

semantic diversity of the items formed by conversion.[10] This is not what we find in conversion nouns, however. Unlike conversion verbs, conversion nouns display a uniformity of semantic class: they are all clearly eventive nouns.

This might be taken to suggest that verb to noun conversion should be analyzed as a species of zero affixation, specifically, addition of semantic structure without concomitant addition of phonological structure. Within a zero affixation analysis, the relevant skeleton would be the one in (6):

(6) possible skeleton for verb to noun conversion[11]
[-material, dynamic ([ ], <base>)]

That is, verb to noun conversion would involve the addition of semantic material that would place the base verb in the class of abstract processual nouns. The Principle of Coindexation would integrate the zero-affixal skeleton with the skeleton of the base. I repeat the Principle of Coindexation as proposed in Lieber (2009, 96):[12]

(7) Principle of Coindexation
In a configuration in which semantic skeletons are composed, coindex the highest non-head argument with the highest (preferably unindexed) head argument. Indexing must be consistent with semantic conditions on arguments, if any.

Given the affixal skeleton in (6) and a verbal base like *repair* or *attack*, we would arrive at the structure in (8):

(8) predicted skeleton for [repair]$_N$ or [attack]$_N$
[-material, dynamic ([$_i$], [+dynamic ([$_i$], [ ])])]

Although this is a plausible enough first analysis, I do not, however, believe that it is the correct one. A number of objections have been raised over the years to the zero affixation analysis of conversion, among them the danger of proliferating phonologically null affixes (Lieber 1981, Kastovsky 2005), the inability to tell whether the proposed zero is prefixal or suffixal (Booij 2007), and the fact that zero affixation undermines the notion of the Saussurean sign (Kastovsky 2005).

---

10. I have made the same argument with regard to morphosyntactic categories. If conversion is a matter of relisting, we should expect that the outputs of conversion should be found in several different morphosyntactic classes (e.g. gender, inflectional class) in languages in which such morphosyntactic categories are overtly marked.

11. This skeleton indicates that the zero affix would create an abstract processual substance, the notional equivalent of an abstract noun. The reader will note that the feature [dynamic] appears in this skeleton without a value; in the framework of Lieber (2004), whether the feature has the [+] value (signifying an eventive reading) or the [-] value, signifying a stative reading, is determined by the broader syntactic context. See Lieber (2004) for a fuller explanation.

12. The framework of Lieber (2004) assumes that all affixes come with an argument, the equivalent of the "R" argument of Williams (1981).

But there is a stronger reason not to adopt the zero affixation analysis that bears specifically on the facts at hand here. As I noted above, there is no evidence to suggest that the first element in Type 2 NDVCs is anything but a verb, whereas the second element in Type 1 compounds is clearly a noun. Nevertheless, in terms of semantics, items like *attack* or *repair* are semantically very much alike whether they occur in first or second position.[13] The analysis in (8) suggests that [attack]$_N$ has more semantic structure than [attack]$_V$, indeed that it has precisely the semantic structure of overt nominalizers like words derived with *-ation*. We would therefore expect that words like [attack]$_N$ should contain semantic nuances or behave differently than [attack]$_V$. But this does not seem to be the case. Although a few conversion nouns are lexicalized as concrete nouns (*drift, spill*), the vast majority of them are purely eventive in nature and lack the result or product meanings that are frequent with nominalizations in *-ation* for example. They are no more prone to such result or product interpretations as the second element in compounds than they are as the first element of compounds. This suggests an analysis in which the semantic structure of conversion items might be the same, even when their syntactic category differs.

An important feature of the framework developed in Lieber (2004) is that there need not be a one-to-one correspondence between lexical semantic categories and syntactic categories. For example, the skeleton [-dynamic ([ ])] can correspond either to an adjective or to a stative verb. Given this ability to map skeletons of various sorts onto more than one syntactic category, we might hypothesize that eventive skeletons need not always correspond to syntactic verbs. If it is possible to map eventive skeletons onto syntactic nouns as well as onto syntactic verbs, we have a way of characterizing a process like verb to noun conversion in which the resulting noun seems uniformly to be eventive in character, but does not show the typical effects of affixation. Noun to verb conversion would therefore be the process by which a skeleton like that in (9) is mapped onto a syntactic noun node:

(9) proposed skeleton for [repair]$_N$ or [attack]$_N$
 [+dynamic ([ ], [ ])]

Readers will recognize that this proposal fits easily into the framework of Distributed Morphology (DM) (Halle and Marantz 1993; Harley and Noyer 1999; Embick and Marantz 2008) or other frameworks like DiSciullo's (2005) or Borer's (2005) in which

---

13. To the extent that there is any difference in interpretation, conversion nouns like *kick* or *attack* frequently have an aspectual nuance that their base verbs lack. That is, they are frequently interpretable as 'an instance of Ving', and therefore have a semelfactive flavor. There is an obvious reason for this, however, following from the fact that nouns have quantificational properties (i.e., they must be count nouns, mass nouns, group nouns, or collective nouns). The quantificational features for count nouns in the framework of Lieber (2004) are the same features that delimit the aspectual class of semelfactive verbs, and the vast majority of conversion nouns are count nouns.

lexical items can be inherently categoryless.[14] Without commiting to any specific syntactic framework, I would claim that while items like *repair* or *attack* can lack underlying syntactic category, they do not lack semantic category. They simply differ from other lexical items in being allowed to map onto either syntactic noun or verb nodes.

4. An analysis

In this section, I will first review the analysis of synthetic compounding that I developed in Lieber (2004, 2009), and then go on to look at how NDVCs may be analyzed in this framework. I begin with synthetic compounds because a comparison of their analysis to that of NDVCs will begin to shed light on the question of why subject-oriented interpretation is so much harder to get with synthetics than with NDVCs.

4.1 Synthetic compounds

Synthetic compounds consist, of course, of a noun as the first element and a deverbal noun containing an overt affix like *-er, -ation, -al, -ure, -ment,* or *-ing* as the second element. In Lieber (2009), I argued that the hallmark of synthetic compounds is that their semantic interpretation depends on the coindexation of an argument of the non-head element with an argument of the head element of the compound.[15]

A synthetic compound like *burrito assembler* would receive the lexical semantic interpretation in (10):

(10) burrito assembler
    [+material ([$_j$])] [+material, dynamic ([$_i$], [+dynamic ([$_i$], [$_j$])])]
      burrito   -er   assemble

Given the presence of an overt affix like *-er* which places no special semantic demands on its R argument, the Principle of Coindexation coindexes the R argument of *-er* with the highest argument of the verb *assemble*. The first element of the compound then preferentially links to the lower argument, yielding the object-oriented interpretation.

---

14. Note that I would say that lexical items – roots in the terminology of DM – *can* lack underlying syntactic category, but not that they *must* lack syntactic category. It remains to be seen in any of the above-mentioned frameworks to what extent an entirely categoryless lexicon can be maintained.

15. In contrast, interpretation of coordinate and root compounds depends upon the matching of features in the semantic bodies of the two compounded elements. I refer the reader to Lieber (2009) for the details of this analysis.

If the second element of the synthetic compound is a deverbal noun derived with the suffix *-ee*, however, another indexing obtains:

(12) *city employee*
[+material ($[_j]$)] [+material, dynamic ($[_{\text{sentient, nonvolitional -i}}]$, [+dynamic ($[_j], [_i]$)])]
    city   -ee   employ

As I argued in Lieber (2004) following Barker (1998), the suffix *-ee* requires its R argument to be both sentient and nonvolitional. Since the highest argument of the verbal skeleton typically is volitional in nature, the R argument of *-ee* links to the lower argument. Therefore, when compounded with another noun, that noun preferentially links to the as yet unlinked highest argument. The compound therefore has a subject-oriented interpretation.

As I said above, it is not impossible for subject-oriented linkings to occur in synthetic compounds, but it is decidedly more rare than in NDVCs. We might ask why this would be the case. Subject interpretations can occur, of course, if the deverbal noun is based on an intransitive verb, as is the case in two of the examples that Bauer and Renouf (2001) cite (*blood pooling, shrapnel flying*). In such cases the only possible linking is between the first element of the compound and the already indexed argument of the base verb:

(13) *blood pooling*
[+material ($[_i]$)] [-material, dynamic ($[_i]$, [+dynamic ($[_i]$)])]
    blood   -ing   pool

With transitive verbs, the subject-oriented interpretation can be found in cases like (14):[16]

(14) a. court ruling, EPA warnings
     b. state decision, wind erosion

As the examples in (14a) suggest, a subject-oriented interpretation is possible when the verbal base of the second element takes a proposition as its second argument. Assuming that a nonpropositional argument cannot link to a propositional argument,

---

16. The examples in (14) can be found in the database of compounds provided as an appendix to Plag et al. (2008).

the subject linking is forced, even though it requires linking the first element of the compound to the already linked highest argument of the deverbal noun:

(15) court ruling
[+material, dynamic ([$_i$])] [-material, dynamic ([$_i$], [+dynamic ([$_i$], <proposition>[17])])]
    court   -ing   rule

The linking in (15) is the only one possible if the second element of a synthetic compound is based on a verb whose second argument is propositional, so we would predict that subject orientation would occur with these types of verb to the extent that they occur in such compounds. For the examples in (14b), however, the subject-orientation is purely a matter of the semantic incompatibility of the initial element with the lower (unindexed) argument of the base verb:

(16) wind erosion
[+material ([$_i$])] [-material, dynamic ([$_i$], [+dynamic ([$_i$], [ ])])]
    wind   -ion   erode

We would expect, of course, that the R argument of *wind* should be indexed to the lower argument of *erode*, as that is the argument that remains unlinked after the affixal skeleton is integrated. However, encyclopedic knowledge (part of the semantic body in the theory of Lieber (2004)) tells us that that indexing would be odd (simply put, wind is not something that can be eroded – cf. *beach erosion*). In Lieber (2004), it is argued that the Principle of Coindexation gives the default linking, but that other linkings are still possible if semantic restrictions on bases or encyclopedic knowledge force them. In other words, a coindexation may be optimal, even if it is not a perfect linking according to the Principle of Coindexation.[18] In the case of *wind erosion* the optimal and indeed only semantically felicitous indexing is the one shown in (16). The same kind of encyclopedic knowledge prevents the expected indexing in the case of the other compounds in (14b) and pushes us towards the subject-oriented indexation.

The answer to the question that we raised at the beginning of this section – why it is difficult (but not impossible) to get a subject-oriented interpretation in synthetic compounds – is clear: the subject-oriented interpretation requires either that the base verb of the second element have a very specific sort of diathesis or that encyclopedic information about the first element precludes the expected indexation.

---

17. Here I am glossing over the proper way of integrating propositional arguments into a verbal skeleton. Nothing hinges on the precise formalization here, though, as the main point is that a non-propositional argument would not link felicitously to a propositional argument, however we represent it.

18. See Lieber (forthcoming) for a discussion of Optimality Theory in the context of the framework of lexical semantic representation of Lieber (2004).

4.2 Non-affixal (de)verbal compounds

How then does our analysis of NDVCs differ from that of synthetic compounds? Let us consider Type 1 compounds first.

We begin with a subject-oriented case. Assuming that the second element of Type 1 compounds has a skeleton consisting mainly of the feature [+/− dynamic] and its arguments (which is mapped to a syntactic noun), when it is compounded with a noun, both of its arguments are initially unlinked. The Principle of Coindexation favors the indexing shown in (17) in which the highest nonhead argument – the R argument of *dog* – is coindexed with the highest argument of the head, in this case, the subject argument. The result is the subject-oriented reading. What is important is that this is the *favored* indexing for structures of this sort; the subject-oriented reading is the result of a default indexing here.

(17) *dog attack*
   [+material, dynamic ($[_i]$)] [+dynamic ($[_i]$, [ ])]
   dog   attack

In the case of (18), the verb *kick* typically requires its first argument to be sentient. As *ball* is an inanimate object, it doesn't fulfill the semantic requirement of the first argument of *kick*, but it can be coindexed with the second argument, which has no special semantic requirements. The resulting interpretation is the object-oriented interpretation.

(18) *ball kick*
   [+material ($[_i]$)] [+dynamic ($[_{sentient}]$, $[_i]$)]
   ball   kick

Finally, for the compound *baby care*, the noun *baby* could in principle be coindexed with the higher argument of *care* giving rise to a subject-oriented reading (think of the compound *mother care*), as there is no strict semantic incompatibility there. But encyclopedic knowledge favors the indexing we see in (19). In other words, our knowledge of the world disfavors the default indexing in this case.

(19) *baby care*
   [+material, dynamic ($[_i]$)] [+dynamic ([ ], [FOR ($[_i]$)]]
   baby   care

Note that with compounds like *robot repair* or *computer design* either subject or object indexing is possible. Whether the subject indexing or the object indexing obtains is a matter context and of our encyclopedic knowledge, in other words what our expectations are about the behavior of robots or computers.

Type 2 compounds follow exactly the same pattern. Although the semantic representation of the first element of the compound is mapped to a verb rather than a noun in this case, it is the same semantic representation as that of the second element in

Type 1 compounds. Thus in a compound like *attack dog* we get the indexed representation in (20):

(20) *attack dog*
    [+dynamic ([$_i$], [ ])] [+material, dynamic ([$_i$])]
       attack   *dog*

The highest argument of *attack* is coindexed with the highest argument of the head *dog*, that is, its R argument, giving rise to a subject-oriented interpretation. Again, the subject-oriented interpretation is the default. If there is semantic incompatibility between the highest argument of the nonhead and that of the head, an alternate indexation obtains. Consider the skeleton for the compound *kick ball* in (21):

(21) *kick ball*
    [+dynamic ([$_{sentient}$], [$_i$])] [+material ([$_i$])]
       kick   *ball*

We start with attempting to index the highest argument of the nonhead *kick*, but this cannot be indexed with *ball*, as *ball* has only its R argument, and it is not sentient. We must therefore pass to the next highest argument, the second argument of *kick*. This can be coindexed with the R argument of *ball*, and therefore the object-oriented interpretation results.

We move, finally, to a case like *washbasin*, which would have the representation in (22):

(22) *washbasin*
    [+dynamic ([$_{sentient}$], [IN ([$_i$])] [+material ([$_i$])]
       wash   *basin*

The highest argument of *wash* must be linked to a sentient argument, but the highest argument of *basin* does not fulfill this requirement. We must therefore move to the lower argument of *wash*, its prepositional argument. This can be felicitously matched with the R argument of *basin*. What we get, then, is the prepositional object-oriented interpretation.

4.3   A comparison

Why then do we get the differing pattern of interpretation for synthetic and NDVCs? The answer apparently has to do with the presence of an overt affix in synthetic compounds which has already bound an argument of the base verb at the time of compounding. Since the default is in all cases to bind the highest nonhead argument to the highest unindexed head argument (assuming semantic compatibility), the highest argument is frequently already bound in the second element of synthetic compounds, and linking the argument of the nonhead typically means linking lower down to an object or prepositional object argument of the base verb. Assuming the structure of NDVCs that I propose here, however, the skeleton of the verb (in Type 1) or the conversion noun (in Type 2) has no prior indexing at the point of compounding, so the default indexing is between the highest argument of the nonhead and the highest argument of the head, one of which will be the subject argument. Other indexations can be driven by semantic requirements on the highest arguments or the effects of encyclopedic knowledge, but indexing of the subject argument is the rule rather than the exception.

5. The classification of compounds

I have argued here that both synthetic compounds and NDVCs involve the interpretation of one element of a compound as an argument of the other element. But in terms of how that argument is interpreted the two types behave differently. These differences lead us to reevaluate the traditional classification of English compounds into root and synthetic compounds. Elsewhere (Lieber 2009) I have suggested that this traditional classification is inadequate in any case, as it leaves no place for coordinate compounds like *scholar-athlete* or *blue-green*, and have proposed instead that English compounds can be classified according to the scheme devised by Scalise and Bisetto (2009). Scalise and Bisetto argue for a tripartite division of compounds into subordinate, coordinate, and attributive compounds. Subordinate compounds are comprised of synthetic compounds, compounds like Spanish *abrelatas* 'can opener' (lit. 'opens-cans') or French *tire-bouchon* 'cork screw' (lit. 'pulls cork'), and other verb-containing compounds. Coordinate compounds contain items like *scholar-athlete* and *blue-green*. In attributive compounds the relation between the two compounded elements is one of modification: English root compounds like *mushroom cloud* or *hardhat* fall into this category. Scalise and Bisetto argue further that each of these major compound categories in turn has endocentric and exocentric exemplars:

(23) The Scalise-Bisetto classification of compounds (2009)

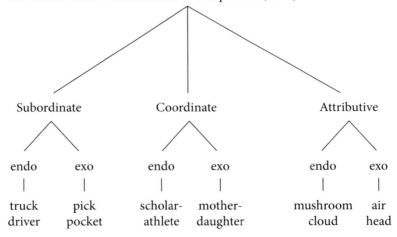

What this paper suggests is that for English at least, subordinate endocentric compounds should be further divided into two types, synthetic and NDVCs, and that each of these can, in turn, be divided into three categories: subject-oriented, object-oriented, and prepositional object-oriented:

(24)

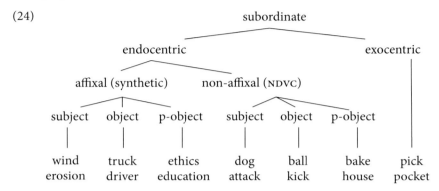

For NDVCs we could further divide each category into Type 1 and Type 2, although I will not do so here.

Scholars have observed for many years that English is a language rich in compounds. It seems that the data I have discussed in this paper simply reinforce that conclusion. Careful attention to a wide variety of compounds, and observations of their occurrence in corpora lead us to see an even more fascinating texture in the data than we would hitherto have expected. Although it might be tempting to consider what I have called NDVCs a subspecies of synthetic compounds, I believe that we are better served by dividing endocentric subordinate compounds into two types, those with overt affixes, traditionally called synthetic, and those without overt affixes, the NDVCs, and by recognizing that their different behavior follows from the presence or absence of an affix.

The examples in Appendices 1 and 2 were extracted from the Corpus of Contemporary American English (COCA), a data base that allows the user to see substantial context with queried items. There are a number of items that are attested multiple times in COCA, and occasionally they are attested with both the subject-oriented and the object-oriented interpretation, in which case they appear in both categories. Quite a few others of the compounds below could potentially be ambiguous. They are categorized according to the meaning they exhibited in the COCA data, however.

Appendix 1

Subject-oriented synthetics in –ation: media attention, media action, staff attention, cavalry action, corps action, staff action, media assumption, media anticipation, media agitation, infantry action, yen appreciation, media creation, media communication, media competition, interspecies communication, aureus colonization, cereus contamination, livestock competition, media concoction, media conversation, staff cooperation, media construction, media condemnation, media characterization, media celebration, media distortion, media deception, staff direction, pike domination, media disruption, media denunciation, media definition, media defamation, media exploitation, media exaggeration, folk explanation, spacecraft exploration, species evolution, media explanation, media expectation, media fascination, media fabrication, media glorification, multimedia intervention, aureus infection, smallpox infection, militia infiltration, multimedia interaction, Marine Corps investigation, deer interaction, folk imagination, species infestation, interspecies interaction, media interrogation, media invention, species interaction, staff infection, people identification, pair interaction, media invocation, media interpretation, media inspection, media infatuation, interspecies interaction, folk interpretation, Peace Corps invitation, chicken pox infection, media manipulation, salmon migration, caribou migration, fish migration, species migration, deer migration, folk migration, whiting migration, tuna migration, sperm maturation, media misrepresentation, media misinformation

Object-oriented synthetics in -ation: data acquisition, data abstraction, sales automation, data accumulation, graphics acceleration, sales administration, media attraction, eel animation, data aggregation, data assimilation, fruit abortion, species aggregation, species adaptation, series approximation, tuna aggregation, statistics administration, staff allocation, staff administration, staff addition, sperm animation, media administration, media acquisition, media accreditation, headquarters administration, grapefruit appreciation, fish addition, deer abortion, data association, data alteration, data administration, aircraft acquisition, media bifurcation, data collection, species composition, sperm competition, fish consumption, media consumption, species conservation, media consolidation, data corruption, media concentration, data connection, people connection, aircraft certification, fish conservation, data classification, data compilation, fruit consumption, fish contamination, aircraft configuration, poultry consumption, series cancellation, species classification, staff coordination, tuna conservation, aircraft construction, azalea collection, coleus celebration, cod consumption, data coordination, data correlation, fish coloration, fruit collection, herring consumption, kin classification, livestock consumption, pair creation, salmon consumption, salmon cultivation, sperm collection, media conglomeration, media collection, livestock conservation, kin compensation, hake consumption, grapefruit cultivation, graffiti collection, sperm donation, species distribution, fish distribution, data distribution, sales distribution, trout distribution, livestock depredation, data destruction, media distribution, species diversification, species depletion, data description, data disaggregation, data dissemination, media deregulation, people distribution, salmon depletion, deer depredation, media direction, sperm dilution, species description, staff desegregation, swine depopulation, species differentiation, species detection, species designation, species demarcation, species definition, series designation, salmon distribution, media destruction, poultry demonstration, people destruction, people deprivation, pair distribution, moose distribution, militia direction, militia demobilization, means destruction, livestock domestication, livestock destruction, fish description, fish demonstration, fish decomposition, livestock demonstration, kid discrimination, fruit distribution, folk deprivation, data detection, data derivation, data democritization, data delineation, data deduction, cod distribution, chub description, bison distribution, aircraft direction, deer concentration, cod concentration, data encryption, data extraction, multimedia exhibition, smallpox eradication, species eradication, people education, corps education, data exploration, data evaluation, staff education, staff excalation, sperm extraction, media exploration, hake exploitation, fish election, fauna exhibition, duck evolution, Druze ethnicization, data elimination, data elicitation, corps evaluation, aircraft exhibition, aircraft evaluation, data fabrication, data fragmentation, infantry formation, aircraft fabrication, media fragmentation, sperm formation, species formation, media filtration, fruit formation, extra-pair fertilization, data falsification, aircraft filtration, data generation, data generalization, sales generalization, quercus germination, media globalization, duck hybridization, blowfish hydration, ethics investigation, media intimidation, data interpretation, sperm injection, graphics interpretation, species identification, data integration, poultry inspection, species introduction, aircraft identification, aircraft instrumentation, Peace Corps investigation, data illustration, fish ingestion, livestock identification, fish identification, media intimidation, salmon interception, sperm incapacitation, staff induction, sperm insertion, sales investigation, salmon introduction, militial intimidation, media integration, means investigation, fruit importation, fish imitation, flora identification, fish inspection, Druze integration, data investigation, data installation, data inspection, data implementation, data identification, cavalry installation, media liberalization, people liberation, folk liberation, media manipulation, data manipulation, media mobilization, staff motivation, staff manipulation, sperm micro-injection, militia mobilization

Prepositional object-oriented synthetics in -ation: works administration, statistics application, sales application, kin affiliation, graphics application, fish affection, ethics action, data communication, ethics consultation, pair correlation, extra-pair copulation, ethics conviction, media connection, sales compensation, kin competition, graffiti communication, aspirin desensitization, starfish decoration, media education, ethics education, statistics education, multimedia exploration, media equation, media experimentation, dynamics education, bison education, aircraft ejection, fish fixation, sales information, smallpox inoculation, species information, multimedia instruction, ethics instruction, smallpox immunization, aircraft information, dynamics information, media instruction, staff information, sperm insemination, species infestation, spacecraft instrumentation, poultry information, measles immunization, ethics information, dice information, data intervention, ethics legislation, species legislation, endangered species litigation

Appendix 2

***Subject-oriented synthetics in* -ment**: folk argument, media accompaniment, media bombardment, cannon bombardment, staff commitment, media encampment, militia encampment, media encouragement, livestock encroachment,Druze enrollment, media harassment, gentry harassment,media investment, media imprisonment, deer movement, buck movement, aircraft movement, fish movement,staff mismanagement, sperm movement, bison movement, corps movement, staff retirement, militia recruitment, media reinforcement, folk treatment, media treatment

***Object-oriented synthetics in* -ment**: media assessment, staff assignment, staff appointment, multimedia assessment, media asset management, graffiti abatement, fruit arrangement, Druze advancement, media bombardment, livestock confinement, species containment, swine confinement, staff development, multimedia development, sales development, aircraft development, sperm displacement, media development, series development, livestock development, chassis development, staff disillusionment, staff deployment, species development, offspring development, militia development, graphics development, ethics development, data development, Marine Corps deployment, species endangerment, ethics enforcement, cavalry engagement, fish excapement, salmon enhancement, salmon escapement, media enhancement, fish entrapment, fish endangerment, Druze embarrassment, data enhancement, staff involvement, ethics improvement, headquarters involvement, media involvement, offspring impairment, sales inducement, livestock improvement, Peace Corps involvement, data management, deer management, people management, data movement, species management, sales management, livestock management, media management, data measurement, fish management, tuna management, salmon management, bison management, duck management, aircraft management, aircraft movement, staff management, public works management, swine management, squid management, quail management, poultry management, herring management, grouse management, caribou management, poultry procurement, graffiti placement, fruit placement, fish procurement, data placement, sales requirement, species replacement, duck recruitment, aircraft retirement, ethics requirement, staff requirement, staff redeployment, staff recruitment, staff reappointment, staff realignment, species recruitment, media replacement, media realignment, means requirement, livestock replenishment, aircraft refurbishment, data refinement, chassis refinement, fish settlement, fruit shipment, data treatment, deer treatment, fruit treatment, grapefruit treatment, smallpox treatment

***Prepositional object-oriented synthetics in* -ment**: ethics agreement, aircraft agreement, headquarters assignment, series commitment, whiting experiment, vole experiment, rhino entertainment, militia enlistment, media engagement, media investment, multi-media investment, livestock investment, media placement, Marine Corps reenlistment, aspirin treatment

The phonology of compounds*

Irene Vogel
University of Delaware

This chapter examines a number of phonological properties of compounds. These include the limitation of many phonological phenomena to the individual members of compounds, the application of others at the juncture of the members of compounds, and the distribution of prosodic properties over an entire compound. Other areas that involve phonological patterns within compounds, linking elements and rules applying within lexicalized items, are also briefly mentioned. Finally, the phonological constituent structure of different types of compounds is examined.

1. Introduction

At first glance, the topic of the phonology of compounds may appear to be somewhat impoverished. It is frequently observed that compounds consist of two (or more) Phonological Words (PWs), and while each member exhibits certain phonological phenomena, these phenomena tend to be blocked across the members of the compound (e.g. Nespor and Vogel 1986, Booij 2007). More thorough consideration, however, also reveals a variety of phonological properties associated with entire compounds.

This chapter first discusses the evidence that the individual PWs of a compound do not interact. Subsequently, other cases are examined in which phonological phenomena apply precisely at the juncture of the members of compounds, and still others in relation to compounds as wholes. Two additional types of phenomena, linking elements and phonological patterns of lexicalized compounds, are also briefly mentioned, although these will not be examined in depth here. Finally, issues relating to the phonological structure of compounds are considered. Both the nature of the PWs that constitute compounds and the larger phonological structure that groups the members of compounds together are examined. Recursive PWs have been posited for the latter purpose in a number of analyses, however, they have several drawbacks. An alternative approach is thus offered whereby the members of compounds are grouped into a constituent between the PW and the Phonological Phrase, the Composite Group (Vogel 2009).

---

*   I am grateful to Geert Booij for his comments on an earlier version of this chapter.

2. Phonological phenomena and the members of compounds

2.1 Phonological properties of the individual members of compounds

Since the members of a compound are typically considered Phonological Words (PWs), any phenomenon that has as its domain the PW will apply within a compound to its individual parts. These include the full range of phonological phenomena, such as phonotactic constraints, segmental rules and non-segmental phenomena (e.g. stress and tone). As PW domain rules are common across languages, it is frequently observed that the individual members of a compound exhibit phonological phenomena that do not spread throughout the compound.

For example, in stress languages, the (phonological) word is the domain of lexical stress assignment. Thus, in compounds, each member bears a lexical stress, whether it has been assigned on the basis of uniquely phonological considerations (e.g. Hungarian: first syllable of PW), a combination of phonological and morphological considerations (e.g. English, Italian), or lexically (e.g. Russian). The retention of the individual word level stresses in compounds is observed in the languages just mentioned, as well as many others, including Yimas, Fijian, Jarawara, Georgian, Turkish and Arrerernte (Dixon and Aikhenvald 2002: 28–29).

In many languages, there are also phonotactic constraints and segmental phonological rules observed at the level of the PW. For example, in Italian, there is a phonotactic constraint on the palatal lateral [λ], written as "gl". It may appear word-internally, and at the beginning of clitics (e.g. *giglio* 'lily' and **gli** *alberi* 'the trees', **gli** *offro* '(I) offer (to) him'), but not at the beginning of lexical items. It thus fails to appear at the beginning of PWs, including PWs that are members of compounds. We therefore find the compound *segna libri* 'book mark' in Italian, but a compound with the structure *segna gl...* would not be possible.

Italian also has segmental rules that apply within each PW of a compound, but not across their juncture. Intervocalic s-Voicing (ISV) in northern varieties voices an "s" between vowels within a PW (e.g. *abra[z]ione* 'abrasion'). It does not apply, however, when the vocalic context is distributed across the PWs in a compound (e.g. *acqua* [s]*anta* 'holy water'). Similarly, in Crow, there is a rule of Identical Vowel Reduction that applies between a root and affix, presumably within a PW, such that there are no more than two moras with the same vowel (i.e. /a/) in a sequence. Three and four mora sequences of /a/ are thus reduced to two moras, as in *íkaa-ák* → *íkaak* 'see ss'[1] and *íkaa-aahi* → *íkaahi* 'see DISTR'. By contrast, we do not observe vowel reduction when the vowel sequence is found across the juncture of the members of a compound, where we may have up to four moras as in *biláa áapchi* 'fire light' (Grayczyk 2007: 26).

Vowel Harmony (VH) phenomena, which may be analyzed as phonotactic constraints or as phonological rules, ensure that the vowels in a given domain share a

---

1. "Ss" refers to the same subject marker.

particular feature (or features). This domain is typically the PW, so we commonly find that VH does not spread across the members of a compound to the entire compound. In Hungarian, for example, all the vowels in a PW must be back or front (e.g back: *Buda-nak* 'Buda-DAT'; front: *Pest-nek* 'Pest-DAT'). When words combine in a compound, however, each component retains its own harmony properties (e.g. *[Buda]$_{PW}$ [pestnek]$_{PW}$* 'Budapest-DAT'). Similarly, in the Gur language, Dagbani, ATR harmony is observed within a PW between a root and a suffix. For example, we find [+ATR] and [-ATR] vowels in *[dirgu]* 'spoon SG', and *[jɔgʊ]* 'lid SG', respectively. In compounds, however, each member forms its own harmony domain, as in *[no sɔ-yʊ]* 'hen coop' (= 'fowl' + 'stall SG'), where the first element, *[no]* is [+ATR] and the second element *[sɔ]* and following suffix are [-ATR] (Olowsky 2003: 210).

Finally, it can be observed in many languages that syllabification processes observed within the individual PWs of a compound are not observed across the juncture of these items. For example, in Dutch (Booij 2007), a sequence such as "lk" is syllabified between the two segments when they fall within a single PW (e.g. *kal.koenen* 'turkeys'), and simply as the final coda (e.g. *balk* 'beam') at the end of a PW. In compounds the sequence exhibits the original distribution of the segments of the individual members. Thus, we find "lk" split into two syllables in the compound *bal kanker* 'testicle cancer' due to the origination of the segments in the different words. By contrast, we find "lk" as a cluster at the end of the first member of the compound *balk anker* 'beam brace' due to its original word final location. There is no resyllabification of the sequence to parallel the distribution in *kal.koenen* (cf. Booij 2007), and thus *bal kanker* and *balk anker* exhibit distinct syllabification patterns. A similar lack of resyllabification across the members of a compound also accounts for the well-known contrast in English between *night rate* and *Nye trait*.

2.2 Phonological phenomena at the juncture of the members of compounds

While they are not instances of phonological phenomena spreading throughout a compound, there are phonological rules that apply precisely at the juncture of the members of compounds. These phenomena seem to involve a variety of rule types, and appear across languages. For example, in Marathi a stop at the end of the first member of a compound becomes a nasal when followed by a nasal at the beginning of the next member of the compound (e.g. /b^{h}əgəwət/ 'god' + /nām/ 'name' → *[b^{h}əgəwnnām]* 'god's name'; *sat* 'six' + *mās* 'month' → *sanmās* 'six months') (Pandharipande 1997: 563). By contrast, this nasalization pattern does not apply elsewhere, for example with the adverb forming suffix *-ne*; instead we find a vowel inserted in this context (e.g. *hāt-āne* 'by hand') (Pandharipande 1997: 504).

Another example of a phonological phenomenon that applies at the juncture of the members of a compound is a vowel lengthening rule in Hausa. This rule lengthens the final element of the first member of verbal compounds, as in *dàfàa-dukà* 'jollof rice' (< *dafà* 'cook' + *dukà* 'all'), *kàarèe-dangì* 'type of arrow poison' (< *kaarè* 'finish' + *dangì* 'relatives') (McIntyre 2006: 54). Such juncture phenomena play a significant role in identifying a particular string in a language as being a compound, with phonological properties that are distinct from those of other types of strings.

2.3 Application of phonological phenomena to compounds as wholes

In addition to the types of phonological phenomena examined thus far that apply to the individual members of compounds or at the juncture of these elements, there are phonological phenomena that apply in relation to an entire compound. While the previously examined phenomena appear to include both segmental and suprasegmental phenomena, those that apply in relation to compounds as wholes appear to be suprasegmental or prosodic phenomena, involving in particular stress and tone.

Perhaps the best known of these is the Compound Stress Rule of English. While the individual members of compounds retain their original internal prominence relations, the first member of the compound typically exhibits the main prominence of the entire string.[2] By contrast, stress in phrases is on the final element. We thus find many minimal pairs that differ only in the presence of compound or phrasal stress (e.g. *White House*, vs. *white hóuse*). Similarly in Dutch, compounds are typically stressed on the first member, while phrases are stressed finally. For example, in the compound *zúurkool* 'sauerkraut' the first element bears the main prominence, while in the phrase *zure kóol* 'sour cabbage' the main prominence is on the final element.

Stress patterns are also distributed in specific ways in Swedish compounds, and dialects may differ in this regard. While North Swedish and East Swedish have many properties in common, the stress distribution in the dialects of the far north is distinct from that of the eastern, and most other, dialects. Specifically, while the common pattern is for compound words to exhibit two stresses, the primary stress relatively early in the compound and the secondary stress relatively late, many compounds in far North Swedish do not exhibit this pattern. Instead, when compound stress applies in these cases, there is a single stress for the entire compound, and it tends to appear on the final element (Bruce et al. 1999).

Languages also exhibit tonal phenomena that apply in relation to an entire compound. This can be seen in Hausa in the same examples that previously illustrated vowel lengthening. Specifically, we also observe in these items a rule of tone lowering that applies at the beginning of the compound (i.e. *dàfàa-dukà* 'jollof rice' (< 'cook' = *dafà*...), *kàarèe-dangì* 'type of arrow poison' (< 'finish' = *kàarè*...) (McIntyre 2006: 54). In Akan, too, there are tonal phenomena that apply in relation to compound formation in the three major dialects: Fante, Asante and Akuapem (Abakah 2006).

---

2. See Plag et al. (2008) for a detailed discussion of where the Compound Stress Rule does and does not apply.

2.4 Other phenomena within compounds as wholes

At first glance, the appearance of "linking elements" between the members of a compound might also seem to be a phonological phenomenon that applies to an entire compound. Closer examination, however, reveals that such elements are often more morphological than phonological in nature. For example, in Dutch we frequently find *-en* or *-s* between the members of a compound. In a case such as *boek-en kast* 'book case', the syllable *-en*, pronounced as [ə], can be seen as breaking up the sequence of two *k*'s. The same element is also found in other items (e.g. *zon(n)-en bloem* 'sunflower' < *zon* 'sun' + *bloem* 'flower') where, however, the sequence *nb* does not appear to be problematic (cf. *tuin bank* 'garden bench'). In some cases, moreover, the linking element actually makes the segmental sequence more complex, as in *schaap-s kop* 'sheep head', and its insertion would thus not be phonologically motivated. Indeed, a similar structure takes the *-en* element: *paard-en kop* 'horse head'. It has been proposed that non-segmental phonological factors (i.e. stress and number of syllables of the members of a compound) may be more relevant in the choice of the linking elements (Neijt and Schreuder 2007). While these phonological properties correspond to observable preferences, it is still not possible to unambiguously predict the appearance of a specific linking element, as illustrated by the comparison of *schaapskop* and *paardenkop*. Given the inconsistent role phonology plays with regard to linking elements, these elements will not be considered further in this chapter.

Finally, it is well known that "lexicalized" compounds tend to exhibit certain phonological phenomena that are not observed in more productive types of compounds. In fact, they often exhibit phonological properties that are more typical of non-compound words, an indicator that they have indeed undergone lexicalization. For example, the English word *holiday* (< *holy day*) has a schwa in the second syllable as would be expected for a PW internal unstressed vowel (cf. *pachyderm*). If this syllable were at the end of a PW, by contrast, we would expect to find the tense vowel [i], as in *holy water*. Since lexicalized compounds exhibit a variety of phonological properties that are not found with more typical compounds, they will also not be considered further here.

2.5 The phonological structure of compounds

In addition to the specific phonological phenomena that apply, or are blocked, in relation to compounds and their components, we must consider the phonological structure of the compounds themselves, a topic that has not received much attention. While the members of a compound are widely assumed to be PWs, a question arises as to the nature of the entire unit. Since it is usually observed that the members of compounds are not simply incorporated into a Phonological Phrase, it is necessary that there be some other means of grouping them. In some analyses it has been proposed that the PWs of a compound are combined into a larger, or recursive, PW, however this type of structure raises a number of problems with regard to both phonological structure and linguistic structure more generally.

3. Compounds and the recursive phonological word

We first examine the motivation for the treatment of compounds as recursive Phonological Words, and then discuss the drawbacks of such an analysis. An alternative analysis is presented in the Section 4.

3.1 The motivation for the recursive phonological word

In English, the sequence "yellow + jacket" can be interpreted as a phrase, with the literal meaning, or it can be interpreted as a compound referring to a type of stinging insect. Since the components in both cases are PWs, they have the same structure: $[yellow]_{PW}$, $[jacket]_{PW}$. Word level stress assignment, which in English is based on a combination of morphological and phonological criteria, places prominence on the first syllable in each of these words. A problem arises, however, in determining the location of stress in the two interpretations, since the phrasal meaning has prominence on the final element, while the compound meaning has stress on the first element, as in (1). Acute accents represent word stress; the small capital font indicates relative prominence within the string.

(1) a. phrase: $[yéllow]_{PW}$ $[JÁCKET]_{PW}$
    b. compound: $[YÉLLOW]_{PW}$ $[jácket]_{PW}$

As such examples show, there are three types of stress assignment in English (i.e. word, compound and phrasal), but there are not three domains available for these patterns. We must thus introduce additional structure to allow us to adequately represent the requisite number of stress domains. In the case of phrasal stress, the obvious candidate is the Phonological Phrase (PPh), where stress is placed on the final element, as in (2a). The compound, however, cannot have the same prosodic structure since this would predict that it will exhibit the same stress properties. It has thus been proposed in some analyses that the members of a compound are grouped into a larger PW, or recursive PW, as in (2b).

(2) a. [$[yéllow]_{PW}$ $[JÁCKET]_{PW}]_{PPh}$
    b. [$[YÉLLOW]_{PW}$ $[jácket]_{PW}]_{PW}$

3.2 Drawbacks of the recursive phonological word

While we now have different structures for the phrasal and compound interpretations of "yellow + jacket", we have also introduced new problems. As mentioned, word level stress is assigned on the basis of morphological and phonological considerations, while in compounds stress is assigned in a much simpler fashion by the well-known Compound Stress Rule – to the first element. If we assume that the individual elements, *yellow* and *jacket*, are PWs, and the entire compound, *yellow jacket*, is also a PW, as in (2b), we predict that all of these items will exhibit the same (PW) properties. That is, since constituents in linguistics are defined by a specific set of properties, if all of the strings in question are labeled as the same type of constituent, the expectation is that they will all behave in the same way phonologically. This is problematic since the properties of the inner and outer PWs are different with respect to stress assignment.

It should be noted that this type of problem is not uncommon. Instead, in many languages it appears necessary to distinguish the phonological properties of compounds from those of single PWs on the one hand, and from those of sequences of words combined into Phonological Phrases on the other hand. As Vigário (2003: 261) notes: "[b]esides the EP (European Portuguese) data, …facts from other languages also suggest that the prominence within … prosodic compounds must be stated independently of… phonological phrase prominence."

The problems that arise when compounds are analyzed as recursive PWs are not limited to stress phenomena, but extend to PW domain phenomena of any type. A variety of phonological phenomena, as seen above, apply within a PW, but not across PWs in a compound. If both the inner and the outer constituents bear the same (PW) label, however, it is expected that the entire compound should exhibit the same phenomena as the internal PWs. This is not what is observed, as illustrated with Italian ISV which applies within the PW domain. Specifically, if compounds are also PWs, we incorrectly predict that the rule should apply to an item such as *acqua santa* 'holy water (*acqua [z]anta), as mentioned above.

The introduction of recursive PW structures for compounds also creates problems more generally with respect to phonological structure, and to linguistic theory. First it should be noted that the labeling of strings with different properties as the same type of constituent violates the definition of "constituent". If it is permitted, phonological constituents can no longer be defined as linguistic strings exhibiting a specific property or properties, in contrast with constituents in other components of grammar.

In addition, by referring to the resulting structures as "recursive" we are violating the definition of "recursion", which "…consists of *embedding a constituent in a constituent of the same type*,[3] for example a relative clause inside a relative clause […], which automatically confers the ability to do so *ad libitum*." (Pinker and Jackendoff 2005: 211). The internal PWs are not embedded in constituents of the same type, since the inner and outer structures exhibit different properties.

The introduction of recursion into the phonological component of grammar also raises problems for linguistic theory in general. That is, recursion has traditionally been the basis for a crucial distinction between the syntactic and phonological

---

3. Italics added here.

components of grammar (e.g. Pinker and Jackendoff 2005; Jackendoff and Pinker 2005; Neeleman and van de Koot 2006), and the loss of this distinction has far-reaching implications. It would affect not only our understanding of phonological structure, but also the relationship among the components of grammar, and the mapping between morpho-syntactic and phonological structure. The consequences of such a fundamental modification have not, however, been carefully examined (Vogel submitted).

Finally, it should be noted that in order to avoid losing the ability to distinguish the behavior of PWs and entire compounds, in some analyses a diacritic has been introduced for the latter case (i.e. PW', PW^{max}). While the use of a diacritic makes it appear that compounds are still a type of PW, in reality, the result here, too, is the introduction of an additional type of constituent, with its own set of properties.[4]

4. Phonological constituent structure of compounds

The foregoing discussion makes it clear that compounds require some type of grouping that is neither the Phonological Word nor the Phonological Phrase. In earlier versions of the prosodic hierarchy (e.g. Nespor and Vogel 1986), there was a constituent between the PW and PPh, the Clitic Group (cf. Hayes 1989 [1984]), however, it has often been excluded more recently. In all analyses of compounds that lack a constituent between the PW and PPh, the problem of how to phonologically group the members of a compound persists, and as seen, the introduction of a diacritically labeled variety of PW only obscures the problem. An alternative approach is presented that recognizes a prosodic constituent between the PW and the PPh, the Composite Group. This constituent replaces the Clitic Group and not only includes compounds, but also clitics and certain types of affixes.[5]

4.1 The composite group and simple compounds

As mentioned, English stress involves three mechanisms: lexical, compound and phrasal stress assignment. Thus, the members of a compound form a lexical stress domain, while the entire compound constitutes the domain for the Compound Stress Rule. Since the recursive PW was shown to have significant drawbacks, and thus appears not to be a viable option, we now examine the approach that involves the Composite Group (CompG). As can be seen in (3), the presence of the CompG between the PW and the PPh in the prosodic hierarchy results in three distinct domains for the

---

4. In fact, Vigário (2008) has recently suggested that European Portuguese compounds be analyzed as a distinct constituent type, the Phonological Word Group, instead of PW^{max}.

5. The Composite Group avoids the problems associated with the Clitic Group with a modification of the Strict Layer Hypothesis that permits a prosodic constituent to dominate constituents more than one level lower in the prosodic hierarchy (Vogel 2009, submitted).

three types of stress assignment. Word stress is indicated by italics, and CompG and PPh stress are indicted by single and double acute accents, respectively.

(3) a. Compound Stress
[[[yellow]_PW [jacket]_PW]_CompG]_PPh
[*yellow*]_PW   [*jacket*]_PW
[*yéllow*   jacket*]_CompG
[*yȅllow*   jacket*]_PPh

b. Phrasal Stress
[[[yéllow]_PW]_CG [[jácket]_PW]_CompG]_PPh
[*yellow*]_PW   [*jacket*] _PW
[*yéllow*]_CompG   [*jácket*]_CompG
[*yellow*   *jȁcket*]_PPh

A similar approach also accounts for other languages that exhibit different stress properties in compounds and phrases. As mentioned, Dutch also typically places prominence on the left element in compounds, but on the right in phrases, seen above with *zúurkool* 'sauerkraut' vs. *zure kóol* 'sour cabbage', which would be represented as *[[zuur]_PW [kool]_PW]_CompG/PPh* and *[[[zure]_PW]_CompG [[kool]_PW]_CompG]_PPh*. According to Kabak and Vogel (2001), in Turkish, too, compounds and phrases can be distinguished on the basis of their stress patterns, and related CompG structures (e.g. compound: *[[açi]_PW [ölçer]_PW]_CompG/PPh* 'protractor'; phrase: *[[[açi]_PW]_CompG [[ölçer]_PW]_CompG]_PPh* '(it) measures (an) angle').[6]

4.2 The composite group and longer compounds

In English, as well as some other languages, it is possible to combine more than two words into compounds, yielding potentially quite long strings. If we adopt the CompG approach, the structure for compounds involving three (or more) words still remains essentially flat, with the same constituent types seen in shorter compounds (i.e. […[PW] [PW] [PW]…]_CompG). The result represents a crucial difference between the phonological and morphological structures of compounds, since the latter are widely assumed to reflect the sequence of the word formation processes, and may thus exhibit considerable depth. This difference is illustrated in (4) for a typical left-branching compound. The Compound Stress Rule applies in (4b), where the main prominence of the compound is placed on the first element of the entire compound in the CompG domain.

(4) a. morphological structure: [[[cake]_N [sale]_N]_N [program]_N]_N
    b. phonological structure: [[*cake*]_PW [sale]_PW [program]_PW]_CompG

---

6. This was originally analyzed as Clitic Group structure in Kabak and Vogel (2001).

It should be noted that the CompG analysis treats all three-word compounds in the same way, regardless of their morphological composition. Thus, a right-branching compound would have the same phonological structure as that in (4b), and it follows that the main prominence would be on the left-most element in this case as well, as illustrated in (5).

(5) a. morphological structure
[[car]$_N$ [[sales]$_N$ [person]$_N$]$_N$]$_N$
b. phonological structure
[[*car*]$_{PW}$ [sales]$_{PW}$ [person]$_{PW}$]$_{CompG}$

It is often assumed that the stress pattern reflects the morphological structure of a compound, which would result here in main prominence on *sales*, instead of *car*. In this scenario, stress is assigned first to the left-most element of the (morphologically) inner compound, and subsequently to the entire compound. Although the left-most member of the entire compound is *car*, this element is passed up and prominence is placed on the element with the highest level of stress, *sales*: *car SALES person*. While this pronunciation seems possible if one is emphasizing the structure of the compound, a non-emphatic reading seems to yield the same prominence pattern as observed in CAKE *sale program*.

Should a difference between the stress patterns be consistently identified, or if both possibilities are observed, this would need to be reflected in the compound structures. For example, we might limit CompGs to two PWs, resulting in the structures *[CAKE sale]$_{CompG}$ [program]$_{PW}$* and *[car]$_{PW}$ [SALES person]$_{CompG}$*. The CompGs and the additional PWs would then be grouped into PPhs and undergo phrasal stress assignment. This would enhance the prominence of the (rightmost) element with the highest level of stress (i.e. CompG stress) in each case, giving *[[CAKE sale]$_{CompG}$ [program]$_{PW}$]$_{PPh}$* and *[[car]$_{PW}$ [SALES person]$_{CopmG}$]$_{PPh}$*.

It should be noted that the CompG approach predicts a flat structure for longer compounds as well. Since languages tend to avoid long strings without varying prominence (i.e. clashes and lapses), it is possible that a phenomenon of rhythmic structuring exists to limit, or restructure, potentially long CompGs to shorter ones, each of which would then be assigned its own prominence. At this point, such possibilities remain speculative; systematic acoustic measurements are needed to further evaluate the properties of compounds with three or more elements.

5. Other types of compound structures

5.1 Phrase + Word compounds

While compounds containing a phrase might pose a challenge for morphology and syntax with regard to their formation, their phonological structure and behavior are more straight-forward. For example in the case of English, the phrasal portion is assigned phrasal stress, and the entire compound is then assigned compound stress, as illustrated in (6).

(6) [[mad cow]$_{NP/PPh}$ disease]$_{N/CompG}$
    [mad *cow*]   Phrase
    [mad *cow*   disease]   Compound

While the relative prominence pattern of a phrase may be retained, the individual words are simply PW constituents in a compound. This would account for the possibility of a shift in stress to the first element, at least in some cases. For example, while the phrase *deep sea* may retain its prominence on *sea* in *deep sea fishing*, it also seems possible to stress the first element as in other compounds (i.e. DEEP *sea fishing*). Longer compounds with phrases are also possible (e.g. *flavor of the month contest*), and it is anticipated that such structures will follow similar principles of stress assignment. Relatively little is known about the phonology of such structures, however, and it thus awaits further systematic investigation.

5.2 Structures with bound stems

At the other end of the spectrum, in a sense, are structures that do not contain independent words at all, but rather consist of combinations of bound elements. It seems useful to distinguish two types of "boundedness": morphological and phonological. What are referred to here as morphologically bound stems are those that do not exist as meaningful words on their own, but acquire meaning in combination with other elements. Well-known cases in English are the first elements in *luke warm* and *huckleberry*. This possibility is more common in languages such as Chinese, where we find compounds with one morphologically bound stem as well as compounds in which both elements are bound stems. For example, in the combination *róu+lìn*, neither element has a meaning of its own, however, together they mean 'trample' (Ceccagno and Basciano 2009). Despite the fact that the elements in question are morphologically bound, phonologically they exhibit the properties of free morphemes. They can thus be considered PWs, and form CompGs, as in (7).

(7) a. [[luke]$_{PW}$ [warm]$_{PW}$]$_{CompG}$ [[huckle]$_{PW}$ [berry]$_{PW}$]$_{CompG}$
    b. [[róu]$_{PW}$ [lìn]$_{PW}$]$_{CompG}$ 'trample'

By contrast, we find stems that are bound phonologically, although we may attribute some meaning to them. This is the case with the stems in so-called neoclassical compounds (e.g. *biology, geography*). Morphologically, there might be some question as to the status of these items as stems, affixes, affixoids, etc. (cf. Ralli this volume), however, phonologically, what is crucial is that do not stand alone, but join into a single (PW) unit.

This can be seen in English, where combinations of bound stems participate together in word stress assignment, as illustrated in (8a). Moreover, if a compound containing two stems is subsequently suffixed, the stress may be adjusted accordingly, as in (8b). An analogous situation exists with similar structures of Italian, as illustrated in (8c-e).

(8) a. [psychó-logy]$_{PW}$
    b. [psychológi-cal]$_{PW}$
    c. [psicó-logo]$_{PW}$ 'psychologist'
    d. [psicológ-ico]$_{PW}$ 'psychological'
    e. [psicolog-ía]$_{PW}$ 'psychology'

In Italian, moreover, the PW domain rule of Intervocalic s-Voicing, which does not apply across the members of compounds with free elements, does by contrast, apply within neoclassical compounds. This follows from the PW analyses of the different types of constructions, as shown in (9).

(9) a. [cromo-[z]oma]$_{PW}$ 'chromosome'
    b. [gira]$_{PW}$ [[s]ole]$_{PW}$ 'sun flower'

Phonologically bound stems are not restricted to combining with other bound stems; they may also combine with other elements – affixes and lexical items. For example, in Italian when a bound stem combines with an affix, typically a suffix, the result is a PW, and stress applies to this combination, as shown in (10a). When a stem combines with a word, it precedes it and is external to the PW. Stress is assigned to the PW as usual, without involving the preceding stem, as in (10b).

(10) a. [gráf-ico]$_{PW}$ 'graphic'
     b. psico [sociále]$_{PW}$ 'psycho-social'

The proposed structure is further supported by the fact that ISV fails to apply between the stem and word in (10b): the /s/ is not between vowels within a PW.

The question that remains now is what the structure of the bound stem is when it is not part of a PW. Since the elements are not independent PWs, the next (smaller) option would be the Foot. As Feet, they may be combined with the PW in a CompG, as shown in (11). ISV does not apply here since the Feet are excluded from the PW.

(11) a. [[psico]$_{Ft}$ [[s]ociale]$_{PW}$]$_{CompG}$ 'psycho-social'
     b. [[cromo]$_{Ft}$ [[s]omatico]$_{PW}$]$_{CompG}$ 'chromo-somatic'

It will be recalled that when the stem *cromo* combined in (9a) with *soma* as a stem, ISV applied since together they formed one PW (i.e. *cromo[z]oma*).

That the stems in question are Feet, as opposed to PWs, is further supported by the stress patterns of items consisting of a stem and word in English. If the stems are

PWs, on a par with the independent words to which they attach, we would have a structure such as that in (12).

(12) *[[neuro]$_{PW}$ [biology]$_{PW}$]$_{CompG}$

Since this is the same structure that is posited for compounds consisting of two words, we would (incorrectly) expect the Compound Stress Rule to assign prominence to the first element. If the stem is analyzed as a Foot, it will exhibit prominence on its first syllable, the head of the Foot, as in (13a), but not the main stress of the entire formation. This applies to longer structures as well, as in (13b), where the bound stems combine with the PW into a CompG. The acute accent indicates the main prominence of the entire item; italics show the heads of the Feet associated with the additional stems.

(13) a. [[*neuro*]$_{Ft}$ [biólogy]$_{PW}$]$_{CompG}$
      b. [[*neuro*]$_{Ft}$ [*psy*cho]$_{Ft}$ [biólogy]$_{PW}$]$_{Comp}$

6. Other phenomena

6.1 Atypical compounds

There are several additional types of constructions that appear to be compounds in that they consist of combinations of PWs, and the PWs are not grouped into PPhs. In some cases, they contain PWs that are affixes or combinations of affixes and other elements, and in some cases strings that are not morphemes at all. While such structures may resolve the specific phonological issues that led to their construction, they raise problems with respect to the structure of compounds more generally. That is, if the PW, as a constituent of the prosodic hierarchy, is part of Universal Grammar, it is crucial that there be cross-linguistic consistency in its construction (via mapping rules from other components of grammar), and its properties.

6.1.1 *Affixes as members of compounds.* In Vigário's (2003) analysis of European Portuguese (EP), we find compounds in which one of the members is an affix. It is argued that since such affixes are not phonologically "weak", but rather have the potential for being stressed, they constitute PWs. They combine with the PW containing the word's root to form a recursive PW structure, where the outer constituent is labeled with the diacritic "max", as shown in (15). The affixes in question are in italics.

(15) a. [[*pos*]$_{PW}$ [sintactico]$_{PW}$]$_{PW}$^{max} 'post-syntactic'
      b. [[alegre]$_{PW}$ [*mente*]$_{PW}$]$_{PW}$^{max} 'happily'

Similarly, we find a number of affixes in Dutch analyzed as PWs (cf. Booij 2007), which then combine with another PW to form compound structures. For example, the suffix

-*achtig* is assigned PW status, while the suffix -*ig*, which is not, based on certain phonological properties of the affixes. While -*achtig* does not allow the final C of a preceding root to form its onset, -*ig* does. We thus find syllable-final devoicing of the /d/ of *rood* 'red' when it combines with the former but not the latter: *roo[t].achtig* 'reddish' vs. *roo.[d]ig* 'reddish'. Although Booij does not explicitly claim that the structure involving the suffix -*achtig* is a recursive PW, as Vigário does for EP, it must be assumed that the affix PW and the PW containing the root form such a structure (i.e. [[rood]$_{PW}$ [achtig]$_{PW}$]$_{PW}$), since the two PWs are not directly grouped into a PPh.

Aside from the general problems seen above in relation to recursive PWs, the EP and Dutch items are problematic with respect to the claim that they are compounds. The bound elements in question are affixes, and thus are distinct from the bound stems seen above which cannot be considered affixes (i.e. *luke, huckle*; Chinese *róu, lin*). In order to maintain this distinction, while attributing the necessary structure to the affixes, we may instead assign them Foot status like the neoclassical stems seen in (13), and allow them to form a CompG with the associated PW (e.[[*pos*]$_{Ft}$ [*sintactico*]$_{PW}$]$_{CompG}$, [[*alegre*]$_{PW}$ [*mente*]$_{Ft}$]$_{CompG}$, [[*rood*]$_{PW}$ [*achtig*]$_{Ft}$]$_{CompG}$).

It should be noted that historically affixes are often derived from lexical items, and may for a period of time retain aspects of their original status, exhibiting a recognizable root and/or the typical phonological properties of a PW in the language in question. For example, we may consider *man* to be in transition in (American) English. That is, we find items such as *mailman* and possible formations such as *telescope man* (i.e. someone who operates a telescope), in which *man* is a pronounced with a full vowel (i.e. [mæn]) and thus may constitute a PW. There are also cases, however, in which *man* has lost the properties of a PW, and is pronounced with a schwa (i.e. [mæn]), behaving more like an affix than an independent word (*postman, fireman*).[7] Thus, it is possible that during a transition we may find affixes that are still considered PWs, although this is not the typical situation. (See Ralli this volume for a detailed discussion of how morphemes may change their status historically; also Booij this volume; Mithun, this volume, among others.)

6.1.2 *Diverse morpheme combinations as members of compounds.* In Dixon and Aikhenvald's (2002: 36–37) analysis of Fijian, we find different types of strings considered PWs and these in turn combine with other PWs to form compound structures. Again, the motivation is a phonological phenomenon, specifically a Diphthongization rule that changes /i/ to a glide after a vowel. It is claimed that this

---

7. It should be noted that in certain words the development has progressed even further, to the point where the root meaning is generally not noticed by speakers, as in *foreman*.

rule operates in the PW, as shown in (17). The "j" in (17c) indicates an "i" that has undergone Diphthongization.[8]

(17) a. [[a   on*a*]_PW [*i*   talanoa]_PW]_PW 'his story'
           article POSS   nom pref tell

     b. [[i na]_PW [on*a*]_PW [*i*   talanoa]_PW]_PW 'in his story'
           P article POSS   nom pref tell

     c. [[i na   j]_PW   [talanoa]_PW]_PW 'in the story'
           P article nom pref   tell

We find, as sisters to the PW containing the root *talanoa* 'tell', a variety of groupings that differ from the usual composition of PWs: article + possessor (17a), preposition + article (17b), and preposition + article + nominalizing prefix (17c). While these structures yield the correct results with respect to Diphthongization, they are problematic with respect to a more general definition of PW, and the universal nature of the prosodic hierarchy. That is, if such varied types of strings may be considered PWs, it is not clear what type of mapping principles from morpho-syntax to phonology could be advanced to construct PWs, and thus compounds, cross-linguistically.[9]

6.1.3 *Non-morphemes as members of compounds.* In addition to analyzing certain Dutch affixes as PWs that then form compounds, Booij (1999) attributes PW status to certain strings that do not correspond to morphological constituents at all. Specifically, monomorphemic words may be broken into two PWs and then combined to form a compound as in (18), where it is assumed that the outer constituent is a (recursive) PW. Again, this is done to accommodate specific phonological properties of the items.

(18) a. [[ant]_PW [woord]_PW]_PW   'answer'
     b. [[aal]_PW [moes]_PW]_PW   'alms'

This type of structure is posited to account for the unexpected stress placement on the first syllable by a rule similar to the English Compound Stress Rule, as well as the superheavy syllable at the end of the first word, a structure that is typically associated with the end of a word.[10]

---

8. Dixon and Aikhenvald do not explicitly argue that combinations of such PWs constitute recursive PWs, however, we may assume this structure on the grounds that grouping the items directly into PPhs appears not to be appropriate, as in Dutch.

9. Dixon and Aikhenvald (2002) suggest that there might not, in fact, be general principles that relate morpho-syntactic (grammatical) and phonological words across languages. Given the view taken here that the PW, and other prosodic constituents, are part of UG, however, it is crucial for there to be at least some core principles for mapping morpho-syntactic structure onto phonological (here PW) structure.

10. I thank Geert Booij for pointing this out.

Neither *ant-* nor *aal-* is a prefix (or word), and the second components of these items, while coincidentally corresponding to words, are not the roots of the complete words. In the case of (18a), there is a chance that speakers may view the structure as a compound since *woord* is a recognizable word in Dutch (i.e. 'word'), and thus perceive a vague relationship between the meanings of 'answer' and 'word'. A similar type of interpretation is not available for (18b), however, despite the fact that here too the second element, *moes*, happens to be a word of Dutch (i.e. 'pulp'). There is not even a vague relationship between *moes* and "alms", so there would be no motivation for speakers to reanalyze *aalmoes* as consisting of two morphemes on the basis of its meaning.

As in the case of affixes being assigned PW status and then forming a compound with another PW, the analysis of words like *antwoord* and *aalmoes* is problematic with regard to the possibility of cross-linguistic generalization. Interestingly, in this case, too, the atypical PWs may be an indication of elements in transition. As Booij (this volume) points out, there is evidence of historical developments in which a portion of a word comes to be analyzed as a meaningful morpheme and subsequently combines as such with other morphemes (e.g. Dutch: *-gate* from *Watergate* may now form compounds with other words with the meaning of some type of scandal: *kippen-gate* 'chicken-gate' = 'scandal concerning chickens').

Finally, it should be noted that positing the same type of prosodic structure for *antwoord* and *aalmoes* and for typical, similarly structured, compounds (e.g. *landheer* 'land owner', *oogarts* 'eye doctor') makes a more subtle, testable, prediction about their properties. Since the first member of typical compounds is an actual word, but that of the atypical compounds is not, we may observe word level phenomena (e.g. word final lengthening) in the former, but not in the latter. An analogous situation may also be observed in other languages. For example, in English the word *kowtow* would appear to lend itself to analysis as a combination of two PWs, which then form a compound, like in the Dutch words. If we compare this with a possible compound *cow chow* (i.e. food for cows), we might, however, observe subtle differences. Again, while the two items are very similar prosodically, there may nevertheless be subtle differences such as word final lengthening at the end of *cow* but not *kow*. If, however, the phonetic properties are the same, this would lend support to an analysis in which they have the same prosodic structure. Given the subtle nature of such a difference, systematic acoustic analysis is called for here.

6.1.4 *Reanalysis of atypical compounds*

As seen, atypical, transitional, PWs may be motivated in some cases, and thus be members of compound structures. In such cases, a constituent between the PW and PPh, is then required, as for typical compounds, specifically the CompG proposed here. It should be noted that this type of analysis locates the idiosyncrasy of the items in question in their prosodic structure, allowing their other phonological properties to operate in a regular manner. An alternative, however, would be to avoid creating atypical PWs and to allow the idiosyncrasies to be accounted for in their lexical representation.[11] Finally, in other cases, where there is less – or no – motivation for atypical or transitional PWs, it is proposed that the elements in question may are grouped into a CompG with a related PW, but as syllables or Feet (e.g. [[*neuro*]$_{Ft}$ [biól-ogy]$_{PW}$]$_{CompG}$, [[rood]$_{PW}$ [achtig]$_{Ft}$]$_{CompG}$ 'reddish', [[pos]$_{Ft}$ [sintactico]$_{PW}$]$_{CompG}$ 'post syntactic', [i na j [talanoa]$_{PW}$]$_{CompG}$ 'in the story').

6.2 Gapping in compounds

The final aspect of compounds we consider here is the phenomenon of "gapping" or "factoring out", removing repeated parts of strings. It has been argued by Booij (1985), and subsequently by others (e.g. Wiese 1996; Vigário 2003) that gapping provides evidence for the analysis of certain affixes as PWs, and thus for the treatment of words containing them as compounds. For example, according to Wiese, the German suffix *-chen* is a PW since it can be factored out, as in (19).

(19) Bruder-*chen* oder Schwester-*chen* → Bruder oder Schwester-*chen*
      brother-dim or sister-dim   '(little) brother or little sister'

The prosodic structure of a word with the suffix *-chen* would thus be a compound, represented as a recursive PW, as in (20).

(20) a. [[Bruder]$_{PW}$ [chen]$_{PW}$]$_{PW}$
      b. [[Schwester]$_{PW}$ [chen]$_{PW}$]$_{PW}$

This analysis not only has the drawback of attributing PW status to an affix, it is inconsistent with the phonological structure of German. Since the PW is the domain of stress assignment, it must contain at least one full vowel. The vowel in *-chen*, however, is schwa, and it may not bear stress.

As mentioned above, while some affixes might constitute PWs, this is not the typical case. Instead, they join with the related PW in a CompG, either as Feet or syllables. Given the schwa in *–chen*, it is likely that this suffix is simply a syllable, yielding the structure: *[[Bruder]$_{PW}$ chen]$_{CG}$ oder [[Schwester]$_{PW}$ chen]$_{CG}$*. Since *–chen* was originally analyzed as a PW to account for the possibility of gapping, if it is no longer considered a PW, a different account is necessary. What appears to be crucial here is the fact that *–chen* is not part of the related PW; it is not necessary for it to constitute a PW on its own.

The more general view of gapping that allows it to apply to elements that are not necessarily PWs (i.e. Feet and syllables), as long as they do not constitute a portion of a PW, also accounts for phenomena in other languages. For example, Vigário (2003) points out that gapping is possible in European Portuguese in structures such as (21a, b), but not (21c).

---

11. See Simon and Wiese (2009) for detailed discussion of the treatment of linguistic exceptions.

(21) a. macro-*economia* e micro-*economia*→ macro- e micro-*economia*
    'macro-economy and micro-economy'
  b. alegre*mente* e triste*mente* → alegre e triste*mente*
    'joyfully and sadly'
  c. mono*grafia* e bio*grafia* → *mono e bio*grafia*
    'monograph and biography'

It was indicated above that bound morphemes such as *macro-* and *micro-*, and suffixes such as -*mente*, that may bear some degree of stress, only need to be analyzed as Feet; it is not necessary to attribute PW structure to such elements. The analysis of the examples in (21) in terms of the CompG, shown in (22), not only accounts for the phonological behaviors of such items, it allows us to see why gapping is possible in the first two cases, but not in the third.

(22) a. [[macro]$_{Ft}$ [economia]$_{PW}$]$_{CompG}$ e [[micro]$_{Ft}$ [economia]$_{PW}$]$_{CompG}$
  b. [[alegre]$_{PW}$ [mente]$_{Ft}$]$_{CompG}$ e [[triste]$_{PW}$ [mente]$_{Ft}$]$_{CompG}$
  c. [[monografia]$_{PW}$]$_{CompG}$ e [[biografia]$_{PW}$]$_{CompG}$

In (22a), what is factored out is the entire PW, not a portion of it. The structure in (22b) is similar to that of German in that the part that is removed is an affix, although it is a Foot here, not a single syllable. In these cases, too, all that is required in order for gapping to be possible is that the repeated element be a constituent on its own, as opposed to being a portion of a PW. In the case in (22c), since we have a combination of two bound roots, it is not possible to factor anything out since the components are both included in a single PW. Removing either part would require the removal of a portion of the PW.

It should be noted that the restriction on gapping proposed here does not predict when gapping will actually take place. It only specifies the conditions that make it possible (or impossible). Even in uncontroversial cases of compounds, we cannot predict that a given item may be factored out. For example, while gapping is possible in (23a), it is not in (23b).

(23) a. They sell doghouses and birdhouses →
    …dog- and birdhouses
  b. They sell doghouses and dollhouses →
    *…dog- and dollhouses

Despite the fact that the compounds in these sentences have identical structures, they do not behave in the same way with respect to gapping. Thus, additional factors must be taken into consideration if we are to effectively predict the application of gapping in clear cases of compounds, and it is suggested that the same may be true with respect to gapping with different types of structures.

7. Conclusions

This chapter has examined different phonological properties of compounds. First, cases were examined that showed that it is common for the components of compounds to exhibit their own phonological properties, or to interact only at their junctures. Next it was shown, however, that certain types of phenomena such as stress and tone may also apply to entire compounds. It was pointed out that there may be phonological considerations involved in the phenomenon of linking elements as well, however, since the phonological aspects are at best inconsistent, they were not examined in depth. In addition, the potentially richer phonological interactions observed in lexicalized compounds were only mentioned but not examined here since they do not represent typical or productive compounds and their phonological properties.

In addition to the phonological phenomena that apply in relation to compounds, the phonological structure of different types of compounds was examined. It was shown that analyses that treat them as recursive Phonological Words encounter a number of problems, and an alternative was proposed that crucially makes use of a constituent between the Phonological Word and the Phonological Phrase, the Composite Group.

Finally, a number of types of constructions that have been referred to as compounds were examined, and it was shown that some required the positing of rather atypical PWs as their components. This lack of consistency is problematic from the perspective of Universal Grammar, which assumes that PWs, and other prosodic constituents, are not only present in all languages, but are the result of the same type of mapping from morpho-syntactic structure onto phonological structure. In some cases, alternate structures were proposed, so that the nature of PWs can remain more consistent across languages. As a result, certain constructions that were previously analyzed as compounds no longer need to be analyzed as such. This approach also offers a way of accounting for gapping that does not require the removed element to be a PW member of a compound.

PART III

Typology and types of compounds

The typology of exocentric compounding

Laurie Bauer
Victoria University of Wellington

On the basis of a survey of types of exocentric compound found in a large number of languages, a small set of basic types is established. Even one of these is considered marginal. These basic types are described and exemplified, with problems of nomenclature and description being discussed. The marginality of exocentricity is discussed. The potential for other, rarer, types is considered.

1. Introduction

Exocentric compounds are usually defined negatively, as the class that is left once the endocentric compounds have been removed (see Scalise & Guevara 2006: 192). Endocentric compounds are defined as compounds which are hyponyms of their head elements. Exocentrics can fail the hyponymy test in a number of ways: they can fail to display a head element; they can function as a member of a word class which is not the word-class of their head element; they can have a head element of the correct word-class, but with apparently the wrong denotation. For the purposes of this chapter, exocentric compounds are identified by this criterion. Despite its relevance, the question of the definition of the term 'compound' is rarely raised in this context, and it is simply assumed that we can recognise a compound. In practice, this problem is solved by taking the definition of the grammar writer: if a particular description states that something is a compound, it is a compound. In light of the well-known difficulties in defining compounds (Bauer 1998; Lieber & Štekauer 2009; Montermini this volume) this side of the question deserves greater consideration.

If we look at Marchand's encyclopaedic *Categories and Types of Present-Day English Word Formation* (1969) we find a small number of types of compound which might be considered to be exocentric. We can exemplify these types as in (1).

(1) $[[pick]_V\text{-}[pocket]_N]_N$
 $[[black]_V[out]_P]_N$
 $[[show]_V[off]_P]_N$
 $[[bird]_N[brain]_N]_N$

Quirk *et al.* (1985) add nothing to this list, nor does Kruisinga (1932). Bauer (1983) adds examples such as

(2) $[[\text{fail}]_V\text{-}[\text{safe}]_{A/Adv}]_A$ (device)
$[[\text{roll}]_{N/V}\text{-}[\text{neck}]_N]_A$ (sweater)
$[[\text{before}]_P\text{-}[\text{tax}]_N]_A$ (profits)
$[[\text{go}]_{?V}\text{-}[\text{go}]_{?V}]_A$ (dancer)
$[[\text{quick}]_{A/Adv}\text{-}[\text{change}]_{N/V}]_A$ (artiste)
$[[\text{tow}]_V\text{-}[\text{away}]_P]_A$ (zone)

Some of these are mentioned by Marchand (1969) and Adams (1973), but not as exocentrics.

The point of the example is that, even in a particularly well-described language like English, most descriptions give a limited set of exocentric compounds. Furthermore, they are words which are available in the lexicon rather than patterns which are productive: the *pick-pocket* pattern is at best marginally profitable in English. The other patterns are probably available, but not particularly profitable. The examples in (2) give rise to many problems of description, and I have elsewhere (Bauer 2007) tried to argue that in many or most cases they are not actually exocentric on deeper consideration (see Section 6 for one such case). But certainly they are superficially exocentric, and worthy of consideration in any serious study of exocentric compounding. If these exocentrics can be missed or masked by major descriptions of a language like English, the chances of finding a full set of exocentrics described for any language chosen at random seem small. At least, we must be prepared for the notion that there will be gaps in the descriptions available to the linguist and that these gaps may prevent a complete typology of exocentrics.

While this is clearly a problem for any approach which, like mine, is based on the analysis of descriptive grammars of a number of languages, it is also a problem for scholars who, like Sergio Scalise or Pavol Štekauer, take a different approach, seeking detailed descriptions of the word-formation possibilities in individual languages based on feed-back from speakers of those languages. Unless you know what to ask questions about, it will be easy to overlook the more marginal categories. And the sporadic attestation of minor categories may, in turn, mask their importance. So I see studies like mine as a necessary precursor to the more detailed kind of study that the project at Bologna has been able to carry out. At the same time, the example of English shows that it may be dangerous to be too complacent about having covered all the relevant types on the basis of a questionnaire or interview data.

The work reported in this chapter was exploratory in nature. I wanted to find out what kinds of exocentric compounds were reported in the literature, and whether languages differed greatly in terms of the patterns that were reported in them. Since I was not interested in questions such as what percentage of languages show what kind of pattern, but simply in identifying the patterns, there was no need for a carefully balanced sample of languages, although it was important that I should have a range of languages both geographically and genetically. Since many of the descriptive grammars I consulted listed no exocentric compound types, it is difficult to say how many relevant languages were considered. The number is greater than 50, with as wide a genetic and geographical spread as I could guarantee from the materials available to me. The languages cited here indicate something of the range, but since most patterns were repeated from language to language, only a subset of the languages considered are actually mentioned.

To my great surprise, I discovered that there were very few recurrent major patterns of exocentric compound types reported in the languages I considered. Even one of these is rather marginal. These patterns represent my own analysis of the data available from the various descriptive grammars. Each of these major patterns contains sub-types, often depending on factors such as the word-classes involved. In what follows, I shall illustrate the various types and sub-types. I have labelled the major types: Bahuvrihi, Synthetic, Transpositional, Exocentric co-compounds, and Metaphorical.

2. Bahuvrihi

There is no surprise in having bahuvrihi compounds as one of the types of exocentric compound – or at least, if there is, it is because the Sanskrit label is sometimes appropriated for exocentrics as a group rather than for one type of exocentric (see, for example, Bloomfield 1935). As is well-known, the label is from Sanskrit, where it exemplifies the type. The elements are *bahu-vrihi* 'much rice' and it means "having much rice" (e.g. of a village) or "one who/which has much rice". The Sanskrit word *bahuvrihi* itself seems to have first been an adjective and then become a noun (Killingley & Killingley 1995: 47). Thus bahuvrihis may act as nouns or as adjectives. The alternative label 'possessive compound' is explained by the example of *bahuvrihi*, glossed as "having" or "possessing" much rice, though there are some examples where the gloss is less obvious: for example, English *red-eye* (with various meanings including "cheap whisky" and "overnight flight") does not clearly denote anything which possesses red eyes, but rather something which causes someone to have red eyes.

Typically, bahuvrihis are made up of a noun (the possessed noun) and a modifier for that noun. Various subtypes are illustrated in Table 1, where the modifier may be an adjective, a quantifier, a verb or a noun, and where the whole may be interpreted as a noun or as an adjective. The head of the compound is indicated with an asterisk.

Table 1. Examples of bahuvrihi compounds

Language	Form	Gloss	Translation	Pattern	Source
Koasati	nakeó-baski	ear + long	mule	N*+A	Kimball 1985: 396
Natchez	ʔaːt-tauːʔiʃ	foot + many	centipede	N*+Q	Mithun 1999: 468
Apache	cʔís-tèł	body + to be wide	terrapin	N*+V	Hoijer 1946: 76
Turkana	e-wur-ù-mosiŋ	smell + rhinoceros	tree sp	N*+N.	Dimmendaal 1983: 293
Finnish	partasuu	beard + mouth	bearded	N+N*(A)	Sulkala & Karjalainen 1992: 361

3. Synthetic

The term 'synthetic compound' is usually restricted to those compounds where the head contains a verb and the modifier contains an argument of that verb; typically, in agentive instances, the head word also contains a morph which denotes the external argument of the verb. A classic example is *bus-driver*, where the head element contains the verb *drive* plus a morph denoting the external argument of the verb, *-er*. The modifying element is an argument of the verb, prototypically, as here, the direct object of the verb (*bus* in this particular example). In the exocentric counterparts of this construction, there is no marking corresponding to the external argument of the verb, yet the compound as a whole denotes the person or entity which performs the role of the external argument. The Romance languages provide a host of good examples, for example French *gratte-ciel* 'scratch-sky, skyscraper'. The compound as a whole denotes the thing which (apparently) scratches the sky, but only the elements of "scratch" and "sky" are overt in the compound.

Bisetto & Scalise (2005: 320) argue that the *gratte-ciel* type are not synthetic compounds, but Marchand (1969: 16) argues that the similarity of English constructions like *watch-maker* and *pickpocket* suggests that their structure should be seen as parallel, and that *pickpocket* has a zero morph where *watch-maker* has the overt *-er* suffix. Because of this similarity, I retain the label 'synthetic' here, though other labels might be employed. Some authors (e.g. Dressler 2006: 38) term this type of compound the 'Romance type', but that seems to be too Eurocentric a label to use in a typological framework.

Some examples of exocentric synthetics are provided in Table 2. In the first two examples we find the expected pattern of a verb with its direct object. In the third example we have a verb and its adjectival subject complement. In the fourth example the direct object of the verb is itself verbal. And in the last example, the whole thing is an abstract noun rather than an agentive. This makes it like English examples such as *whale watching, grouse shooting*, which denote activities and not agents.

Table 2. Examples of exocentric synthetic compounds

Language	Form	Gloss	Translation	Pattern	Source
Babungo	mè-vǝlú'	swallow + eggs	snake sp.	V*+N	Schaub 1985: 249
Japanese	tsume-kiri	nail + cut	nail clipper	N+V*	Hinds 1986: 366
Damana	mʉnzisa-kuaga	viscous + appear	gum	A+V*	Trillos Amaya 1999: 71
Italian	lascia-passare	permit + to pass	a pass	V*+V	Maiden & Robustelli 2000: 33
Korean	sal-in	kill + person	manslaughter	V*+N	Sohn 1994: 414

4. Transpositional

In the synthetic compounds outlined above, the meaning of the compound as a whole can be deduced from the meaning of the verb, its argument and the unexpressed agent or action. In the cases of transposition that fall under this next heading a similar situation arises, but it is only the word-class of the finished compound that is not overt, there is no semantic feature such as 'agentive' or 'action' involved in the interpretation.

Some examples are given in Table 3. The first two of these illustrate two adjectives being interpreted as a noun. Note the different semantic patterns involved in these two instances. The third examples has two verbs being interpreted as an adjective. The fourth example has two nouns being interpreted as a verb. (In this example the relationship between the two nouns and the denotation of the whole is not compositional, as it is in many of the other examples.) In the fifth example a sequence of verb and adjective is interpreted as a noun: an interpretation as a verb or an adjective might be expected by an outsider. In the final example, something which looks like a synthetic compound is interpreted as an adverb.

Table 3. Some examples of transpositional compounds

Language	Form	Gloss	Translation	Source
Khmer	khɔh trəw	wrong + right	morality	Ourn & Haiman 2000: 484
Turkana	ŋi-karì-mɔjɔŋ	thin + old	The Karimojong tribe	Dimmendaal 1983: 294
Damana	tua kuaga	to see + to live	visible	Trillos Amaya 1999: 72
Vietnamese	°bà con	grandmother + child	be related	Thompson 1987: 127
Swahili	ujauzito	come + heavy	pregnancy	Maina 1987: 2
Mandarin	zhuǎn-yǎn	turn + eye	'instantly'	Li & Thompson 1981: 79.

5. Exocentric co-compounds

Almost no co-compounds are endocentric. Of the types listed by Bauer (2009), only two may be endocentric, eleven are exocentric. The most frequent endocentric co-compounds are the appositional type illustrated by English *singer-songwriter*, where it possible to say of the person thus denoted that they are both a singer and a songwriter. On the other hand, such a person is not made up of a singer and a songwriter in the way that Budapest is made up of Buda and Pest, so this is not a dvandva compound (Bauer 2008). Of these, Adams (2001: 82) says of these that they "are arguably… phrases, not complex words", but unfortunately fails to spell the argument out beyond saying that the elements are coordinated. This moves the problem of their status from morphology to syntax. Haspelmath (2002: 89) treats these as exocentric, just like other co-compounds. Fabb (1998: 67) says that the elements in such constructions "share head-like characteristics", without it being clear what this means in practice. Plag (2003: 147) follows others and suggests that these constructions are right-headed in English, because they take plural marking on the right end of the construction: *singer-songwriters/*singers-songwriter(s)*. This argument does not seem to hold, however, since right-edge inflection is a default in English, even where it is not associated with a grammatical head: *trade-offs, pickpockets, model Ts, mother-in-laws* (this last is normal in colloquial English, though frowned upon by purists). In any case, this inflectional pattern is not universal for equivalent constructions. Clearly, there is disagreement in the literature on this point, and a final decision on whether or not such compounds are classified as exocentric depends on the solution to this disagreement. My own feeling is that if they are coordinated, they should have the same status with regard to headedness, but even this does not solve the impasse.

Table 4. Some examples of exocentric co-compounds

Language	Form	Gloss	Translation	Classification	Source
Chantyal	nɦe tɦara	milk buttermilk	dairy products	co-hyponymic	Noonan 2003: 328
German	Schleswig-Holstein			additive, names	
Lezgian	kar-k'walax	job work	job, business	co-synonymic	Haspelmath 1993: 108
Sanskrit	keśaśmasurú	hair beard		additive, common N	Burrow 1955: 217
Old Uyghur	ulug-i kičig-i	big-its little-its	size	scalar	Wälchli 2005: 138
English	blue-green		compromise		

Be that as it may, the vast majority of co-compounds are not endocentric. Korean *puwu-ca* 'father son' (Sohn 1994: 417) does not denote a type of *father* or a type of *son* but a unit made up of a *father* and his *son*. The same is true for the other examples given in Table 4. The classification of co-compounds in Table 4 is from Bauer (2008), except for the term 'scalar' which is from Wälchli (2005).

The scalar type has already been illustrated with an example from Khmer in Table 3. Bauer (2008) calls these 'exocentric', which they are, but the label is clearly not distinctive enough. The point of them appearing both in Table 3 and in Table 4 is that they appear to be instances of transposition, but are also coordinative. Not illustrated in Table 4 are additive adjective and verb compounds, and other types of coordinated adjective and verbal compounds parallel to the nominal examples in Table 4, which are nevertheless exocentric; for examples of these see Bauer (2008).

6. Metaphorical

This final major class of exocentric compound is perhaps the most controversial, but is added here for completeness. It arises when a compound fails the hyponymy test which is supposed to define endocentrics because the head element of the compound or the compound as a whole has a metaphorical interpretation.

The example which drew this class to my attention is one cited by Søgaard (2004), that *dust bowl* is an exocentric compound. The argument is unimpeachable. If we define *bowl* as "deep dish" and *dust bowl* as "an area with no vegetation", then a dust bowl is not a bowl, and there is no hyponymy; if there is no hyponymy the compound must be exocentric. Benczes (2006) takes this whole area a lot further, looking at compounds with a metaphorical head (*firedog* "iron support for burning logs"), where the complete compound is metaphorical (*catlick* "quick wash"), and where the head is metonymic rather than metaphorical, as in *phone neck* ("pain in the neck caused by using the phone") or the whole compound is metonymic (*bear skin* "hat worn by certain soldiers"). There is a major theoretical problem in dealing with such matters, even if there is no practical problem in using the relevant compounds.

My personal feeling about these is that the notion of 'exocentricity' is not helpful here. Just as we do not say that *ass* is exocentric if someone says *My teacher is an ass*, so we should not call compounds like *dust bowl* exocentric. Nevertheless, it is clearly true that compounds of this type fit the (rather loose) definition of exocentric compound, and have to be considered in any serious survey of compounding.

7. Exocentrics as exceptions

The definition of exocentric compounds given above means that exocentrics are a remnant after a well-defined group has been removed from the relevant field of enquiry. In this sense they are exceptions. They are also exceptions in other ways. Dressler (2006) claims that exocentrics are marked with regard to endocentrics: less common cross-linguistically and less common in word-classes in which they occur in individual languages. On the whole, this seems to be true, though there are individual languages (Kayardild (Evans 1995), Turkana (Dimmendaal 1983), Seediq (Holmer 1996), for example) where exocentric compounds appear to be the most frequent compound type, and languages like Italian where the most productive type of compounding is exocentric (as is pointed out to me by a referee). This suggests that there are new things for which we might seek explanations: what causes exocentric compounds to be more frequent that endocentric ones in particular word-classes, or in particular languages? What factors might encourage the growth of exocentrics? Such questions have not yet been taken seriously. It should be noted that, even if the meaning "one having ~" is one which seems to be found useful in many languages, there is no necessary corollary that this will lead to the use of exocentric compounds. There are many languages (including Burushaski (Berger 1998), Kayardild (Evans 1995) and Lezgian (Haspelmath 1993)) which have derivational means of creating such words. A typological study of the incidence of the two methods of marking the relevant meaning and the distribution of examples between them might turn out to be enlightening.

8. Conclusion

Given the remnant-like status of exocentrics, it is surprising if it is possible to classify them into such a small number of basic types. So the basic finding of this chapter is not at all an expected one. Of course, as was said at the beginning, this apparent simplicity may be the result of insufficient description of the languages considered, and there may be a more complex picture yet to be uncovered. This will, however, require a different methodology, and the insights of linguist-informants who are sensitive to the presence of rare categories. I would thus encourage descriptive linguists not to assume that what is presented here is all there is to be found. At the same time, this survey is based on descriptions of so many languages, that it seems it must give a fairly robust description of the most common categories of exocentric compound.

Coordination in compounding

Giorgio F. Arcodia, Nicola Grandi and Bernhard Wälchli[*]
University of Milan Bicocca, University of Bologna, University of Bern

This chapter deals with the expression of coordination relations in compounding. Two macro-types of compounds are identified, namely hyperonymic coordinating compounds (co-compounds), where the referent of the compound is in a superordinate relationship to the meaning of the parts (as Mandarin *dāo-qiāng* 'sword+spear, weapons'), and hyponymic coordinate compounds, where the referent is in a subordinate relationship to the meaning of the parts (as English *actor-director*). The chapter also argues that the distribution of these two macro-types is not random but, rather, areally skewed: whereas co-compounds are common in the Eastern part of Eurasia, New Guinea and Mesoamerica, they seem to be absent in Standard Average European languages, where hyponymic coordinating compounds are formed quite freely. Moreover, while co-compounds may belong to different word classes, hyponymic coordinating compounds are (probably) never verbs.

1. Introduction

Coordination in compounding is typologically more diverse than commonly believed. Coordinating compounds have been given different names, the most time-honoured being Sanskrit *dvandva*, and several labels have been proposed to identify subclasses of them (see, among others, Ten Hacken 2000, Olsen 2001). Here a "coordinate compound" is understood as one in which two or more units share the same status (Eng. *bittersweet*), as opposed to the kind of relation in which the units have an asymmetrical relation, as in subordinating compounds (Germ. *Lippenstift* 'lipstick'; see Haspelmath 2004: 3). This

---

[*] Although this work is the outcome of a joint project, Sections 1, 3, 5 and 6 were written by Giorgio Francesco Arcodia; Section 2 by Bernhard Wälchli; Section 4 by Nicola Grandi. Bernhard Wälchli was funded by the Swiss National Science Foundation (PP001–114840). We would like to thank an anonymous reviewer for insightful comments on a draft of the present chapter.

is, admittedly, a very broad definition; unfortunately, the exact delimitation of coordination in morphology is even more difficult than in syntax.[1]

We will argue here that there is a major dichotomy between hyperonymic coordinate compounds (such as Mandarin *dāo-qiāng* 'sword + spear, weapons', Wälchli's 2005 *co-compounds*) and hyponymic coordinate compounds (such as Spanish *lanza-espada* 'spear + sword, a spear with a blade, a spear which is a sword at the same time'). Both have a coordinate relationship between the parts of the compound, but while the former express superordinate-level concepts, the latter express subordinate-level concepts. The two types of coordinating compounds not only differ in their meaning, but also exhibit different areal distributions. While the hyponymic ones are common in Standard Average European (SAE) languages, co-compounds are common especially in East and South East Asia.

This chapter is structured as follows. Section 2 gives a survey of the typology of co-compounds and argues that they constitute a phenomenon of their own from a typological point of view. Section 3 is devoted to the analysis of co-compounds in the languages of East and South East Asia. Section 4 concentrates on SAE languages where the hyponymic coordinating compounds dominate. Section 5 deals with the interaction of number marking and referential properties in Noun-Noun coordinating compounds. To conclude, we shall provide our areal generalizations on the distribution of semantic types of coordination and on the "division of labour" between morphology and syntax in the expression of coordination relations. Due to the limited space, we shall focus mainly on noun-noun constructions.

2. The typological approach to co-compounds

Following the Sanskrit grammarians, traditional morphology considers any compound whose syntactic paraphrase is a coordination ("*ca-arthé* 'and-denoting'") to be a coordinate or dvandva-compound, thus disregarding that coordination can be manifested in very different ways in compounds. Here it is argued that it is indispensable to consider the meaning of the whole compound in order to define compound types. While subordinate compounds (sub-compounds) typically denote subordinate-level concepts (Mari [Uralic] *kid-tup* 'hand + back, back of the hand'), a wide-spread type of coordinate compounds is used for the expression of superordinate-level concepts (Mari *kid=jol* 'hand + foot, hand and feet, limbs'), which has first been noted in the description of coordinate compounds in American Sign Language (Klima & Bellugi 1979). Following

---

[1]. The precise definition of "coordination" is a debated issue in the literature on syntax (see Haspelmath 2004: 33–37) and, to our knowledge, there is no clear solution to the problem, especially as far as mismatches between semantic and structural coordination are concerned; "[I]t remains difficult to operationalize the basic undisputed intuition that coordination involves symmetry, while subordination involves asymmetry" (Haspelmath 2004: 37).

Wälchli (2005), the term *co-compound* will be restricted here to such compounds denoting superordinate-level concepts and does not extend to compounds with a coordinate and appositional relationship between the parts which denote subordinate-level compounds, such as intermediate-denoting compounds (*southwest*), appositional compounds (French *wagon-restaurant*) and complex numerals (*twenty-three*). Such forms will be discussed in Section 4. Co-compounds further have in common that they express *natural coordination* (rather than accidental coordination), the coordination of things or events that often occur together with characteristic lexical domains including pairs of relatives (Rural Tok Pisin *papa-mama* 'father + mother, parents', *brata-susa* 'brother + sister, siblings'), body parts (*han-lek* 'hand + foot, limbs') and clothes (*su-soken* 'shoe + sock, footwear' Mühlhäusler 1979: 377).

It is hardly ever sufficient to consider the relationship between the parts of a co-compound without considering *the relationship between the parts and the whole*. This becomes particularly manifest in semantic subclassifications of co-compounds. A compound consisting of the parts 'day' and 'night' can be additive (> '24 hours') or generalizing > 'all the time'. In (1), a proverb from Komi, it has yet another contextual meaning 'future'.

(1) Komi (Uralic; Finnic; Timušev 1971: 37)
    Myj   *lun=voj*   vaj-e,   ńinem   on   ted
    what *day=night*   bring-PRS3SG nothing NEG:2S know
    'Nobody knows what the *future* will bring'

In synonymic co-compounds, where the parts and the whole all have very similar meanings, there is still a strong tendency to express superordinate-level meaning, even though this contradicts a narrow definition of synonymy. Synonymic compounds are typically used in generalizing and collective contexts. For instance, Vietnamese *bạn hữu* 'friend + friend, friends' is typically used in plural contexts, see Wälchli (2005: 143–146) for more examples.

Morphological work is often restricted to the analysis of complex lexemes or word-forms in isolation. For co-compounds *context matters* as can be seen in Example (2) from Arapesh and (3) from Erźa Mordvin. After Eastern Eurasia, New Guinea is the second large linguistic area with many languages with a moderate or high level of co-compounding. A characteristic co-compound in New Guinea is 'pig + dog' originally meaning '> (domestic) animals', since pigs and dogs are the most prototypical domestic animals in this area. In Example (2), however, the compound is used metaphorically to indicate people who can be treated like animals without objecting:

(2) Arapesh (Torricelli, Kombio-Arapesh; Conrad & Wogiga 1991: 185)
    ...o apak   *buwul nubat.* m-a-kli   orait
    and we:PL *pig   dog*   1PL-REAL-say   OK
    ...and we "ordinary people", we said "OK"...

Example (3) is from a context where somebody complains about the lack of medical treatment in a Mordvin village. This co-compound is a *hapax legomenon* (occurs only once in the text); 'injection + powder' does not generally mean 'minor forms of medical treatment', the use of the co-compound is triggered by the generalizing and emphatic context outside of which it cannot be interpreted correctly.

(3) Erźa Mordvin (Uralic, Finnic; Doronin 1993: 338)
    ...eŕva   ukol-onť=poroška-nť   meľga
    every   injection.GEN:DEF-powder.GEN:DEF   after
    arď-tńe-k-a   Kaćelaj-ev.
    ride.FREQ.IMP2SG.EMPH   Katselay.LAT
    '(even) for every injection and powder one has to go to Katselay'.

In traditional morphology, dvandva compounds are tertiary categories defined by way of the primary category of word and the secondary category of compound. Below it will be argued that co-compounds are the primary notion, manifested as a cross-linguistically recurrent class type, sharing identical form with other types of compounds only incidentally due to recurrent zero-marking. It is further argued that the notion of word as a strict delimitation is too narrow for co-compounds. Co-compounds in many languages have some phrasal properties even though they tend toward the tight pole of the word-phrase continuum. Thus, co-compounds are generally word-like, but not generally words (for a similar issue in incorporation see Mithun this volume). This becomes particularly manifest if prosodic phonology is considered. Only in very few languages, such as Modern Greek, co-compounds are phonological words (see 5 below). Co-compounds are only one of many phenomena between words and phrases exemplifying a fundamental non-isomorphism between form and function, among them compound types in many languages, clitics, suspended affixation, transpositional inflection (Haspelmath 2002: 230). As a consequence we need two different approaches to compounds: a formal approach, focusing on particular formal properties of compounds, and a functional approach, considering functional class types such as co-compounds irrespective of their concrete formal manifestations. Due to non-isomorphism, co-compounds are not coextensive with any unit of prosodic phonology: they exhibit different prosodic phonology in different languages and there may even be different prosodic types within the same language (Wälchli 2007a:167).

A particularly clear instance of co-compounds which are not words are *discontinuous co-compounds*, as they are common in Hmong, Khasi, Karen, Chinantec, Mixe and many other languages. The Hmong Daw synonymic co-compound *teb chaws* 'land + land, land' is often interrupted by a repeated element C according to the formula CACB or ACBC where C can be different things such as a classifier (*kuw lub teb lub chaw*[2] 'I CL land CL land, my land') or even a proper name (*Yawm Pus teb Yawm Pus*

---

2. Final "consonant" graphemes mark tones in Hmong orthography, the alternation of zero and *s* in *chaw(s)* is due to tone sandhi.

chaw 'Yau Pu's land'; Bisang 1988: 36, 56, 37; Wälchli 2005: 102). Like Germanic bare binomials (Lambrecht 1984) often contain non-analyzable parts, such as **kith and kin**, **to and fro**, many co-compounding languages have imitative co-compounds, where one part is restricted to co-compounds. (4) exemplifies a discontinuous imitative co-compounds from Khasi. Note the general abstract meaning of the verb and the iterative context, both favouring the use of co-compounds:

(4) Khasi (Austro-Asiatic, Khasian; Rabel 1961: 149)
...kii la   juu wan hiar   ša ka   prthey
they PST HAB go   descend to DEF:FEM earth
ban *rep*   ban *riaŋ*
to   *cultivate* to   IMI
'they used to go down to earth in order to cultivate'

Co-compounds share with other types of compounds a recurrent cross-linguistic tendency for zero-marking: in many languages there is no overt marker; the construction is characterized simply by mere juxtaposition of two elements. According to the isomorphism principle, made explicit by John Haiman and implicitly held by most linguists: "recurrent identity of form between different grammatical categories will always reflect some perceived similarity in communicative function" (Haiman 1985: 19). Applied to compounds, this means: different types of compounds are recurrently formally identical in many languages which is why compounds are a general category with closely related meanings of all subtypes. However, even though there is recurrent identity in form, the shared form is not characteristic (zero) and zero marking of co-compounds is not arbitrary, the tight construction iconically reflects the tight semantic relationship of natural coordination. Isomorphism is therefore not sufficient to determine the nature of the category so that it is highly doubtful whether compounds are a uniform cross-linguistic category type at all. Interestingly, co-compounds tend to have different marking from other types of compounds if there are overt markers. While sub-compounds tend to have traces of dependent (genitive) and head marking (possessive affixes), co-compounds may contain traces of coordinators or often exhibit symmetric double marking which is iconic for coordination (Haiman 1985, Wälchli 2005: 54). This can be manifested in different ways, by discontinous co-compounds as in (4) or by double marking of inflection as in Mordvin in (3). Symmetric double marking is not characteristic of sub-compounds.

Interestingly, co-compounds are not only claimed to belong to compounds but also to other large vaguely defined phenomena for which zero marking is recurrent. Many scholars who discuss serial verbs list verbal co-compounds as a minor type of serial verbs (Bisang 1992: 49, Durie 1997: 337) since any V V construction lacking overt markers of coordination and subordination can qualify as a serial verb construction according to the traditional definition. According to Inkelas & Zoll's (2005) morphological doubling theory, co-compounds are, however, an instance of reduplication, and in the literature on parallelism, co-compounds are a form of parallelism

(Nguyễn 1965: 125 for Vietnamese, Lewy 1911 for Uralic). The basic mistake in all these accounts is that construction types cannot be sufficiently characterized only negatively, that is by features they lack.

As shown above, the meaning of the whole is important to a category and neither sub-compounds nor serial verbs nor reduplication nor parallelism share with co-compounds the feature of expressing superordinate-level concepts and natural coordination. However, that all these are different phenomena becomes clear especially in a typological perspective, as they do not occur in the same languages or only to a very limited extent. Intrinsically related phenomena exhibit strong typological correlations. Different types of word order, such as verb-object and noun-adposition order, are well known to correlate cross-linguistically, but word order does not correlate with particular phonological features, to which they are not related. Co-compounds show a strongly areally determined distribution (eastern Eurasia, New Guinea, to a lesser extent Mesoamerica, Wälchli 2005, ch. 6), the other zero constructions do not cluster in the same areas (Wälchli 2005: 176, 231; 2007). However, it can be shown that co-compounds correlate within themselves. The extent to which a language uses co-compounds in some contexts makes it more likely that it uses compounds also in other contexts. In a study based on parallel texts, Wälchli (2007a:157) shows that co-compounds are not distributed randomly across languages. Even though there are no strict hierarchies, co-compounding languages exhibit characteristic profiles depending on the frequency level of co-compounds. Languages with higher frequency of co-compounds have a higher proportion of synonymic co-compounds (Wälchli 2005: 195). Typology is thus indispensable to establish co-compounds as a class type.

What makes it particularly difficult to establish a typology of co-compounds is their particular frequency distribution. Every typological feature has its characteristic typological frequency distribution. Word order, for instance, has a strongly bimodal distribution: most languages have almost only order XY or order YX and there are very few languages without a clear order preference. This makes it possible to characterize word order accurately for most languages in terms of dominant order (Wälchli 2009). In co-compounds, however, there is no characteristic cut-off point. Many languages have very few co-compounds which does not mean, however, that the pattern is non-existent or impossible and the languages with more than a few co-compounds vary greatly in their frequency level of co-compounds. This is why the question "Does a language have co-compounds?" is pretty much useless in typology, the much more relevant question is "How many co-compounds does a language use?" and this can be investigated only on the basis of texts. Since there is also much intra-language variation across styles and registers it is important to keep the register constant which makes it even more difficult to investigate frequency levels of co-compounds (Wälchli 2005, ch. 6).

The zero-marking of co-compounds makes it also difficult to investigate the diachrony of the category. Even though there is evidence at least from some languages that co-compounds grammaticalize from phrasal coordination, it cannot be excluded that a simple juxtaposition construction develops spontaneously. This makes co-compounds particularly available as a contact phenomenon. Even though British and American English have no or very few co-compounds, Indian English can take over co-compounds characteristic of Indian languages more easily than other features of Indian languages ('*However we can help our father-mother that is what it is for us to do*'; Rushdie 1981/1995: 228). The title of Ang Lee's famous film *Eat Drink Man Woman* consists of co-compounds even in English. Other features of Chinese grammar cannot be transferred to English so easily. There is thus no different parameter setting in European languages that causes a lack of co-compounds in West European languages, as it has sometimes been claimed (McCawley 1974: 33; Fanselow 1985: 303). The particular behavior of co-compounds is reflected in their typological frequency distribution. While it is easy for a language to acquire few co-compounds, it is more difficult to acquire a high frequency of co-compounds because in every context of use there is a local competition with other lexical means of expression. Co-compounds are a coherent phenomenon because the use of co-compounds helps co-compounds in other domains to win their local competition in the lexicon. However, co-compounds are not represented as a single coherent phenomenon in the mental lexicon. Some co-compounds are highly lexicalized and stored as chunks, while others, such as 'injection-powder' in (3), are occasional formations produced by a morphological rule.

Table 1 summarizes the arguments of this section for a typological approach to co-compounds as opposed to the traditional taxonomic approach.

In what follows, we shall analyse both co-compounds and coordinating structures expressing subordinate notions, providing evidence for the areal bias in the distribution of such forms.

Table 1. Typological vs. taxonomical approaches to co-compounds

	Traditional view	Typological approach to co-compounds
(a)	Dvandvas are defined by way of their syntactic paraphrase: the 'and-denoting'	Co-compounds express natural coordination; they express superordinate level concepts but not subordinate level concepts
(b)	The meaning of a type of compounds is determined by the semantic relationship of the meanings of the parts	The meaning of a type of compounds is determined by the semantic relationship between the parts and the whole
(c)	Compounds can be studied in isolation	Compounds must be studied in their natural context (in texts)
(d)	Compounds are words	Many compounds are intermediate between word and phrase; compounds are tight patterns ("word-like")
(e)	Top-down taxonomical definition of compounds	Bottom-up definition of class types with recurrent cross-linguistic behavior
(f)	Form and function are isomorphic	Form and function are not isomorphic; formal groups of compounds do not correspond directly to functional groups of compounds.

Traditional view	Typological approach to co-compounds
(g) If two phenomena have the same form or the same construction in a language they are instances of the same category	Compounds are often zero-marked and zero-marking is not a reliable criterion for establishing a category
(h) Co-compounds are compounds (Alternatively: Co-compounds are reduplication / Verbal co-compounds are verb serialization / Compounds are a form of parallelism)	Co-compounds are a category type of their own
(i) A language has or lacks a particular type of compounds	Languages can be classified according to their frequency level of co-compounds
(j) Co-compounds are impossible words in some languages due to particular parameter setting	Co-compounds can be built from scratch. What inhibits them from being used frequently in texts is local competition in lexical domains
(k) Word formation patterns are represented as rules in competence	Co-compounds are an emergent phenomenon in texts; they cluster to groups because their members have a related fate in performance
(l) Typology is not needed to define category types	Typology is indispensable to define category types

3. Coordination in NN compounds in East and South-East Asia

The region of East and continental South East Asia is an often-quoted example of *Sprachbund*, since it contains languages belonging to several different families (Sino-Tibetan, Hmong-Mien, Mon-Khmer, Tai-Kadai, Austronesian, Japanese and Korean) sharing many common features, such as obligatory noun classifiers, none or limited inflectional morphology, etc. (see Goddard 2005 for an overview). In Wälchli (2005), the frequency of co-compounds in a number of languages of Eurasia has been calculated in parallel texts (*The Universal Declaration of Human Rights* and *the Gospel according to Mark*) and languages have been arranged on a scale from 0 to 6, 6 being the highest frequency class for co-compounds. In the two top classes, 5 and 6, we find Mandarin, Vietnamese, White Hmong (a language spoken mainly in South-Western China and in Thailand), Tibetan, Lahu (a Lolo-Burmese language), Burmese, Thai, Khmer, Khalkha (i.e. Standard Mongolian of Mongolia) and Tuva, a Turkic language which has had intense contact with Khalkha Mongolian. Besides, both Japanese and Korean fall in class four (or upper moderate level) and although many of the co-compounds in these languages are composed of lexemes borrowed from Chinese (e.g. Japanese *fū-fu* 'husband and wife'), we have indeed several examples of co-compounds even in the native stratum of the lexicon, such as Korean *o-nwui* 'brother and sister' or *son-pal* 'hand and foot' (Sohn 1999: 245).

From the semantic point of view, the coordinate constructions which we find in languages from this area are indeed rich and varied. In what follows we will not provide an exhaustive exemplification but, rather, we will describe briefly the types of co-compounds which are most interesting for our comparison, which mostly seem to be also the most basic and widespread types, according to Wälchli (2005).

One quite widespread type of co-compound is called *additive*, where the meaning of the compound as a whole is simply the sum of the meaning of the parts, such as the above mentioned Japanese example *fū-fu* 'husband and wife' or the Korean word *son-pal* 'hand and foot', representative of the *paring* subtype, which may be either related to the same person, as in Khmer *ʔɜwpuk mədaaj* 'father + mother, parents' (Antelme 2004: 163) or have a converse reference, such as in Japanese *oya-ko* 'father and son'.

Wälchli's *non-pairing* type includes "collection complexes which are exclusively listed by the parts" (2005: 139), such as Chinese *dāo-chā* 'knife and fork'. If a compound designates a collection complex which rather is not exclusively listed by the parts, then it falls into the class of *collective* co-compounds, fairly common in languages of this area: examples of this class might be Vietnamese *bàn ghế* (table + chair) or Khmer *tok tuu* (table + closet), both for 'furniture', where two instances of the category are made metonymically representative of the set as a whole.

In Chinese, compounds belonging to the latter subtype may have a specific, determined referent, such as *Gǎng-Ào* 'Hong Kong and Macao', which is simply the juxtaposition of the abbreviated names of the two Special Administrative Regions of China (note the hyperonymic component and the natural coordination in *Gǎng-Ào*). They have something in common with the *Australian-American relationship* type (example quoted from Bauer 2001: 700), termed *relational compounds* by Wälchli, which usually act as determiners of an attributive compound, as it often happens with the *Gǎng-Ào* 'Hong Kong and Macao' type, but relationships are not restricted to natural coordination. The interpretation of the relationship between the members of the compound may be 'between…and', as it actually is in the English example given above, for constructions such as *Zhōng-Rì guānxì* 'Sino-Japanese relationship' (see also Olsen 2001 on this topic) or may also be simply conjunctive (logical operator AND), such as in *Gǎng-Ào-Tái-qū* 'The Hong Kong-Macao-Taiwan area', somehow similar to the *Alsace-Lorraine* type. A feature of these constructions in Chinese is that a disjunctive interpretation seems to be also possible, as in *Gǎng-Ào-Tái hùzhào* 'Hong Kong, Macao or Taiwan passport(s)':[3] the existence of a disjunctive relationship in compounding is

---

3. This point might be controversial and deserves further clarification. A compound such as *Gǎng-Ào-Tái hùzhào* in normally seen at the passport check counter of a Chinese (P.R.C.) airport: the interpretation, therefore, could be 'those bearing either Hong Kong or Macao or Taiwan passports' (disjunctive) or 'all those bearing Hong Kong, Macao and Taiwan passports' (conjunctive). We believe that, although the "AND" interpretation is possible, the "OR" interpretation is in no way excluded.

far from being an exception in the languages of East and South-East Asia, and it seems to be a feature common also to some languages of India with co-compounds, as we will see below (but cf. Section 4.).

Indeed, one of the categories which have been proposed by Wälchli is that of *alternative co-compounds* which, as the name suggests, are based on a disjunctive relationship. In Mandarin Chinese, we have compound forms such as *shèng-fù* 'victory or defeat', 'success or failure' where only one of the alternatives may be true (akin to *exclusive disjunction*; see Dik 1968):

(5) Mandarin Chinese (Sino-Tibetan; Sinitic)
zhè chǎng zhànzhēng de   shèng-fù   juédìng-zhe
this CL   war   POSS victory–defeat decide-PROG
guójiā de mìngyùn
country POSS destiny
'the outcome (<victory or defeat) of this war will decide the country's destiny'

In this kind of co-compounds, the function of disjunction is to blur the contrast; in an 'either A or B' compound, the meaning of the whole is more general than the meaning of the parts. A possible context for the development of this kind of construction are indirect questions: for *shèng-fù*, it could be something like 'whether there is victory or defeat'. However, compounds belonging to this type may also, sometimes and in certain contexts, be interpreted as additive (i.e. 'victory and defeat').

Lastly, we will briefly discuss *scalar co-compounds*, which typically have as a referent some scalar property such as height, weight and the like. Their constituent lexemes are the two adjectives which signify the extreme poles of the scale: an ordinary expression for 'length' in Chinese, for instance, is *cháng-duǎn*, lit. "long+short". The constituents of scalar compounds are in a disjunctive relationship as for the alternative type; here, however, they seem to follow an exocentric pattern, the output being systematically a noun: $[cháng]_{ADJ}$ $[duǎn]_{ADJ}$ > $[chángduǎn]_N$ (for exocentric compounds, see Bauer this volume). Scalar co-compounds evolve in contexts where there is the question of a choice: 'the question of A or B / the choice of A or B', which is, in a way, a set of A and B. A likely source for *scalar co-compounds* are the above mentioned *alternative co-compounds* employed in direct and indirect questions (Wälchli 2005: 153–4).

Let us now turn to the examination of coordinating structures in languages of the SAE area, taking into account both "prototypical" compound words and other word-like constructions (such as e.g. binomials).

4. Hyponymic coordinating compounds and the SAE area

As stated in the introduction, co-compounds are not the only kind of coordinating compounds. As it is well known, if syntax is taken into account coordination is not limited to the expression of a natural tie between the coordinands. Many other coordinate constructions are attested, expressing different semantic relations, and displaying various formal patterns.[4] Therefore, it is not surprising that also in morphology the range of coordinate constructions is wider than that suggested in the previous paragraphs. In this section, we will focus on coordinate compounds expressing subordinate-level concepts, cursorily mentioned above, in particular compounds with the structure [N N]$_N$:

(6) Standard Average European coordinate compounds
English
[*singer*]$_N$ [*actor*]$_N$ > [*singer actor*]$_N$
Italian
[*studente*]$_N$ [*lavoratore*]$_N$ > [*studente lavoratore*]$_N$
'student + worker, student worker'
French
[*chanteur*]$_N$ [*auteur*]$_N$ > [*chanteur auteur*]$_N$
'singer + author, singer author'

This compounding scheme, labelled 'coordinate endocentric' by Bisetto & Scalise (2005 and 2009), seems to be cross-linguistically quite uncommon and its distribution appears to be areally restricted mainly to Western and Central Europe, the so called Standard Average European linguistic area (cf. Haspelmath 2001 for a general survey).[5]

In § 2, we argued in favour of a typological approach to co-compounds. As for the pattern of coordinate compounding exemplified by English *singer actor*, further research is needed before a similar approach may be applied to it as well; the literature on this issue does not offer as much typological perspective as that on co-compounds. Also, the fact that hyponymic coordinating compounds could be a phenomenon mostly limited to the SAE area makes a large-scale typological approach (arguably) less desirable.

As shown in the previous paragraphs, as far as conjunction is concerned, no significant difference should be expected between syntactic constructions and morphological ones: a conjunctive coordinate construction including two or more nouns should designate an entity which is the the "arithmetical sum" of the meanings of the constituents. As far as syntax is concerned, all the examples discussed by Haspelmath (2004) and (2005) support this claim:

(7) Iraqw (Afro-Asiatic, Southern Cushitic)
Kwermuhl, nee Tlawi, nee Dongobesh, nee Haydom nee Daudi
Kwermuhl and Tlawi and Dongobesh and Haydom and Daudi
'Kwermuhl, Tlawi, Dongobesh, Haydom, and Daudi [place names]'

---

4. Cf. Haspelmath (2004) and (2007) for a general picture.

5. It is also very common, however, in Standard Russian (and standard languages in Eastern Europe influenced by Russian) due to influence from French, but it is less common in Russian dialects, where co-compounds occur.

The coordinate construction indicates the addition of all the single places designated by the coordinands.

Moving to morphology, a similar behaviour characterizes co-compounds, discussed above. But, perhaps unexpectedly, in SAE languages a compound pattern as the one underlying co-compounds as Khmer *ʔəwpuk mədaaj* 'father + mather, parents' (cf. § 3) is unproductive in nominal compounding. On the contrary, a different compounding schema with a high degree of productivity is widely attested, for which we gave some examples in (6). The interpretation of these compounds is quite "anti-iconic": they do not designate a pair of people (thus they are not the result of the addition of coordinands), but a single person sharing features designated by both coordinands. In this case, the relation of modification is bidirectional: a *singer actor* is both a kind of singer and a kind of actor. Hence, the compound designates a subordinate concept with respect to the meaning of its constituents; in other words, it is a hyponym of its members. So, "hyponymic coordinate compounds" express subordinate-level concepts, just as subordinate or attributive-appositive compounds and are thus opposed to co-compounds. This peculiarity gives reason of the fact that in hyponymic coordinate compounds, the only semantic type attested with a high degree of productivity is conjunction. As for disjunction, a slight difference between co-compounds and hyponymic coordinate compounds is attested. As it is well known, a disjunctive binary construction is true only if one of the two alternatives is true: if a coordinate compound designates a superordinate concept which includes both alternatives (as in the case of co-compounds; cf. 5), this interpretation is possible; however, it is hardly compatible with a costruction in which the coordinands express two simultaneous properties of a single referent. It is quite unplausible for two properties perceived as alternative to be predicated of the same referent. Adversative coordination is never expressed in coordinating compounds. As for co-compounds, this is rather predictable, since adversative coordination presupposes contrast, which does not go together with tight constructions. For hyperonymic coordinating compounds, the very notion of adversative coordination clashes with the basic function of a noun, which is reference: you just do not have a label meaning 'A but not B' (Caterina Mauri, p.c). In a compound such as *gentleman thief* there is some sort of contrast implied, but only at a pragmatic level: usually a gentleman is not supposed to be stealing, but this does not concern the structural and semantic levels ('gentleman AND thief'). So, it must be overtly stated that the label 'hyponymic coordinate compound' implicitly means 'conjunctive compound'.

As to the formal features, it is worth mentioning that in co-compounds constituent order usually displays a high degree of internal cohesion and is often constrained by socio-cultural variables; therefore, it can hardly be inverted. On the contrary, the order of the constituents in most "hyponymic" conjunctive compounds is usually a matter of pragmatics. As a consequence, their internal order is quite free and can be inverted without significatively affecting their referential meaning. For instance, a web search reveals that in Italian the compound *studente lavoratore* 'student worker' is found in educational environments, whereas the inverted sequence *lavoratore studente* 'worker student' is more likely to appear in work- or market-related contexts. Example (8) is particularly thrusting. Two compounds made up by the same constituents occur in the same sentence with two different internal structures, revealing that the first slot is filled up by the constituent that is perceived as more relevant in the extra-linguistic context:

(8) Italian (newspaper *La Repubblica*, 23/12/2008)
    La Fortezza [...] deve prendere rimbalzi, recuperare palloni
    LF   must get   rebounds,   steals
    e   avere in Boykins una **guardia-play**,
    and use B. as a   point guard – play maker
    non un **play-guardia**   che   inizia e
    not as a play maker – pointguard who just starts and
    finisce   il   gioco
    concludes the game
    'La Fortezza [a basketball team] must get rebounds, steals and use Boykins as a pointguard–playmaker, not as a playmaker–pointguard who just starts and concludes the game.'

It must be pointed out, incidentally, that this situation prevents us from identifying a semantic head on the basis of positional criteria, that is, we cannot identify the head of such a compound with its first constituent simply recalling that Italian is a head initial language.[6] This example, like many other similar constructions, reveals that in "hyponymic" conjunctive compounds pragmatic constraints are stronger than formal ones. Possibly, forms as that in (8) weaken even the opportunity of identifying a head within a coordinate compound. As it is well known, the notion of head was, originally, purely syntactic: "the intuition to be captured with the notion of head is that in certain syntactic constructs one constituent in some sense 'characterizes' or 'dominates' the whole" (Zwicky 1985: 2). So, it holds only for linguistic constructions that are hierarchically organized. This necessary precondition seems to contradict the definition of coordinate construction, whose members, according to Haspelmath (2004), must have the same status and can be insensitive to their reciprocal positions. Not by chance, reversibility of internal order is strictly forbidden in hierarchical compounds, that is in compounds in which the identification of a head is uncontroversial.[7]

The different degree of "internal stability" of coordinate compounds is a possible consequence of the semantic relations they encode. In a general perspective, the closer

---

6.   Note, however, that in Example (8) the different order of constituents, *guardia-play* vs. *play-guardia*, triggers a different gender in the indefinite article (*una* vs. *un*), suggesting an analysis of the left-hand consitutent as a categorial head. For a general picture on the notion of head in compounding, cf. Scalise and Fábregas (this volume).

7.   Constituent order reversibility constitutes a valuable test to disambiguate unclear cases such as *woman doctor*, the interpretation of which can be both coordinative and appositive. If constituent order is reversible, then the compound is certainly coordinate.

the semantic connection between two (or more) elements, the more cohesive the linguistic construction that expresses it. The labels "tight coordination" and "loose coordination" can be employed to describe different levels of internal cohesion of coordinate constructions. On the semantic ground, loose and tight coordination seem to be preferably associated to natural and accidental coordination, respectively. In the tight/natural case, the coordinands form a conceptual unit; in the loose/accidental, the coordinands are thought of as separate units (cf. Wälchli 2005, ch. 3).

As shown above, co-compounds usually express natural coordination and, as a consequence, are expected to be often more cohesive than conjunctive coordinate compounds encoding a hyponymic relation, as English *singer actor*, which typically encode accidental coordination. Therefore, co-compounds can be defined as tight coordinate constructions expressing a natural tie between coordinands. Hence, they usually display a rigid order of constituents. On the contrary, conjunctive compounds in (6) are instances of morphological loose coordinate constructions, expressing an accidental connection between coordinands. So, their internal structure is far more flexible and their reciprocal order can be inverted. Morphological tight coordinate constructions (co-compounds) and morphological loose coordinate constructions of SAE languages as *singer actor* correspond to exocentric and endocentric coordinate compounds, respectively, in Bisetto & Scalise's (2005, 2009) terminology.

Difference and similarities between the two compounding patterns analysed so far are summarized in Table 2.

Table 2. Differences and similarites between co-compounds and hyponymic coordinating compounds

	Co-compounds (Hyperonymic coordinating compounds)	Hyponymic coordinating compounds
Overt / covert marking of coordination relation	Various patterns	Zero is predominant
Part-whole relationship	Referent of the compound is in a superordinate relationship to the meaning of the parts	Referent is in a subordinate relationship to the meaning of the parts
Semantic sub-type of coordination	Conjunction and, occasionally, disjunction	Conjunction
Semantic sub-type of conjunction	They express natural coordination (they form a conceptual unit)	They express accidental coordination (they are separate units)
Coordinands' word class	The constituents of a coordinate compound usually belong to the same word class	
	Any word-class	Nouns or adjectives (?)
Constituent order	Mostly irreversible	Reversible

What is really puzzling about these kinds of constructions is that, often, they do not co-exist in a language. In other words, what distinguishes coordinate compounds from subordinate and attributive / appositive ones is that in coordinate compounds endocentric and exocentric forms tend to be mutually exclusive. In languages in which compounds productively express natural coordination,[8] accidental coordination is usually expressed by binomials[9] or other structural types further from the prototype of word than compounds. But SAE languages behave contrarily to this tendency: natural coordination seems a prerogative of binomial constructions (which are usually irreversible), whereas coordinative compounds express accidental coordination (and are reversible):

(9) Italian
 a. Coordinate compounds
 $[studente]_N$ $[lavoratore]_N$ > $[studente\ lavoratore]_N$
 'student + worker, student worker'
 $[lavoratore]_N$ $[studente]_N$ > $[lavoratore\ studente]_N$
 'worker + student, worker student'
 b. Binomials (from Masini 2006)
 punto e virgola   su e giù   anima e corpo
 'full stop and comma, semicolon' 'up and down'   'soul and body'
 *virgola e punto   *giù e su   *corpo e anima

Thus, in a cross-linguistic perspective, in encoding accidental and natural coordination syntax and morphology seem to be in complementary distribution: if accidental coordination is expressed through morphological strategies, then natural coordination is encoded by syntactic means (and *vice versa*).

Moreover, the distribution of these two compounding patterns among the World's languages seems highly conditioned by strong areal biases. Whereas in languages of the core SAE area the productive model is the hyponymic type (cf. *singer-actor*), in languages outside it coordinating compounds typically designate a superordinate level concept. The situation can be summarized as follows:

Table 3. Some correlations between types of coordination and marking patterns

	SAE pattern	Cross-linguistic trend
Hyperonymic	Looser	Tighter
Hyponymic	Tighter	Looser

---

8. That is, in languages in which co-compounds have a plain productivity: eastern Eurasia, New Guinea, Mesoamerica, above all.

9. "Binomial constructions are generally defined as constructions that consist of two (or sometimes more) coordinated items that belong to the same lexical category, are linked by a conjunction and display a certain degree of conventionality and fixity" (Masini 2006: 2).

Note, however, that this is to be understood as a trend, rather than as an absolute universal. In fact, many languages of Russia with co-compounds have occasional instances of hyponymic coordinative compounds, borrowed from standard Russian (cf. Footnote 5). The correlation could also be historically motivated, as hyponymic coordinative compounds are largely restricted to Europe.

The distribution of coordinate compounds productively formed by means of the hyponymic pattern exhibits many similarities with that of features that usually identify the SAE linguistic area. More specifically, this pattern of compounding shows the highest degree of productivity in languages placed in the core area of the SAE *Sprachbund*: Italian, French, English, Dutch, German, etc. Moving away from it, these compounds scatter: both their frequency and productivity decrease. Maltese has just few of them in some hybrid construction such as *student-haddiem* (student worker) in which Italian influence is evident. Basque has mostly compounds designating superordinate level concepts.

Therefore, we can put forward the hypothesis that the formation of coordinate compounds through hyponymic patterns is an areal feature of SAE languages. This hypothesis seems supported by the fact that when a SAE language comes out of this linguistic area, it usually loses this feature. For example, even though English is a language in which hyponym conjunctive compounds display a high productivity, in Indian English the pattern expressing superordinate level concepts is attested, as the *father-mother* example given at the end of § 2 reveals. Moreover, also in English-lexified pidgins and creoles co-compounds seem to be the default pattern, as confirmed by the Tok Pisin data discussed above. The case of contact languages is very interesting, since they are usually included in the situations "where the complexity of modern languages is disrupted or impaired" and where "elements of the protolanguage still emerge" (Jackendoff 2009).[10] So, if Jackendoff is true in asserting that contact languages can be to some extent compared to the protolanguage, the emerging of co-compounds in their formation, independently of the type of coordinate compounds of the lexifier language is not meaningless. It probably indicates that compounds expressing superordinate level concepts have some sort of cognitive prominence over hyponymic ones.

Let us now have a closer look to the referential properties both of hyponymic and hyperonymic coordinating compounds (i.e. co-compounds), comparing them to the kinds of coordinating compound attested in some languages of India (both Indo-Aryan and Dravidic), in "peripheral languages" of Europe, such as Basque or Armenian, and in Western European SAE languages.

---

10. Here Jackendoff uses the term "protolanguage" in the sense assigned to it in Bickerton (1990): the "protolanguage" should be an evolutionary stage of the language capacity earlier to the language, with no syntax or morphology.

5. Reference and number in NN coordinating compounds

As we have said in the preceding section, coordinating compounds in the languages of Western Europe seem to belong to the hyponymic type, where the entity designated by the compound as a whole is, in a sense, more specific than its constituents: *singer-actor* is a more specific notion than those of *singer* and *actor* themselves, bringing thus these compounds closer to attributive compounds.

Under the label *karmadhāraya* compound, "made up of two nouns, each of which independently refers to some aspect of the entity denoted by the compound as a whole" (Bauer 2001: 698–9) are thus included compounds that actually seem to be attributive or, at least, closer to the attributive type, such as *woman doctor*, which is usually understood as 'a doctor belonging to the female sex' (note that the word *doctor* has no feminine form in English; compare Italian *dottoressa*), rather than 'someone who is both a woman and a doctor', although this statement would not be false (cf. footnote 7). The same may be said about a complex word such as Spanish *hombre rana* (man+frog) 'diver', corresponding to English *frogman*, which is indeed a man (see Olsen 2001): note also that the constituent meaning "man" is located in the standard head position for both languages (and the same goes for the the Italian and French equivalent compounds, and for *doctor* in *woman doctor*). We think that these examples are analogous to "classical" attributive compounds such as *snail mail*, where the feature "slow" is the only relevant one in the attributive function of the *snail* constituent (Scalise, Bisettto & Guevara 2005: 142[11]): similarly, in *frogman* only the semantic feature "amphibian" of the frog is relevant for the characterization of *man*. This does not seem to be the case with compounds such as *singer-actor* or *washer-drier*, where the semantic representation of the constituents (the *body*, in Lieber's framework; cf. footnote 12) is the same to a great extent: this means that we are designating an entity which is actually both "A" and "B". As mentioned earlier (cf. 4), such compounds may have a reversible order of the consitutents: e.g. Hungarian *nadrágszoknya* (trousers+skirt) 'culottes' is also attested as *szoknyanadrág* (Gouesse 2004: 137), just as for Modern Greek χιονόβροχο *chionó-vrocho* 'snow+rain, sleet', the reverse order of constituents βροχόχιονο is also attested (Ralli 1992).

We have already mentioned the Khmer additive compound *ʔɜwpuk mədaaj* 'parents' in Section 3 above, which is made up of the two semantic constituents of the entity designed by the compound as a whole, qualifying thus for the definition of "hyperonymic" compound. In Chinese, a language with no morphological marker for number in nouns and adjectives but with obligatory nominal classifiers, such compounds may refer to one individualized member of the pair, such as e.g. *yí-ge jiě-mèi* 'one sister', where the co-compound *jiěmèi* is made of the constituents 'elder sister' and 'younger sister' (a typical pattern for languages where the age distinctions among members of a family are codified in the lexicon). If reference is made to, for instance, both parents in

---

11. Here reference is made to Lieber's *Lexical Semantics*; see Lieber 2003.

a family, then the classifier would have to be *duì* 'pair' as in *yí-duì fūmǔ*. The constituents of these compounds may be "visible" for syntactic reference, individually, a feature which has been pointed out in the literature for Japanese co-compounds (i.e. by McCawley 1974): in this language, we find sentences such as *kyōdai wa otagai tatakau koto* 'the fact that (the) brothers fought with each other'. This seems to be impossible for hyponymic compounds, since reference is made to a single entity with two identities (as for singer-actor); in co-compounds as well reference is made to a single entity, but its constituent parts are, in a sense, separable.

Note, however, that most languages of the East Asian area are classifier languages with no count nouns and no morphological marking of number (cf. 3). There are some languages located between Western Europe and East Asia which have both hyponymic compounds and number marking, such as Pāli. In Pāli, a coordinative compound is marked for the plural and takes the gender and declension of its last member if the constituents of the compound are considered separatedly, such as *samaṇabrāhmaṇā* 'samanas and brahmins' or *candimasuriyā*, 'the sun and the moon'. If a compound takes the form of a neuter singular, whatever the number of its members, it becomes a collective, like *kusalākusalam* 'good and evil'; however, even this kind of collectives may take a plural marker and, in fact, the grammarians regards those which go only in the neuter singular and those which may be marked also for plural as two separate classes (respectively, *samāhāra* and *vikappasamāhāra*) and only the former are always considered collectively (Duroiselle 1997: 130). We see here how number (singular vs. plural) plays a role in the interpretation of a coordinating compound: plural marking matches best an additive interpretation, something like 'the As and the Bs, considered separately', whereas singular marking triggers the collective interpretation, 'the set of A(s) and B(s)'. In Basque, co-compounds such as *errege-erreginak* 'king and queen' are always plural, with reference to a single couple of monarchs, wheras a few compounds such as *ur-ardoa* 'water with wine' are marked for singular, as their referent is a mass entity (Hualde 2003). A similar situation is also that of Marathi, where co-compounds behave as a plural phrase (Pandharipande 1997). In Malayalam, the humble plural marker *–maar* is obligatorily marked on co-compounds, as in *acchanammamaar* 'father and mother', but it is optional if a non-humble equivalent is chosen (Asher & Kumari 1997). The positive correlation between singular number and collective interpretation, on one side, and that between plural number and additive intepretation, on the other, however, is far from being a rule. In many Uralic languages, for instance, both consituents of a co-compound are normally marked for dual (or for plural, in those languages which have lost the dual as a category) in natural coordination, ignoring the distinction between additive and generalizing (Wälchli 2005: 51–52).

Number marking may influence the interpretation of a coordinate construction even in English: as Wälchli (2005: 77–78) points out, a phrase such as *my relatives and friends* would by default be understood as 'all the people that are my relatives or my friends' (additive interpretation), but if the number were singular, as in *my relative and friend*, there can be only a single referent.[12] As in *singer-actor*: the additive interpretation is normally excluded. In Chinese, a construction such as *xuésheng gōngrén*, the juxtaposition of the words for 'student' and 'worker', will normally be understood as 'student(s) and worker(s)', with the number depending on the context (and even an attributive reading is possible), whereas an explicit conjunctive marker *jiān* is required if the 'student-worker' interpretation is expected (*xuésheng jiān gōngrén*).

In Modern Greek, where both hyponymic and hyperonymic compounds are attested, we see again different structural patterns for the two types of coordinative constructions: co-compounds such as γυναιχόπεδα *gynaichó-peda* 'women and children' or the often quoted example ανδρόγυνο *andró-gyno* 'married couple', lit. 'man+woman' are undoubtedly compound words (note the unexpected neuter gender of the compound); hyponymic constructions such as ηθοποιός τραγουδιστής *ithopoiós tragoudistís* 'actor singer' may receive internal inflectional markers and are two phonological words, but behave as syntactic atoms and cannot have an independent syntactic reference, thus lying somewhere between words and phrases, but further from morphology than co-compounds are (Ralli 1992).

Curiously, Ancient Greek did not distinguish structurally these two kinds of coordinative constructions, i.e. the hyponymic and the hyperonymic ones: a hyponymic coordinating compound such as ιατρόμαντις *iatró-mantis* 'physician-diviner' seems to qualify as a word (Grandi & Pompei, forthcoming). Also, in Armenian we have a compound form such as *goyavazak* 'pickpocket-bandit' which, according to Donabédian (2004: 12–13)'s account, could also be interpreted as a hyperonym ("la cátegorie des voleurs et des brigandes pris ensemble"). However, such forms are rare in the language. These are the only exceptions which we have found in our sample to the tendency represented in Table 3. Note, however, that for hyponymic coordinating compounds we collected mostly areally-biased data; so, the fact that languages employ some strategy to distinguish formally hyponymic and hyperonymic coordinating compounds should be taken as a tendency, rather than as a universal.

6. Conclusion

To sum up, we find a great variety of constructions between "pure" morphology and syntax which fall in the domain of coordinating compounds (in the broadest sense of the word).

---

12. See Wälchli (2005: 77–78) on the distinction between *overlapping* and *non-overlapping* coordination.

In Section 2, we focussed on co-compounds only, arguing for the advantages of a typological approach to them, as opposed to the traditional one (see Table 1).

The suggestion stated in Section 4, namely that hyperonymic coordinating compounds (co-compounds) are the more "basic" type of coordinating compounds is consistent with the data surveyed, since all of the languages outside the SAE area which we have tested seem to have co-compounds with no marker or a morphological marker for coordination, whereas hyponymic coordination normally requires a heavier form, mostly closer to syntax.[13] However, it must be noted that our survey of hyponymic coordinating compounds was essentially limited to languages of the SAE and East and South-East Asian *Sprachbünde* and to a number of languages of Europe and India, (both Indo-European and non-Indo-European). Our proposal that co-compounds represent the basic type here can be proved only areally; a proper typological sample should be investigated to verify this claim.

What the data has shown is that languages actually tend to choose either the hyponymic or the hyperonymic relationship as the one with the tightest (i.e. morphological) marking: a case in point is Modern Greek which, as we have seen (paragraph 5), has co-compounds which are clearly words, whereas hyponymic compounds are syntactic atoms but do not show morphological and phonological cohesion. The borderline between the two semantic types of coordination, i.e. hyperonym and hyponym, may be blurred in syntax and might be influenced by number, as it has been shown with the English example *my relatives and friends* but, usually, it is unambiguous in morphology: a potential exception is the Armenian example *goyavazak* 'pickpocket-bandit', where both a hyponymic and a hyperonymic readings may be possible, but the model should not be productive and frequent in the language. In languages with no morphological marking of number, there is usually no ambiguity between the hyperonymic and hyponymic reading in syntactic coordination (see the Chinese 'student(s)-worker(s)' Example, 5).

The marking patterns for number are various. In some languages with co-compounds and number marking (as e.g. some languages of India and Basque), we see a tendency to inflect compounds for plural, when they designate a sort of union between two separate entities (as in the Basque *senar-emazteak* 'husband and wife' example) and for the singular / neuter when the union of the constituents builds up a unitary notion or substance (as in Pāli *jarāmaraṇam* 'old age and death' or Basque *ur-ardoa* 'water with wine', which we already quoted before). In other languages, such as Marathi, co-compounds always behave as plurals; in some Uralic languages (e.g. Mansi, Khanty), a dual marker is added to both coordinands in natural coordination.

---

13. Bauer (2001) claims, on the basis of a 36-languages sample, evenly divided between 6 major geographical areas, that there is no areal bias in the presence or absence of *karmadhāraya*-type coordinating compounds: however, his data and ours are not readily comparable, since the category of *karmadhāraya* includes many compounds which are, in our perspective, rather attributive compounds, as we said before (5). Also, Bauer considers all word classes, wheras we focussed only on noun-noun compounds.

As for referentiality, it is interesting to note how in additive co-compounds such as the Japanese *oyako* 'father and son' separate reference may be made to each constituent, although the marking pattern of coordination is clearly morphological (and, indeed, other kinds of coordination are marked by syntactical means: *jochū-**ken**-ryōrijin* 'maid and cook'; cf. Kageyama 2009: 514). The question seems to be non-existent for hyponymic compounds, since here a single entity is designated.

As expected, we have found no examples of adversative coordination expressed in compounds in our sample, since the contrast inherent in such kind of coordination does not allow tight constructions. "Or-type" compounds seem to be rarer than "and-type" compounds; also, the latter are richer in semantic subtypes than the former.

Our survey concerned mainly nominal hyponymic compounds while in the discussion of co-compounds, instances of V-V could be easily included. In fact, hyponymic coordinating compounds do not extend to verbs in any of the languages considered, which suggests that this is a further difference between hyponymic and hyperonymic types of coordinating compounds. While the former do not easily go together with verbs, the latter do not exhibit equally strong word class restrictions.

Parasynthetic compounds
Data and theory*

Chiara Melloni and Antonietta Bisetto
University of Verona and University of Bologna

This chapter is dedicated to parasynthetic compounding, a word-formation phenomenon consisting of the merger of two lexical stems (forming a non-existent compound) with a derivational suffix. On the basis of several classes of data pertaining to Slavic and Romance, we outline a formal analysis of the phenomenon in question and show that a constructionist account, recently developed within the Construction Morphology framework, cannot be applied to a particular set of compounds. We show that a configurational analysis of these (pseudo)compound-affixed forms formulated along the lines of Ackema and Neeleman (2004) which applies a severe mapping between the morpho-syntactic and semantic structure, is not only able to account for the challenging data at issue, but also refines our comprehension of the synthetic compounding phenomena commonly attested in most I.E. languages.

1. Introduction

This chapter focuses on a class of compounds which have been dubbed 'parasynthetic compounds' because of their peculiar ternary structure (cf. Serrano Dolader 1995 and, more recently, Bisetto and Melloni 2008).

Parasynthesis is usually analysed as a derivational phenomenon consisting of the simultaneous adjunction of a prefix and a suffix to a nominal (cf. *bust-a* 'envelope', in the Italian example below) or adjectival (*dolc-e* 'sweet') base.

(1) a. im-bust-are   'to put in an envelope'
    b. ad-dolc-ire   'to sweeten'

Whatever analysis is applied to these derivatives (cf., among the many, Darmesteter 1877, Tollemache 1945, Corbin 1980, 1987, Alcoba Rueda 1987, Scalise 1994), their

---

*   This chapter is the result of research supported by the Italian Ministry of the University and Research (Bologna – PRIN Project 2005, COMPONET).

internal structure is necessarily 'ternary' because the binary steps of these forms are unattested as autonomous lexemes, as shown in (2).

(2) a. *in+busta   *bust(a)+are
    b. *a+dolce   *dolc(e)+ire

Similar properties are shared by complex forms such as English *able bodied*, or *blue eyed*. Like the parasynthetic verbs in (1), these words are ternary constructions since they are formed through the concatenation of two lexical stems and a derivational suffix. They differ from synthetic compounds, which are also ternary complexes, because they entail both compounding and derivation, which cannot be neatly separated. In other words, neither the 'compounds' formed by the two stems nor the affixed constituents are existent lexemes in the language in question (cf. *able body* and **bodied*). This is why, in accordance with Serrano Dolader (1995), we have dubbed these compound-affixed forms parasynthetic compounds.

Though similar formations are attested in several Indo-European languages, parasynthesis in compounding represents a marginal phenomenon in most Germanic and Romance languages. This blend of compounding and derivation, however, is a productive means for the formation of new lexemes in Slavic, where compounds generally exhibit ternary structures (with the exception of calques and borrowings from non-Slavic languages).

It is our goal to discuss and provide an analysis for these complex forms starting with the Germanic data, and from there we focus on a challenging set of Slavic data. Furthermore, we propose to extend the configurational analysis proposed for Slavic languages to a group of prepositional compounds in Romance languages, alternatively analyzed either as exocentric compounds or as prefixed forms, and generally understudied in the literature.[1]

This chapter is organised as follows. Section 2 contains an introduction to the phenomenon of parasynthesis showing its differences and similarities to synthetic compounding. Section 3 outlines two recent analyses of (para)synthetic compounds, one framed within Ackema & Neeleman's (2004) morpho-syntax model, the other developed within the Construction Morphology framework. Section 4 proposes a formal account of some challenging compounding patterns in Slavic languages which are not explicable in constructionist terms.[2] Section 5 deals with a set of Italian data for which a parasynthetic analysis is called again into question. In Section 6, some concluding remarks are presented.

---

1. A recent, syntactic analysis is Bok-Bennema & Kampers-Manhe (2005).
2. For discussion of other relevant data, cf. Bisetto and Melloni (2008).

2. Parasynthesis in compounding

Parasynthetic compounding phenomena share the relevant properties of the oft-debated synthetic compounding patterns, since both involve (category-changing) derivation in addition to compounding (cf. Gaeta, this volume, for thorough discussion of synthetic compounding). These two processes, however, are commonly assumed to be autonomous or independent steps in synthetic compounds, traditionally analysed as NN constructions containing a deverbal head (e.g. English *coffee maker* = *coffee* + [*make*+*er*]).[3] In this case, derivation would thus 'precede' compounding according to a synchronic perspective.[4] In parasynthetic compounds the two word formation processes, however, seem to be intrinsically fused, since the derived constituent is a bound form (-*eyed* in 3) while the complex base is not independently attested as a compound.

(3) *blue-eyed* *[blue-eye] / *[eyed]

Cases showing this mismatch are primarily found within the adjectival and nominal word-formation domains and are cross-linguistically attested, as shown by the adjectival and nominal formations in (4–5):

(4) Dut. blauwogig 'blue-eyed' *blauwog+ig / blauw +*ogig
    Eng. red-blooded *red blood+ed / red +*blooded
    Gr. kokinomalis 'redhaired' *kokin-o-mal+is / kokin-o- +*malis
    Lat. albicapillus 'white-haired' *alb-i-capill+us / albi+*capillus

(5) It. pescivendolo 'fish seller' *pescivend(ere)+olo / pesci+*vendolo
    Lat. veriverbium 'the telling of the truth' *ver(i)verb+ium / veri+*verbium
    Pol. obcokrajowiec 'foreigner' *obc(o)kraj +oc / obc(o)+*krajoc
    Sp. quinzeañera 'fifteen-year-old girl' *quinzeañ(o) +era / quinze+*añera

These forms represent bracketing paradoxes because of the mismatch between their structural makeup and the internal relation of semantic scope. The affix seems to be merged with the second constituent following its own usual selection and allomorphy patterns, thus suggesting a [α + [β + γ]] analysis, however, semantically it has scope over the complex base, supporting an opposite [[α + β] + γ] analysis. This mismatch, in fact, is what establishes a direct parallel between parasynthetic and synthetic compounding.

---

3. The synthetic compound *coffee-maker*, for instance, has been analysed as the combination of the deverbal head *maker* with the non-head *coffee* (cf. Selkirk 1982, Di Sciullo and Williams 1987 and Booij 1988), which is in turn analysed as the direct internal argument of the verb. See discussion below for a different analysis of the phenomenon.

4. Furthermore, an existing compound can be itself derived as in It. *guardarobiera* 'cloakroom attendant'. This complex form is analysed as the merger of the nominalising suffix -*ier(a)* with the existing compound *guardaroba* 'to look + stuff, wardrobe, cloakroom'.

Under the Binary Branching Hypothesis (cf. Aronoff 1976 and Booij 1977), complex forms such as *coffee maker* have in fact been subject to two alternative analyses:

(6) a. [coffee [make-er]$_\alpha$]
 b. [[coffee make]$_\beta$- er]

As mentioned above, synthetic compounds have been analysed as NN complexes, more precisely, as the combination of a deverbal head (*maker*) and a non-head (*coffee*), the latter representing the internal argument of the head's verbal base (i.e., solution 6a., proposed by Selkirk 1982, Booij 1988 and Lieber 1992). This rationale is based on the notion of 'inheritance of argument structure', proposed by Booij (1988), who argues that the deverbal noun *inherits* the internal argument of the base verb, whose thematic role (Patient / Theme) is then assigned to the non-head constituent.

Alternatively, synthetic compounds have been regarded as the merger of a NV complex with a derivational suffix (i.e., solution 6b., defended by Lieber 1983, Fabb 1984 and Sproat 1986). While this proposal guarantees a strict form-semantics mapping, as the affix has scope over the complex base, it has been criticised mainly because NV compounding is an unproductive pattern in English and other Germanic languages. In fact, *(to) coffee-make* is a non-attested and, arguably, impossible verb (Ackema and Neeleman 2004 for discussion of this point). It is also worth noting that this is precisely the situation arising in the case of *blue-eyed*, whose base *blue-eye* is not attested as a compound. Under the (6b) analysis, therefore, *coffee-maker* and *blue-eyed* would be instances of the same word formation pattern, only differing in the categorial status of their constituents.

3. Recent accounts of (para-)synthetic compounds

In recent years, two alternative accounts, developed within radically different frameworks, have innovatively reinterpreted the analysis of synthetic compounding previously proposed by Lieber (1983), Fabb (1984) and Sproat (1986). Both attempt to overcome the productivity issue posed by the unattested compound base in synthetic compounds. We will provide a short outline of these proposals which, although based on deeply divergent theoretical assumptions, exhibit converging aspects.[5]

---

5. Synthetic compounding has been analysed in syntactically-oriented frameworks (c.f., a.o., Kayne 1994, Roeper 1999, Ferrari Bridgers 2005b, Harley 2009). Though we acknowledge the theoretical relevance of these studies, we will disregard them here not only due to space limitations, but also because they are less directly related to the parasynthetic formations at issue in this chapter.

3.1 Ackema and Neeleman's analysis[6]

Ackema & Neeleman (2004) (hereafter A&N) have dedicated a great deal of attention to synthetic compounds because these complex forms constitute important evidence in favour of their idea of a competition between morphology and syntax for the generation of structures, which is one of the crucial hypotheses underlying their framework. In particular, A&N's proposal is that Phrasal Syntax and what they define 'Word Syntax' (i.e., morphology) are independent generative mechanisms, and are both able to create structures from a given set of nodes. Syntactic generation is the unmarked choice with respect to morphological generation, and the former, thus, prevails over the latter.[7] In A&N's view, morphological merger of two nodes, α and β, is only an option when there is no syntactic competitor. This situation arises under three conditions:

a. when morphological merger results in semantics that cannot be expressed by syntactic merger of two nodes, as in the case of root compounding in Germanic;
b. when either α or β is an affix which, as such, requires morphological merger;
c. when a head and a dependent element that cannot normally be merged morphologically, nevertheless show up as a morphological complex when embedded under a category-changing affix. This can be seen in the comparison between (7) and (8), where there is no actual competition between word and phrase syntax. In (8), α and β are directly merged, whereas in (7) the merger takes place between an extended projection of β and γ (i.e., a derived lexeme headed by the suffix γ, taking α as its base).

(7)

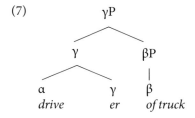

---

6. Cf. Ackema and Neeleman, this volume, for a presentation of the framework and specific discussion of synthetic compounding.

7. Competition between syntax and morphology is restricted to structures in which two nodes (α and β) are merged. Furthermore, to have competition, the semantic relation between α and β must be identical in the syntactic and morphological structures. For instance, if β is interpreted as α's adjunct in the morphological structure (cf. *code* and *colour* in *to colour-code* = to code *with* colours) but as an internal argument in the syntactic one (*to code colours*), A&N's framework predicts there will be no blocking effect by the latter over the former.

(8)

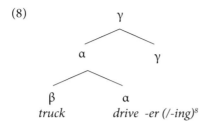

Therefore, A&N interpret synthetic compounding as the derivation of a non-free NV root compound, i.e. a complex whose merger would not be licensed in isolation. Without an affixal trigger, according to A&N, syntactic merger of the two categories would be the unmarked choice. The relevant synthetic feature consists, within this framework, of the restriction that a certain compound formation with compositional semantics is only possible in the case of a co-occurring derivational process. It is worth stressing that this rationale does not hinge on the actual occurrence of the derived form, *driver* (or *driving*), thus annulling the assumed difference between synthesis and parasynthesis in compounding. Thus, *truck driver* and *blue-eyed* would thus be subject to the same type of configurational analysis, cf. (8).

As we will see below, A&N's rationale seems to be particularly appropriate in accommodating the Slavic and Romance data at issue in this chapter.

3.2 The construction morphology rationale

Although based on a different view of the lexicon and morphology, the Construction Morphology (CM) account of parasynthetic compounding also denies the existence of a difference between synthesis and parasynthesis in compounding. Booij (2005/a, 2007) proposes to re-interpret the structural analysis provided by Lieber (1983), replacing morphological structures with word formation templates that can become fused or *conflated* under specific conditions.[9] In particular, Dutch words such as *brand-bluss-er* 'fire extinguisher' or *gif-meng-er* 'poison mixer, poisoner' would be derived, according

---

8. The reverse order of the constituents, according to A&N, indicates that the merger of α and β in (8) is morphological, in accordance with the Right-hand Head Rule (cf. Di Sciullo and Williams 1987), a morphological principle distinguishing morphological combinations from syntactic ones. Observe, however, that while the Right-hand Head Rule appears as a correct generalisation concerning headedness in Germanic complex words, it does not fully apply to Romance languages where, as pointed out by Scalise (1983), Corbin (1980, 1987) and Varela (1990a), compounding is typically left-headed (cf. It. *pesce spada* 'sword-fish', *carro bestiame* 'cattle truck').

9. Booij (this volume) explains: "In order to use the notion of conflation, we need templates or schemas for the specification of these recurrent combinations of word formation patterns. Such templates, in which both variable and lexically specified positions occur, are in fact constructional idioms at the word level, and thus provide additional evidence for a constructional approach to morphology."

to Booij (2007), by means of the conflation of NV compounding and the suffixation of -er to these compounds. In particular, it is the unification of the independently attested templates [NV]$_V$ and [V-er]$_N$ that yields the synthetic template [[NV]$_V$ -er]$_N$.

Template unification preserves the idea of a structural hierarchy in these constructs, since attachment of the suffix to a NV compound guarantees the correct semantic mapping, with the affix having semantic scope over the complex base. Booij suggests that this explanation is able to overcome the productivity problem raised by the unavailability of the NV template in isolation, as conflation would be responsible for the productivity of the unified [[NV]$_V$ -er]$_N$ template, regardless of the non-productivity of [NV]$_V$. Quoting Booij (2007: 43), 'the observed productivity boost of NV compounding in de-verbal word formation can be expressed by unification of the relevant templates.'

Concerning this point, however, we observe that if the special productivity pattern of synthetic compounding is strongly motivated in A&N's analysis, where, in a specific configuration (cf. 8), the affix licenses the morphological merger of the complex base, it surfaces as a mysterious phenomenon in the CM account, raising several questions. In particular, it is not immediately clear why a conflation pattern would trigger the productivity of a template which is unproductive by itself, and to what extent, in general, productivity plays a role in the identification of the basic constructional idioms and of the processes applying to them, within the lexicon (or *constructicon*) of a given language.

Booij's analysis of standard synthetic compounds also extends to adjectival parasynthetic compounds like the Dutch *blauwogig* 'blue-eyed' or *langharig* 'long-haired', where conflation involves the independently attested word-formation templates of [A+A]$_A$ compounds and of denominal adjectives in -*ig* (which are indeed productive constructions in Dutch). Booij maintains that °*ogig* 'eyed' is a possible well-formed word and as such it can instantiate the second stem A in the template in (9):

(9)   [A+A]$_A$ [N+*ig*]$_A$
                         \   /   relation of UNIFICATION
                      [A   [N-*ig*]$_A$]$_A$ having N with property A
                       /   \   relation of INSTANTIATION
      blauw-og-ig 'blue-eyed'   *lang-har-ig* 'long-haired'

To explain the non-occurrence of the derived constituent °*ogig*, Booij (2005/b: 218–9) invokes the pragmatic constraint of *Non Redundancy* (proposed by Ackerman & Goldberg 1996, and Goldberg & Ackerman 2001). Specifically, the non-occurrence of adjectives such as °*eyed*, °*haired*, or °*nosed* (cf. *crook-nosed*) is due to the fact that it is expected that human beings have body parts such as eyes, hair or nose, thus the coinage of such adjectives would express redundant information. A possible way to use these adjectives is to modify the base noun, in order to express a specific property of the possessed body part. And this is actually what we find in the complex forms at hand.

As we will see below, there are cases in Slavic languages where this pragmatic constraint cannot be argued to be responsible for the non-occurrence of the derived adjective.[10]

4. Parasynthesis in Slavic

In Slavic languages, complex words where compounding and derivation are simultaneously attested represent the core pattern of compounding. Compounding and derivation are considered 'simultaneous' processes in the following cases:

i. both [Stem1+Stem2] and [Stem2+affix] are non-existent lexemes,
   cf. Rus. strel   + obraz + n – yj   'arrow-shaped'
             arrow + shape + Suf.$_A$ - infl$_{MASC/SG/NOM}$
   with *strelobraz / *obraznyj;
ii. [Stem2+affix] is an independently occurring lexeme, but the suffix takes scope over the complex base, rather than just over the second stem, causing scopal ambiguity effects to arise, i.e. bracketing paradoxes, such as the following:
   Rus. železn - o + dorož + n – yj   'rail-road related'[11]
         iron$_A$ + road + Suf$_A$ - infl$_{MASC/SG/NOM}$

The second case is represented by the template in (10), with lexical stems connected by the linking vowel -o (recently analysed as a compounding marker, cf. Ralli 2008b)[12] and the concomitant presence of a derivational affix.

---

10. See also Gaeta (2006) for a similar approach to Italian and German formations.

11. The compound adjective is derived through suffixation of the lexicalised adjectival phrase *železnaja doroga*, lit. iron$_A$ road, 'rail road'. As observed by Booij (2005/b) regarding similar formations in Dutch, the derived constituent can be a possible, well-formed though non-attested word. Therefore, it can be plausibly assumed that these Slavic compounds are 'instantiations' of conflated schemas of compounding and derivation.

12. An anonymous reviewer has questioned the status of the linking element in Slavic languages, proposing a genitive Kase analysis along the lines of Ferrari Bridgers (2005/a) for *-i-* in Italian forms such as *pescivendolo*. Although we do not have an analysis for the linking element in Slavic languages, we doubt that a Kase analysis could capture the role of this element on both formal and semantic grounds. Formally, *-o(/e)-* does not coincide with the genitive suffix in most Slavic languages (which, differently from Romance languages, tend to preserve mophological Kase). There are few compounds containing a genitive marker, such as (Czech) *pomst-y-chtivy* 'revenge-gen-wanting, desirous of revenge' (Pavel Štichauer, p.c.) but the genitive marker, consistently, is *-y-*. On a semantic level, moreover, it is not clear what meaning the genitive Kase would express in Slavic compounds, since the linking element is attested in both subordinate and coordinate compounds, whose intrinsic semantic relations deeply diverge, and cannot be uniformly reduced to the possessive semantics of genitive Kase (cf. Kayne 1994).

(10) [Stem1 + linking vowel + Stem2 + derivational affix-inflection]
Rus. *kratk-o-vrem+enn-yj* 'short+time+Suf$_A$, short in time'

Slavic compounds are therefore similar to the standard cases of Germanic (and Romance) parasynthetic compounding studied in the relevant literature: either template conflations or the morphology-syntax competition could be taken as explanatory hypotheses for these patterns.[13] As we will see in the next section, however, there are problematic cases of compounding in Slavic languages that pose a major challenge for the constructionist analysis, whereas they are instead amenable to A&N's analysis.

4.1 Bahuvrīhi compounds

In most Slavic we find compound formations lacking an overt derivational suffix but taking instead an (adjectival) inflectional morpheme:

(11) [A+ **linking element** + N - infl$_A$]$_A$
Cz. *modrook-ý*   'blue-eyed'
Rus. *goluboglaz-yj* 'blue-eyed'
Pol. *niebieskook-i* 'blue-eyed'
Bul. *blakitnavok-i* 'blue-eyed'

These adjectives replicate the Indo-European pattern of *bahuvrīhi* compounds, i.e. exocentric compounds typically expressing a possessive relation:

(12) Lat.   *albicapill-us*   'white-haired'
An.Gr. ἀσπρόσαρχ-os   'with white complexion-pale face'

The *Non-Redundancy Constraint* invoked by Booij for the Dutch data cannot justify the simultaneity of compounding and derivation in this set of Slavic parasynthetic compounds. With respect to *blue eyed* or *blauwogig*, in fact, we find in Slavic languages a derived constituent instantiating a non-occurring word-formation pattern. Specifically, to become adjectives, Slavic Nouns require an overt derivational suffix. Therefore, the forms in (13) are not only non-attested but cannot be possible (i.e., well-formed) words.

(13) *[N + infl$_A$]$_A$
Cz. *ok-ý
Rus. *glaz-yj
Pol. *ok-i
Bul. *vok-i

If the CM rationale, for similar constructions, is based on the occurrence of templates of compounding [A+A] and derivation [N+Suf$_A$], the absence in most Slavic languages of a derivational pattern [N+infl$_A$]$_A$ (that is, conversion of nouns into adjectives

---

13. See Bisetto and Melloni (2008) for further discussion of this issue.

through an inflectional morpheme) represents a serious problem for the constructionist explanation.

4.2 Analysis and discussion

Although the present analysis focuses on *bahuvrīhi* and a class of (Russian) nominal compounds, most Slavic compounds fall exactly under the pattern of (para-)synthetic compounding: *free morphemes that cannot independently form a morphological complex can instead do so when embedded under a derivational affix*. In other words, certain compound formations, i.e. root compounds with compositional semantics, are only possible in the case of a co-occurring derivational process. The following patterns, all drawn from Russian, represent ternary constructions whose 'compound' base is not attested as an independent lexeme:

(14) [N+V+SufN]$_N$ *domostroenie*   'house + build + ing, house building'
                                              pis'monosec   'letter + carry + er, letter carrier'
      [A + N+ Suf$_N$]$_N$ *legkomyslie*   'light + thought + ing, superficiality'
      [Pro + N + Suf$_N$]$_N$ *svoevolie*   'own + willing + ness, stubbornness'
      [A+N + Suf$_A$]$_A$ *ravnopravnyj*   'equal + right + ing, having equal rights'
      [N+V + Suf$_A$]$_A$ *metallorežuščij*   'metal + cut + ing, metal-cutting'
      [N+N + Suf$_A$]]$_A$ *kubovidnyj*   'cube + aspect, cubiform'
      [N+V + Suf$_A$]$_A$ *bronenosnyj*   'armor + bear + ing, armor-bearing'
      [Num$_A$+ N + Suf$_A$]$_A$ *desjatikilometrovyj* 'ten + kilometer + Suf$_A$, ten kilometer long'
      [P+N+SufA]$_A$ *bezbožnyj*   'without + god + Suf$_A$, scandalous'

Independently of the (non-)existence of the derived constituents in the data in (14) (cf. *stroenie* vs. **nosec*), we emphasise that a derivational suffix is obligatorily present in these constructs. The restriction posed by (para)synthetic phenomena, i.e. the concomitant presence of a compound and a derivational, category-changing affix, is explained by A&N's analysis, which thus seems particularly appropriate for explaining the Slavic cases at issue.

Due to space limitations, the data in (14) will not be analysed here.[14] We shall start our analysis with a discussion of *bahuvrīhi* compounds, and then we move to other challenging cases of (para)synthesis in Russian.

---

14. See Bisetto and Melloni (2007 and 2008) for discussion of the challenging type of Slavic data in (14).

4.2.1 Bahuvrīhi compounds in Slavic

Let us begin with a general observation about [A+N]$_N$ compounds, specifically that this pattern, which is minimally productive in Slavic languages, is usually characterised by non-compositional semantics, in Slavic as well as in Germanic and Romance languages.

(15) Rus. suchofrukty   'dry+fruit, dry fruit'
     Pol. ostrosłup   'sharp+column/pile, pyramid'
     Bul. frensko grozde 'french+grapes, currants'
     Dut. zoethout   'sweet+wood, liquorice'
     It.   altoforno   'high+furnace, blast furnace'

Assuming A&N's idea of competition between morphology and syntax (cf. 3.1 above), the fact that the meaning of the AN complex is idiosyncratic explains why morphological merger is not blocked by syntactic merger. The latter would in fact produce a compositional result, yielding an interpretively different output.[15] The transparent meaning of the AN complex is preserved, however, in all those cases where a derivational affix attaches to the noun constituent (cf. 10). We thus contend that [A+N]$_N$ root compounding can be licensed by a (c-commanding) category-changing affix, generating a configuration in which competition between morphology and syntax is suspended, despite the compositional meaning of the [A+N]$_N$ complex.

(16)

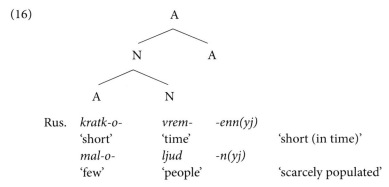

Rus. kratk-o-   vrem-   -enn(yj)
      'short'   'time'   'short (in time)'
      mal-o-   ljud   -n(yj)
      'few'   'people'   'scarcely populated'

Crucially, the structural configuration in (16) directly accounts for the semantic scope of the suffix over the complex base, rather than over the noun stem, independently of the autonomous occurrence of the denominal adjective (vremennyj 'time related' and ljudnyj 'people related'). With regard to the bahuvrīhi compounds discussed above, we propose that they instantiate the same configurational pattern, differing only in the phonological shape of the suffix which remains unspelled in the complexes in question:

(17) Rus.   [[bel   -o-   golov-] Ø-yj]   'white-headed'
            'white'   LE   'head' -Infl

---

15. Cf. case (a) in Section 3.1.

Pol. [[wąsk -o- biodr- Ø-y] 'narrow-hipped'[16]
'narrow' LE 'hip' -Infl

As commonly observed in the literature, *bahuvrīhi* compounds express a possessive semantics, which can be glossed as 'having N specified by A'. The special nature of the complex forms in (17), however, lies in the fact that the nouns in these complexes refer to inalienably possessed body-parts of humans or animals. As put forward in Bisetto and Melloni (2008), the covert nature of the adjectival suffix is descriptively captured by Haiman's principle (1983: 795): 'In no language will the phonological expression of inalienable possession be bulkier than that of alienable possession'. In a functionalist perspective, a possible explanation for this phonological pattern is proposed by Haspelmath (2004a). Specifically, Haspelmath argues that, since inalienable nouns occur in possessive constructions more often than alienable nouns do, the possessive use of inalienable nouns is more expected (that is to say, predictable) by hearers. Consequently, speakers can afford to 'economise' on inalienable constructions by means of a phonologically empty coding element. The covert nature of the suffix in parasynthetic *bahuvrīhi* compounds, expressing the possession of body parts is thus expected, at least at the processing level.[17]

Another complex built on body part nouns is $[P+N+Suf_A]_A$, where the first constituent is a preposition expressing a locative meaning. For these cases, we again suggest the configurational analysis proposed in (16) above:

(18) Rus. [[vnutri myšeč-] n-yj] 'inframuscular'
'infra muscle' Suf_A
[[pod kož-] n-yj] 'underskin'
'under skin' Suf_A

It is worth noting that, although N refers to a salient body part, the compound-affixed complex does not express a possessive meaning, but preserves the locative interpreta-

---

16. Concerning the Polish data, Szymanek (2005) points out that, whereas the derived adjective is independently attested with a specific overt derivational suffix (-ow- or -at-, cf., the Polish compound in (17) with the derivational pattern *biodr-o* 'hip' → *biodr-ow-y*), the adjective in the compound form systematically lacks an overt derivational morpheme (cf. *-biodr-y*). A similar situation holds in Czech as well (Pavel Štichauer, p.c.).

17. The adjectival affix is usually spelled when N does not refer to body parts, cf. Polish *długo+ziarn+-ist-y* 'long + grain + Suf_A, long-grain(ed)' or Russian *dvuch+etaž+n-yj* 'two + store + Suf_A, two storied'.

tion conveyed by the preposition. Accordingly, the overt realisation of the suffix is expected in these complexes.[18]

4.2.2 Nominal compounding in Russian

To conclude the present analysis of Slavic languages, we examine a set of nominal compounds denoting concrete entities, which, from a formal viewpoint, are obtained through the attachment of a range of suffixes to a complex base. The following examples are all from Russian and include nominalising affixes such as -ok, -ovik, -ka, usually employed for the expression of concrete nouns in isolation. It is noteworthy that these suffixes typically select verbal bases (cf. for instance snim-ok 'photograph' from snim-at' 'to take a photograph') or attach to the first stem of a lexicalised phrase, as in otkrytoe pis'mo 'open letter' becoming otkryt+ka 'postcard', with the noun element dropped. In the cases below, however, the base is represented by a locative (or privative) preposition merged with a nominal stem:

(19) na+perst+ok   'on + finger + Suf$_N$, thimble'
     pod+berjoz+ovik   'under + birch + Suf$_N$, brown mushroom'
     bes+kozyr+ka   'without +peak + Suf$_N$, peakless cap'

These compounds are parasynthetic constructs in virtue of the non-occurrence of the complex base and of the derived noun (*naperst /*perstok). We propose that they should be understood as cases of PN root compounds embedded under a derivational affix.

Other cases of Russian compounds (but note that similar patterns are also attested in other Slavic languages) can be reduced to the same configurational pattern: in all these constructs the presence of an overt or covert derivational affix can be seen as the trigger for the merger of stem 1 and stem 2, as suggested by the semantic scope relation of the affix over the complex base and by the non-occurrence of the derived form. In (20), for example, we find [N+V] complexes which can be overtly or covertly suffixed, but in all these cases [V+Suf$_N$] (del, vodec, datel' and čist-ka) is an unattested lexeme.

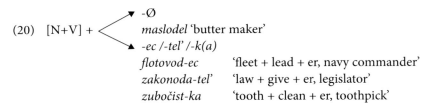

(20) [N+V] + -Ø
              maslodel 'butter maker'
              -ec /-tel' /-k(a)
              flotovod-ec   'fleet + lead + er, navy commander'
              zakonoda-tel'   'law + give + er, legislator'
              zubočist-ka   'tooth + clean + er, toothpick'

---

18. Note that when the preposition overtly expresses (lack of) possession as in the case of bez(/s) 'without,' and appears with nouns referring to body parts, the affix is again not overt, signalling the overall semantics of the complex. On the contrary, when N refers to alienably possessed objects, the adjectival suffix is present: bez+golos+yj 'without + voice + Ø$_A$, voiceless' vs. bez+bilet+n-yj 'without + ticket +Suf$_A$, ticketless'.

Molinsky (1973: 122) notes that a few Russian compounds reflect the underlying animate-inanimate opposition (cf. (21)), where the covert affix is associated with animacy). In general, however, there is no specific syntactic-semantic feature that can distinguish covert from overt agentive suffixes in these complexes:

(21) a. *duše-gub-Ø*   'soul/breath + destroy, murderer'
     duše-gub-ka   'canoe / mobile gas chamber'
   b. *xlebo-rez-Ø*   'bread + cut, bread-cutter (person)'
     xlebo-rez-ka   'bread cutter (instrument)'
   c. *kryso-lov-Ø*   'rat + catch, rat-catcher (dog)'
     kryso-lov-ka   'rat-catcher (dog, instrument)'

We thus conclude that the existence of the minimal pairs in (21) strongly supports our analysis, which argues for the necessary presence of a derivational affix as the trigger of the base root compound.

4.2.3 Preliminary conclusions

Our proposal offers a uniform analysis of the Slavic compounds previously examined as the expression of the configurational pattern of (para)synthetic compounding in (8), specifically, a merger of two stems licensed by a structurally prominent derivational suffix. Several forms can be accommodated under this configuration given the range of variation associated with the different nodes, where α (= Stem 1) can be an Adjective, Noun or Preposition (Numerals and Possessives are also possible first stems, cf. Bisetto and Melloni 2008), and β (= Stem 2) can be either a Noun or a Verb, while node γ is a c/overt Nominal or Adjectival suffix.

5. Parasynthesis in Romance languages

In this section, we develop an original account of a set of morphological constructs attested in the Romance domain, although we shall limit our analysis to Italian for reasons of space.

Not only in Germanic and Slavic languages, but also in Italian specific word formation patterns are attested that can be analysed as instances of (para)synthetic compounding. Adjectival AN complexes such as *terzomondiale* 'Third-World related' and *cortocircuitale* 'concerning short circuits' have been previously analysed by Gaeta

(2006) within the framework of Construction Morphology. In the remainder of the chapter, we instead address a different set of data, represented by [P+N]$_N$ compounds such as *soprammobile* 'ornament' and [P+N+Suf$_A$]$_A$ compounds such as *soprarenale* 'lit. over-renal'. We propose that both classes of complex forms are instances of parasynthetic compounding given that the morphological merger of the base is licensed by a c/overt derivational affix.

5.1   Italian P+N compounds

PN compounds represent a relatively small number of nouns traditionally analysed as exocentric, that is, they lack a formal and semantic head. Examples are *sottotetto* 'under+roof, attic', *soprammobile* 'over+furniture, ornament', *lungolago* 'along+lake, lakeside promenade', *senzatetto* 'without+roof, homeless'. These nouns are created via the merger of a disyllabic preposition with locative meaning (e.g. *sopra* 'over', *sotto* 'under', *lungo* 'by the side of', *senza*[19] 'without') and a noun. The N constituent, however, is not responsible for the categorial and interpretive features of the complex. Interpretively, in fact, the noun expresses the *location*, while the compound refers to the *locatum*. Furthermore, while it shares the category with the N constituent, the complex is usually characterised by a distinct set of syntactic-semantic features (cf. *sottoscala* 'under+stairs, space under a staircase', which is [−feminine] with *scala* [+feminine], and *senzatetto* 'without+roof, homeless' [+human, ±feminine] with *tetto* [-human, -feminine]). The formal and interpretive features of these compounds, thus, cannot be solely accounted for through the merger of the two constituents. We argue instead that a phonetically null nominalising constituent is the licensing head that determines the category and interpretation of the whole compound.

Similar to exocentric VN compounds (i.e. *portalettere* 'mailman'), where a (covert) nominalising suffix has been argued to bind the external argument of the V constituent (cf. Bisetto 2006), the covert nominalising suffix of PNs can be argued to bind the external argument of the P constituent. However, in contrast to VNs, which are mainly agentive, the interpretation of these constructs is extremely heterogeneous. This fact depends on the different nature of the external arguments of Vs and Ps: whereas the prototypical external argument of a verb is an Agent (in particular in the case of Italian VNs), the N external argument of a P can denote a person (*senzatetto*), a location (*sottotetto* 'loft'), a path (*lungolago*) or an object (*soprammobile*).

---

19.   PN constructions with P = *senza* can be grouped together with 'locative' compounds if, following Lakoff & Johnson (1985), one accepts that this preposition metaphorically expresses lack of location, namely 'not being in possession of' where 'possession' is interpreted as location. Also *senzadio* lit. 'without God' (pointed out to us by an anonymous reviewer) can be interpreted this way: *senzadio* refers to someone who does not 'possess' God, namely, God is not 'located' in him/her.

In accordance with A&N's proposal, we suggest that PN compounds be analysed as in (22), with a ternary structure split into a double binary branching one.

(22)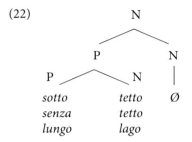

This configurational pattern differs from A&N's with respect to the head of the first merger, which we argue is the left constituent, P, rather than N in compliance not only with the left-headedness of Italian (Romance) root compounds (cf. Scalise 1984) but also with the parallel behaviour of Ps in syntactic phrases. The formal features of the complex, however, are determined by the features of the covert constituent. We wish to emphasise that the analysis of a covert affix at play in these constructs is cross-linguistically supported since, as we have seen in the preceding section, Russian has a number of PN compounds which are overtly suffixed (cf. 18), showing that the parasynthetic pattern is overtly attested in other languages.

5.2 Italian P+N+Suf$_A$ compounds

Other data for which we suggest a (para)synthetic analysis are adjectival formations such as *soprarenale* lit. 'over-renal' and *sottocrostale* 'sub-crust+Suf$_A$', often analysed as prefixed adjectives, rather than compound forms. Although *renale* and *crostale* are existing (relational) adjectives, we are inclined to propose a parasynthetic structure like that in (23) for them, hence choosing a configurational analysis which preserves the form-semantics mapping:

(23) [[sopra ren(e)] ale]$_A$
       'over' 'kidney' Suf$_A$

This analysis is motivated by the following considerations. First, as in other bracketing paradoxes, the meaning of the complex highlights the fact that the adjectival suffix (*-ale*) takes scope over the PN structure (*soprarenale* is used to refer to an X (located) over the kidney). Furthermore, with regard to the prefixal analysis of these adjectives usually found in the literature, we point out that prefixes that are phonologically identical to prepositions usually tend to lose their locative meaning, following a diachronic de-semantisation pattern cross-linguistically attested (cf., for instance, the case of Slavic prefixes in verb formations, as well as the semantic drift of Latin prefixes along their evolution into Romance). *Sopra*, for example, as a prefix, acquires a quantitative meaning, roughly, 'in excess' (cf. *sopravvalutato* 'over-estimated' which means *excessively* estimated), while *sotto* conveys an 'inferiority' meaning, as in *sottocommissione* 'subcommittee', denoting a 'committee with a *smaller* number of members'.[20] In forms such as *soprarenale*, however, the element *sopra* keeps the meaning it has in its syntactic use as a preposition. In contrast with the prefixal analysis, we therefore argue for the (unbound) lexeme status of this element.

These parasynthetic formations are similar to cases of derived compounds, such as *sopracciliare* 'superciliary' and *sovrastrutturale* 'superstructural', obtained through suffixation of an existing complex (exocentric) lexeme (*sopracciglio* 'eyebrow' and *sovrastruttura* 'superstructure' respectively). However, °*soprarene* 'over kidney' and °*sopracrosta* 'over crust' do not exist as autonomous complex lexemes, but rather are the outputs of the merger of a P and a N triggered by the adjectival affix. Hence, the concomitant concatenation of a derivational affix supports a (para)synthetic analysis for the *soprarenale*-type formations.

Within the *soprarenale* class we include adjectives such as *intrapelvico* 'intrapelvic' and *postconciliare* 'after council+Suf$_A$', formations in which the first (Latinate) constituent is usually analysed as a prefix (cf. Iacobini 2004a). These complexes too are instances of bracketing paradoxes in that they manifest a mismatch between form (24a) and meaning (24b):

(24) a. [intra$_{pref}$ [pelvico]$_A$]$_A$ [post$_{pref}$ [conciliare]$_A$]$_A$
     b. [[intra pelv(i)]-ico]$_A$ [[post concili(o)]-are]$_A$

With respect to the preceding class of data, we point out that *intra* and *post* cannot form syntactic constructions (viz. PPs), because they are *bound*, rather than free

---

20. This explains why forms such as *sottocultura* 'subculture' and *sottosviluppo* 'underdevelopment', pointed out to us by an anonymous reviewer, are excluded from the present analysis. These words are not compounds, but prefixed nouns (the head constituent is the noun) where the first element, *sotto*, does not preserve its (prepositional) locative meaning but assumes the quantitative meaning 'inferior/minor': a *sottocultura* is a 'culture of a minor level', and does not refer to something located 'under the culture'. From a formal viewpoint, *sotto*, being a prefix, rather than a lexical element, does not retain the property of being a two-argument element in such constructions (cf. Bisetto & Scalise 2007).

prepositions. The corresponding free prepositions are *dentro* 'inside' and *dopo* 'after' respectively, which predominantly appear in PPs (e.g. *dentro la pelvi* 'in/to the pelvis', *dopo il concilio* 'after the Council' vs. **intra la pelvi* and **post il concilio*). Bound Ps, in fact, can only merge with a noun in morphological constructions when licensed by a derivational suffix. They are thus ternary constructions that give rise to (para)synthetic compounds. In A&N's framework, which assumes a separation between morphological structure and phonological form (regulated by a set of rules for the structure-PF mapping), the PF choice of bound, rather than free Ps should be seen as an indicator of the morphological status of these constructs. In other words, if the lexicon of a given language is provided with stems that are marked as requiring morphological rather than syntactic merger, we expect that these stems will be chosen in parasynthetic compounds to express the morphological status of these objects.

Among ternary, parasynthetic, formations we also include the adjectival constructions involving a neoclassical (ancient Greek or Latin) numeral, such as *bisillabo* 'disyllabic' (which has a derived mate: *bisillabico*), *bilingue* 'bilingual', *monoalbero* 'single-shaft', and *monoposto* 'single-seat'. The nouns *lingue*, *albero* and *posto* cannot be interpreted as adjectives in isolation and the (bound) numerals (*bi-*, *mono-*) cannot be merged with a noun to form a free-standing endocentric (nominal) compound. Consequently, for all these constructs, we argue in favour of a parasynthetic analysis: specifically, these forms can only surface if a c/overt adjectival affix licenses and heads the whole complex.

(25)

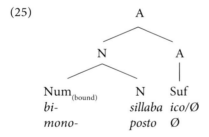

Specifically, (25) shows that a noun can merge with a bound numeral and be used as an adjective only if a derivational affix, responsible for both categorisation and merging of the two lexemes, is hypothesised. The rationale of the overt vs. covert nature of the licensing suffix is an issue that remains for future research.

6. Conclusions

The theoretical issue raised by (para)synthetic compounding is not new in morphological theory. In this chapter, however, we have aimed to show that a formal account of a challenging set of data, drawn from Slavic and Romance languages (i.e. Italian), can contribute to our understanding of synthetic compounding phenomena in general terms. Specifically, we have proposed that (para-)synthesis in compounding, far from being restricted to AN compound adjectives such as *blue-eyed*, can instead accommodate several complex forms, ranging from common bracketing paradoxes to alleged exocentric compounds (alternatively analyzed, in the relevant literature, as prefixed words).

The discussion began with emphasising the parallelism between deverbal synthetic compounds such as English *truck driver / truck driving* and denominal parasynthetic compounds in other Germanic languages. Both classes of data are amenable to an analysis along the lines of A&N's (2004) proposal (cf. also Lieber 1983, Fabb 1984 and Sproat 1986), i.e., a morphological merger of two stems (with compositional semantics) which is licensed by the presence of a category-changing affix. We have shown that a constructionist approach not only fails to account for the productivity issue posed by deverbal synthetic compounds, but it also cannot easily account for the class of Slavic *bahuvrīhi* compounds. We have therefore implemented A&N's analysis of synthetic compounding, extending the relevant configurational pattern to other Slavic and Romance (i.e. Italian) data.

Since it supports A&N's view of the architecture of language, the analysis outlined in this chapter argues in favour of a competition between syntax and morphology or, in other words, between syntax above and below X^0, where the latter emerges as a last-resort generative system activated under specific conditions (cf. Ackema & Neeleman, 2004 and this volume). In particular, from this perspective, parasynthetic compounding surfaces as one of the relevant configurations in which the morphological merger of two elements does not compete with (hence, is not blocked by) the syntactic merger because it is embedded under a structurally prominent affixal head.

Synthetic compounds
With special reference to German*

Livio Gaeta
University of Naples "Federico II"

This chapter focuses on a traditional issue of word formation, namely synthetic compounds. The three basic approaches to the question will be reviewed and analyzed with the help of a large text corpus. The latter is of paramount importance for the analysis because dictionaries usually are not reliable for investigating highly productive word formation patterns and especially German compounding. It is shown that purely syntactic approaches do not cope well with the data, whereas a lexical approach like Construction Morphology is able to grasp the fine-grained distributional properties displayed by compounds. Furthermore, the corpus-based analysis allows us to shed some light on the complex network of semantic properties guiding the selective solidarity between deverbal head and nominal modifier by representing argument structure as a bundle of Dowty's base-roles.

1. Introduction

Synthetic compounds have a long history in the grammatical terminology, although the concepts of synthesis and of its cognate parasynthesis have been used with varying success in the different linguistic traditions. For instance, while in Italy (and partially in France), the concept of parasynthesis is fairly well established, the exact correspondents of the Italian parasynthetic derivatives are completely neglected in the English and German tradition – at least in modern times. On the other hand, our main object of investigation, namely synthetic compounds, are either completely neglected or simply assigned to compounding in Italy (and in France). To understand what is synthetic in a synthetic compound, it is usually referred to a double operation which

---

* This chapter results from a research developed within the PRIN-project COMPONET co-ordinated by Sergio Scalise (2005–07). I am deeply indebted with the editors and with an anonymous reviewer for helpful comments. Needless to say, opinions expressed and remaining mistakes are of my own responsability.

seems to take place at once: an operation of compound formation, in which the verb/
noun relation naturally looks like being of an argumental nature, and an operation of
deverbal noun formation. The latter may give rise to agent or action nouns, as in the
German examples *Taxifahrer* 'taxi driver' and *Wasserladung* 'water loading'.

Actually, this interpretation of synthesis slightly diverges from the old grammatical usage, which basically translates into linguistic parlance the Kantian concept of synthetic judgements. The latter are distinct from the analythic ones because they imply the increase of the information content of the judgement, or assertion. Well aware of this usage, Tollemache (1945: 9) writes:

> "Se prendiamo a esaminare un composto greco per es. l'aggettivo θεοφιλής, ci accorgiamo che esso si compone di due temi forniti di desinenza aggettivale. Se proseguiamo il nostro studio, vedremo che da una parte è la desinenza che determina la natura grammaticale del nuovo composto, e che dell'altra questo è sintetico, contiene, cioè, più idee di quelle inerenti ai soli membri componenti ... Ora, poiché per queste due proprietà esso si sottrae alle regole ordinarie della sintassi, i grammatici lo denominano asintattico".[1]

The part of the definition which is reminiscent of Kant's synthetic judgement refers to the fact that θεοφιλής 'dear to the gods' contains more ideas than those inherent in the single compound members. By this we can understand the argumental relation between head and modifier in the compound as in *Taxifahrer* above. On the other hand, the grammatical problem raised by θεοφιλής is given by the fact that the derivational operation causes the coming into existence of a new combination of morphemes, in that *φιλής as such is not attested, whereas the adjective φίλος 'dear' occurs. This word formation mechanism is termed asyntactic because it cannot be simply explained away as resulting from the juxtaposition of morphemes, which is typical of a number of other compounds like Latin *respublica* 'republic', *terraemotus* 'earthquake', etc. (cf. Gaeta 2008). The latter sort of compounds is accordingly called syntactic and analytic. Thus, we have two different aspects of synthesis: on the one hand, a semantic "more", which is the argumental relation between the members, and on the other a formal "more", which is the special combination of morphemes, which does not occur outside of the synthetic formation. This latter aspect is shared by the so-called parasynthetic formations like It. *in-forn-are* 'to put into the oven'.[2]

---

1. [If we examine a Greek compound like the adj. θεοφιλής, we notice that it consists of two themes provided with an adjectival desinence. If we proceed with the analysis, we observe that on the one hand it is the desinence which determines the grammatical nature of the new compound, and on the other it is synthetic, namely, it contains more ideas than those inherent in the single compound members ... Now, since these two properties keep this compound distinct from the normal rules of syntax, the grammarians call it asyntactic] (my translation).

2. Notice that since in the French tradition (cf. Arnaud 2004) complex words containing prepositions or particles (i.e., prefixes) are assigned to compounds, it turns out that what in Italy is considered to be a parasynthetic derivative is assigned to (para-)synthetic compounding in France.

At least, three possible analyses have been suggested to account for the simultaneous double operation traditionally labeled synthesis:
– Incorporation, i.e. lexical derivation via suffixation of a verb;
– Lexical derivation and subsequent composition;
– Lexical derivation via suffixation of a word group.

In what follows I will review the three different approaches with the aim of (i) establishing their adequacy to cope with synthesis and (ii) considering the theoretical implications which result from it. I will take German as main object of the investigation, because this language is traditionally known to be particularly rich in compounds. Furthermore, I could have access at large text corpora which will provide the empirical basis of my analysis. This is an essential aspect of the research, because corpora may help us overcome a general difficulty connected with the investigation of compounds and more in general with any extremely productive word formation pattern. If one does not want to rely solely on speakers' intuition and dictionaries are used, the problem arises that the latter usually discard the completely regular and transparent formations, because "dictionary-users need not check those words whose meaning is entirely predictable from its elements, which by definition is the case with productive formations" (Plag 1999: 96). In what follows, I will make use of a large text corpus (DEWAC01) developed within the Wacky-Project (cf. Bernardini, Baroni & Evert 2006) and containing about 170 million tokens extracted from the Web. Even though the reliability of the corpus is not optimal, in that it is difficult to evaluate a Web-corpus in terms of text types and distribution, its large size allows me to aspire to a certain significance of the results.

2. Incorporation in German?

Because of the enhanced polysynthetic potential exploited in the course of the German linguistic history (cf. Wurzel 1996), several proposals have been made for explaining synthetic compounds with the help of a mechanism of incorporation. This implies that the argumental relation between head and modifier is accounted for by making reference to an intermediate derivational stage, in which a verbal compound is generated. In fact, verbal compounds are usually considered to be the main characteristics of incorporating languages (cf. Aikhenvald 2007). There are two different versions of this approach, a radical and a moderate one.

The generalized incorporation suggested by Siebert (1999) translates the traditional idea of synthesis, which was asyntactic as shown above, into a strictly syntactic view. Morphology is equated with syntax: there are no (X-bar) principles specific for morphology. Accordingly, synthetic compounds are the result of syntactic head-movement, as depicted below (1999: 127):

(1) [ein [Roman$_i$leser [[t$_i$]$_{NP}$]$_{DP}$]$_{NP}$]$_{DP}$

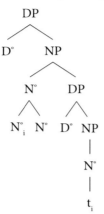

The structural difference between a compound like *Romanleser* 'novel reader' and the corresponding phrase *der Leser des Romans* 'the reader of the novel' is merely given by the head-to-head movement of *Roman* to a Chomsky-adjoined higher node (the sister position of the DP). This extends to all compounds, independent of the deverbal nature of the head. Thus, a similar structural analysis is suggested for a compound like *Romanautor* 'novel author' with respect to the phrase *der Autor des Romans* 'the author of the novel', in which the head *Autor* cannot be claimed to be deverbal. This approach implies that the traditional difference between synthetic and analytic compounds is lost, and that every compound is taken to be synthetic. Moreover, incorporation is taken to occur independently of the true formation of a verbal compound.

Siebert tries to find support for her approach by making reference to general properties of incorporation which are supposed to be relevant for German compounds. Thus, Baker's (1988: 64) Government Transparency Corollary is called into question, whereby "[a] lexical category which has an item incorporated into it governs everything which the incorporated item governed in its original structural position". The effect of this corollary are taken to be mirrored in the compound *der Härte$_i$grad t$_i$ des Wassers* 'the degree of hardness of water' which corresponds to the phrase [*der Grad* [[*der Härte* [*des Wassers*]]]. However, this is not generally true, as shown by the impossibility of **Direktor$_i$foto t$_i$ der Schule* 'the photo of the director of the school'. To cope with this, Siebert's (1999: 142) tentative answer is to relate the effect of the corollary to the transparency of the head. Only abstract nouns are transparent enough to allow for argument inheritance, as shown by the following Google-examples:

(2) a. *In den Worten von Chinas Verhandlungs$_i$leiter t$_i$ mit der WTO, Long Yongtu,...*
'In the words of China's leader of the negotiation with the WTO, Long Yongtu,...'

b. *Was klingt wie eine Einladung für Piraten, sich Geiseln als unkomplizierte Einnahmequelle zu suchen, hat seinen Sinn im Krisenmanagement und der Verhandlungs₁leitung t₁ mit den Entführern.*
'What sounds as an invitation for pirats to look for hostages as an uncomplicated source of income, makes sense in crisis management and in the conduction of the negotiation with the kidnappers'.

Notice that this also implies that not every compound can be taken to be synthetic, but only those which are sensitive to argument structure, i.e. abstract nouns. In other words, a mechanism of lexical derivation must be postulated for at least a subset of compounds, although we are not precisely told which sort of compounds are lexically or syntactically derived.[3] In fact, while on the one hand a deadjectival noun like *Härte* is claimed to be sensitive to argumental inheritance, on the other a simplex like *Autor* must be taken to display an intrinsic argument structure, which is exploited at a syntactic level.

Finally, it can be objected against this strictly syntactic view that a governed adjective cannot be moved to a higher position, nor can it stay *in situ*, thus violating Baker's (1988) corollary:

(3) a. *Versuch eines tödlichen Attentats auf den Papst*
'attempt at an assassination of the pope'
b. **tödlicher₁ Attentats₁versuch t₁ t₁ auf den Papst*
c. **Attentats₁versuch tödlichen t₁ auf den Papst*

Notice that this restriction doesn't apply when the allegedly incorporated noun is a complex lexical unit like *generative Grammatiktheorie* 'generative grammar theory', which gives rise to a classical example of bracketing paradox (cf. Spencer 1991: 398–417). These paradoxes can only be explained by making reference to an autonomous lexical status of the phrase *generative Grammatik*, which is then combined into a compound (cf. Schlücker and Hüning 2009). In other words, *tödliches Attentat* is not lexical enough to give rise to such a bracketing paradox. Thus, the abstractness of the head cannot be the reason for incorporation to take place. Rather, the lexical status of the modifier is of relevance.

Besides the problems relating to the overgeneration induced by this approach, which also force us to assume a parallel mechanism of lexical compounding, there are other classical issues traditionally arisig from such strictly syntactic analyses, and in particular linking elements (*Fugenelemente*, cf. Fuhrhop 1996 among others). In this light, the general question for a strictly syntactic approach to compounds sounds: If

---

3. As pointed out by an anonymous reviewer, this is generally true for all compounds, because there are ambiguities between readings requiring the non-head as an argument and readings where this does not make sense. For instance, in a compound like *Alkoholfahrer* the non-argumental reading 'drunken driver' is clearly preferred over the argumental 'driver who transports alcohol', whereas in *Schmuckräuber* the argumental reading 'someone who robs jewellery' is preferred over the non-argumental 'thief wearing jewellery'.

compounding can be reduced to a purely syntactic operation, where are the allomorphic aspects of word formation to be dealt with? An answer can be sought in an approach sharing the separation hypothesis like split morphology, in which the actual derivation of compounds is conceived as separated from its "phonological" implementation (cf. Anderson 1992, Beard 1995). However, besides the standard arguments against split morphology (cf. Booij 1994), a specific problem is provided by German linking elements. On the one hand, there are cases which are productive and not relatable to the inflectional properties of lexical items like the so-called unparadigmic -s-: [[[V]-*ung*]s[N ~ Adj]$_Z$]$_Z$ (cf. *Bildungssystem* 'education system', *erklärungsbereit* 'ready to explain'). On the other, there are cases which appear to be strictly related to the inflectional properties of the modifiers, and also give rise to meaning effects: *Buchdecke* 'book cover' vs. *Bücherregal* 'books-shelf' (cf. Libben, Boniecki, Martha, Mittermann, Korecky-Kröll & Dressler 2009). It is not trivial to treat these alternations in a strictly split-morphology approach. At least, inherent vs. contextual inflection should be distinguished (cf. Booij 1996 and the discussion there).

Although similar objections of a formal nature apply to Rivet's (1999) moderate approach to incorporation, let us briefly review it, because it has at least the advantage of assuming incorporation only for deverbal nouns via an intermediate stage of verbal compounding:

(4) [$_N$ [$_V$ *Roman*$_N$ *les*$_V$] -*er*$_{NAf}$]

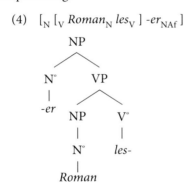

The crucial assumption in this approach is the empty intermediate step of a verb like **romanlesen*. Evidence in support of this analysis is claimed to come from other cases, in which the verbal compound is attested like *haushalten* 'to economize', *ehebrechen* 'to commit adultery', etc. (cf. Wurzel 1998 for a detailed investigation). Moreover, Rivet observes that in spite of the nonoccurrence of **romanlesen* as a verb, its nominalized form is attested, as in the following Google-example:

(5) *Hier führt Kant aus, daß das Romanlesen die Einheit des Denkens aufhebt.*
    'Here Kant points out that reading novels destroys the unity of thought'.

This is surely true, but there is general consensus (cf. Wurzel 1998) that it is the nominal compound that provides the trigger for backderiving a verb, and not the other way around. This explains fairly well the fact that only in a restricted number of cases a verbal compound is attested in the face of the large amount of nominal compounds headed by a deverbal noun or a nominalized infinitive. Thus, adopting Rivet's approach flows us again into the sea of overgeneration.[4]

3. Lexical derivation and subsequent compounding

A second way to deal with the two-faced nature of synthetic compounds is via derivation followed by compounding. Thus, a synthetic compound is taken to have the format $[[N][V\text{-}Suff]_Y]_Y$. As for the argumental relation between head and modifier, two different options are available: either lexical derivation is coupled with a syntax-driven operation which is responsible for argument inheritance, or argument inheritance simply results from semantics.

Oshita (1995: 180) adopts the first approach, and provides a lexico-syntactic definition of synthetic compound, which is "[a] compound whose nonhead satisfies the obligatory argument requirement of the head, irrespective of the latter's morphological origin". In his mind, English synthetic compounds like *whale-hunting* are accounted for by an alteration of the argument structure of the input verb, which is not suppressed by the morphological process:

(6) Suffixation of *-ing* (complex event)
    a. Morphological Process: $]_V \text{-}ing]_N$
    b. A-Structure Alteration: $(x\,(y)) \rightarrow Ev\,(x = \%\,(y))$

Accordingly, "[t]he a-structure is retained, except that the original (external) argument x is now suppressed. The remaining argument y still needs to be projected" (Oshita 1995: 185). Notice that in this view only gerunds form synthetic compounds in English, whereas the cases like *taxi driver* are not synthetic, in that the head/modifier relation is not argumental. In the following representation "[b] expresses the nullification of the original a-structure with the angle brackets" (Oshita 1995: 186):

(7) Suffixation of *-er*
    a. Morphological Process: $]_V \text{-}er]_N$
    b. A-Structure Alteration: $(x\,(y)) \rightarrow R = x\,\langle(x\,(y))\rangle$

Extending this view to German compounds, however, leads us into troubles, because both sorts of compounds manifest the possibility of preserving the subcategorization properties of the deverbal nouns, as we have seen above in (2).

Another problem of this approach is the role played by the so-called internal argument y, which – in Oshita's mind – basically is the direct object of transitive or the

---

[4]. There are other problems related to Rivet's approach, e.g. concerning an alleged condition on stress, but they will not be discussed here for the sake of brevity.

subject of unaccusative verbs. Accordingly, it should be automatically selected, provided that the argument structure of the verb displays it. As pointed out by Maling (2001: 455), however, this is not the case because of a number of transitive verbs which do not freely form synthetic compounds:[5]

(8) *Krankenbesucher   'one who visits the sick'
    *Königbediener   'one who serves a king'
    *Gasteinlader   'one who invites a guest'
    *Richterbitter   'one who pleads the judge'

She argues that this is due to the semantic role associated with the direct object, which implies that the argument structure must be much richer than the rather poor frame based on syntactic functions suggested by Oshita. The semantic roles expressed in the argument structure determine the selectional restrictions of the synthetic compounds. In this light, internal arguments are not all equal: those linked with a goal role (i.e., in her view: recipients, experiencers and beneficiaries) encoded as accusative cannot form synthetic compounds.

In order to verify the suggestion that argument inheritance is sensitive to the semantic roles encoded by the syntactic functions, several verbs selecting a goal argument as a direct object were investigated in the corpus DEWAC01. The two verbs *einladen* 'to invite' and *besuchen* 'to visit' are representative respectively for a three-place predicate in which the direct object is linked with a goal and a further locative role is present, and for a two-place predicate in which the direct object is linked either with a goal or a locative:

(9) a. *Karl hat seinen   Freund zu einer Party eingeladen.*
       Karl has his-ACC friend to a-DAT party invited
       'Karl has invited his friend to a party'.

    b. *Karl hat seinen   Freund besucht.*
       Karl has his-ACC friend visited
       'Karl has visited his friend'.

These findings are interesting from a double perspective. On the one hand, Maling's idea that semantic roles play a role in forming synthetic compounds seems to be confirmed, in that the selection clearly displays a preference for locatives instead of beneficiaries. On the other hand, this also requires to extend the idea that it's not argument selection that is relevant within a synthetic compound, but rather the semantics of the arguments involved. Thus, locatives are clearly preferred over beneficiaries, so that in the few divergent cases a locative interpretation is contextually available. This may give

---

5. This doesn't exclude that such compounds may be sporadically attested, as in the Google-example: *Der Krankenbesucher von der Personalabteilung hat heute versucht mit Ihnen zu sprechen* 'The visitor of the sicks from the personnel division has tried today to talk to you'. I thank an anonymous reviewer for this observation. As will be shown below, a corpus analysis is meant to partially solve the question of what is possible (and attested) and what is marginal or unattested.

Table 1. Synthetic compounds formed from *einladen* 'invite' and *besuchen* 'visit' in DEWAC01

[[X] *einlader*]	2	Locative: *Volksfest*- 'inviter to folk fests'	1
		Others: *Gefälligkeits*- 'pleasure i.'	1
[X [*einladung*]]	20	Agent: *Regierungs*- 'government's invitation'	1
		Beneficiary: *Selbst*- 'self i.', *Presse*- 'i. for the press'	2
		Locative: *Hochzeits*- 'i. to the wedding', *Konzert*- 'i. to a concert'	16
		Others: *Ferien*- 'i. during the holidays'	1
[N [*besucher*]]	166	Locative: *Konzert*- 'visitor of concerts', *Wien*- 'v. of Vienna'	157
		Others: *Durchschnitts*- 'average v.', *Zufalls*- 'occasional v.'	8
		Recipient: *Prostituierten*- 'v. of prostitutes'	1

rise to meaning effects like with *Prostituiertenbesucher* 'visitor of prostitutes', the only case of recipient in Table 1, in which prostitutes are degraded to a sort of locative!

Furthermore, notice that the preference for locatives over beneficiaries is independent of the syntactic function encoding the semantic role: it can be a direct object as in the case of *besuchen* or a prepositional object as in the case of *einladen*. This finding is at odds with most syntactically-oriented treatments of synthetic compounds, e.g. those based on incorporation, which usually allows only for structural cases to undergo head-to-head-movement of the kind depicted above, excluding the rest of the argument structure. Clearly, it is always possible to discard compounds like *Volksfesteinlader* 'inviter to public festivals' as generated via a different mechanism, which excludes the intervention of the reference to argument structure. This is also the line taken by Siebert and Oshita, as we have seen above. However, in the light of the argumental nature of the role encoded by the modifier, this move does not help much in assessing the status of these compounds, because it simply stipulates them to be different.

If semantics plays a crucial role in determining the selective possibilities of synthetic compounds, the question arises as for which sort of semantics is required. In this regard, Maling's view does not make predictions about the fact that except for beneficiaries the other semantic roles which are quite low in the thematic hierarchy are fairly well attested.

Instead of assuming a categorical restriction for goals as suggested by Maling, one may try a different approach to argument structure along the lines proposed by Primus

(1999).⁶ She distinguishes three main proto-roles, which are hierarchically ordered, by making reference to Dowty's (1991) base-roles: Agent > Recipient > Patient. The latter reference is crucial for establishing such a hierarchy, in that a recipient is defined as the "first participant of a thematic predicate and this predicate is embedded in the thematic representation of the second participant of a higher thematic predicate such as CONTROL or CAUSE. The first property also characterizes Proto-Agents, the second property also specifies Proto-Patients" (Primus 1999: 55). This idea can be illustrated by the following representation which characterizes in broad terms the argument structure of two verbs displaying respectively recipients and beneficiaries:

(10) a. *Hans gab seiner Frau einen Apfel.*
Hans gave his-DAT wife a-ACC apple
'Hans gave his wife an apple'.
$\forall x \forall y \forall z [\text{GIVE}(x,y,z) \rightarrow \text{P-CONTROL}(x, \text{BECOME}(\text{POSS}(y, z)))]$

b. *Peter half seiner Frau.*
Peter helped his-DAT wife
'Peter helped his wife'.
$\forall x \forall y [\text{HELP}(x,y) \rightarrow \text{P-CONTROL}(x, \text{BECOME}(\text{EXPER}(y)))]$

This approach allows us to look at semantic roles as bundles of interacting semantic properties or predicates. Accordingly, the semantic roles "are not distinguished by different basic thematic predicates, but only by their dependency relative to each other" (Primus 1999: 52). On this basis, we can formulate a preference to account for the tendency observed above for the selection of semantic roles which are quite low in the thematic hierarchy. Namely, the acceptability of synthetic compounds increases with the increase of the distance of the involved argument from the agentive prototype, which is defined as +human, +intentional, +individual, or, in Dowty's terms, which occurs as first argument of the highest base-roles.

From this preference, two predictions follow. The first prediction foresees that modifiers encoding semantic roles which are quite distant from the agentive prototype should be allowed in a synthetic compound. This can be shown to hold true on the basis of synthetic compounds containing verbs like *teilnehmen* 'to participate' and *fahnden* 'to search'. In the case of *teilnehmen*, the second argument encodes a locative role via a prepositional phrase, while the second argument of *fahnden* is a patient, encoded as a prepositional phrase:

(11) a. *Karl hat an der Tagung teilgenommen.*
Karl has at the-DAT conference participated
'Karl has participated at the conference'.

---

6. See Szigeti (2002) for an approach which also goes beyond mere argument inheritance in that it reflects the connection between word formation and the generation of concepts.

b. *Die Polizei hat nach dem gestohlenen Geld gefahndet.*
   The police has after the-DAT stolen money searched
   'The police has searched for the stolen money'.

As shown in Table 2, modifiers encoding semantic roles which are quite distant from the agentive proto-roles are in fact richly attested, irrespective of the syntactic function (direct or prepositional object, see also Table 1) present in the argument structure of the base verb.

The second prediction entails that dative-marked arguments should not be categorically excluded. Rather, they should be possible, displaying the same pattern observed so far of distance from a prototypical agent role. Recall that this is in contrast with what is claimed by Maling (2001), who sees a categorical restriction on the occurrence of the goal role in synthetic compounds. To assess this question, a detailed analysis of the synthetic compounds headed by the *-er*-derivatives of a typical dative-verb like *helfen* 'to help' proves useful (cf. (10b) above).

Although the majority of modifiers selects locatives (either in a concrete or in an abstract sense), a significant number of beneficiaries is attested. However, if we look at the single cases, we observe that they are distributed along well-defined semantic classes, which can be nicely captured by the idea laid down above of an agentive prototype characterized by a number of semantic properties. Recall that the preference entails that deviations are considered to be possible, but should accumulate at the margin of the prototype, thus displaying prototypical properties like + human, + intentional, + individual to a reduced degree. The beneficiaries occurring as modifiers

Table 2. Synthetic compounds formed from *teilnehmen* 'participate' and *fahnden* 'search' in DEWAC01

[[N] *teilnehmer*]	271	Locative:	259
		Kongress- 'congress participant', *Safari-* 'safari p.'	
		Copulative:	4
		Laien- 'lay p.', *Pilot-* 'pilot p.'	
		Others:	8
		Dauer- 'permanent p.', *Fach-* 'professional p.'	
[X [*fahnder*]]	23	Patient:	19
		Drogen- 'drug searcher', *Kunst-* 'art s.'	
		Others:	4
		Ziel- 'targeted s.', *Polizei-* 'police's s.'	
[N [*fahndung*]]	33	Agent:	2
		Interpol- 'interpol search', *Polizei-* 'police s.'	
		Patient: *Drogen-* 'drug s.', *Terroristen-* 'terrorists s.'	21
		Others:	10
		Serien- 'serial s.', *Sofort-* 'immediate s.'	

Table 3. Synthetic compounds formed from *helfen* 'help' in DEWAC01

[[N] *helfer*]	184	Beneficiary	22
		Self compound: *Helfershelfer* 'accomplice'	
		Individuals: *Arzt-* 'doctor's assistant', *Pfarr-* 'pastor's a.', *Teufels-* 'devil's a.'	
		Groups: *Alten-* 'elderly a.', *Behinderten-* 'handicapped a.', *Flüchtlings-* 'refugee's a.', *Jugendgruppen-* 'youth a.', *Suchtkranken-* 'addict a.'	
		Collectives: *Gemeinde-* 'community a.', *Jugend-* 'youth a.', *Familien-* 'family a.', *Gestapo-*, *Luftwaffen-* 'air force a.', *Marine-* 'marine a.', *Nachbarschafts-* 'neighborhood a.', *Partei-* 'party a.', *Polizei-* 'police a.', *Rotkreuz-* 'Red Cross a.'	
		Abstracts: *Geist-* 'spirit helper'	
		Copulative	6
		Laien- 'lay assistant', *Bäcker-* 'a. baker', *Drucker-* 'a. printer', *Koch-* 'a. cook', *Maler-* 'a. painter', *Schreiner-* 'a. carpenter'	
		Abstract goal	107
		Locative	30
		Others	19

headed by *Helfer* are reported in Table 3. Apart from the self compound *Helfershelfer*, which is quite opaque, the modifiers are mainly given by groups (mostly formed by non-intentional individuals, like *Behinderte* or *Flüchtling*), or collectives. Notice that the only three cases of modifiers constituted by individuals are peculiar in that they might be partially treated on a par with what I tentatively classified as copulative compounds in Table 3 because their meaning comes close to be intersective rather than subordinative.[7] Thus, while an *Arzthelfer* cannot be categorized as a doctor, because it lacks some essential properties for being considered a doctor (for instance a completed degree), a *Kochhelfer* can be considered copulative if we perceive an assistant cook to be a cook, although still an apprentice. And, we can discuss whether a *Teufelshelfer* has undergone the process of becoming completely demonic or not.

Notice finally that most cases of modifiers headed by *Helfer* are abstract goals, like *Pflegehelfer* 'cure helper' or *Terrorhelfer* 'terror helper'. While this copes fairly well with the approach adopted here, because abstract goals are quite distant from the agentive prototype, this is problematic both for Maling's view and for the syntactically-based approaches which refers to incorporation. In fact, on the one hand an abstract goal should be categorically excluded anyway, unless it is considered a sort of locative, which is hard to claim in view of true cases of locatives like *Küchenhelfer* 'kitchen assistant'. On the other, such abstract roles are likely to encode true arguments, and not

---

7. See the discussion in Gaeta & Ricca (2009) about the continuum between the two different compound types.

merely adjuncts, as shown by the following Google-examples, in which the dative-marked argument is flanked by an instance of true adjunct:

(12) a. *Wird das der Pflege helfen [...]?*
'Will this help the cure?'
b. *Kinder können bei der Pflege helfen.*
'(lit.) Children can help at the cure'

This evidence supports the view of a semantic approach to synthetic compounds which is sensitive to the argument structure of the base verb. The argument structure must be understood in a wide sense, namely taking into consideration the semantic roles involved in the conceptualization of the event. The thematic hierarchy, irrespective of the syntactic coding, is a good predictor of synthetic compounds formation.

4. Lexical derivation via suffixation of a word group

Let us discuss the third possible approach to synthetic compounds, which is in a way the mirror-image of the incorporation approach depicted above, namely the lexical derivation via suffixation of a word group: $[[X\ Y]_Y\ Z]_Z$. Traditionally (cf. Erben 2006: 37–38), two types are distinguished in dependence of the relation between X and Y. This can be of a morphological or of a syntactic nature:

(13) a. *Zusammenbildung*: [[*Klavier-spiel*] *-er*] 'piano player'
b. *Zusammenrückung*: [[*saure Gurken*]*zeit*] 'time of sour gherkins'

In (13a) the synthetic compound results from the compounding of *Klavier* and *Spieler*. However, via a mechanism of backderivation a verb *klavierspielen* 'to play piano' is derived as hinted at above, which can then be reanalyzed as the base of *Klavierspieler*. The case of the so-called *Zusammenrückung* reminds us of the bracketing paradoxes mentioned above. The remarkable property here is that the adjective *sauer* 'sour' syntactically modifies the head *Zeit* (cf. *das Ende der sauren Gurkenzeit* 'the end of the time of sour gherkins', in which the adjective inflects in agreement with the head), but it clearly forms an onomasiological unit with the modifier *Gurke* 'gherkin' which must be stored as such in the lexicon.

We already pointed out above that backderivation has to be preferred over incorporation as a viable solution because the latter gives rise to severe problems of overgeneration, whereas on the other hand backderived verbs only occur in the presence of a nominal compound. The problem is that we also find cases in which a synthetic compound occurs which cannot be explained away as resulting from compounding, but needs to refer directly to a deverbal derivation. Thus, in *Todsagung* 'declaration of death' and *Verhaftnehmung* 'arrest' no deverbal nouns like **Sagung* or **Nehmung* occur based on *sagen* 'to say' and *nehmen* 'to take'.

Recently, research developed within the framework of Construction Morphology (Booij 2005, Gaeta 2006) has suggested to explain similar facts by making crucial reference to the idea of a rich lexicon, which contains not only idiomaticized expressions, but any kind of entrenched unit. On this basis, abstract schemas are analogically extracted, which may also be partially elaborated, and conflated with other schemas of a different nature. Thus, synthetic compounds like *Todsagung* result from the conflation of the schemas of compounding and of suffixation of abstract nouns:

(14) $[X\ X]_N$ $[[X]_V\ ung]_N$
       \\   /
      $[X\ [[X]_V\ ung]_N]]_N$ 'the action of $[X\ X]_V$'
       /   \\
      Todsagung   *Verhaftnehmung*

As pointed out by Booij (2005: 129), "this template does not introduce a new formal type of complex words, but it expresses that it is the combination of two independently motivated word formation processes that systematically and productively co-occur".

If these premises are true, a number of predictions follow. First, we should expect that conflation effects should be sustained by recurrent input patterns, which favor the mechanism of entrenchment. As a matter of fact, the frequent activation of a certain of pattern enhances its direct access and sustains therefore its storage in the lexical memory. A second prediction we can make on the basis of a constructionist approach is that the single conflation patterns should be centered around highly entrenched models, which give rise to series of derivatives (*Reihenbildung*). Finally, because of their entrenchment, conflations should not strictly undergo principles like lexical blocking which have been shown to be highly sensitive to lexical frequency (cf. Rainer 1988).

As for the first prediction, we can search our corpus for cases like *Todsagung* above, and check for their type- and token-frequency. This is exemplified below on the basis of the conflation schema [X [V ung]] for the three highly frequent *geben* 'to give', verbs *machen* 'to make', *tun* 'to do', which do not normally form the respective abstract nouns *Gebung, *Machung, *Tuung.

The entrenched pattern seems to be provided by the schema [X [*machung*]], which is robustly present with 127 different types. A detailed analysis of the token frequency

Table 4. Synthetic compounds with -*ung* formed from *machen* 'make', *tun* 'do' and *geben* 'give' in DEWAC01

	typ.		tok.
[[Adv] *machung*]	121		
[[N] *machung*]	6		
[[Adv] *tuung*]	1	*Genug-* 'enough'	331
[N [*gebung*]]	2	*Kund-* 'known'	1071
		Frei- 'free'	1

Table 5. Synthetic compounds with -*ung* formed from *machen* 'make', tun 'do' and *geben* 'give' and their basic recurrent patterns in DEWAC01

	tok.	[Adv+V]$_{V^\circ}$	[Adv V]$_{V'}$
Bekanntmachung 'making known'	2814	756	987
Geltendmachung 'm. valid'	2156	1	8452
Kundmachung 'm. known'	907	8	20
Wiedergutmachung 'm. good again'	546	76	42
Glaubhaftmachung 'm. believable'	247	1	828
Mobilmachung 'm. mobile'	144	1	46
Rückgängigmachung 'm. regressive'	142	0	726
Zugänglichmachung 'm. accessible'	130	67	1249
Nutzbarmachung 'm. usable'	77	0	255
Sichtbarmachung 'm. visible'	58	0	468
Kenntlichmachung 'm. knowable'	54	2	206
Genugtuung 'satisfaction'	331	1	44
Kundgebung 'demonstration'	1071	25	5
Freigebung 'liberation'	1	1649	172

is presented in Table 5 above. For the other two cases, we record only two types, in which however respectively *Genugtuung* 'satisfaction' and *Kundgebung* 'demonstration' display a considerable token frequency. Let us see whether these synthetic compounds are likely to rely on highly recurrent patterns. Two possible input patterns occur, which are given below with the help of the usual Google-examples:

(15) a. [Adv+V]$_{V^\circ}$ *bekanntmachen* 'to make known'
      hat man sich miteinander bekanntgemacht.
      'we introduced to each other'.

   b. [Adv V]$_{V'}$ *bekannt machen* 'id.'
      Filme, die Oliver Stone bekannt gemacht haben.
      'Films, which have made Oliver Stone known'.

Clearly, the first pattern shows a higher lexical entrenchment than the second one. In Table 5 the single compounds are given with their respective token number and flanked by the token frequency of the two possible patterns on which they rely.[8]

---

8. For the sake of brevity, only the cases of the pattern [X [*machung*]] which display a token frequency higher than 50 are reported in the table. Moreover, only the adjacent sequences were searched, although German is known to display a highly constrained word order, in which the finite verb forms obligatorily occupy the second position in main declarative sentences. At any rate, including also these cases would only have the effect of increasing the frequency of the single patterns.

Table 6. Synthetic compounds formed from *geben* 'give' in DEWAC01

	typ.		typ.
[[N] *gebung*]	287	[N [*gabe*]]	113
[[Adj] *gebung*]	70	[Adj [*gabe*]]	80
Others	3	Others	26
Tot.	360	Tot.	219

On average, the frequency values seem to confirm the idea that the compounds are based on recurrent patterns. Furthermore, notice that conflation chain effects occur, as in the following cases:

(16) a. [[*Kampf*]*unfähig*[*machung*]]   'making unable to fight'
     b. [*Wieder*[[*gut*]*machung*]]   'amend, lit. making good again'

Especially the second case is very telling of the idea of recurrent patterns because the intermediate derivational stage °*Gutmachung* is not attested in the corpus.

As for the second prediction, we may observe that conflation patterns usually crystallize starting from single models which are robustly attested and give rise to *Reihenbildungen*. By doing so, lexical blocking may be overcome because the recurrent pattern forces the instantiation of productive mechanisms of word formation.

Let us investigate in detail the synthetic compounds based on the verb *geben* 'to give'. In spite of the fact that the robust occurrence of the opaque apophonic derivative *Gabe* 'giving, gift' (1864 tokens) blocks the derivative *Gebung* 'id.', which nevertheless shows up twice in the corpus, the numbers in Table 6 are essentially different if the conflation patterns are taken into consideration.

The high number of compounds headed by *Gebung* is mainly given by conflation chains built on the most frequent model *Gesetzgebung*, which displays a high token frequency (2758) and gives rise to 221 compounds of the type [X [*gesetzgebung*], namely about 60% of the total. Notice that the opaque counterpart *Gesetzgabe* is not attested at all. Thus, the entrenched model gives rise to a considerable series of derivatives which in their turn reinforce the presence of the pattern in the lexicon. On the other hand, the compounds based on the opaque but frequent derivative *Gabe* are clearly recessive against the productivity of the conflation pattern.

5. Conclusion

To sum up, the first conclusion that comes to mind is that corpora are of growing relevance for morphological analysis. Especially for highly productive word formation patterns like German synthetic compounds, a corpus-based analysis may shed some light on the intricacies of their selectional properties and of their distribution. They provide evidence for an approach based on the idea of a rich lexicon, which contains schemas of growing abstractness.

Second, this view is at odds with a strictly syntactic approach like incorporation, because the latter is not able to account for the fine-grained selectional properties of compounds. Instead, a framework provided with a rich semantic information like Dowty's base-roles is required for capturing the spectrum of possible modifiers within synthetic compounds.

Finally, corpora also provide invaluable data for assessing the degree of entrenchment of the single patterns which sustain the conflation of different word formation models which are well accomodated within the framework of Construction Morphology. This can be said to capture the essence of synthetic compounds like the Greek θεοφιλής seen at the start, which are at the heart of the lexicon-syntax interface.

Corpus data and theoretical implications
With special reference to Italian V-N compounds*

Davide Ricca
University of Turin

> The chapter aims at showing the usefulness of quantitative, corpus-based investigations to get a better understanding of a word formation procedure, taking as a case study the Italian VN compounds found on a large newspaper corpus. Corpus data make it possible to compare the weight of the process with respect to competing derivational strategies, and to evaluate the relevance of tendential phonological and morphological restrictions. Moreover, the hapax data, being a powerful tool to distinguish empirically between production and lexicalization/storage, may offer a new insight into the long-debated issue of the output category of this word-formation rule. It is argued that while the Unitary Output Hypothesis may basically hold for the lexicalized items, it cannot be adequate to describe the formation procedure itself.

1. Introduction

Verb-Noun (hereafter also VN) compounds in Italian and more generally in Romance languages have been extensively studied both theoretically and empirically (for Italian, cf. Tollemache 1945, Zuffi 1981, Dressler & Thornton 1991, Scalise 1992, Vogel & Napoli 1995, Bisetto 1999, Guevara & Scalise 2004, Ferrari-Bridgers 2005, Ricca 2005 among others; for a thorough review of the issue in the whole Romance perspective, see e.g. Gather 2001). They are also often cited as one of the best instances of a productive exocentric formation (e.g. Scalise & Guevara 2006, Bauer, this volume), although not all authors agree on this point (cf. e.g. Bisetto 1999: 508–520).

The main motivation for investigating this interesting word-formation procedure once again is given by the recent availability of data coming from very large textual corpora, which may be quite relevant from a theoretical perspective as well. On the one hand, they allow us to provide a well-founded assessment of the overall relevance

---

* This chapter originates from the CompoNet research project coordinated by Sergio Scalise (PRIN 2005–2007).

of the process within the general picture of Italian word-formation, especially with respect to the competing derivational strategies (§ 3). Moreover, it becomes possible to check on real data the validity of the hypothesized morphological or phonological constraints on VN compound formation (§ 4).

Perhaps more importantly, looking in depth at the output of a given word-formation rule in a very large corpus makes it possible to identify the really productive meanings/functions within the formation procedure itself, especially on the basis of hapax data, because hapaxes in a large corpus are the best way to observe, so to say, a word-formation rule at work (cf. Baayen & Renouf 1996: 74–75). Italian VN compounds are well-suited as a case study in this respect, since – as in other Romance languages – they display a very wide semantic spectrum, summarized in (1):

(1) a. Agent N: $[[porta]_V [lettere]_N]_N$ 'carry + letters, postman'
 b. Instrument N: $[[apri]_V [scatole]_N]_N$ 'open + cans, can opener'
 c. Event N: $[[bacia]_V [mano]_N]_N$ 'kiss + hand, hand-kissing'
 d. Location N: $[[sparti]_V [acque]_N]_N$ 'separate + waters, water divide'
 e. Qualifying A: $[[mozza]_V [fiato]_N]_A$ 'cut + breath, breathtaking'
 f. Relational A: *(cannone)* $[[spara]_V [neve]_N]_A$ 'shoot + snow, snow (cannon)'

In particular, since (1e-f) belong to a syntactic category different from (1a-d), the polysemy in (1) also raises the theoretical question of the validity of the Unitary Output Hypothesis (Scalise 1984: 137), which, contrary to most general restrictions proposed within the lexicalist framework, has remainend relatively unchallenged in the subsequent theoretical debate (see § 5.1 for a necessarily brief discussion).

It will be shown in § 5.2 that if we compare the distribution of nominal and adjectival subtypes in (1), we get very different results among the high-frequency formations – i.e. the entrenched words – and among the hapaxes. This suggests that the behaviour of a word-formation rule *as a purely morphological procedure* has to be kept distinct from its evaluation as a lexicalization device.

2. The corpus

The database for this investigation is given by virtually all VN compounds (both hyphenated and written with a single word)[1] occurring in the large corpus *La Repubblica/ SSLMIT*, which comprises sixteen years of the Italian newspaper *La Repubblica*, from

---

1. Compounds written as two separate words, as *macchina mangia barattoli* 'can-eating machine', could not be included in the VN compound sample, but they should not change much the picture: they have been extracted "manually" for 15 among the most productive verb bases, yielding less than 5% of the types' total from the same bases.

1985 to 2000, totalling about 330 million tokens (Baroni et al. 2004).[2] The frequency list of all wordforms in the corpus was automatically matched with a list of the over 9000 verb bases recorded in DISC, a medium-sized Italian dictionary (Sabatini & Coletti 1997), selecting all wordforms beginning with a sequence identical to any of the verb bases. After filtering out automatically the forms involving the main inflectional and derivational suffixes and/or clitic sequences, a final and very time-consuming phase of "manual" cleaning has been necessary. Only a few items of clear metalinguistic/jocular nature have been excluded from the counts.

Lemmatization has been done manually as well. The following forms have been grouped under one single type:
- all nominal and adjectival (i.e. noun modifier) uses;
- all forms occurring with singular and plural N, irrespective of the number of the whole compound, e.g. *fermacravatta* 'hold + tie, tiepin(s)' (11 singular and 2 plural occurrences) with *fermacravatte* 'hold + ties, tiepin(s)' (12 singular and 6 plural);[3]
- forms with and without hyphen, e.g. *portacontainer* 'carry + container(s), container ship' (125 occurrences) with *porta-container* (24);
- forms with and without elision, e.g. *strappa-applausi* 'pull out + applauses, applause-drawing' (11 occurrences) with *strappapplausi* (11);
- the very rare instances of phonetic/graphic variants, e.g. *strappalagrime* 'pull out + tears, tear-jerking' (1 occurrence) with *strappalacrime* (166).

3. Overall data on VN formation: Some comparisons with derivation

The total number of tokens, types and hapaxes of Italian VN compounds in the *Repubblica* corpus is given in (2):

(2) Tokens: **102 204** Types: **2270** Hapaxes: **1350**

---

2. I am very grateful to Marco Baroni and Eros Zanchetta for allowing me an easy access to the data in the SSLMIT corpus (available at http://sslmit.unibo.it/repubblica), and for providing me with the basic cues to handle them. The corpus is often described as containing 380 million tokens; however, punctuation marks are included. The linguistically relevant wordform total is about 330 million and has been used for relative frequency data.

3. This is unproblematic whenever the two forms are clearly variants of the same lexeme, as in the instance given; however, there are very few cases like *portauovo* 'carry + egg, egg cup' vs. *portauova* 'carry + eggs, egg box/holder' (Zuffi 1981: 37), which in the singular usally denote two quite distinct (kinds of) objects, by shape, material and function. The plural *portauova* may refer to both, thus troubling the picture. As a single exception, VN compounds ending in *-tutto* ('everything') have been separated from those ending in *-tutti* ('all:PL', nearly always [+animate]). Anyway, just two items in the whole corpus occurred in both series.

Data in (2) show that VN compounding is unlikely to be the most productive compounding device of Italian, contrary to what has often been said (e.g. Bisetto 1999: 503). Even A–A compounds, recently studied by Grossmann & Rainer (2009) on the basis of the same corpus, display much higher figures (about 13,000 types and 8,500 hapaxes).

The hyphenated orthography is irrelevant token-wise (only 1627 tokens, 1.6%), but, not unexpectedly, becomes much more relevant considering the types and particularly the hapaxes: 39.7% of them are written with an hyphen.

As said in § 1, corpus data allow us to evaluate the weight of this formation with respect to competing derivational strategies. Although no single Italian derivational affix covers the full meaning extension of VN compounds, we may compare the VN compound formation rule with the whole inventory of the deverbal derivational affixes in Italian which have Nouns or Adjectives as outputs. Table 1 shows the results for that comparison at the token level, exploiting the data from Gaeta & Ricca (2003), who provide quantitative data for an extensive sample of Italian derivational affixes, taken from a different corpus, namely three years (1996–1998) of another newspaper, *La Stampa*.[4] For the three deverbal suffixes *-mento*, *-tore* and *-trice*, the relative frequencies have been calculated also with reference to the same *Repubblica* corpus, to check – with satisfactory results – the reliability of the comparison between data on relative token frequencies from different newspaper corpora.[5]

From Table 1, it can be seen that the impact of VN compounding at the token level is very marginal within Italian word-formation: the process is ranked well below the token frequency displayed by each one of the most important deverbal derivational suffixes. Moreover, since almost all of the main Italian deverbal suffixes are included in Table 1, the sum of their relative frequencies gives an estimation of the token relevance of the whole Italian deverbal derivation vs. VN compounding: the resulting ratio is about 100:1.

VN compounds may also be compared with competing denominal strategies. The most productive denominal agentive suffix in today's Italian is *-ista* '-ist', and this suffix again displays a much higher relative token frequency in the *Repubblica* corpus: 2.5‰, more than eight times the token frequency of VN compounds.

A different kind of comparison concerns quantitative productivity. There is too little space here to discuss this issue in any detail (for a very recent survey, see Baayen 2009). In a few words, the main quantitative approaches to morphological productivity

---

4. The data for the suffixes in Table 1 include the formations derived from allomorphic stems (typically a stem formally identical with the Past Participle – as in *fusione* 'melting' from *fondere*, PPt. *fuso* – or with a "Latinate" form of it). For any details, see Gaeta & Ricca (2006: 75–79). Among the lacking suffixes, the most important ones are *–ata*, forming semelfactive Event nouns, and the V→N conversion processes mainly forming Event nouns.

5. Differently from the other cases, the line for *–tore* includes only the non-allomorphic formations, which basically constitute the only productive segment of the word formation rule. These data are given independently, although they obviously refer to a subset of the formations listed under *-(t)ore*, because they will be used in the following Tables 2 – 4.

Table 1. Relative token frequency of VN compounds compared with the main deverbal derivational suffixes

suffix	main meaning	Relative token frequency (‰)	
		La Stampa 96–98 (Gaeta & Ricca 2003)	La Repubblica 85–00
-(z)ione	V → Event N	13.9	
-(t)ore	V → Male Agent N / Instrument N	3.7	
-mento	V → Event N	3.4	3.7
-nza	V → Event N	2.8	
-tore	V → Male Agent N / Instrument N	2.1	2.1
-bile	V → A, '-able'	1.4	
-(t)ura	V → Event N	0.85	
VN compounds			0.31
-trice	V → Female Agent N / Instrument N	0.32	0.25
-aggio	V → Event N	0.29	
-evole	V → A	0.25	
-(t)orio	V → A	0.19	

in the last two decades start from the notion of vocabulary growth curve $V(N)$ in a very large corpus: the number V_{affix} of different words formed by a given affix (or, more generally, morphological procedure) is seen as a function of the number N_{affix} of its tokens, which increases as long as the corpus sampling proceeds. The slope of the $V(N)$ curve then gives a way of measuring the speed at which new types can be formed in the language, provided that the corpus is large enough to approximate the conditions of real language production. Therefore, the slope is a measure of productivity p. It can be mathematically shown that $p_{affix} = h/N_{affix}$, i.e. the ratio between the number of hapaxes and the number of tokens of a given affix in the corpus (Baayen 1992). Since the values of p necessarily decrease as N increases, Gaeta & Ricca (2006) have proposed to calculate the value of p keeping N_{affix} constant for all the affixes being compared. Baayen (2009: 905–906) includes this measure among those reflecting the "expanding productivity", judged as producing plausible productivity rankings, and contrasts it with the different meaning of the "potential productivity" measured by his original procedure (which calculates p for the full corpus size, i.e. at the endpoint of the $V(N)$ curves, irrespective of the high differences in token frequencies between the affixes to be compared).

In Table 2, the values of p for a fixed value of N_{affix} have been calculated applying the binomial interpolation algorithm available in the *zipfR* package (http://zipfr.r-forge.r-project.org/), developed by Evert & Baroni (2007) within the

R-environment.[6] By this procedure, it is possible to plot the expected values for the affix's types and hapaxes as a function of N_{affix}, taking as input the full frequency spectrum of the given affix in the whole corpus. The fixed value chosen for N_{affix} is 100,000, which is the highest possible for VN compounds and had already been used in similar productivity calculations for the major Italian derivational affixes in Gaeta & Ricca (2003).

The results in Table 2 show that in this case VN compounds are ranked well above even the most productive Italian derivations (not only the deverbal ones). Again, some calculations made in Gaeta & Ricca (2003) have been repeated for the *Repubblica* corpus to check data comparability.

The very high value for the quantitative productivity of VN compounds in Table 2 reflects both the high number of hapaxes and the scarcity of entrenched formations among the compounds with respect to the main derivational affixes. This is made more explicit in Table 3, which compares the two extremes of the frequency spectra for the VN compounds and four highly productive competing suffixes in the same *Repubblica* corpus: eventive *-mento*, deverbal agentives *–tore*, *-trice* and denominal agentive *-ista*.

Table 2. Productivity of VN compounds compared with the most productive Italian derivational affixes

	Quantitative productivity $p(‰) = h/ N_{affix}$ at $N_{affix} = 100{,}000$		
affix	main meaning	La Stampa 96–98 (Gaeta & Ricca 2003)	La Repubblica 85–00
VN compounds			13.3
-mente	A → Adv, '-ly'	6.4	
-ismo	A, N → N, '-ism'		5.4
-bile	V → A, '-able'	4.1	
-ista	N, A → N, A '-ist'	3.8	3.6
-ità/-età	A → Quality N	3.7	
-tore	V → Male Agent N /Instrument N		3.2
-trice	V → Female Agent N /Instrument N		3.1
-mento	V → Event N	3.1	2.8
-(z)ione	V → Event N	2.7	
ri-	V → V, 're-', 'back';	2.3	
-ese	place N → ethnic A	2.2	
-ale/-are	N → relational A	1.9	
-oso	N → A 'having N, plenty of N'	1.0	

---

6. In particular, the functions employed are those named *spc.interp* and *vgc.interp* in the *zipfR* package, which are are implementations of binomial interpolation, using equations (2.41) and (2.43) from Baayen (2001). I am grateful to my students Marco Angster and Valentina Cuminale for helping me perform some of the calculations involved.

Table 3. Hapaxes and high-frequency items for VN compounds and four competing suffixes in the *Repubblica* corpus

Number of	VN compounds	-mento	-tore	-trice	-ista
– hapaxes	1350	580	538	308	681
	(59.5%)	(28.3%)	(29.4%)	(31.7%)	(30.2%)
– items with rel. tok. freq. $\geq 10^{-6}$ (freq. $\geq$ 330)	45	311	185	40	213
	(2 %)	(15.2%)	(10.1%)	(4.1%)	(9.5%)
Total number of types	2270	2050	1833	972	2253

4. The scarcity of verb bases and the role of restrictions

4.1 Few verb bases

As shown in Table 3, the total number of VN compound types is approximately of the same order of that of a single major derivational affix, like -*mento*, -*tore* or -*ista*. Although much higher than the one for the tokens in Table 1, the figure is still rather low, considering that the compounding rule involves two open class items: comparing its output with those of a derivational rule is like comparing the points on a plane (a two-variable function) with those on a straight line.

A main reason for this scarcity of types is given exactly by the fact that the VN compounding process can hardly be considered a full-fledged two-variable function, since the verb bases really involved in the process are not very numerous. This is a well-known fact in all Romance languages (Gather 2001: 11). The evidence, however, usually comes from lexicographic sources, and finds here a strong confirmation on the basis of corpus data.

Of the over 9000 verb bases potentially available in the starting list from DISC, only 399 occur in the corpus. This figure may be compared with:
- the 6386 verbs of "common use" in GRADIT (De Mauro 1999);
- the 1899 verbs assigned to the basic lexicon in DISC (Sabatini & Coletti 1997);
- above all, the number of verb bases for the derivations by -*mento*, -*tore*, and -*trice* in the same *Repubblica* corpus (2050, 1833, 972, as reported in Table 3).

The low number of bases suggests to look for relevant restrictions which may limit the productivity specifically of this morphological process, at least as strong tendencies if not as absolute constraints.

A first possibility involves syntax: the syntactic constraints limiting VN compounds to transitive (Scalise 1992: 191, Gather 2001: 76–79) and agentive (Varela 1990b: 67–71, Bisetto 1999: 511) verb bases are extensively discussed in the literature. However, this kind of restriction alone cannot be quantitatively decisive. Taking – as will be done in all this section – the DISC list of 1899 verbs belonging to the "basic lexicon" as a standard of reference, only 358 verbs in that list (18.9%) have exclusively intransitive/copulative uses, and 50 (2.6%) are exclusively non-agentive.

Therefore, the VN compound formation rule makes little exploitation of its conceivable verbal domain, even considering its reduction by virtue of the syntactic constraints above. Two further restrictions seem to play a role, even if as tendencies only, and they will be dealt with in the following subsections.

4.2 A phonological restriction: The preference for bisyllabic verb bases

VN compounds show a massive preference for bisyllabic verb bases: 59.9% of the 399 attested bases are bisyllabic, and on average they are also more productive than the others, since 74.9% of the types are formed with them. Of course, proper standards of comparison are needed to state that a 60% preference for bisyllabic bases is the result of a tendential restriction specific for this morphological procedure, and not the by-product of some more general statistical distribution. This is done in Table 4, in two different ways. First, lines a. and b. show that such a percentage of bisyllabic bases is certainly not what we would expect from a random selection among the DISC reference list of common verbs: in that list the bisyllabic bases amount to less than 30% of the total, and their number further decreases slightly, if we take into account a more appropriate set of comparison, namely the transitive and agentive verbs. Cf. Thornton (2007: 254–256) for a similar count on data from GRADIT.

However, the preference for two-syllable verbs in VN compounds might simply be due to a general tendency to avoid too long words, a factor obviously much less relevant for the verbs in isolation. Luckily, we are in the position of ruling out this possibility as well, since Italian derivational morphology has several "heavy" derivational

Table 4. The prevalence of bisyllabic bases as a constraint specific to VN formations

Sample: set of …	total of types	number of two-syllable Vs	%
a. all basic DISC verbs	1899	526	27.7
b. transitive & agentive basic DISC verbs	1491	392	26.3
c. -*trice* derivations in corpus	893	169	18.9
d. -*tore* derivations in corpus	1833	389	21.2
e. -*mento* derivations in corpus	2050	264	12.9
f. all different V bases of VN compounds in corpus	399	239	**59.9**
g. all VN compounds in corpus	2270	1701	**74.9**
h. VN compounds with bisyllabic N only	1054	845	**80.2**
i. all different V bases of VN compound hapaxes in corpus	319	187	**58.6**
l. all VN compound hapaxes in corpus	1350	940	**69.6**

suffixes to compare with, whose outputs are phonologically quite similar to VN compounds, as shown in (3) for the three bases *batti-* 'beat', *conta-* 'count' and *lucida-* 'polish':

(3)   a.   VN compound
           battipanni 'beat + clothes, carpet beater'
           contagocce 'count + drops, dropper'
           lucidalabbra 'polish + lips, lipgloss'
      b.   V-derivative
           battimento 'beat'
           contatore 'counter'
           lucidatrice 'floor-polisher'

Lines c.-e. in Table 4 show that the derivatives like those in (3b) do not display any preference for bisyllabic bases.[7] On the contrary, the percentages for all three suffixes are lower than what should be expected from a random selection from the DISC reference list, despite the fact that these derivatives are as long as the VN compounds with bisyllabic N (the most common pattern). Notice that restricting the VN compound sample to those with bisyllabic N, to fully match the syllabic structure of the derivatives, yields an even higher percentage of bisyllabic Vs, as seen at line h. in Table 4.

Finally, lines i. and l. show that the phonological restriction on bisyllabicity is almost equally effective when the sample is limited to hapaxes, i.e. to non-established formations, which means that it is not much influenced by lexicalization preferences.

Therefore, it can be safely said that the preference for two-syllable verb bases is specific of VN compounding and opposes it to deverbal derivation.

4.3   A minor morphological restriction: The disfavouring of *-isci-* verb bases

As is well known, in Italian the verb base occurring in VN compounds coincides formally (obviously not semantically) with the form of 2nd singular Imperative. For most verbs of the *-ire* inflectional class, like *pulire* 'clean', *finire* 'finish', this form displays an augmented stem: *pulisci*, *finisci*. The reluctance of these *–isci-* bases to form VN compounds has been often discussed (e.g. Bisetto 1999: 513–515), and is confirmed by corpus data. Only three bases occur (0.75% of the total): *pulisci-* (e.g. *pulisciforno* 'clean + oven, oven-cleaner'), *ripulisci-* 'clean up' and *distribuisci-* (*macchinette distribuisci-soldi* 'distribute + cash, cash-dispensing machines'), with 10 types in total.

By the same reasoning made in § 4.2, it can be said that this low figure is linguistically significant, because the rate of *-isci-* verbs in the reference list of DISC basic transitive and agentive verbs is 6%, so in the absence of morphological conditioning a total

---

[7]   The number of types for *-trice* in line c. is lower than in Table 3 because the derivatives from allomorphic bases identical to the Past Participle, like *lettrice* 'woman reader' (cf. PPt. *letto* 'read'; see also note 4) have been excluded from this count, since they yield a shorter syllabic pattern. They are absent for the other two suffixes considered.

of *-isci-* bases eight times greater would be expected. On the other hand, this very figure of 6% says that the overall impact of this restriction is quite limited.

Moreover, we are not dealing with an absolute constraint, contrary to what is sometimes stated in the literature. Sampling a larger corpus would inevitably give new instances of VN compounds built on *-isci-* bases. A full search – although limited to the hyphenated compounds which were technically easier to retrieve – was made on a 2-billion-tokens Web corpus of Italian (the *itWAC* corpus, Bernardini et al. 2006; updated information at http://wacky.sslmit.unibo.it/) and yielded the VN compounds listed in (4), all hapaxes in adjectival function:

(4) *demolisci-magistratura* 'magistracy-destroying', *farcisci-curriculum* 'CV-stuffing', *lenisci-tosse* 'cough-soothing', *rapisci-bambini* 'child-kidnapping', *restituisci-gettoni* 'token-returning', *scandisci-tempo* 'time-beating', *stordisci-sordi* 'deaf-deafening', *tradisci-parole* 'word-distorting',

together with 17 different nominal and adjectival types with *pulisci-*, the only *-isci-* base whose productivity has always been recognized (Dressler & Thornton 1991: 15, Vogel & Napoli 1995: 371, Bisetto 1999: 514). Moreover, a Google search (26/4/09) gave 20 different types for a single semantically promising pattern like *macchina distribuisci-N* 'N-delivering machine'.

Thus the *-isci-* VN compounds are not agrammatical, and often they aren't particularly odd when they are met. But as a matter of fact, they are massively avoided in real usage, which is not without linguistic significance.

It is true that *-isci-* bases are also "long", i.e. non-bisyllabic, so they would be disfavoured anyway by virtue of the phonological tendency discussed above in § 4.2. However, their avoidance cannot probably be explained only by phonological factors, because in the corpus there are still much less *–isci-* compounds than one would expect if they were a proportional fraction of VN compounds formed by long bases. The quite salient divergence between the compound base and the augmentless stem occurring in derivatives (e.g. *pulitore* 'cleaner'), which is characteristic of these verbs, probably plays a stronger role (Dressler & Thornton 1991: 15, Bisetto 1999: 515). Support to this view is brought by the occurrence in the *itWAC* corpus of some competing formations from the augmentless stem, like *pulivetri* 'glass cleaner', *puliorecchie* 'ear cleaner', also mentioned in Thornton (2007: 258). For other bases, analogous evidence may be found on the Internet: *guaritutto* beside *guariscitutto* 'all-healing', *scanditempo* beside *scandiscitempo* 'time-beating', *sgranchigambe* beside *sgranchiscigambe* 'leg-stretching' (26/4/09).

4.4 The really productive verb bases

Not only relatively few verbal bases are involved in the VN compounding process; most of them are only very marginally involved. If the verb bases are ordered according to the number of different types they form in the corpus, the resulting distribution (a sort of "second order spectrum" for the verb bases) is very skewed. Again, this fact has been previously noticed for most Romance languages on the basis of lexicographical evidence (Gather 2001: 12), and finds clear confirmation in the corpus data, although the leading bases do not fully overlap, as will be shown below. More than half (52.8%) of the 399 verb bases are represented in the corpus by just one compound, while at the other edge of the spectrum, the 9 highest ranked bases emerge neatly from the rest and are responsible for about 40% of both the types and the hapaxes.

In (5) the first 10 verb bases are listed in decreasing order of number of types occurring in the corpus (for each verb, the figures in brackets give types and hapax number). Nearly all the leading bases have high rates of hapaxes (the exception is *para*-), which means that they are currently very productive.

(5) *porta*- 'carry' (214/103), **salva**- 'save' (152/98), *mangia*- 'eat' (104/69), **acchiappa**- 'catch' (100/62), **ammazza**- 'kill' (93/70), *copri*- 'cover' (72/43), *taglia*- 'cut' (55/33), *para*- 'block, protect' (46/13), **spacca**- 'break' (44/25), *trita*- 'mince' (29/19).

The bases highlighted in boldface are ranked much lower in similar lists obtained from dictionary sources like the GRADIT (Ricca 2005: 471). These bases play indeed a relevant role in nonce formations with noun modifier function, but do not seem to build many firmly lexicalized items (this distinction will be discussed in detail in § 5).

For some of the most frequent bases, there may be some potential for grammaticalization into (quasi-)affixes (cf. Bauer 2005: 98–99, Booij this volume). In particular, *porta*- 'carry' and *mangia*- 'eat', when occurring as first elements in the compound, may display specific meaning changes which can be expressed in terms of loss of semantic features of V and/or selectional restrictions on N. In compounds, *porta*-, besides its usual lexical meaning as in (6a), often means 'contain', 'hold', with no motion capability implied, as in (6b):

(6) a. *portabandiera* 'carry + flag, standard-bearer'
 b. *portacenere* 'carry + ash, ashtray', *portalampade* 'carry + lamps, lamp socket'.

Mangia-, besides its literal sense of 'eat' in (7a), has developed two further productive meanings. In (7b), meaning 'destroy', 'waste', V has lost the restriction on [+animate] subjects, while in (7c), meaning 'fierce opponent of', it typically selects [+animate] objects, opposite of its literal use. At least type (7c) is almost restricted to compounds.

(7) a. *mangiarane* 'eat + frogs, frog-eater'
 b. (*candela*) *mangiafumo* 'eat + smoke, smoke-eating (candle)', *mangiasoldi* 'eat + money:PL, money waster'
 c. *mangiapreti* 'eat + priests, dogged anticlerical', *mangia-arbitri* 'eat + referees, referee hater'.

5. Corpus data and the Unitary Output Hypothesis

5.1 Theoretical "no-adjective" proposals

As said in § 1, VN compounds are an interesting field to test the Unitary Output Hypothesis, already implied by Aronoff (1976: 22) and made explicit by Scalise (1984: 137). Indeed, at least for what concerns the syntactic category of the output, this constraint has been seldom questioned even outside the lexicalist framework, and the formal parallelism between the Unitary Base and the Unitary Output Hypotheses has been often reversed into what appeared to be a characteristic asymmetry in word formation (cf. e.g. Rainer 1993: 113): contrary to the UBH, the UOH has been considered empirically very solid, or even "inherent in an output-oriented approach" like the one of Plag (1999: 243).

Concerning Italian (and Romance) VN compounds, there is little doubt that they can be extensively used as noun modifiers, as already shown in (1e) and (1f); for Romance data, see e.g. Gather (2001: 155–159). This does not automatically imply a substantial violation of the UOH, however. Many instances of VN compounds acting as noun modifiers, for instance *nave portacontainer* 'container-carrying ship', can be treated in various ways which would "save" the UOH. As a first solution, the whole unit can be transferred to morphology (cf. Zuffi 1981: 18), by considering it a "loose compound", as in (8):

(8)   [[*nave*] $_N$ [*portacontainer*] $_N$] $_N$

Alternatively, *portacontainer* can be viewed as being in appositive relation with *nave* 'ship', which keeps the VN compound among nouns altogether; or it may be considered as acquiring the adjectival categorial status only indirectly, as the output of a N → A conversion process starting from the identical – and well attested – nominal compound *portacontainer* 'container carrier'. In the latter case, a two-step process is needed, as in (9):

(9)   a.   [*porta*]$_V$ [*container*]$_N$ → [*portacontainer*]$_N$
      b.   [*portacontainer*]$_N$ → [*portacontainer*]$_A$

Differently from (8), solution (9) is able to account for the common instances of separation between the head noun and its VN compound modifier, as in the following corpus examples:

(10)   a.   *telecamera mobile acchiappacattivi* 'lit. bad (drivers)-catching mobile camera'
       b.   *scatola d'argento portafiammiferi* 'lit. matches-holding silver box'

The solutions sketched above seem to satisfy the authors of most theoretically-oriented descriptions (especially in the Italian tradition, cf. Scalise 1992: 191, Bisetto 1999, Guevara & Scalise 2004; less unanimously in Spain, as discussed for instance in Gather 2001: 155–165). The crucial point, however, is that they all share a common presupposition: the corresponding nominal formation should be attested (and hopefully also more frequent/ancient/ established); or – at the very least – it should be quite natural as a "possible word". If a sizeable amount of VN compounds used as noun modifiers cannot be easily related to a parallel nominal use, a reductionist approach complying with the Unitary Output Hypothesis becomes much less convincing (similar considerations for Spanish are found in Rainer 1993: 273).

Lexicographical data tend to support the prevalence of nominal formation (Gather 2001: 155, Ricca 2005: 471), as dictionaries list very few gradable qualifying adjectives with no nominal use (like *mozzafiato* 'cut + breath, breathtaking' or *spaccatimpani* 'break + eardrums, exceedingly loud'). Clearly, these rare but clear-cut instances of adjectival VN compounds hardly derivable from nominal bases already constitute a problem, but only if the Unitary Output Hypothesis is taken rigidly (i.e. as exceptionless). However, the corpus data are much more interesting in this respect, as shown below.

5.2 VN compounds as noun modifiers: The corpus data

The corpus data are by no means uniform, depending on whether high- or low- frequency items are considered. Data for high–frequency items confirm the prevalence of nouns, as shown in Table 5. Among the highly entrenched words (as in Table 3, the threshold has been put, somewhat arbitrarily, at the relative frequency of 1: 10^6), most VN compounds occur only as nouns, and some of them also display a marginal use as a noun modifier with relational meaning, as is the case for instance of *contagocce* 'count + drops, dropper', which occurs just once in the corpus as a modifier, in *tappo contagocce* 'drop-counting cap'.[8] It is clear that such cases are easily dealt with in terms of conversion or appositive uses, along the lines of (9), and for them there is no need at all to posit Adjective as a direct output of the VN compound formation rule.

Table 5. Nominal and adjectival VN compounds among the highest-frequency items

items with relative token frequency...	Tot.	only N	N and (marginally) A	both N and A	A and (marginally) N	only A
$\geq 10^{-6}$ (freq. $\geq$ 330)	45	29 88.9%	11	4	0	1
between 10^{-6} and 10^{-7} (freq. < 330 and $\geq$ 33)	138	70 75.4%	34	21	7	6

---

8. Since even high-frequency VN compounds do not normally occur in thousands in the corpus, it was a feasible task to scrutinize all their contexts of occurrence "manually" to find out possible uses as modifiers. Only for the first five ranked VN compounds, just the first 1,000 occurrences were checked, giving no modifier use at all, as expected for items like *portavoce* 'spokesman', *portafoglio* 'wallet, portfolio', *passaporto* 'passport', *marciapiede* 'pavement', *grattacielo* 'skyscraper'.

In this highest-frequency group, only *mozzafiato* 'breathtaking' is a full-fledged adjective with no nominal use, and only four other VN compounds have relatively frequent uses as noun modifiers as well: *rompiscatole* 'break + boxes, bore', *portafortuna* 'bring + fortune, lucky charm', *lanciamissili* 'launch + missiles, missile-launching' as a relational adjective, and the somehow special case of *colabrodo* 'strain + broth, colander', which is nearly always used metaphorically, and in this sense is common also as a modifier with clear adjectival properties ('leaking, unreliable': cf. the coordination in *apparato giudiziario ansimante e colabrodo* 'gasping and inefficient justice system').

In the logarithmic frequency class immediately below, the percentage of items with exclusive nominal use, or nearly so, is a little lower, but still clearly dominant (75.4%). Examples of the different uses of VN compounds as noun modifiers in this class, according to their classification in Table 5, are given below:

(11) a. chiefly noun, marginal use as an adjective (34 items):
   (casco) asciugacapelli 'dry + hair:PL, hair-drying (helmet)'
b. current both as noun and adjective (21 items):
   rubacuori 'steal + hearts, charmer/charming'
c. chiefly adjective, marginal use as a noun (7 items):
   (cannone) sparaneve 'shoot + snow, snow (cannon)'
d. only attested as adjective (6 items):
   spaccagambe 'break + legs, very tiring, exhausting'

On the contrary, a totally different picture is found at the other end of the frequency spectrum. The 1350 VN compound hapaxes distribute almost equally between the nominal and the noun-modifying function, as reported in Table 6.

Before discussing the neat discrepancy between Tables 5 and 6 in more detail, the subclasses in Table 6 deserve some closer inspection.

As for the noun subclasses, the hapax count confirms the well-known high productivity of both Agent and Instrument nouns, with no marked preference. No further examples are needed here. On the other hand, Location nouns as *spartiacque* 'water divide', very rare in general, are practically not represented among hapaxes and low-frequency items. Event nouns, however, are a limiting case and are worth of some illustration. This

Table 6. Nominal and adjectival VN compounds among the hapaxes

VN hapaxes in nominal function		VN hapaxes in noun-modifying function	
Agent nouns	344	Qualifying adjectives	68
Instrument nouns	272	Relational adjectives	274
Event nouns	29	Other modifiers	359
Other	4		
All Nouns	649 (48.1%)	**All modifiers**	701 (51.9%)

kind of semantic output is often said not to be productive anymore (e.g. Bisetto 1999: 509), implying that it enjoyed a different status in earlier stages of the language.

The corpus data are not really decisive about this issue. The number of hapaxes – although very limited compared to Agentive and Instrumental VN compounds – should suggest that productivity cannot be ruled out in this semantic domain as well. On the other hand, the "peripheric" status of Event new formations is enhanced by the fact that many of them seem to be built on strict analogical models well established in the lexicon, like *bacia-anello* 'kiss + ring, ring-kissing' on *baciamano* 'kiss + hand, hand-kissing', *stringimani* 'grip + hands, hand-shaking' on *battimani* 'clap + hands, applause', and so on. However, there are other instances which seem better described in terms of rule-governed productivity, independent from strict analogical parallels, although tracing the border is not easy, and perhaps also unfeasible in principle (cf. Booij this volume). One could subsume under a wider concept of analogy, for instance, cases like (12), which belong to two rather well definable semantic niches characteristic of many Event VN compounds, namely the events involving parts of the human body, or denoting game activities:

(12) a. *un ta-trac d'* **accavallagambe minigonnate**
'a ta-trac of *[miniskirted leg]-crossing*'
b. *Si passa dunque alla gara del* **piantachiodi**
'We come then to the *nail-driving* contest'

The fact that there are undoubtedly very few new formations with Event semantics (2.1% of the hapax total) with respect to both Agentive and Instrument VN compounds is not enough to state that the former have undergone a substantial loss of productivity, because they are a minority among established words as well (4.8% of all the non-hapax types), and it is likely that this semantic output has always been marginal in the history of Italian.

Coming to the VN compounds occurring as noun modifiers, they will be illustrated in greater detail, as their high rate of occurrence is perhaps unexpected. The three subclasses outlined below are not always easily separable in real data; therefore the figures in Table 6 must be taken as indicative. The total figure for noun modifiers, however, would not change anyhow.

The less problematical subclass from the perspective of the Unitary Output Hypothesis is given by the relational adjectives, since several of them can be easily related to an elsewhere attested – or reasonably possible – Instrument/Agent noun. Predictably, favoured heads are *macchina* 'machine' (62 hapaxes alone) and other nouns denoting broad classes of object/instruments, as *battello* 'boat' in (13a). But also human/animate beings (13b-c), dynamic forces (13d) and even abstract nouns (13e) occur as heads:

(13) a. *battello raccattaschifezze* 'rubbish-collecting boat'
b. *ragazzi pompa-benzina* 'petrol-pumping boys'
c. *cani annusadroga* 'drug-sniffing dogs'

d. *gas divora-ozono* 'ozone-devouring gas'
e. *azione copri-odore* 'smell-covering action'

Relational VN compounds are separable from their heads through other, non-compounded, relational adjectives, as in (10a) above, or PPs in classifying function, as in (10b). Two of them can even be hierarchically juxtaposed, as in *orologio segnatempo timbra-cartellino* 'card-stamping time-marking clock'.

Qualifying adjectives are also well represented among hapaxes, and are definitely a more serious challenge for a reductionist approach aiming at deriving them from nouns. Sometimes syntactic evidence can confirm their status (for application to VN compounds of the usual tests of adjectivality, see e.g. Gather 158–159, Ricca 2005): they may occur in coordination with an established qualifying adjective (14a), in predicative use (14b), or separated from the head by another qualifying adjective (14c):

(14) a. *Roma scettica e scansaguai* 'sceptical and trouble-avoiding Rome'
b. *un ruolo [...] considerato ammazza-voci* lit. 'a role [...] considered as voice-killing'
c. *aria querula e lacrimosa tiraschiaffi* 'slap-drawing querulous and tearful expression'

However, most VN compound modifiers which cannot be considered as relational adjectives (since they have no classifying function) could hardly be labelled as qualifying adjectives either. Rather, they express a looser kind of modification, with transient/eventive character, sometimes bordering on the function of a (reduced) relative clause.[9] They have been put in the "other modifiers" subclass in Table 6. Two instances are given in (15):

(15) a. *con il colpo di testa **fissa-risultato** di Fonseca*
'with Fonseca's *result-securing* header'
b. *alludendo alla ventilata astensione **salva-Prodi***
'alluding to the proposed *Prodi-saving* abstention'

The compounds in (15) are puzzling if the application of a morphological rule is equated with lexeme formation. Indeed, they obviously share the same formation process with the preceding subclasses, but they are extremely poor candidates to lexical storage. Notice that they often keep the referential autonomy of the noun intact, which is patent when a proper noun is involved, as in (15b), but holds for (15a) as well. Such formations are definitely not relatable to putative VN compound nouns, and strongly

---

9. Notice that the transient character associated with these formations runs counter to the generalization that in Romance VN compounds the V should convey habitual or generic aspect (Varela 1990b: 65, and recently for Italian, Ferrari-Bridgers 2005: 70–71). This could be a further proof that properties holding for the lexicalized items do not necessarily belong to the formation process proper, as discussed in § 5.3 below.

suggest the opportunity to keep separate the two levels of morphological formation and lexicalization.[10]

Incidentally, a different kind of evidence for non-lexical VN compounds is given by the notorious instances of V-NP compounds. In the corpus they are not very numerous (1.1% of the types: one instance has been given in 12a), but interestingly, they are not limited to frozen/idiomatic/lexicalized NPs, and can give rise to syntactic ambiguities resolved only by world knowledge, as in (16):

(16) *Clinton ha confuso i missili antimissili Patriot, gli **ammazza-Scud di Saddam**, coi missili intelligenti Cruise*
'Clinton mistook the Patriot anti-missile missiles, the [*Saddam's Scud*]-*killers*, with the Cruise intelligent missiles'.

5.3 Concluding remarks: One or two output categories?

It seems that in Tables 5 and 6 we are faced with a divergent behaviour simply because we are observing two different phenomena. The data in Table 5 do not describe VN compound formation proper, but rather the distribution of firmly lexicalized items. Unavoidably, they are the only kind of data available if the investigation is based on lexicographical sources; but also when investigations are essentially founded on linguists' introspection, these sort of data will arguably be dominant, as they can be most readily retrieved from the native speaker's mental lexicon. On the other hand, the data in Table 6 focus on the compound formation "in real time", looking at how the outputs of a dedicated morphological procedure are produced, irrespective of their chances of acquiring a stable position in the (mental) lexicon.

VN compound hapaxes in a large corpus are necessarily morphological objects, because they are all built via a rule – or constructional pattern – unknown to Italian syntax[11]; however, most of them are not (yet) lexical units. Some will become fullfledged lexical units, i.e. they will be stored in the mental lexicon, but many never will. If we want to describe the features of a given morphological procedure, hapaxes are the best evidence to look at, because they are insensitive to all kinds of factors which may influence the lexicalization chances of an item, not to speak of the idiosyncratic semantic changes that many long-established words undergo after coinage.

In this perspective, the reason for the clear nominal preference in the well-established items can hardly be ascribed to the formation rule/pattern itself. A relevant

---

10. For a wider discussion on this issue, clearly not limited to VN compounds, see Gaeta & Ricca (2009). On the non-lexical character of some compound types cf. Hohenhaus (2005: 365–357) and Montermini (this volume, § 3.3).

11. This point should deserve more space than is allowed here. At any rate, for most current analyses – not all, of course – the obligatory absence of the determiner ensures that VN compounds are not built by the same syntactic rule which builds VPs (cf. e.g. Gather 2001: 55), even in the case of V-NP compounds like the ones in (12a) and (16) above.

factor in play may be the difference in "naming force" between nouns in general (as referential entities) and adjectives in general (as property concepts), which, all other things being equal, should enhance the lexicalization potential of the former.

On the whole, there is some undesirable ambiguity in the ubiquitous use of expressions like "word-formation rule": if it is meant to incorporate also post-coinage effects determining the stabilization in the lexicon, then the Unitary Output Hypothesis may keep some validity – as a strong, but not exceptionless tendency – in describing the Italian, and probably Romance, VN compound formation process. If, however, by "word-formation rule" it is meant only the morphological procedure involved, it becomes difficult to maintain that VN-compounding yields basically only Nouns as output. One is left with two alternatives which cope better with the facts:

a. assume two distinct formation rules (or patterns) with different outputs N and A, as proposed for instance by Rainer (1993: 274) for Spanish;
b. leave the output category underspecified and basically context–dependent. This requires the price of violating the Unitary Output Hypothesis, but seems preferable since it avoids the high redundancy – a point made e.g. in Gather (2001: 160–161) – implied by a., because the two putative rules do not seem to show any distinct semantic, morphological or phonological behaviour.

To conclude, I think that the point raised by these data goes beyond the descriptive issue concerning a specific morphological procedure of Italian. A similar approach might be fruitfully applied to several derivational procedures which are challenging for the Unitary Output Hypothesis, as their outputs have frequent adjectival uses besides the nominal ones: suffixes like -*ista* '-ist', and the two agentive deverbals -*tore* and -*trice* are cases in point for Italian.

More generally, a relevant contribution corpus data may bring into the theoretical debate is that they are very helpful to distinguish empirically between production and lexicalization/storage. The output of a formation rule (or a constructional pattern) can be well approximated by looking at hapaxes in a very large corpus; and some statements which may be valid at the level of stored items (in this particular instance, "VN compounds are basically nouns"), cannot be automatically extended to the formation rules. Others, like the preference for bisyllabic bases, can on the contrary be shown to apply to the formation procedure proper. In Rainer's (2005: 350) words, "No field of linguistics can draw more profit from these new tools than the study of word formation".

PART IV

Quantitative and psycholinguistic aspects of compounding

Frequency effects in compound processing

R. Harald Baayen, Victor Kuperman and Raymond Bertram
University of Alberta, Edmonton – Stanford University – Turku University

This chapter discusses the role of compound token frequency, head and modifier token frequency, and head and modifier compound family sizes (type frequencies) in the comprehension of English and Dutch compounds, using data from word naming, visual lexical decision, and eye-tracking studies. Using generalized additive regression modeling, it is shown that these frequency measures enter into many complex interactions. These interactions argue against current staged models and argue for morphological processing as part of a complex dynamic system.

1. Introduction

The entry of the Collins English Dictionary for the word index offers as its first subentry the meaning 'an alphabetical list of persons, places, subjects, etc., mentioned in a printed work...'. The second subentry is a pointer to a compound: 'see thumb index'. Ever since Taft and Forster (1976), this setup of dictionary entries has served as a model for decompositional theories of lexical processing. According to these 'prelexical' theories, lexical access to the meaning of a compound such as *thumb index* is crucially mediated by a representation of its modifier (*thumb*).

The Collins English Dictionary also provides separate main entries for many compounds. A main entry for *house*, for instance, is supplemented by a main entry for *houseboat*. This set-up has also served as a model for rival theories of lexical processing. According to these theories, access to the meaning of *houseboat* might just as well be guided by a separate orthographic access representation for the compound word itself. In the parallel dual route model of Baayen et al. (1997), the meaning of *houseboat* can be retrieved either directly through the access representation of *houseboat*, or indirectly through the access representations of *house* and *boat*.

What these rival theories have in common is their assumption that a frequency effect observed in an experiment for modifier, head, or compound reflects the activation of a lexical representation for that lexical unit. What they disagree about is the temporal order in which these representations become activated. In prelexical theories, the compound representation is activated only after its constituents have been accessed. In 'supralexical' theories (see, e.g., Giraudo and Grainger, 2001), the constituents are accessed following the activation of the whole word. In the parallel dual route framework, access representations for compound, head and modifier are accessed in parallel, and which interpretational route is the first to complete depends on the distributional properties of all three forms, including their frequencies. The goal of the present study is to introduce evidence that all these theories underestimate the complexities involved in understanding compound words. We first discuss evidence from large-scale visual lexical decision and visual word naming studies carried out with English compounds. We then proceed with a reanalysis of an eye-tracking study of compound processing in Dutch.

In what follows, we investigate the predictivity for lexical processing of the following variables: (1) compound frequency (the summed frequencies of the compound and its inflectional variants), (2) head frequency and modifier frequency (also summing over inflectional variants), (3) head and modifier compound family size (the number of different compounds in which the head (or modifier) occurs as head (or modifier), and as a final control variable (4) the length (in letters) of head, modifier, and the compound.

2. Lexical decision and naming latencies

From the set of compounds with nonzero frequency in the CELEX lexical database (Baayen et al., 1995) consisting of two monomorphemic nouns, those compounds were selected for which lexical decision and naming latencies were available in the English Lexicon Project (Balota et al., 2007), resulting in a set of 1252 words. On the basis of the information in CELEX, the following information was extracted or calculated for each compound: the frequency of the compound, the lemma frequency of the head, the lemma frequency of the modifier, the constituent family size of modifier and head and the lengths of both constituents in characters. Frequencies and family sizes were log-transformed in order to reduce artefactual outlier effects. Given the high collinearity of this set of predictors (the condition number is 29.44), the constituent frequency measures were residualized on the corresponding family sizes, and the length measures were residualized on the family size and constituent frequency measures. The residualized measures were all highly correlated with their original counterparts (all r > 0.75). After decorrelation, the collinearity was no longer harmful, as indicated by the low value of the condition number 8.49.

The response latencies in both naming and lexical decision deviated substantially from normality. This deviance was corrected by a reciprocal transformation. We used the transformation -1000/RT so that larger values in the transformed dependent variable correspond to larger values of the original variable.

2.1 Lexical decision

Figure 1 summarizes a regression model fitted to the lexical decision latencies, given the assumption that the effects of the predictors are linear in nature (the adjusted R-squared of this model is 0.33). The frequency of the compound itself emerges as the predictor with the largest effect size: The greater the frequency of the compound, the shorter the response latencies. Intermediate effect sizes come with the lengths of the constituents: Greater lengths for head and modifier lead to longer response latencies. Slightly smaller, facilitatory effect sizes can be seen for the compound family sizes. The smallest effect sizes are those for the head and modifier frequencies. All partial effects graphed in Figure 1 were highly significant (all $p < 0.002$), with the exception of the frequency of the head ($p = 0.31$).

Previous research has shown that the assumption of the effects being linear may be too restrictive (see, e.g. Baayen et al., 2006). Nonlinearities can be modeled efficiently using restricted cubic splines (see, e.g., Harrell, 2001; Wood, 2006). A second implicit assumption underlying the present regression model is that there are no interactions between the different numerical predictors. In other words, the model shown in Figure 1 assumes that the effect of one predictor is the same irrespective of the value of any of the other predictors. Although interactions between factors and between a factor and a numeric predictor are routinely explored in analysis of variance and analysis of covariance, interactions between two (or more) numeric predictors are seldom investigated. There are two reasons for this neglect. First, when we consider interactions between numerical variables, we are effectively searching for a solution in a potentially nonlinear, highly complex multidimensional space. Harrell (2001) gives as practical advice not to explore interactions between numerical variables, unless they have already been reported to be relevant in the literature. This paradoxical advice – someone has to take the first step to explore and report such interactions – illustrates the conservatism that characterizes much research using multiple regression.

Second, modeling interactions between two or more numerical predictors is not a trivial enterprise. Within the standard linear regression framework, one can include a so-called multiplicative interaction, which effectively amounts to including as a new variable the product of the two predictors for which an interaction is required. For an interaction of compound frequency and modifier frequency, for instance, a new variable is created that, for each word, multiplies the compound frequency of that word with the frequency of its modifier. This new variable is then entered into the regression equation along with the other predictors.

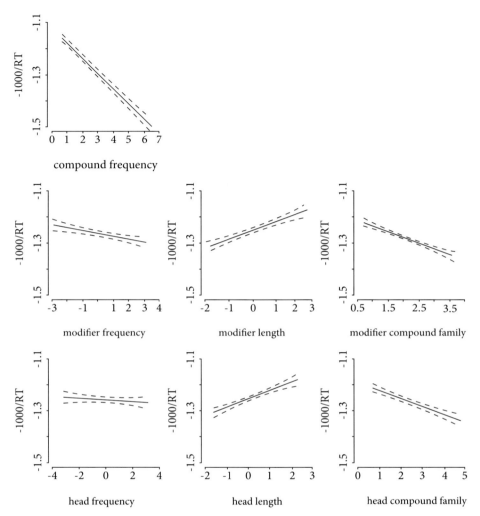

Figure 1. Partial effects of compound frequency, modifier and head frequency, length, and compound family size, in a simple regression model fitted to the (transformed) lexical decision latencies of 1252 two-constituent compounds as available in the English Lexicon Project

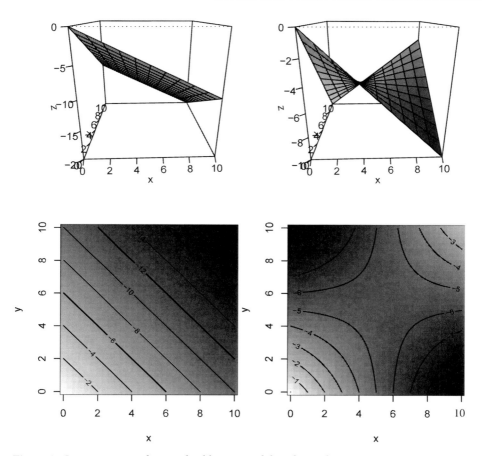

Figure 2. Interactions in the standard linear model. Left panels: no interaction, right panels: a multiplicative interaction. The top panels present 3-D perspective plots, the lower panels the corresponding contour plots, with darker shades of grey representing larger (less negative) values. In the right panels, the dependent variable z varies substantially depending on the specific combination of values of x and y

The problem with this multiplicative interaction is that it imposes a very specific functional form on the interaction, as can be seen in Figure 2. The left panels show simulated data where the dependent variable z is a straightforward linear function of the predictors x and y, without an interaction. The top left panel shows the resulting plane in 3-D, the bottom left panel presents the corresponding contour plot, with darker shades of grey representing more negative values. Note that the contour lines run in parallel.

The top right panel illustrates a multiplicative interaction. For small x, the effect of y is facilitatory, for large x, it is inhibitory. The bottom right panel presents the corresponding contour plot. Note that the two corners on the main diagonal are dark (large negative values), that the other two corners are light (representing negative values closer to zero), and that the center of the graph is intermediate between these extremes. Depending on the range of values of the predictors and the strength of the interaction, the interaction plot can show full reversals as illustrated here, or only part of this twisted but otherwise quite regular surface.

Given that the multiplicative interaction captures only a small subset of possible regression surfaces, we need to explore more flexible ways of understanding interactions between distributional variables in lexical processing. Sometimes it is possible to replace a multiplicative interaction by a theoretically motivated alternative. Kuperman et al. (2009a), for instance, observed that an interaction of suffix productivity by base family size, emerging in the eye-movement record for Dutch derived words, could be more economically modeled by considering the entropy of the families of suffix and base word. In the present study, we explore a more general and more flexible alternative, namely, Generalized Additive Models, henceforth GAMs.

A generalized additive model consists of two parts, a parametric part identical to that of standard linear models, and a non-parametric part that provides non-parametric functions for modeling wiggly surfaces in two or higher dimensions. In what follows, we make use of so-called tensor products to model wiggly surfaces, for details, the reader is referred to Wood (2006).

The tensor product functions are non-parametric in the sense that we will not be interested in the parameters that these smoothing functions use internally, but only in how well these mathematical black boxes succeed in capturing the wiggliness of a given surface. When fitting tensor smoothers to the data, it is crucial to avoid both undersmoothing and oversmoothing. We have used the Restricted Maximum Likelihood option of the MGCV package of Wood (2006) (version 1.5–5) to obtain the optimal balance between undersmoothing and oversmoothing. To evaluate whether a smooth function is contributing significantly to the model, we inspected the Bayesian p-values that the MGCV package documentation provides.

The upper panels of Figure 3 summarize the tensor smoothsof the GAM fitted to the lexical decision data. All smooths shown are highly significant ($p < 0.0001$). The Head Frequency measure never reached significance. Other interactions were also considered, but turned out not to be robust predictors and were removed from the model specification. The adjusted R-squared for this model is 0.37. In Figure 3, darker shades of grey represent more negative transformed response latencies, and hence shorter response latencies in the original untransformed ms scale. The small dots represent the individual data points.

First consider the top left panel. As Compound Frequency (horizontal axis) increases, we see darker shades of grey, indicating shorter response latencies, as expected: Frequency effects are usually facilitatory. The effect of Compound Frequency is modulated by Modifier Frequency, but only for lower-frequency compounds. Here we see that latencies decrease to some extent for compounds with higher-frequency modifiers. Note that this facilitation tends to level off for higher modifier frequencies.

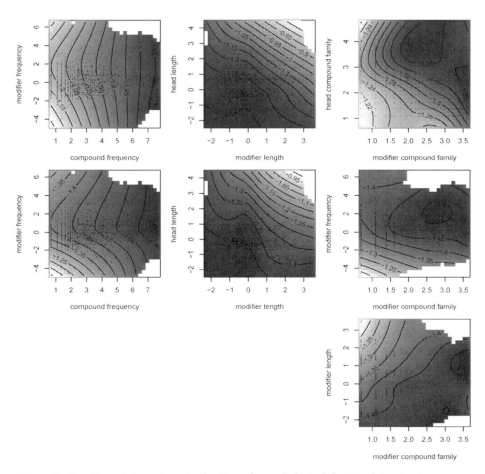

Figure 3. Nonlinear interactions in the (transformed) *lexical decision latencies* (top panels) and *naming latencies* (lower panels) to 1252 two-constituent noun-noun compounds as available in the English Lexicon Project. Lighter shades of gray indicate longer latencies. Dots represent data points. Grid nodes that are too far away from actual data points are excluded from the plot and show up in white

The top center panel visualizes the interaction of the orthographic lengths of head and modifier. Most observations are located in a fairly flat and somewhat irregular area between contour lines -1.3 and -1.2. The relatively small number of compounds with both larger left and right constituents elicited longer response latencies. Clearly, constituent length comes with increased processing costs.

The upper right panel depicts the interaction of head and modifier family size. The effect size of this interaction is small: Contour lines are 0.02 units apart, instead of

0.05 units as in the two preceding panels. Facilitation for both family size measures is visible, but what strikes the eye is that facilitation is most pronounced for high values of one family size given intermediate values of the other family size.

2.2 Word naming

The English Lexicon Project also provides the naming latencies for the present data set. The last two rows of panels in Figure 3 summarize the generalized additive model fitted to the naming data. As for the lexical decision data, all tensor smooths were highly significant ($p < 0.0001$). The adjusted R-squared of this model was 0.36.

The pattern of results obtained for the interaction of Compound Frequency and Modifier Frequency, and for modifier and head orthographic length, resembles that obtained for the lexical decision latencies. The effect of the frequency of the modifier seems to be somewhat stronger and more persistent for higher compound frequencies. It also seems to level off more substantially for higher modifier frequencies.

The effect of the family size measures emerges as qualitatively different from that observed for lexical decision. First, and not shown in Figure 3, a significant facilitatory effect of head family size was present (modeled with a restricted cubic spline), that was not modulated by the family size of the modifier as in lexical decision. This effect was linear for all but the highest head family sizes, for which it leveled off.

Second, the effect of the family size of the modifier was modulated by both modifier frequency and modifier length. This modulation was captured by a three-way tensor product, which outperformed a model with two pairwise tensor products. Figure 3 visualizes this complex interaction by means of the two pairwise interactions in the central and lower right panels. In the central rightmost panel, the contour lines are more horizontally oriented than vertically oriented, indicating that most of the effect in this panel is carried by Modifier Frequency. Modifiers with higher frequencies elicited somewhat shorter naming latencies, but this facilitation leveled off for higher modifier frequencies. The evidence for facilitation from the modifier family size is much stronger in the lower right panel, especially so for longer modifier lengths.

3. The eye-tracking record

The data from the English Lexicon Project, although informative, remain silent about the time course of information uptake during reading. As a consequence, it remains unclear whether the effects of compound frequency and effects linked to distributional properties of the head and modifier occur simultaneously or whether they are staggered in time. Early studies argued that constituent effects preceded whole word effects (Taft and Forster, 1976). As mentioned in the introduction, the reverse position, with whole-word effects preceding constituent effects in time, has also been argued for

(Giraudo and Grainger, 2001). Eye-movement studies offer more fine-grained insight into the moments in time at which the different kinds of information carried by a compound are absorbed, and may help resolving this theoretical conflict.

Classic eye-tracking studies replicated results from lexical decision and naming studies suggesting a role for both constituents and whole words in lexical processing (see, e.g. Andrews et al., 2004; Bertram et al., 2004). Pollatsek et al. (2000) observed that the frequency of the head and the frequency of the compound emerged in later measures of compound processing, after the first fixation on the word. The study by Hyönä et al. (2004) also suggested that for long compounds such as dishwasher there is early activation of the left constituent (dish) and only later activation of the right constituent (washer).

In what follows, we re-analyze the data of a recent study (Kuperman et al., 2009b) with generalized additive models. As GAMs currently do not integrate well with mixed-effects models, our analyses are carried out on by-compound mean durations, averaged over participants. In our reanalysis, we focus on compound frequency, head and modifier frequency, head and modifier compound family size, and head and modifier length, all defined in the same way as in the study of the lexical decision and naming latencies in the English Lexicon Project. For details on the decorrelation of these predictors, the reader is referred to (Kuperman et al., 2009b). The materials comprise 1250 Dutch compounds, written without hyphens or intervening spaces, for which at least one of the immediate constituents was itself morphologically complex. The length in letters of these compounds ranged between 8 and 12 characters.

Figure 4 summarizes the effects observed at the first fixation (left panels, all $p < 0.0001$), the subgaze duration on the modifier (central panels, all $p < 0.0001$), and the total gaze durations (all $p < 0.003$). In this figure, contour lines are all equidistant. Going from left to right, the overall shades of grey become lighter, indicating longer durations (as expected for increasingly cumulative measures). Contour lines are all 0.1 unit apart, so that the size of the different effects can be gauged.

First consider the top three panels, which visualize the development of the effects of the orthographic lengths of head and modifier. The effects of the lengths are very small during the initial fixation. Notably the effect of modifier length becomes highly prominent in the modifier subgaze measure, to ebb away in the gaze durations with the exception of compounds with long heads. Note, furthermore, that the effect of modifier length is facilitatory during the initial fixation, inhibitory during subsequent fixations on the modifier as witnessed by the subgaze duration measure, and emerges as facilitatory in the overall gaze durations. Apparently, an initial short fixation on the modifier is followed by more refixations, balancing a first superficial scan by more thorough visual processing. From the very beginning, this process seems to be modulated by the length of the head. The longer the head, the less superficial the initial scan is. The same holds, albeit to a lesser degree, for subsequent subgazes on the modifier. This suggests that knowing more substantial processing is going to be required for the right part of the visual input induces the system to invest more in understanding the

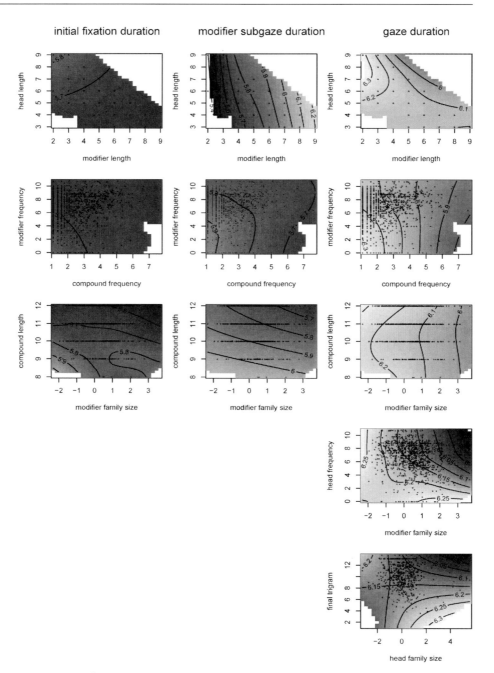

Figure 4. Nonlinear interactions in the eye-movement record

left part of the word. In the overall gaze durations, the earlier investment in longer subgazes on longer modifiers pays off in the form of a modest overall processing advantage that manifests itself most clearly for compounds with more than average head lengths. Within the area for which the present experiment offers data, we see slightly elongated gaze durations for compounds with short modifiers and long heads, and perhaps also for compounds with short heads and long modifiers. Apparently, at this late processing stage, the system has optimized processing for heads and compounds of average length. Finally, it is noteworthy that the effect of head length is already apparent at the very first fixation. This effect should probably be interpreted as an approximate indicator (based largely on parafoveal information) of the amount of visual information that remains to be scanned.

The effect of orthographic length that emerges from the eye-tracking record of this Dutch experiment is remarkably different from the effects observed above for the English lexical decision and naming latencies. For the English experiments, latencies increased as both head and modifier increased in length. Two possible explanations may help understand this discrepancy. First, English writes many of its compounds with intervening spaces, and does so without exception for more complex compounds. Dutch, like German or Danish, consistently write compounds, however complex, without spaces. This language difference may lead to different reading strategies. Second, the English and Dutch data sample the space of lengths differently. The Dutch data are tightly constrained by the length of the compound, which varied between 8 and 12 letters. The English compounds vary in length between 6 and 14, and offer more compounds for which both head and modifier are relatively long. As a consequence, the Dutch data are more restricted in their exploration of the consequences of constituent length in compound processing. Further research is clearly required.

The second row of panels of Figure 4 summarizes the joint effects of compound frequency and modifier frequency. Moving from left to right, the number of contour lines increases, notably for compound frequency, indicating that especially this whole-word frequency effect increases in magnitude as we move from early to late measures of information uptake. As the visual information about the full compound becomes available mostly after the first fixation, this increase in the magnitude of the compound frequency effect is as expected. A comparison with the English lexical decision and naming data shows roughly similar patterns in both sets of latencies and in the gaze durations. This suggests that the frequency effects that emerge in the response latencies are more or less fully developed at the point that the eye leaves the word.

An important question is, however, why the compound frequency effect emerges as early as it does, already at the first fixation duration. One potential explanation is to assume that compounds have some full-form orthographic access code that can be activated on the basis of partial matching information for the initial constituent, combined with parafoveal information about the compound's length, following, e.g., Pollatsek and Rayner (1982). This explanation fits well with parallel dual route models of lexical access in which orthographic representations for constituents and whole words are activated in parallel. Interestingly, the present evidence for an early effect of compound frequency, also observed for Finnish compounds in the regression study of Kuperman et al. (2008), is incompatible with 'postlexical' staged models of lexical access according to which properties of a complex word as a whole would become accessible only after access to their constituents has been completed.

There are several problems with the assumption of whole-word orthographic access representations mediating the activation of word meaning. First, whole-word frequency effects are much more robust than constituent frequency effects, and have been observed even for very low-frequency complex words (Baayen et al., 2007). The presence of whole word frequency effects in the absence of constituent frequency effects for low-frequency complex words would, under the traditional interpretation of frequency effects in psycholinguistic theories, deny a role for constituents in lexical access to many very low-frequency words, a conclusion that does not make sense from both linguistic and computational perspectives. It makes more sense to understand full-form frequency effects as tapping into the reader's knowledge about the joint probability of modifier and head, possibly in the form of memory traces for previous experience in parsing the compound into its constituents. Given that only partial information is available at the earliest stages of visual information uptake, the effect of compound frequency is, under this alternative, expected to increase over time and to produce its greatest effect in the gaze duration measure.

The third row of panels of Figure 4 brings together the contour plots for the family size of the modifier, which is also already present at the first fixation. Here, an inhibitory family size effect for short compounds levels off for longer compounds. Subsequent fixations on the modifier reverse the effect into facilitation independently of compound length. In the gaze durations, a modest facilitatory effect of modifier family size remains visible. For small-family modifiers it appears to be somewhat less facilitatory for medium-length compounds. The facilitation in the gaze durations mirrors the facilitation observed in the naming and lexical decision latencies.

The early presence of a family size effect in the eye-movement record is interesting in the light of the suggested semantic nature of this effect (De Jong et al., 2000). Although an early family size effect can be interpreted as a form effect relating to familiarity with parsing a word out as a modifier in a compound, as argued by Kuperman et al. (2009b), one would expect facilitation rather than the inhibition actually observed at the initial fixation, the prime moment for visual parsing.

It is therefore worth considering the possibility that with the modifier family size effect we are actually observing an index of early semantic processing, which would harmonize well with the very early stages at which semantic effects have been demonstrated to arise (Feldman et al., 2009). Instead of assuming a form-then-meaning architecture for morphological processing and strictly serialized processing of constituents, we may need to consider more flexible architectures in which the link between form and meaning in reading is much tighter than has often been assumed.

Possibly, the constituent and compound frequency effects documented in the present study should also be interpreted as – at least partial – indices of meaning activation. The development over time of the interaction of compound frequency by modifier frequency, with an initially stronger effect of modifier frequency that later gives way to a compound frequency effect would then represent an initial understanding of the modifier by itself that then gives way to an integrated understanding of the compound as the unification of the meanings of modifier and head.

There are two further interactions at work in the gaze durations. The one but last panel of Figure 4 graphs the joint effect of modifier family size and head frequency. For compounds with low-frequency heads, the effect of the modifier family size is slightly inhibitory. For compounds with higher frequency heads, the majority of the compounds in this experiment, the effect reverses. The effect of head frequency shows a similar reversal, with facilitation for higher modifier families, but inhibition for smaller modifier families. The gaze durations, as a global measure of information uptake, therefore suggest a trade-off, perhaps even some form of competition between the head and the modifier. Possibly, modifiers with large families are stronger competitors for the functional interpretation as head of the compound.

The final interaction, shown in the lower right panel of Figure 4, concerns the modulation of the head family size by the token frequency of the word-final trigram. Word beginnings and word ends are visually the most salient part of the word. Kuperman et al. (2009b) therefore included the initial and final trigrams as control variables in their study. The pattern that emerges in the gaze durations suggests that the final trigram affords shorter gazes for compounds with intermediately-sized head families. Conversely, compounds with highly salient final trigrams are the ones for which facilitation from the head compound family is present. This suggests that in long compounds, a salient constituent ending is essential for boosting the head family size effect.

We conclude this reanalysis of the data of Kuperman et al. (2009b) with a methodological comment. The GAM models fitted to the durational measures from the eye-tracking record confirm the main patterns uncovered with the help of standard linear models with multiplicative interactions. Across models, we find, however, that the GAMs offer slightly more precise models that explain significantly more variance (6% in the case of the gaze duration measure, for instance). Furthermore, the GAMs are able to detect interactions that are not visible to standard models with linear interactions (in the case of the gaze duration analysis, this is the case for the interactions of the frequency of the head by modifier family size, and head family size by final trigram).

4. General discussion

If one thing is clear from the present analyses, it is that the processing system is much more complex than previously thought. Psycholinguistic theories of morphological processing have been dominated by staged models, with different frequency effects reflecting different processing stages.

The independent effects illustrated in Figure 1 for a straightforward main effects linear model would seem to offer support for such an approach. For instance, the effect of Compound Frequency in Figure 1 seems independent of all other effects, and thus can be argued either to be accessed prior to, or posterior to the access to its constituents, following either Giraudo and Grainger (2001) or Taft (1979).

However, the enhanced precision obtained by carefully considering interactions suggests a fingerprint not of a simple sequence of processing stages, but rather the hallmark of a complex dynamic system. Even for straightforward lexical decision and naming latencies, Figure 3 illustrates a much more intricate interplay of factors. The effect of Compound Frequency, for instance, is modulated by the frequency of the modifier. This is not what either prelexical or postlexical theories of morphological processing predict. Yet it fits well with the observation that high-frequency words may have different distributional properties than low-frequency words (see Ricca, this volume). The decrease in facilitation from constituent frequencies, or even its reversal into inhibition as seen in the eye-tracking record may reflect the increased independence of high-frequency complex words with respect to their constituents. For an experimental investigation of specifically the role of semantic transparency in compound processing and how transparency may modulate the effects of compound and constituent frequencies, see Kuperman and Baayen (2009c).

The eye-movement record clarifies that this interaction of compound frequency and modifier frequency can arise early, already at the initial fixation duration (see Figure 4). Even at this early stage of information uptake, when the modifier is fixated, the processing system is already anticipating the possibility that this modifier may be part of a larger compound structure.

Our data suggest that understanding the compound frequency effect as simply reflecting the activation of some unstructured, holistic lexical representation may be misguided. As explained by Kuperman et al. (2008), it is worth considering this effect as tapping into dynamic knowledge about the joint probability of head and modifier and their combinatorial semantics.

Our data further suggest that multiple sources of linguistic information are used dynamically as soon as they become available. These multiple sources include not only information from the fixated modifiers, but also information from the embedding compounds, and, also present from the initial fixation duration, information coming from the modifiers' morphological families, which are now known to play important roles for compound interpretation (Gagné & Shoben 1997, see also Gagné & Spalding, this volume), the selection of interfixes in Dutch (Krott et al. 2001) and compound stress assignment in English (Plag et al. 2008).

Computational issues in compound processing

Vito Pirrelli, Emiliano Guevara and Marco Baroni
ILC / CNR – University of Oslo – University of Trento

Understanding compounds is a challenging computational task, cutting across multiple levels of linguistic analysis and touching upon intricate issues of representation, grammar architecture and algorithmic processing. At the same time, compounds raise all these problems in the most direct and exemplar way. From this perspective, they are an ideal probe into core issues of language architecture, making us pause about the need for advanced processing models and multi-disciplinary approaches to long-lasting linguistic *cruces*. This chapter reviews some of the lessons that can be learned from reading twenty years of computational literature on the topic and assesses them against the background of germane theoretical and cognitive issues.

1. Introduction

Lexical compounds have been described as syntactically complex units which behave in a syntactically simple way (Matthews 1974). Starting from their syntactic simplicity, it seems indisputable that they normally behave in syntax like simple words. Given two words like *milk* and *breast milk*, there are in general no constructions in which the compound can appear, but not the simpler constituent *milk*. On the other hand, it is fairly uncontroversial to say that a compound like, e.g., *blackbird*, exhibits the same construal of the corresponding phrasal unit *black bird*. The only grammatical difference is, arguably, that the phrase has been collapsed into one constituent with a single main stress. Moreover, even if the *blackbird* pattern is not very productive (there is no *whitebird* or *redbird*), and even if not every *blackbird* is actually black (the female is brownish), the semantic relation between the two constituents of the compound is akin to the modifier-head relation between the two elements of the corresponding phrase. Finally, there is an unmistakable sign of the wide range of productivity of word composition: recursion. There are embedded layers of compounds which are like layers of syntactic embedding, as exemplified in (1) below:

(1) a. [*child language*]
　　b. [[*child language*] *acquisition*]

c. [[[child language] acquisition] research]
d. [[[[child language] acquisition] research] group]
e. [[[[[child language] acquisition] research] group] member]

Such a hybrid status, halfway between a simple lexical unit and a complex construction, and the ensuing controversy on its proper theoretical account, are accompanied by an intriguing processing paradox, which will be the main object of inquiry of the present chapter. Although compounds are flourishing in modern language (Leonard 1984, Biber & Clark 2002), especially in more formal genres such as news and academic writings, and although compounding is apparently common to all human languages (cf. Scalise & Vogel, this volume), compound parsing remains an exceedingly hard case for most current Natural Language Processing (NLP) systems. We suspect that this is due to a failure of traditional NLP architectures to deal with complex interface domains of language competence like lexical compounding. Moreover, as NLP architectural choices (such as serial order of parsing levels, decoupling of lexicon and grammar, domain insensitivity, insensitivity to frequency effects, to mention but a few) are often dictated by theoretical requirements, a better understanding of the limitations of current computational systems is bound to shed light on broader theoretical issues.

The enormous interest raised by the connectionist view on morphological computation over the last several years (Rumelhart & McClelland, 1987 McClelland & Patterson 2002, Pinker & Ullman 2002) showed that no theoretical model of language can nowadays be decoupled from an algorithmic view of (i) how it develops through maturational steps during language acquisition, (ii) how it is put to use in on-line parsing. No seriously explanatory morphological theory can nowadays exist without a testable running model, and no processing model can go much further without supporting theoretical and empirical evidence (Culicover & Nowak 2003, Rogers & McClelland 2004, Westermann & Plunkett 2007). In this chapter, we explore the view that, by testing theoretical issues through well-established computational tools, we can gain novel insights into aspects of representation, organization and understanding of lexical compounds.

Hereafter, we shall mostly focus on productive **NN compounds** for various reasons. First, this is the most productive compounding type (Boase-Beier 1987, Becker 1992, Kiefer 2001, Olsen 2000) and lends itself quite naturally to **recursive word formation mechanisms** (see (1) above) which, in turn, raise non-trivial parsing issues. At the same time, unlike other more syntactically-flavored compound types like Prep+N (e.g. Italian *sottoscala* 'under+stairs, closet (under the stairs)') or V+N (Italian *apriscatole* 'open+cans, can opener'), NN compounds are not amenable to strongly compositional approaches to semantic interpretation. They have also been the focus of the cognitive literature dedicated to **concept combination**, as they provide somewhat "pure" instances of this process and an ideal test-bed for comparing alternative hypotheses. Indeed, as we shall see in more detail in Section 3, there is a lot to be gained in dealing with compounds from a **multi-disciplinary perspective**.

The chapter is structured as follows. Section 2 contains an overview of the main issues in compound parsing addressed in the computational linguistic literature. This will give us the opportunity to point out possible connections with more theoretical issues and will pave the way to Section 3, entirely devoted to the central problem of NN compound interpretation. Section 4 discusses the implications of this work for both theoretical and computational Morphology.

2. Parsing issues: a bird's eye view

In the computational linguistic literature, compound parsing has been the focus of intensive investigation for a number of reasons. Firstly, compounds may play tricks to parsers. In those languages where compound constituents are (or can be) written as distinct words separated by blanks, compounds are often difficult to demarcate in context and may generate unusual or highly ambiguous sequences of part-of-speech tags (exemplified by the three consecutive nouns in *child language acquisition*). Conversely, one-word compounds (e.g. German *Lebensversicherung* or English *boyfriend*) raise problems of lexical recognition and segmentation. Since compounding is both productive and frequent, particularly in technical writing, closed-list strategies of fully stored compounds are of limited use.

Another related issue rests on the impact of compound identification on high-level parsing stages. With the only exception of the compound head, all compound constituents syntactically depend on other compound constituents only. Moreover, they are unlikely to govern words which are not part of the compound, in keeping with the well-known observation that compounds are **syntactically atomic units**, impervious to external syntactic dependencies. Early identification of compounds in context can thus simplify syntactic parsing considerably, by reducing the number of available landing sites for dependency links.

Finally, compounds are often used to refer to highly salient and accessible concepts that are characteristic of both domain and content of their embedding texts. Hence, it is difficult to overestimate their importance for **document indexing** and **classification**. Their interpretation requires considerable domain knowledge and is often based on recurrent, quasi-lexicalized interpretive schemata (see Section 3.3 below), leading to subtle differences in translating a compound from one language to another (Baldwin & Tanaka 2004), as shown by the following English examples and their corresponding Italian translations:

(2) a. *a paper cup* => *un bicchiere di carta*
 b. *a paper document* => *un documento cartaceo*.
 c. *a tea cup* => *una tazza da tè*
 d. *a cup of tea* => *una tazza di tè*

The compounds in (2a) and (2b) above, in spite of their lexical and semantic similarities, are translated as two different syntactic constructions in Italian (respectively, NP+PP and NP+AP). Conversely, the compound in (2c) and the phrase in (2d) receive translations sharing the same structural makeup (NP+PP) but differing in the choice of preposition.[1]

Over the past twenty years, researchers in Computational Linguistics have addressed at least five different tasks that have to do with compounds: 1) identification of compounds from amongst other text; 2) syntactic analysis of structurally ambiguous compounds; 3) prediction of prosodic features of compounds; 4) directly translating compounds in one language to phrases in another; 5) assignment of implicit semantic relations. The remainder of this section is devoted to a concise overview of the two most basic steps in compound parsing: i) compound identification in context and ii) assigning structure to compounds. Both steps are preliminary and conducive to full **compound interpretation** (an issue we shall turn to in Section 3), but they are also instrumental in addressing application-specific issues, such as Machine Translation problems, and non trivial aspects of compound recognition in speech processing, such as compound prosody.[2]

2.1 Issues in compound identification

Tokenization is the preliminary step in automatically parsing a raw text. It amounts to assigning a string of characters the status of single token, where a token is the most basic parsing unit, approximately corresponding to a linguistic word, but also including non-lexical units such as dates, addresses, proper names, acronyms, measuring expressions etc. In languages where orthographic words are separated by blanks or punctuation marks this is often a relatively simple task. But in languages like Japanese or Chinese, where words are chained together in written form, tokenization requires a considerable amount of pre-processing, relying on a large repository of word forms, and must often invoke complex context-sensitive constraints over large text spans.

For tokens to be identified as independent words and assigned their corresponding part-of-speech tag (or grammatical category), their set of morpho-syntactic features, and their lemma (or lexical exponent), they have to undergo a level of morphological parsing. In its simplest instantiation, **morphological parsing** requires the existence of

---

1. Admittedly, the examples barely scratch the surface of the difficulties posed by compounds in Machine Translation, even between two relatively similar and related languages such as English and Italian.

2. Suffice it to cursorily point out at this juncture that issues of compound interpretation have a bearing on compound stress patterns. Even structurally unambiguous compounds may vary their accent contour depending on the specific relation holding between compound constituents (Sproat, 1994), confirming that "[…] semantics is the most important factor in the prediction of the stress pattern of a given compound" (Plag et al. 2008).

large repositories of word forms, where each form is glossed with a set of inherent morpho-lexical features. From this perspective, compounds in text cause a few parsing hiccoughs in those languages where they can be written as one word, as shown by the following German example (borrowed from Anderson and Lightfoot, 2002):

(3) *Lebensversicherungsgesellschaftsangestellter*
    life insurance company employee

No German lexical repository can be expected to be large enough to contain all possible compounds of this kind. A principled solution is to split (3) into its simple constituent words (*Leben + versicherung + gesellshaft + angestellter*), for the latter to be looked up in a lexical database as individual entries. Nowadays, **compound splitting** is a well-understood but not completely solved parsing problem in as diverse languages as German, Swedish, Estonian, Korean and Bengali (Koehn & Knight 2003, Friberg 2007, Dasgupta et al. 2005, among others). It can be addressed by either resorting to traditional rule-based finite-state technology (Koskenniemi 1983) or frequency-based, probabilistic splitting models (Koehn & Knight 2003) or memory-based machine-learning tools such as TiMBL (Friberg 2007), or a combination of the above-mentioned approaches (Park et al. 2004).

When a compound is written as a sequence of independent words embedded in a larger context, the complementary issue arises of demarcating its boundary constituents, thus determining its text span. To get an intuitive grasp of the nature and extent of this problem, known in the literature as **compound identification**, consider a sentence like the following:

(4) *The CPU signal interrupts transfer activity.*

Upon parsing (4), any NLP system would balk at the morpho-syntactic ambiguity of the form *interrupts*, which can be either a noun (plural) or a verb (present indicative, third person singular). Furthermore, the word *transfer* exhibits an analogous range of morpho-syntactic ambiguity. A parser will thus output, at least, the two alternative structures in (5):

(5) a. [*The CPU signal*]$_{NP}$ [*interrupts*]$_V$ [*transfer activity*]$_{NP}$
    b. [*The CPU signal interrupts*]$_{NP}$ [*transfer*]$_V$ [*activity*]$_{NP}$.

There is no straightforward answer to the comparatively neglected problem of choosing between (5a) and (5b). Arens et al. (1987), among the few technical papers devoted to compound identification, analyze the input text by searching for phrasal patterns that match fragments of it, and by replacing the fragments with the conceptual template associated with the pattern. Patterns of this kind may differ in degrees of abstraction, as they can be specified for as diverse linguistic information as part-of-speech, individual word entry and concept class. Ambiguous verb-noun sequences such as (4) are tackled heuristically, by resorting on limited look-ahead for a morpho-syntactically unambiguous noun to be found in the sequence, and by checking number agreement constraints.

This and similar approaches are based on the reasonable assumption that identifying a compound requires information about the local syntactic context where the compound occurs. All such information must be available – to use Saussure's phrase – *in praesentia*. Other approaches, such as Marcus (1980) and Lauer (1995), implement the idea that compound identification is based upon knowledge available elsewhere in other comparable contexts (*in absentia*). For example, given the noun sequence *ABC*, the relative acceptability of possible noun-noun pairs (e.g. *AB*, *BC*) is assessed by observing the likelihood of each such pair in other similar usages. If both *AB* and *BC* are already attested pairs, then *ABC* is a likely compound too. The use of paradigmatic information of this kind is an important factor in determining the internal structure of a compound. It is to this issue that we turn now.

2.2 Finding structure in compounds

Once a compound is located in context, we are left with the task of (i) bracketing and eventually (ii) labeling its internal structure. The two steps are interlocked. The compound parsing history defines levels of structural embedding (as in Example (1) above), which, in turn, are assumed to reflect the scope of the semantic relations holding between compound constituents. From this perspective, compounds that are made up of two nouns trivially show no structural ambiguity: by application of rule (6), a compound like *child language* will only receive the structure in (7).

(6) N → N N
(7) [*child*$_N$ *language*$_N$]$_N$

Things get more complicated as soon as (6) applies recursively. In a three-word compound like *child language acquisition*, one can assign structure by recursive application of rule (6) to the leftmost N to yield (8). Alternatively, expanding the rightmost N in (6) we get (9).

(8) [[*child*$_N$ *language*$_N$] *acquisition*$_N$]$_N$
(9) [*child*$_N$ [*language*$_N$ *acquisition*$_N$]$_N$]$_N$

The structure in (8) is said to be **left-branching**, and the structure in (9) **right-branching**. The two structures receive two different interpretations: (8) is compatible with the meaning of the phrase *acquisition of child language*, while (9) is better paraphrased as *the acquisition of language by a child*.

The choice between left-branching and right-branching compounds is not a dichotomous one. All intermediate combinations are theoretically possible (*pace* Marcus 1980), as shown by the following examples:

(10) a. [[*bone china*] [*tea service*]]
      b. [*pilot* [[*teacher training*] *course*]]

Nonetheless, the corpus-based literature agrees that left- and right-branching structures are largely prevalent (Resnik 1993, Lauer 1995, Berg 2007), with left-branching compounds being attested twice as often as right-branching ones in right-headed compound families (e.g., in Germanic languages). These distributions are strikingly skewed and have prompted scholars to look for explanations.

Berg (2007) puts forward a parsability argument. In left-branching compounds, every leftmost sequence of two or more words is a compound itself (see (1) above). This allows listeners, upon hearing the *i*th compound constituent, to reuse the compound structure built up on the sequence $w_1, \ldots, w_{i-1}$. Compounds that are easier to understand are more frequent overall.

Lauer (1995) states the problem in probabilistic terms. The two structures in (8) and (9) presuppose the dependency chains illustrated in (11) below, where each pointed arc represents a 'dependant → head relationship'. Given two relations such as *child → language* and *language → acquisition*, the three words can give rise to one compound only: *child language acquisition*. In contrast, the pair of dependencies *child → acquisition* and *language → acquisition* can in principle produce two equally likely compounds: *child language acquisition* and *language child acquisition*. This means that *child → acquisition* and *language → acquisition* can generate twice as many compounds as *child → language* and *language → acquisition* do. If this is true in general, it implies, by straightforward application of Bayes' rules, that, given a compound *ABC*, the probability that it has a left-branching structure is twice the probability that it has a right-branching structure. This is what corpus data tell us.

(11) [[child$_N$ language$_N$] acquisition$_N$]$_N$ [child$_N$ [language$_N$ acquisition$_N$]$_N$]$_N$

How can a parser choose between the different bracketing structures in (11)? Work in the 80's and early 90's (Finin 1980, McDonald 1982, Gay & Croft 1990, Vanderwende 1994) proposes to deal with the problem through knowledge intensive algorithms. The key idea is that the concept defined by the compound head defines a **schema** with **slots** (or attributes) and that the non-head constituent should fill one of these slots. For example, since a *sanctuary* is a reserved area for protecting animals, its concept is interpreted as having an HABITAT-FOR attribute with value *animals*. Syntactic and semantic analysis is then required to decide that *birds* in *birds sanctuary* should occupy that slot. The method relies on the availability of rich lexical knowledge bases, which can either be encoded manually for small domains (Finin 1980) or acquired from dictionary definitions (Vanderwende 1994).

More recently, distributional approaches have suggested that the lexical knowledge required for compound bracketing can be looked for directly in large corpora. The simplest of these algorithms is reported in Pustejovsky et al. (1993) and Bourigault (1993). Given an *ABC* compound, a search is conducted elsewhere in the corpus for the two possible pairs *AB* and *BC*. Whichever is found is then chosen as the most closely bracketed pair.

More sophisticated variants of the same idea capitalize on Smadja's work. Smadja (1993) shows how statistical methods offer reliable means of acquiring domain specific expectations concerning the joint distribution of words in sufficiently large training corpora. Association measures such as **Pointwise Mutual Information** (Church & Hanks 1989) have become standard utilities to measure the degree of collocational association of word pairs in context, by exploiting the intuition that words belonging to the same bracketed pair will co-occur in corpora significantly more often than what would be expected under a model of chance co-occurrence (based on the frequency of the individual words). Liberman and Sproat's (1992) propose using pointwise mutual information to compare all possible word pairs in a compound. Along similar lines, Resnik (1993) bases pair comparison on the contribution of one pair member to the **conditional entropy** of the other.

All these approaches assess the acceptability of only adjacent pairs of nouns. Lauer (1995) departs from this assumption to observe that the choice of either bracketing in (11) is contingent upon the acceptability of the underlying dependency links. The correct left branching structure in (11) depends on *child* being understood as a **modifier** of *language* rather than as an **argument** of *acquisition*. Note that adjacent pairs would not be able to discriminate between the two interpretations, since both *child language* and *language acquisition* are equally likely.

Lauer's point is important as it establishes a strong connection between parsing and **relation-based** approaches to compound interpretation. Unlike the schema modification models mentioned above (requiring the selection of particular dimensions or attributes within the representation of the compound head), relation-based compound interpretation assumes that nouns are combined by determining a fairly general thematic relation holding between them (e.g. LOCATION, PURPOSE, TOPIC), and that there is a relatively small set of such relations (Downing 1977, Levi 1978). Unlike dimensions that are necessarily part of the head-noun schema, thematic relations can be conceptualized as construction-driven functions, that operate during conceptual combination much like dependency links during syntactic parsing. As we shall see in the coming section, this view permeates most recent work in compound interpretation, both in the computational and in the psycho-cognitive literature.

3. Interpreting NN compounds

To linguists and cognitive scientists, NN compounds are simple prototypical instances of lexical composition and **concept combination**. To computational linguists, they are the hardest such instances to parse, as they show little if any trace of overt syntactic structure. Over the last few years, all these communities have appeared to independently work on a strikingly similar conceptualization of the task of compound interpretation that consists in guessing the thematic relation holding between the compound constituents. In this section we will review three different approaches to the computational treatment of compound noun semantics: they are available as two doctoral dissertations (Lauer 1995, and Ó Séaghdha 2008) and a journal article (Baroni, Guevara & Pirrelli 2007). All of these approaches are inspired by work on theoretical classification of compound-noun relations; most notably Levi (1978), Warren (1978) and Bisetto & Scalise (2005).

3.1 Lauer (1995)

Lauer's dissertation explores statistical models for language learning, using compound nouns as a test bed for a series of experiments in parsing and semantic classification. As such, it is, to the best of our knowledge, the first extended work on compound analysis from a statistical/corpus-based perspective. The main tenet of Lauer's approach is the theory of meaning distributions, according to which "the process of language interpretation begins with knowledge of the possible intended meanings in the form of semantic expectations [...] we know, for example, that a sentence describing the diet of animals is to be expected in an encyclopaedia and that one describing the diet of shoes isn't. Given two arbitrary propositions, we can choose which of the two is more expected" (Lauer 1995: 61). In particular, semantic expectations can be modeled as probabilistic distributions that are highly context dependent and combined with lexical and grammatical constraints. One can thus select the most probable interpretation for a sequence of words given that enough prior knowledge is available from a corpus in the form of contextual co-occurrence cues.

Lauer adopts Warren's (1978) inventory of prepositional paraphrases (excluding verbal-nexus and copula compounds), according to which an English NN compound can be successfully paraphrased by using one out of only eight prepositions (*of, for, in, at, on, from, with, about*) in the template **head-preposition-modifier**. This allows use of unsupervised statistical learning methods that require little human engineering effort and which can successfully be implemented using readily available resources. For example, a compound like *baby chair* is paraphrased as *a chair for babies*, and *war story* as *a story about war* (cf. Lauer 1995: 155). For compound interpretation, the problem is to decide which of the eight possible outcomes is the preferred paraphrase given any sequence of two nouns (e.g. *a chair of/for/... babies*). This decision is taken by training a probabilistic model that counts how many times each constituent is found in a corpus, either followed or preceded by each preposition, and then chooses the preposition that is maximally likely to occur between the constituents at stake.

Lauer's approach does not reach a high level of accuracy (47% for the best model), although it is significantly better than the baseline. The main problem is data sparseness, especially given the modest size of the training corpus (The New Grolier Multimedia Encyclopaedia 1992, approx. 8 million words). This difficulty may be overcome if the algorithm is trained on a larger corpus.

3.2 Ó Séaghdha (2008)

Ó Séaghdha's (2008) dissertation is the most recent extended work dedicated to computational compound interpretation. We focus on this study also because it is representative of current trends in computational linguistics, as applied to the study of compounds: creation and rigorous validation of an annotated gold standard, adaptation of state-of-the-art supervised machine learning approaches, use of different corpus-based measures of semantic similarity, based on paradigmatic and syntagmatic patterns.

Ó Séaghdha's study of automated NN compound interpretation makes an important technological contribution by applying sophisticated machine learning techniques to the task. It is however also of interest to the broader community of linguists and cognitive scientists for two main reasons. First, the author annotates 2,000 NN English compounds extracted from the widely used 100-million word British National Corpus (BNC: http://www.natcorp.ox.ac.uk). In the resulting database, the compounds are classified into 6 classes: BE *(guide dog, rubber wheel)*, HAVE *(family firm, star cluster)*, IN *(air disaster, dawn attack)*, INST *(cereal cultivation, foot imprint)*, ACTOR *(army coup, project organizer)* and ABOUT *(history book, house price)*, plus various "trash bin" categories (lexicalized, unknown, etc.). An innovative aspect, with respect to other categorization schemes, is the definition of the two broad INST and ACTOR categories, that contain compounds that either describe the relation between an event and a participant in the event *(cereal cultivation)* or the relation between two participants in an event *(honey bee)*. With respect to classifications that distinguish participant-event and participant-participant relations, this scheme does not have the problem of classifying so-called "synthetic compounds" like *truck driver*, where, arguably, the head stands for both a participant (the driver) and an event (the driving). The compound is labeled as either INST or ACTOR depending on whether the more active role is filled by a non-sentient or sentient entity, respectively. For example, *blaze victim* is labeled as INST because the non-sentient *blaze* plays a more active role in the underlying event (killing or injuring) than the sentient *victim*.

Independently of the specific scheme he proposes, Ó Séaghdha sets high standards for compound annotation, as annotators are presented with compounds in context (sentences from the BNC), and provided with an annotation manual that spells out detailed classification criteria (appended to the thesis). Moreover, the database is publicly available (http://www.cl.cam.ac.uk/~do242/resources.html). Ó Séaghdha also reports agreement figures for two independent annotators on a subset of the database. Agreement is at 66.2%, or 62% when correcting for chance. This shows that even with detailed annotation instructions and relatively broad classes, compound classification is a very difficult task for expert human annotators. In turn, the expert agreement level sets a realistic upper bound for what we can expect automated methods to achieve.

The second main contribution of Ó Séaghdha's thesis concerns the cues that his algorithms use to classify compounds. Ó Séaghdha adopts a supervised paradigm in which a program (called a **classifier**) extracts statistical generalizations about such cues from manually labeled compounds, and it is then evaluated in terms of accuracy in classifying unseen compounds.

Ò Séaghdha uses two kinds of cues: **lexical similarity** and **relational similarity**. Lexical similarity is based on the idea that typical heads and modifiers of a certain class are similar. For example, many BE compounds have mass nouns denoting materials as modifiers and countable concrete objects as heads. If our training data contain *silver necklace* labeled as BE, and the algorithm must classify the unseen *platinum ring*, it could guess the BE class based on pairwise *silver-platinum* and *necklace-ring* similarities. A standard automated way to approximate semantic similarity between two words using corpus data (e.g., Sahlgren 2006) involves recording the patterns of co-occurrence of the two targets with other words in a corpus, and measuring how similar the resulting co-occurrence profiles are (the intuition being that similar words like *necklace* and *ring* will share similar contexts). Ó Séaghdha takes this approach, extracting the relevant co-occurrence statistics from the BNC (using a larger and noisier corpus produced slightly worse results).

Lexical similarity relies on the co-occurrence patterns of the target heads and modifiers independently of each other (we can obtain a meaningful measure of lexical similarity for *silver necklace* and *platinum ring* even from a corpus in which no pair of these words ever co-occurs), whereas relational similarity is based on the comparison of the contexts in which the head and modifier of the compound co-occur. The intuition – essentially the same as in Lauer's method, and based on the original insight of Levi (1978) and others – is that when head and modifier occur in non-compound usages, other elements in the sentence might be informative about the relation linking them For example, fragments like *necklaces made of silver* and *rings made of platinum* are good cues of the fact that *platinum ring* is the same type of compound as *silver necklace*. Ó Séaghdha estimates relational similarity by extracting and comparing fragments containing the strings connecting head and modifier as well as left and right contexts (*a ring made of platinum* results in the fragment *a H made of M* to be used as a feature in the relational representation of *platinum ring*). Relational data are extracted from the BNC and from the 2-billion Gigaword corpus (available from the Linguistic Data Consortium).

In Ó Séaghdha's automated classification experiments, lexical similarity greatly outperforms relational similarity (61% vs. 52.1% accuracy), but the two information sources are at least partially complementary, so that top accuracy is achieved by combining them. The resulting accuracy of 63.1% is approaching the human annotators' agreement rate.

3.3 Psycho-computational issues

From a cognitive perspective, compound interpretation requires integration of the conceptual representations associated with the compound constituents. It is tempting to conceive of such an integration as a straightforward information transfer from the non-head to the head of a compound. Conceptual representations of the compound constituents are first independently accessed and then integrated on the basis of the head selectional requirements. This simple picture, however, has recently been called into question. Access to the conceptual representations of compound constituents is now believed to be more dynamic and context-sensitive, so that the whole compound appears to prompt a process of selective activation of contextually-relevant semantic properties. Shoben (1991), Gagné & Shoben (1997), Gagné (2002) suggest that speakers use the distributional knowledge of how nouns have previously combined to interpret a novel combination. For example, when *mountain* is used as a modifier in a compound, it typically instantiates a locative relation (e.g., *mountain resort, mountain goat*). As a result, people tend to interpret a novel combination such as *mountain fish* by using their knowledge that *mountain* is typically used as a locative modifier. From a strictly computational standpoint, constraint-satisfaction approaches (Costello & Keane 1997) make the interesting suggestion that the interpretation of a complex concept is not carried out on the basis of one-off inferential steps. Rather, it makes use of pre-compiled, schematized information, which is memorized in the mental lexicon and applied probabilistically in the on-line interpretation of novel compounds.

In a similar vein, Baroni, Guevara & Pirrelli (2007, henceforth BGP) have recently argued that understanding Italian NN compounds requires a construction-driven strategy and that the interpretation process does not apply uniformly across compound types, but makes use of asymmetrical constraints, depending on the compound type. They deal with two basic types of compounds (Wisniewski 1996, 1997, Bisetto & Scalise 2005, Pirrelli and Guevara forthcoming): so-called **attributive** (or property) compounds predicate two different concepts of the same entity, e.g. a *ball fish* is a fish round like a ball; **relational** (or subordinative) compounds, on the other hand, establish a conceptual relation between two independently predicated entities, e.g. a *bread knife* is a knife for cutting bread (note that "relational" in this section is used for this compound type, and not for relational similarity as in 3.2 above).

In an attributive compound like *pesce palla* ('fish + ball, blowfish'), the intended interpretation 'a fish shaped like a ball' depends on shape being a highly salient property of *palla*. The same interpretation is shared by all Italian compounds with *palla* as rightmost constituent and can be represented as a **Lexicalized Interpretation Schema** (LIS), *X_palla*, where *X* is any (concrete) noun and *palla* is called the interpretative *pivot* of the schema. Conversely, understanding a relational compound like *ufficio cambi* ('office + exchanges, exchange office') is based upon the conceptual structure of the head *ufficio*, which is the pivot of the LIS. This is confirmed by the high productivity of *ufficio_X*: *ufficio reclami* 'complaint office', *ufficio stipendi* 'wage office', etc.

There are some measurable consequences of this view. First, the emergence of a given LIS in the lexicon should follow from recurrent distributional properties of the members of a LIS-sharing family. This means that, in relational compounds, heads should recur more systematically than non-heads. The prediction for attributive compounds is that the reverse distributional pattern obtains.

BGP test these predictions in clustering experiments where Italian relational and attributive compounds are classified in an unsupervised fashion on the basis of purely distributional cues of the constituents both inside compounds and in other syntactic contexts. These cues measure, in particular, the tendency of relational compounds to have both a highly specialized head (consistently acting as a head in both compounds and NPs) and the tendency for both head and modifier to occur in explicit syntactic relational constructions, linked by overt prepositions (cf. Lauer's approach). Conversely, attributive compounds are characterized by non-heads that specialize as compound modifier.

BGP extract statistics about these cues from large amounts of Web-mined text (in the order of 2 billion tokens) and they use them to perform an unsupervised clustering of a set of 119 frequent corpus-extracted compounds (24 attributives and 95 relationals). Of the two clusters that emerge from the statistical analysis, one has perfect purity, being composed of 75 relationals. The other contains all 24 attributives (that are thus correctly grouped entirely within one cluster) together with the remaining 20 relationals. The error analysis shows that at least some of the problematic relationals are characterized by specialized modifiers, such as *radio* in *radio station* or *press* in *press conference*, which explains the confusion with the attributives (that are also characterized by specialized modifiers), and suggests that there are special LISs that have a relational semantics but that are at the same time modifier-driven like attributives. In any case, the general results suggest that speakers can at least get a good head start on acquiring the distinction between frequent relational and attributive compounds on the basis of the distributional behavior of their constituent nouns and their tendency to specialize as (relational) heads or (attributive) modifiers.

BGP go on to show that their model of relational/attributive asymmetries can also predict the acceptability of newly generated compounds. Without getting into details, they present the results of an online acceptability experiment showing, among other things, that it is easier to generate acceptable compounds by changing the modifier of an attested relational compound while keeping the head fixed than vice versa, whereas for attributives the reverse pattern holds (it is better to change the head than the modifier). This confirms the pivot role of heads for relational compounds and modifiers for attributive compounds. With this experiment, BGP also illustrate a promising methodology for future studies of this sort, namely one that verifies predictions of a computational simulation with behavioral studies (as opposed to the more common route of simulating results of already performed behavioral investigations in a post-hoc manner).

4. Discussion

Interpreting compounds in context is a challenging computational task, cutting across multiple levels of linguistic analysis and touching upon intricate issues of representation, grammar architecture and algorithmic processing. At the same time, compounds raise all these problems in the most direct and exemplar way. For this reason, they are an ideal probe into core issues of language architecture, making us pause about the need for novel, integrated processing systems and multi-disciplinary approaches to long-lasting linguistic *cruces*. In this concluding section, we summarize some of the lessons we learned.

Competence & use: People understand, memorize and parse compounds in a construction-driven way. Not only do speakers keep track of token-based information such as frequency of individual, holistically stored compounds, but they are also able to organize them into paradigm-like structures, or *compound families*, whose overall size is an important determinant of ease of lexical access and interpretation (De Jong et al. 2002). Moreover, speakers seem to be able to successfully generalize over compound families by means of lexicalized interpretive schemata (LIS) in such a way that their acceptability judgments on newly-coined compounds appear to strongly correlate with substitution of semantic cognates in the non-pivotal position of a LIS. Quantitative and analogy-based approaches to automatic compound interpretation lend support to this view, capitalizing on stable correlation patterns that link distributional entrenchment of lexical pivots with productivity and ease of interpretation. This provides a clear indication for a promising converging trend between computational and cognitive lines of scientific inquiry, ultimately blurring the traditional dichotomy between language competence and language use.

Lexicon & Grammar: The evidence reviewed in this chapter is hard to reconcile with a notion of lexicon in the sense of "a raw set/list of words", but rather lends support to a dynamic, generative notion of the lexicon as a productive grammar component (Anderson & Lightfoot, 2002). The emergence of compound schemata from the lexicon is the by-product of a process of active organization of stored compounds as complex constructions. The mixed status of a LIS, halfway between a truly compositional process and a lexicalized pattern (see infra), appears to support the view of a feeding interaction between grammar and lexicon which is at odds with the classical **grammar-lexicon divide**.

Weak vs. Strong Compositionality: Compounds are understood as the output of productive, lexicalized templates, containing variables whose semantic type is constrained by the template as a whole. The semantic relation conveyed by the template is not simply derived compositionally from its lexical fillers and their embedding structure, but is profiled by the pivot-sharing schema underpinning an entire compound family. It is useful, in this connection, to make a distinction between a traditional notion of **strong compositionality**, which derives the meaning of a complex construal on-line, on the basis of the meanings of its constituents and their local, syntagmatic relations, and a **weak** notion of **compositionality**, based on non-local, paradigmatic relations, that are inferred from an entire family of similar constructions. From an interpretive standpoint, routinely created compounds behave like weakly compositional constructions.

Parsing issues: Of late, the machine-learning literature has thrown in sharp relief the importance of usage-based statistical patterns in modeling a number of language parsing tasks as **classification problems**. Even an elusive linguistic task such as compound interpretation can be reduced to choosing the contextually appropriate semantic relation holding between members of a pair out of a limited set of such relations. Tractable stochastic classification algorithms like those based on the Maximum Entropy Principle (Berger et al. 1996, Ratnaparkhi 1998), for example, can estimate the probability of having a particular relation assigned to a noun pair, given a characterization of the pair and its context in terms of a set of "active" linguistic features. Such features may pertain to multiple levels of linguistic analysis, ranging from word position in a text window, to grammatical category and agreement features, lemmas, concept classes and degree of semantic association between concepts. A stochastic classifier solves the problem by calculating, for each relation, the conditional probability of having that relation instantiated in context, given an appropriate feature-based representation of that context.

The approach reflects a notion of parsing as the search for an optimal solution to a classification problem, given a set of both **syntagmatic** (i.e. locally available) and **paradigmatic** (i.e. inferred from other contexts) constraints. Such constraints are violable and probabilistic and can be viewed, rather conservatively, as traditional categorical rules which are statistically weighted to be more readily applied in context. In our view, however, there is much more to them than it meets the (conservative) eye. They prompt the view that grammatical competence is acquired through minimal inferential steps, shaped up by inherently probabilistic knowledge, and defining a grammatical gradient ranging from strongly lexicalized patterns to sweeping generalizations. Compound processing takes a level of generalization lying halfway between these two extremes.

Acknowledgments

Much of the work reported in this chapter was carried out in the framework of the Italian CompoNet project, headed by Sergio Scalise. The authors thank the book editors for their kind invitation, gratefully acknowledge the insightful comments received in the reviewing process and remain accountable for all outstanding errors.

Relational competition during compound interpretation

Christina L. Gagné and Thomas L. Spalding
University of Alberta

The meaning of an endocentric compound (e.g. *snowball*) is derived not just from its constituents (*snow* and *ball*) but also from the relation between them (e.g. noun MADE OF modifier). We propose that, during the interpretation of an endocentric compound, various relational structures compete for selection, and that the fewer competitors the required relation has, the less time it takes the system to settle on that relation. We present results from three streams of empirical research. The first stream indicates that the availability of relational structures influences ease of processing. The second indicates that relations inhibit each other. The third indicates that relation availability is specific to a constituent's use in a particular morphosyntactic role. We conclude by presenting a theoretical framework of compound interpretation.

1. Introduction

Noun-noun compounds are the most productive compound type in English (Lieber 1992) and the vast majority are endocentric (Bauer 1983, 2009, this volume; Spencer 1991). Although each constituent of an endocentric compound contributes to the overall meaning of the compound (e.g. *apple pie* is a type of pie that is made with apples), the process by which a compound's meaning is derived is complex and not yet fully understood. An important aspect of establishing a meaning for an endocentric compound is determining how the constituents are related. For example, *olive oil* can be paraphrased as "oil derived from olives", but this relation does not apply to *baby oil*. Although compounds and phrases can have multiple interpretations (e.g. *cat rash* could be a rash on a cat, or a rash caused by a cat), typically only one meaning is intended by the speaker/writer. Whenever multiple interpretations are available, the listener/reader must settle on the most likely interpretation in order to correctly understand the utterance in which the compound appears. Taft (2003: p. 127) has noted that although some of a compound's meaning can be derived from the constituents, "… other information is needed as well". We propose that the "other information" consists of the conceptual knowledge that is used to construct a relational structure during the interpretation of a compound. In this chapter, we present empirical evidence that suggests that the ease with which an endocentric compound can be interpreted is influenced by the relative availability of competing relational structures.

There have been several attempts to characterize the specific link that exists between the constituents (e.g. Downing 1977; Finin, 1980; Lees 1963; Levi 1978; Li 1971; Warren 1978). Although the relations proposed by these researchers vary, the common assumption is that the underlying structure of compounds and modifier-noun phrases provides information about how the constituents are linked and that this structure plays an important role in determining the meaning of the whole compound/phrase. Although, some linguists have rejected the assumption that compounds rely on a restricted set of relations and argue that a given compound can potentially have an infinite number of interpretations (Coulson 2000; Kay & Zimmer 1976; Lieber 1992), existing empirical evidence suggests that compounds do not typically assume a wide range of meaning. For example, Štekauer (2005) asked participants to propose and rate as many possible meanings as they could for novel compounds, and found that almost all compounds had one reading that was clearly dominant. Furthermore, even Kay and Zimmer (1976) and Downing (1977) propose that a small set of relations can be used to describe most compounds.

This convergence in meaning might arise due to compounds being viewed as long-term category labels rather than as deictic phrases. Apple-juice seat (which was a phrase originally used to refer to a particular place at a table) is an example of a deictic phrase in that it expresses a temporal state and "… does not imply the existence of a subcategory of seats known as apple-juice seats, of which this particular seat is a member" (Downing 1977: 819). The constraints on deictic compounds are not the same as those that govern compounds that are used as long-term category labels. The existence of deictic compounds does not a priori rule out the possibility that compound processing might involve relation linking and does not preclude the use of a set of common relations in psychological research. Indeed, Downing's results indicate that people prefer to interpret compounds as long-term category labels, rather than as deictic phrases. Hence, the focus of the research discussed in this chapter is on this usage.

2. Evidence for the use of relational structures

2.1 Relation availability is influenced by the modifier's general usage

An important theoretical question that arises from the debate about the internal structure of a compound concerns the psychological reality of relational structures. The notion of an underlying relational structure has been part of the linguistic literature for some time, but to what extent is the processing of compounds and noun phrases affected by their relational structure? Shoben and Medin (as reported in Shoben 1991) were among the first to investigate the psychological reality of relational structures. They proposed that some relations are more complex than others and that this variation in complexity might influence ease of processing; for example, causal relations (noun CAUSES modifier; modifier CAUSES noun) appear to have more primitives than the MADE OF relation. However, they failed to find support for this complexity hypothesis in that there were no systematic differences in processing time that could be attributed to relational category.

Shoben and Medin focused exclusively on the complexity of the relations and did not consider the possibility that relational effects might be constituent-dependent. In contrast, Gagné & Shoben (1997) proposed that the availability of relational information varies from constituent to constituent. For example, language users might know that *chocolate* is usually used in a compositional sense (MADE OF), but also is used occasionally in an ABOUT relation. If so, then some relations might be more readily available than others and this difference in availability might influence the time required to interpret a compound. It should be easier to interpret a compound that requires a relation that is highly available (i.e. a relation that is a strong competitor) than to interpret a compound that requires a relation that is less available (i.e. a relation that is a weak competitor).

To test this prediction, Gagné & Shoben (1997) estimated the competitiveness of various relations for particular constituents by creating a set of potential phrases by crossing 91 modifiers and 91 head nouns. They determined whether each pairing had a sensible literal interpretation and classified these 3,239 sensible modifier-noun phrases in terms of Levi's (1978) categories. For example, *plastic bee* was classified as noun MADE OF modifier. Next, the frequency with which various modifiers and head nouns were used with each of these relations was calculated by counting the number of times that a particular modifier-relation pairing was used, and the number of times that a particular head noun-relation pairing was used. For example, the modifier *plastic* appeared in 38 phrases. Of these, 28 used the noun MADE OF modifier relation, 7 used the noun ABOUT modifier relation, 2 used the noun DERIVED FROM modifier relation, and 1 used the modifier CAUSES noun relation. A relation distribution was calculated for each modifier and each head noun.

These distributions were used to select items whose relations were either highly competitive or less competitive for an individual modifier or head noun. Relations were considered a good competitor for a particular constituent if that relation was among the set of relations that was used for 60% or more of all phrases in the corpus using the constituent in question. All other relations were considered low availability relations. Compounds were selected to fit one of three experimental conditions. HH compounds were defined as compounds for which the underlying relation was among the set of highly competitive relations for both the modifier and head, HL compounds were compounds for which the underlying relation was among the set of highly competitive relations for the modifier only, and LH compounds were compounds for which the underlying relation was among the set of highly competitive relations for the head noun only. In Experiment 1, the individual words were controlled in that the identical words were used in all three experimental conditions. In Experiment 2, the relation was controlled such that there was an equal number of each relation type in each condition. Nonsense filler items (e.g. *plastic rain* and *scarf soda*) were included. Each item was presented on a computer screen and participants indicated, by pressing a key, whether the item had a sensible literal interpretation.

In both experiments, responses to the HH and HL phrases were faster than responses to the LH phrases, indicating that it was easier to determine that the phrase had a sensible interpretation when the underlying relation was among the set of highly-competitive relations for the modifier than when it was a less competitive relation. Responses in the HH and HL conditions did not differ, indicating that the availability of the relation for the head noun constituent did not strongly affect response time. This pattern of results was observed in both an ANOVA in which the items were categorized as high and low in terms of relative relation availability as well as in a regression analysis which used a continuous measure of a relation's competitiveness.

Recently, Wisniewski & Murphy (2005) have suggested that Gagné & Shoben's (1997) findings are due to differences in familiarity and plausibility rather than to relation availability. This claim was based on the observation that subjective familiarity and plausibility judgments were correlated with response times. It is well known that the objective familiarity (i.e. frequency) of a compound can affect ease of processing (see, e.g. Andrews, Miller & Rayner 2004). However, Gagné & Spalding (2006) show that objective familiarity (i.e. frequency) did not differ across Gagné & Shoben's experimental conditions. In addition, they found that subjective familiarity ratings were affected by relation availability; noun-noun phrases were more likely to be viewed as familiar when preceded by a item with the same relation than by an item with a different relation. This finding is inconsistent with the claim that subjective familiarity is a cause rather than an effect; if subjective familiarity were a causal factor then it should not have been influenced by relation availability. Finally, the influence of relation availability remained even after subjective familiarity and plausibility were statistically controlled.

A second concern that has arisen is that relation frequencies based on Gagné & Shoben's relational distributions might be not be consistent with relation frequencies calculated using an actual corpus (Maguire, Devereux, Costello & Cater 2007). Contrary to this claim, there is a close linear relationship (r =.87) between the relation frequencies derived by Gagné & Shoben and those based on the British National Corpus (Spalding & Gagné 2008).

2.2 Relation availability is influenced by the modifier's recent usage

Gagné & Shoben's (1997) data indicate that a modifier's relational distribution, which is based on long-term experience with the modifier concept, influences ease of interpretation, but does a modifier's recent usage also influence interpretation? This question was examined in a series of experiments that used a priming procedure; a novel noun-noun compound (e.g. *student vote*) was preceded by one of several prime compounds. The primes were manipulated such that the prime shared either the same modifier or head noun (Gagné 2001). In addition, the primes used either the same general relation as the target combination (e.g. *student accusation* and *employee vote* both can be paraphrased using the noun BY modifier relation) or a different relation (e.g. *student car* and *reform vote*). A neutral prime used a different head noun and modifier than the target, but used the same relation. Each participant saw each target phrase only once during the experiment, but across all participants each target phrase was seen an equal number of times with each prime. The task was to indicate, by pressing one of two computer keys, whether the phrase had a sensible interpretation. Nonsense filler items (e.g. *stair moon*) were included so that the participants could not determine whether the intended response was sense or nonsense prior to the presentation of the stimulus.

If a person has just used a particular relation in the context of a modifier (e.g. if noun BY modifier was used to link *student* and *accusation*), then this recent activity should make that relation a more successful competitor, and it should be easier to reuse that relation during the interpretation of a subsequent combination (e.g. *student vote*) with the same modifier. The data confirm this prediction; it took less time to interpret a phrase when it was preceded by a prime using the same modifier and the same relation than when preceded by a prime using a different relation.

The process of selecting a relation and constructing a unified representation is obligatory for novel compounds because the compound is not part of the lexicon (i.e. it has no pre-established representation). But what about compounds that have already entered the language? Are their meanings directly retrieved, or does deriving the meaning of familiar compounds involve the same meaning computation process as do novel compounds? If the latter is true, then the ease of processing familiar (i.e. lexicalized) compounds such as *necklace* should be affected by relation availability. Gagné & Spalding (2004) examined this issue by presenting target compounds after a prime compound containing the same modifier. The target combinations were lexicalized compounds that were randomly selected from a larger set of compounds found in the Brown corpus (Francis & Kučera 1982). Prime items were constructed for each target compound (e.g. *snowball*); the same relation prime (e.g. *snowfort*) used the same relation (MADE OF) as the target and the different relation prime (e.g, *snowshovel*) used a different relation. Participants saw each item on a computer screen and indicated, by pressing one of two computer keys, whether the item had a sensible literal interpretation. Nonsense filler items were also included.

As was the case for novel compounds, participants took less time to respond to the target compound when it was preceded by the same relation compound than when it was preceded by the different relation compound. This same pattern of results was obtained when a lexical decision task was used (Gagné & Spalding 2004) and when all of the primes were restricted to existing compounds (Gagné & Spalding 2009). These findings suggest that recent exposure to the prime compound altered the competitiveness of the relational structures and, consequently, influenced the time required to interpret the target compound.

3. The nature of the relation priming effect

The data discussed in Section 2 indicates that the required relation is more available in the same-relation prime condition than in the different-relation prime condition. This issue requires further exploration because this difference in relation availability could have two different sources. First, a repeated relation might affect relation selection by increasing the availability of the required relation (facilitation). Second, because the relations compete, the different relation prime might increase the availability of a relation other than the one required, thus making the relation selection process harder and slower than it otherwise would have been (inhibition). In processing novel phrases, one would expect both facilitation and inhibition. In processing familiar compounds, priming should be primarily due to inhibition because the same-relation prime is unlikely to greatly facilitate the pre-established meaning.

To investigate this issue, we again used the same-relation and different-relation conditions, but also included a new baseline condition that does not explicitly require the use of any particular relation. The baseline condition used only the first constituent of the target compound. Presenting only the modifier should activate the modifier's whole relational distribution, but should not activate any particular relation above its normal baseline within that distribution. We also selected this baseline because it controls for priming due to lexical repetition of the modifier constituent. Thus, for the target *snowball* (ball MADE-OF snow), the baseline prime was *snow*, the same-relation prime was *snowfort* (fort MADE-OF snow), and the different-relation prime was *snowshovel* (shovel FOR snow).

If the priming effect is due purely to facilitation, then the same-relation condition should be fast, and the different-relation and the baseline modifier-only condition both should be slow. If the effect is due purely to inhibition, then the different relation condition should be slow and the same relation condition and baseline both should be fast. If there is both facilitation and inhibition, then the same relation condition should be fast, the different relation condition should be slow and the baseline should be in the middle. These predictions were tested in two experiments using the same design and materials. Experiment 1 used a sense/nonsense task. Experiment 2 used a lexical decision task – participants indicated as quickly as possible whether the item presented on the computer screen was a real English word. The results are consistent with inhibition. In both experiments, recent presentation of a compound using a different relation made it more difficult to interpret the target compound, whereas responses in the same-relation and modifier-only prime conditions did not differ.

4. Access to relational information is dependent on the constituent's morphological role

The experiments presented in Sections 2 and 3 indicate that relational availability affects ease of interpretation. However, this research did not directly address the question of the relation between morphosyntactic assignment and relation selection. This is a relevant question because the use of relational structures has two aspects; the activation of the relational frame (e.g. X MADE OF Y) and the specification of the arguments (e.g. equating X with *rabbit* and Y with *chocolate* during the interpretation of *chocolate rabbit*). Argument specification involves identifying the morphosyntactic role played by each constituent (e.g. *chocolate* is the first constituent and modifies the head noun, and *rabbit* is the second constituent and is the head noun). Should theories of compound interpretation view morphosyntactic assignment and relation selection as two distinct psychological processes?

To address this question, we conducted three experiments to determine whether prior usage of a constituent in a different role affects the ease of processing a noun phrase (Gagné, Spalding, Figueredo & Mullaly 2009). We used a priming paradigm and manipulated whether the prime used the same relation as the target. In Experiment 1, the shared constituent moved from the modifier position in the prime to the head noun position the target. For example, the target *research mouse* was preceded by either *mouse trap* (same-relation prime) or *mouse whisker* (different-relation prime). In Experiment 2, the shared constituent moved from the head noun position (in the prime) to the modifier position (in the target). For example, *summer car* (FOR) and *metal car* (MADE OF) served as primes for the target *car port* (FOR).

If relation availability is dependent on the particular constituents in a particular role, relation priming should occur only when the repeated constituent is in the same position in both the target and prime. That is, responses to *reading lamp* (lamp FOR reading) should not be aided by the recent presentation of *lamp shade* (shade FOR lamp) relative to the recent presentation of *lamp light* (light PRODUCED BY lamp) even though they are based on the same relation because *lamp* moves from the modifier role in the prime to the head noun role in the target. In contrast, if relations are accessed independently of the constituents (as suggested by Estes 2003; Raffray, Pickering & Branigan 2007), then responses to the target item should be faster following a prime containing the same relation than following a prime containing a different relation regardless of whether the repeated constituent is in the same position. Our results support the first hypothesis. Neither experiment revealed evidence of relation priming; the response time to the target was unaffected by whether the preceding prime item shared the same relation.

In Experiment 3, the design included a same-position condition, and allowed us to determine whether there is any benefit to repeating a constituent in the same morphosyntactic position, and, if so, whether this benefit is tied to the re-use of a particular relation. The prime compounds used the target's modifier in either the same position or in the different position. In addition, we manipulated whether the prime used the same relation as the target. These two factors were crossed, and, thus, four prime compounds were created for each target item. In the case of the target *fur gloves* the same-relation primes were *fur blanket* and *acrylic fur*, and the different-relation primes were *fur trader* and *brown fur*. In addition to the experimental materials, all experiments included nonsense filler items (e.g. *arm fog*).

We found that relation priming was contingent on the morphosyntactic role of the shared constituent. In all three experiments, repeating the relation with the constituent in a different morphosyntactic role did not speed processing of the target. Experiment 3 confirmed that the same-relation prime only benefited the processing of the target combination when the shared constituent remained in the same position. Thus, the prime *fur blanket* was more beneficial than *fur trader* during the processing of the target *fur gloves*, but *acrylic fur* was not more beneficial than *brown fur*. These data indicate that relational information about the constituents is accessed in the context of the constituent's morphosyntactic role. For example, during the interpretation of *snowball*, conceptual knowledge that is relevant to thinking about *snow* as a modifier and conceptual knowledge that is relevant to thinking about *ball* as a head noun becomes available.

In terms of the role of morphosyntactic information, we found that processing of the target was faster when the shared constituent was in the same position in both the prime and the target. Importantly, this benefit occurred regardless of the relation similarity. To illustrate, both *fur blanket* and *fur trader* aided the processing of *fur gloves*. It could be the case that the link between each constituent's conceptual representation and the relation is strengthened due to presentation of the prime. Raffray et al. (2007) for example, suggest that the concept associated with each word is directly linked to a particular relation. However, this explanation would not account for the finding that responses in the same-position condition were faster than in the different-position condition when the relation was different. Instead, this finding points to a process in which the constituents are assigned morphosyntactic roles without reference to any particular relational structure.

5. Theoretical framework

The data presented in Sections 2 and 3 indicate that the availability of relational structures influences the ease of interpretation and that the influence of a prime compound on the subsequent processing of a target compound is primarily due to inhibition from competing relations rather than to facilitation of a repeated relation. The data presented in Section 4 indicate that the ease of interpreting compounds depends on the ease of mapping constituents to particular morphosyntactic roles (as indicated by the finding that responses in the same-position condition are faster than responses in the different-position condition), and on the ease of selecting an appropriate relational structure (as indicated by the finding that relation priming does occur when the shared constituent is used in the modifier position). Taken together, the findings point to a framework of compound interpretation that involves the coordination of lexical, morphological, and conceptual information. Our proposed framework is based on the CARIN theory of conceptual combination (Gagné & Shoben 1997; Spalding & Gagné 2008). The CARIN theory focuses on the conceptual system, but assumes that the lexical representations of the constituents are accessed and assigned to the modifier and head noun role. Thus, Section 5.1 contains a brief discussion of lexical and morphological information.

5.1 Use of lexical and morphological information

For over 30 years, the question of how morphologically complex words are represented in the mental lexicon has been a topic of psycholinguistic research (for overviews see Frost, Grainger & Rastle 2003; Gagné 2009). This debate focuses on whether morphologically complex words (e.g. *teacup*) are represented as whole-units, or by their constituents (e.g. *tea* and *cup*), and on the point at which the representations of the constituents become available. We found that repeating a constituent led to faster responses to the target compound even when the repeated constituent was in a different position in the prime and target, and even when a different relation was used for the prime and target. This aspect of our data suggests that compounds are represented in terms of their individual constituents and that these representations are available during the initial processing of a compound.

After becoming activated, the lexical representations are then mapped onto a morphosyntactic structure (see Sandra 1994, for an extensive discussion of why the mental lexicon might be organized morphologically). Modifier-head structures can be embedded. For the phrase *oak cabinet store*, the first two constituents form a phrase in which *oak* is the modifier and *cabinet* is the head-noun. This phrase is then used as the modifier of the larger phrase for which store is the head-noun. Although in the case of two-word phrases, the process of morphosyntactic assignment appears, a priori, to be trivial, the same-position effect observed in Gagné et al. (2009) indicates that this process can be speeded. Moreover, the position effect occurred in both the same and different relation conditions, which indicates that this effect is purely morphosyntactic; that is, the identification of a constituent as modifier versus head noun is, initially, not associated with any particular relational structural.

5.2 Use of conceptual information

In the linguistic literature, there is growing evidence that the semantic relation between a compound's constituents is determined by the semantic-encyclopedic information that is associated with the constituents (Scalise & Bisetto 2009; Lieber 2004,

2009a). For example, the semantic/pragmatic body of the constituent *cookbook* includes the knowledge that cookbooks contain recipes, and the body of the constituent *bed* includes the knowledge that beds are used for sleeping. In terms of the psychological literature, this information is viewed as part of the conceptual system because it is involved in a number of cognitive functions (such as reasoning, categorization, and perception) in addition to communication (Komatsu 1992). In our theoretical framework, conceptual knowledge plays a vital role in compound and noun phrase interpretation; it is used to select and evaluate relation structures.

Relation availability is not affected by the mere usage of a relation; otherwise, relation priming should have occurred in the absence of semantically similar constituents (Gagné 2001; Gagné et al. 2009; Gagné, Spalding & Ji 2005). Instead relation availability is associated with concepts in a particular role, as demonstrated by the data discussed in this chapter. To account for this finding, we propose that the search for suitable relations is triggered only after the constituents have been assigned to their respective morphosyntactic roles. If the concept is accessed in the context of being a modifier, then aspects of the concept that are useful for identifying how it can be used to modify other concepts are particularly relevant. Conversely, if a concept is accessed in the context of being a head noun, then information about how it can be modified (e.g. knowledge about the kinds of sub-categories that it permits) is particularly relevant. Relational structures are simultaneously constructed and evaluated. These structures compete with one another and ease of interpretation depends on how quickly a single relation structure can be identified as the most likely candidate.

5.3 Evaluation of competing relations

As relations become activated, each interpretation must be evaluated for plausibility. We assume that the evaluation process occurs beyond the level of conscious awareness, though this assumption is mostly the product of intuition. An important aspect of evaluation concerns the ability of the constituents to function as arguments for a given relation structure. A constituent must fit the entailments required to fulfill a particular function within a particular relation. Consequently, the constituent *snow* can function as a modifier in the MADE OF relation because it is a material. Likewise, the constituent *planet* can theoretically work as the head noun of a LOCATIVE relation because planets can be in a physical location.

However, evaluating each constituent's ability to serve as an argument in a particular relation is not sufficient because the restrictions are co-determined. To illustrate, the MADE OF relation requires that the modifier be a material, but not just any material. It must be a material that is appropriate for the head noun. *Snow sculpture* satisfies these restrictions, but *snow hospital* does not. This aspect of the evaluation process replies on world knowledge; the interpretation *planet LOCATED mountain* is rejected as a possible interpretation of *mountain planet* because planets are too large to be located in the mountains (Gagné & Shoben 1997; Spalding & Gagné 2008). Levi

(1978) refers to this type of knowledge as extralinguistic knowledge and she outlines several semantic and pragmatic considerations that are used to determine the contextually most plausible reference for a given compound (see also Downing 1977; Finin 1980; Meyer 1993; Štekauer 2005, 2006, 2009).

Our psycholinguistic framework outlining the process of interpretation differs somewhat from current linguistic frameworks that propose that semantic-encyclopedic information plays an important role in determining the meaning of a compound (Lieber 2004, 2009a; Scalise & Bisetto 2009). According to Lieber's lexical-semantic analysis, the head noun selects aspects of the non-head. For the compound, *apple cake*, the constituent *apple* includes the feature "can be an ingredient", and this feature corresponds to the "made with ingredients" feature of *cake*. Each constituent contains many features that can be considered and coordinated. Given the vast amounts of knowledge that people potentially have about various constituents, the consideration of the various properties of the constituents must be constrained. We argue that semantic-encyclopedic knowledge about the various constituents is accessed and considered in light of particular relations. Thus, when evaluating the plausibility of *snowball* as "a ball made of snow", information relevant to this particular relation is used to guide and constrain the use of conceptual knowledge. Consistent with this prediction, we found that activating information relevant to the particular relation structure (and constituents) makes verification of that relational interpretation easier (Spalding & Gagné 2007). A second reason for proposing that the coordination of modifier and head noun features, per se, is not the primary basis for combining constituents is that the features of the constituents are not fully available prior to the interpretation of a compound/phrase (Springer & Murphy 1992; Gagné & Murphy 1996).

5.4 Relations are activated and evaluated in parallel

The CARIN theory claims that relations are activated in parallel and compete for selection; this aspect of the theory was mathematically instantiated using a ratio which has the frequency (represented as a proportion) of the selected relation in the numerator and the sum of the frequency of the three strongest competitors and the selected relation in the denominator (Gagné & Shoben 1997). An exponential function was applied to each proportion. More recently, Maguire et al. (2007) have suggested that this ratio does not embody competition. However, Spalding & Gagné (2008) demonstrate that the ratio makes strikingly sharp distinctions between items on the basis of the number of competing relations that are stronger than the selected relation, and that these distinctions become sharper with increasing numbers of competitors. In addition, Spalding & Gagné (2008) present three mathematical models that instantiate sensitivity to number of competitors; these models fit the data better than a model that includes only frequency of the selected relation. This result indicates that competition, in general, and the number of strong competing relations, in particular, influences ease of compound interpretation.

To further evaluate whether the evaluation of relations involves all relations or just a smaller set of the strongest relations, and whether evaluation is a serial process, Spalding and Gagné (2008) compared the relative ability of the number of stronger competitors and the rank of the selected relation to fit the data. The number of stronger competitors was based on the three strongest relations in a given modifier's relational distribution because Gagné & Shoben (1997) found that including more than the three strongest relations in the denominator of the strength ratio did not improve the fit of the model. The number of stronger competitors fits the Gagné & Shoben (1997) data as well as (or better than) the rank of the selected relation (Experiment 1, $r = .47$ for rank and .45 for number of competitors, and Experiment 3, $r = .25$ for rank and .36 for number of competitors). If the process of ruling out relations is serial, then rank should be a much better predictor, as it should be able to pick up any variance associated with ranks beyond 4, while number of competitors will not do so. Interestingly, this seems not to be the case; competitors that are ranked below 4 have little impact on ease of processing.

Overall, the data are consistent with a parallel process in which the number of strong competitors matters greatly, but the number of weak competitors (but still stronger than the required relation) does not matter as much. This might be because such weak competitors require very little negative evidence from the head to rule them out, while strong competitors might require substantial negative evidence from the head. Thus, perhaps low frequency relations (for either constituent) are hard to accept and easy to reject. This pattern would also make sense on a parallel account in which the amount of activation to a given relation is a function of its frequency for the modifier, and in which the difficulty of ruling out an activated relation is related to its level of activation.

5.6 Elaboration of a relational interpretation

The relational interpretation is the framework around which a more detailed interpretation can be constructed. Many relational interpretations will need to be elaborated to be useful in various contexts. As one extremely simplistic example, if one is reading through a children's story and comes across the compound *snowman*, it might be enough to understand that this is a man MADE OF snow until the reader reaches the part where the snowman starts dancing around when the children put that old silk hat on his head. To fully understand the story, the representation of *snowman* must have been elaborated such that a *snowman* should not be able to dance around. Without this elaboration, the dancing snowman is not magical (or even surprising). The required elaboration depends strongly on the relation (i.e. dancing on the part of a snowman interpreted as a man who shovels snow would not be magical, though it might be amusing) but the elaboration is not carried out by the relation, nor by the relational information. Elaboration of the meaning depends on the relation, but draws on knowledge beyond the relation.

5.7 Assumptions about nature of relational information

We make three primary assumptions concerning the nature of relations. First, relational information is assumed to be associated with the conceptual representations of the constituents, not with their lexical representations. Because relational information is associated with the conceptual level, similar effects are likely to obtain across (at least some) languages. Indeed, the influence of relation availability has already been demonstrated with Mandarin (Ji & Gagné 2008) and Indonesian (Storms & Wisniewski 2005) compounds. Also, because concepts that are semantically similar are likely to have similar relational information, relational priming can be obtained from semantically similar constituents (Gagne 2002).

Second, this framework is agnostic with respect to representation of the relations themselves. Because the relations are inherently parts of other structures, it is not clear whether the kinds of relations that are used in relational interpretations require separate representation, or whether they are recovered for use from their existence within existing relational interpretations. It is certainly the case that people must have some representations for semantic information that is similar to these relations. For example, clearly people must have a concept of causality, but the question is whether this separate concept of causality is necessarily implicated in the activation of the relation CAUSE during conceptual combination.

Third, the set of relations used in constructing the experimental materials were based on Levi (1978). The theory, however, is not reliant on relations at any particular level of generality, though the experimental results indicate that this level is sufficiently specific to give rise to reliable and consistent effects. We suggest that relations are hierarchically organized (as are concepts themselves) in level of generality. Thus, a chihuahua is not identical to a beagle, but both are still usefully characterized as dogs, as they share much of their meaning, both with each other and with other dogs. In the same way, there might be sub-relations of a particular relation such that, for example, HAS-PART and HAS-POSSESSION are both examples of a HAS relation.

6. Concluding remarks

The empirical findings discussed in this chapter indicate that the meaning of a compound is actively constructed. Interpreting a compound involves specifying a relation to link the constituent concepts, and the ease of interpretation is influenced by the availability of this relation. The fewer competitors the required relation has, the less time it takes the system to settle on that relation. We have outlined a theoretical framework in which relations compete for selection as the system attempts to find a relation that satisfies semantic and pragmatic restrictions, with the head noun concept being evaluated with respect to a particular modifier and particular relation.

Where does our psycholinguistic framework stand with respect to linguistic frameworks? In her overview of linguistic approaches to English compounding, Lieber (2009b) notes that theories can be classified into two sets. One set takes a purely syntactic or morphological prospective (e.g. Bauer 1978; Lees 1963; Levi 1978; Lieber 1992), whereas the other proposes that interpretive processes are not tied to syntactic processes but, instead, rely on lexical-semantic structures (e.g. Allen 1978; Lieber 2004, 2009a; Ryder 1994; Selkirk 1982). Our framework integrates these two approaches in that it relies on a compound's morphosyntactic structure as well as on conceptual knowledge about the constituents.

Sign languages and compounding

Irit Meir, Mark Aronoff, Wendy Sandler and Carol A. Padden
University of Haifa/ SUNY Stony Brook/ University of Haifa/
University of California San Diego

Compounding is one of the few sequential word formation processes found across sign languages. We explore familiar properties of compounds in established sign languages like American Sign Language, as well as a modality-specific type of simultaneous compounding, in which each hand contributes a separate morpheme. Sign languages also offer the opportunity to observe the way in which compounds first arise in a language, since as a group they are quite young, and some sign languages have emerged very recently. Our study of compounds in a language that came into being only about 75 years ago (Al-Sayyid Bedouin Sign Language) provides insight into the way in which compounds arise and acquire structure. We find in our data a relationship between conventionalization and grammaticalization of compounds: as particular forms become conventionalized in the community, both morphological and phonological structures begin to emerge.

1. Introduction

What could be special about compounds in sign languages? What might they tell us about language in general? Sign languages share two important properties. The first is modality; the second is their age. Each plays a role in the structure of sign languages and each has an impact on the formation of complex words.

Sign languages are produced by the hands, accompanied by the face and body, and are perceived by the eyes. The hands move in a three-dimensional space. The motion of hands in space is a basic building block of signs in any sign language. Because they can make use of space, sign languages show quite distinct types of morphology, which make them typologically distinct from spoken languages (Aronoff, Meir, and Sandler

2005, Meir, Padden, Aronoff, and Sandler 2007).[1] In addition, sign languages but not spoken languages have two independent but identical articulators, the two hands. What are the effects of these physical characteristics on the structure of compounds in sign languages? Do sign languages have compounds? Are they different in structure from spoken language compounds? Are there compound types found in signed but not in spoken languages? The questions raised by modality differences are discussed in Section 2 of this chapter.

The second property shared by sign languages is age. Sign languages can be young, since they come into being when there is a group of deaf people interacting regularly with each other in a particular location. Typically, there are two major types of circumstances that lead to the emergence of a sign language (Meir et al. in press). One type, Deaf community sign languages, arises from bringing together unrelated deaf people of different backgrounds in locations such as cities or schools. The second type, village sign languages, develop within small communities or villages where genetic deafness is transmitted within and between families, resulting in a community with a relatively high percentage of individuals with congenital deafness.[2] In both cases, a sign language emerges at a specific point in time, the point at which deaf people are born to a community or form a community. The conditions leading to the emergence of a sign language recur to the present day, and offer linguists the rare opportunity of watching a language develop almost from its inception. Focusing on compounds, the study of new languages may shed light on the emergence and development of complex words of this type in language generally. Studies of new spoken languages, pidgins and creoles, show that compounding is the type of productive word formation process that develops earliest in the life of a language (Plag, 2006). Yet what are the properties of these early compounds? Do compounds in early stages of a language show different characteristics than compounds in later stages? How are they formed? Are they built up, by combining a sign to another, or are they compacted down from larger strings of words? How do they acquire structure? Which comes first, the sequencing of individual signs, or the structure itself into which signs are inserted?

We have been privileged to study a very young sign language. Al-Sayyid Bedouin Sign Language (ABSL) emerged with the birth of a few deaf children into the Al-Sayyid Bedouin community about 75 years ago. By studying the compounds found in the language productions of second and third generations of signers in this language community, to which we turn in Section 3, we can start to answer some of the questions raised above.

---

1. The issue of modality and its impact of language structure in signed vs. spoken languages have been dealt with in numerous works. See Meier et al. (2002) and Sandler and Lillo-Martin (2006) for in-depth discussions about the role of modality in the various linguistic domains, and Emmorey (2003) and Vermeerbergen et al. (2007) on more language specific structures.

2. For a somewhat different typology, see Fussellier-Souza (2006).

2. Modality

A survey of sign languages reveals that the one highly productive word-formation device that they share is compounding. Most compounds combine words sequentially and are similar to the sorts of compounds found in spoken languages. Yet the signed modality offers a possibility for compounding which is impossible in spoken languages: simultaneous compounding. Since the manual modality has two articulators, the two hands, compounds might in principle be created by simultaneously articulating two different signs, one by each hand. However, straightforward simultaneous combinations of this type are very rare (Section 2.2).

a. Sequential compounding
Properties of sign language compounds: As mentioned above, compounding is widespread in sign languages. It appears in every sign language studied to date. Some illustrative examples of lexicalized compounds from different sign languages are given in Table 1. As in spoken languages, sign language compounds also display word-like characteristics. In their seminal study of compounds in American Sign language (ASL), Klima and Bellugi (1979: 207–10) describe several properties which are characteristic of compounds and which distinguish them from phrases. First, a quick glance at the examples in Table 1 shows that the meaning of compounds in many cases is not transparent.[3] The ASL compound BLUE^SPOT does not mean 'a blue spot', but rather 'bruise'. HEART^OFFER (in Israeli Sign Language, ISL) does not literally mean offering one's heart but rather volunteering, and NOSE^FAULT ('ugly' in Australian Sign Language) has nothing to do with the nose. Since the original meaning of the compound members may be lost in the compound, the following sentences are not contradictory (Klima and Bellugi 1979: 210):

(1) BLUE^SPOT GREEN, VAGUE YELLOW
 'That bruise is green and yellowish'.

(2) BED^SOFT HARD
 'My pillow is hard'.

Compounds are lexicalized in form as well, in the sense that they tend to have the phonological appearance of a single sign rather than of two signs. For one, they are much shorter than equivalent phrases (Klima and Bellugi 1979: 213), because of reduction and deletion of phonological segments, usually the movement segment of the first member of the compound (Liddell & Johnson 1986, Sandler 1993a). The transitional movement between the two signs is more fluid. In some cases, the movement of the second member is also deleted, and the transitional movement becomes the sole

---

3. As is conventional in sign language linguistics, signs are represented by English glosses in capital letters.

Table 1. Examples of compounds in sign languages

American Sign Language	BED^SOFT	'pillow'
(Klima and Bellugi 1979)	FACE^STRONG	'resemble'
	BLUE^SPOT	'bruise'
	SLEEP^SUNRISE	'oversleep'
British Sign Language	THINK^KEEP	'remember'
(Brennan 1990)	SEE^NEVER	'strange'
	WORK^SUPPORT	'service'
	FACE^BAD	'ugly'
Israeli Sign Language	FEVER^TEA	'sick'
(Meir and Sandler 2008)	HEART^OFFER	'volunteer'
	RESPECT^MUTUALITY	'tolerance'
Australian Sign Language	CAN'T^BE-DIFFERENT	'impossible'
(Johnston and Schembri 1999)	RED^BALL	'tomato'
	NOSE^FAULT	'ugly'
Al-Sayyid Bedouin Sign Language	CAR^LIGHT	'ambulance'
(Aronoff et al 2008)	PRAY^HOUSE	'mosque'
	SWEAT^SUN	'summer'
Indo-Pakistani Sign Language	FATHER^MOTHER	'parents'
(Zeshan 2000)	UNDERSTAND^MUCH	'intelligent'
	POTATO^VARIOUS	'vegetable'
New-Zealand Sign Language	NO^GERMS	'antiseptic'
(Kennedy 2002)	MAKE^DEAD	'fatal'
	READY^EAT	'ripe'

movement of the compound, resulting in a monosyllabic sign with only one movement, like canonical simplex signs (Sandler 1999).

Changes contributing to the single-sign appearance of compounds are found not only in the movement component, but also in hand configuration and location. If the place of articulation of the second sign is the non-dominant hand, that hand may take its position at the start of the whole compound. In many cases, the handshape and orientation of the second member spread to the first member as well by a kind of anticipatory assimilation (Liddell & Johnson 1986; Sandler 1989, 1993b).[4]

Morphological structure: Compounding takes advantage of linear structure, but it also involves reorganization and restructuring. The members of a compound may exhibit different types of relationships. In endocentric compounds, compounds that have a head, the head represents the core meaning of the compound and determines its

---

4. Similar phenomena have been attested in Australian Sign Language (Auslan). Johnston and Schembri (1999: 174) point out that in lexicalized compounds phonological segments of the components are often deleted, and suggest that they might be better characterized as blends.

lexical category. A compound such as *scarecrow* is exocentric (see Bauer, this volume). Neither of its internal components is the head: a scarecrow is neither a type of a crow nor a "scare" but rather originally something that scared crows. The meaning of exocentric compounds is often opaque, and the word class of the compound is determined lexically for each compound, disregarding the word class of the constituents. Endocentric compounds are further classified according to the position of the head in the compound: right-headed and left-headed. It is commonly assumed that the position of the head in compounds is systematic in a language (Fabb 1998). English, for example, is characterized as right-headed, while Hebrew is left-headed. However, there are languages in which both orders are possible. For example, in Japanese and Vietnamese, both of which historically borrowed words heavily from Chinese (in the same way that English borrowed a large portion of its vocabulary from Latin and French), native compounds are left-headed, while compounds containing words that were originally borrowed from Chinese are right-headed (Goddard 2005. See also Booij, and Scalise and Fabregas, this volume).[5]

Not much has been written on headedness in sign language compounds. Of the ASL examples presented in Klima and Bellugi, many are exocentric, e.g., SURE^WORK 'seriously', WILL^SORRY 'regret', WRONG^HAPPEN 'accidentally'/ 'as it turns out', FACE^STRONG 'resemble'. In other cases, it is difficult to determine whether a compound is exocentric or endocentric. EAT(FOOD)^NOON 'lunch', THINK^ALIKE 'agree', FLOWER^GROW 'plant', are such cases. In more straightforward endocentric constructions, headedness is not fixed. SLEEP^SUNRISE 'oversleep' is left-headed, but BLUE^SPOT 'bruise' is right-headed. In ISL, compounds that have Hebrew counterparts are usually left-headed (PARTY^SURPRISE 'surprise party'), though for some signers they may be right-headed. Native compounds in that language, compounds that do not have Hebrew counterparts, are often exocentric, e.g., FEVER^TEA 'sick', SWING^PLAY 'playground'. Verbal compounds are often right-headed, as in HEART^OFFER 'volunteer', and BREAD^FEED 'provide for'.

A third type of compound structure is coordinate compounds (or co-compounds, see Bauer, this volume), where the members are of equal rank, as in *hunter-gatherer*, someone who is both a hunter and a gatherer. In a special type of coordinate compounds, the members are basic category-level terms of a superordinate term. The meaning of the compound is the superordinate term. This class of compounds, called also *dvandva* compounds,[6] is not productive in most modern European languages, but occurs in languages of other families. Such compounds exist in ASL (Klima and Bellugi 1979: 234–5): CAR^PLANE^TRAIN 'vehicle', CLARINET^PIANO^GUITAR

---

5. Both types of compounding are quite productive in both Japanese and Vietnamese. Native speakers are not confused, because the vocabulary is quite strictly segregated in much the way that English is.

6. The etymology of the term is from Sanskrit *dvamdva*, literally, a pair, couple, reduplication of *dva* two -- more at TWO.

'musical instrument', RING^BRACELET^NECKLACE 'jewelry', KILL^STAB^RAPE 'crime', MOTHER^FATHER^BROTHER^SISTER 'family'.[7] Like other compounds, they denote one concept, the movement of each component sign is reduced, and transitions between signs are minimal. However, ASL consultants report that there is a lot of individual variation in form and in the degree of productivity of this type of compounding. Younger signers use them very little, and consider them to be old fashioned or even socially stigmatized.

b. *Simultaneous compounding*

Compounding is traditionally defined as combining two (or more) words to create a new word. We have described sign language compounds of this type in the previous section. However, we have also pointed out that the presence of two potentially independent articulators opens up possibilities not present in spoken languages, and that, while each articulator typically contributes a meaningless phonological unit to the word, it may also represent a meaningful morpheme. Sign languages do exploit these opportunities in word formation processes that some researchers have described as simultaneous compounds, although they are not compounds in the traditional sense, as the morphemes are bound. We use the term 'simultaneous compound' as used in the literature we are citing, but in so doing we take no position as to whether or not these are compounds in the usual sense.

Examples of one mechanism for simultaneously combining signs are exceedingly rare. Two BSL example are mentioned in the literature: MINICOM (a machine which allows typed messages to be transmitted along a telephone line, Brennan 1990: 151), and SPACE^SHUTTLE (Sutton-Spence and Woll 1999: 103). The compound MINICOM is composed of the sign TYPE and the sign TELEPHONE produced simultaneously: the right hand assumes the handshape of the sign TELEPHONE, but is positioned over the left hand, that produces the sign TYPE.

However, according to some analyses, a different kind of simultaneous compounding is very widespread in sign languages. Signs in any sign language may be produced by one hand or by both hands. Two handed signs are symmetrical or asymmetrical. In symmetrical signs, the two hands have the same handshape and they articulate the same kind of movement at the same location (or at mirror locations on or near each side of the body). In asymmetrical signs, one hand (the preferred or dominant hand) articulates the sign, while the other hand (the nonpreferred or nondominant hand) is static and functions as the location of that sign. In these signs, the handshape of each hand may be a transparent representation of some meaning aspect of the sign. In a sign such as WRITE (in ISL and many other sign languages), the dominant hand has a handshape depicting the handling of a long thin object (a pen or pencil), and the nondominant hand in a handshape represents a flat surface, a sheet of paper in this case.

---

7.   One unusual feature of the coordinate compounds of ASL is the fact that they often have three members. The classic coordinate compounds of spoken languages have two members only; hence the term *dvandva* of ancient Sanskrit grammar (from the Sanskrit work *dva* 'two').

Since each hand carries its own meaning, in a sense, such signs can be regarded as compounds of two meaning-bearing units. Such an analysis is presented in Brennan (1990), who uses the term 'classifier compounds' for signs in which the non-dominant hand assumes a handshape of a classifier morpheme that occurs elsewhere in the language.[8] It should be pointed out, though, that these signs, however they originated, are lexical signs in every respect, and under most analyses, they are not regarded as compounds synchronically.

The simultaneous structures described in this section are necessarily unique to the signed modality. The spoken modality, with one articulator, cannot produce forms that call for simultaneous use of two articulators, each conveying a different word or morpheme. But the sequential compounds, described in Section 2.1, are very much like spoken language compounds. They show word-like rather than phrasal properties on all levels: phonology, morphology, syntax and semantics. We turn now to the second property characterizing sign languages, their youth. This property will allow us to examine compounds from another angle – how they come into being.

2. Language age: Compounding in a new language

The newness of sign languages may also shed light on the nature of compounds. We will therefore focus on compounding in a sign language that is less than 75 years old and used in a fairly small, closed community: Al-Sayyid Bedouin Sign Language (ABSL). Compounding is the type of productive word formation process that develops earliest in the life of a language, and it is abundant in pidgins and creoles (Plag, 2006). It has been suggested that compounds are a manifestation of very early stages in the evolution of syntax in human language (Jackendoff 2002). Yet little thought has been given to the way in which compounds might arise. What are the stages in the emergence and development of compounding? ABSL, as a young language, offers us the possibility of studying such questions by observing actual language use in a community. We will address three questions here: (a) How do compounds arise? (b) How do they get conventionalized? (c) What kind of structure do they get, and how? As we shall see, compounds may arise in more than one way: not only by combining (as suggested by the very term) but also by reduction of longer strings of words (Section 3.3).

---

8. Classifier morphemes are handshapes that stand for a class of referents, representing some salient visual or semantic properties of these referents. For a survey and analysis of classifier constructions in different sign languages, see Emmorey (2003). Classifier constructions are constructions that combine classifier morphemes (handshapes) with a movement morpheme. The main function of such constructions is to depict the motion of an entity in space. Although these constructions resemble compounds at first glance, they are much more complex, and their linguistic status has been a matter of discussion and controversy for a few decades now. We will not discuss them here. The reader is referred to Sandler and Lillo-Martin (2006) for an overview and an analysis.

In addition, we find remarkable variation, both in terms of the lexical items used in a compound and their structure – variation that must be eliminated in the lexicalization process (Section 3.4). Our data suggest that there is a correlation between conventionalization in choice of compound members and grammaticalization of form: those compounds that are more conventionalized are also characterized by more clear-cut structural and other compound-like properties (Section 3.5).

a. *The Al-Sayyid linguistic community*
The Al-Sayyid Bedouin group was founded about two hundred years ago in the Negev region of present-day Israel. The group is now in its seventh generation and numbers about 3,500 members, all of whom reside together in a single closed community.

As a result of consanguineous marriage, within the past three generations, approximately 150 individuals with congenital deafness have been born into the community, all of them descendants of two of the founder's sons. Thus, the time at which the language originated, and the number of generations through which it has passed, can be pinpointed. Members of the first generation of deafness are deceased. We have worked with second and third generation signers, people in their late forties, down to children as young as five and six years old.

Many of the signers in this community are hearing (Kisch 2004). This is quite typical of sign languages that arise as a consequence of recessive deafness in a closed community (Lane, Pillard and French 2000). One result of the recessiveness is that there is a proportionately large number of deaf individuals distributed throughout the community. This means that hearing members of the community have more daily contact with deaf members, and consequently signing is not restricted to deaf people.[9]

In previous works we have shown that ABSL developed a consistent SOV word order in clauses and Head-Modifier order within phrases by its second generation (Sandler et al. 2005). It also developed a lexicon with open-ended categories of content words, the equivalent of prototypical nouns, verbs, adjectives and adverbs, as well as a few function words (Aronoff et al. 2008). However, we have not found inflectional morphology in the language (Aronoff et al. 2004). It appears that the most productive and prevalent morphological device in the language is compounding.

b. *Compound elicitation*
In order to elicit vocabulary items in ABSL, we used two tasks: picture-naming and translation from Hebrew. In these tasks, signers quite often responded in multi-word strings. In such cases, we had to deal with two questions: first, whether a response was a phrasal description of the target concept or a compound, that is a conventionalized

---

9. The linguistic situation in the Al-Sayyid community is rich and complex. Deaf members in their 40s and 50s are monolingual in ABSL, but all other members typically have access to more than one language, and master it to varying degrees of proficiency. Hearing members' mother tongue is the local Arabic dialect, and they may know Hebrew and ABSL. Younger deaf members may know ISL, and written Hebrew or Arabic. See Kisch (2008) for a description of communicative interactions in the community.

multi-word lexical item; and second, whether the compound was lexicalized or a nonce form created on the spur of the moment. Neither distinction is easy to draw, even in languages which have been studied in detail over a long time, such as English. For example, an English string of the form A N can be either a phrase (*red shoe*) or a compound (*redwing*). Conveniently, some (but not all!) English compounds have a different stress pattern from phrases, which usually allows us to decide which is which, but some strings, like *french fries* can be stressed on either the first or the last element, so we need to resort to further tests before we decide that *french fries* is a compound (because we cannot insert another element in between the two). Furthermore, whether a particular compound is new is an even harder determination to make, because it depends on the individual, although in the case of written languages, one can use listing in a dictionary as a substitute for knowing the mind of the speaker. In a new language, the difficulties are greater. We do not have diagnostic criteria for distinguishing a compound from a phrase and we have no dictionaries to fall back on for determining what is new from what is lexical. Notice that ABSL is new in two senses: it is a young language, and it is also newly studied. Therefore, we can't make any assumptions about whether compounds exist in the first place, and what structure they may take. Where do we start, then?

One possible point of entry into the system is uniformity. As lexical items, we might expect that compounds should be conventionalized and uniform across signers, as we expect with simplex signs. However, this criterion is problematic for two reasons. First, uniformity is expected only in lexicalized compounds. If compounding is a productive process in a language, then novel compounds should occur, and these are, by definition, not uniform across the community, as they are invented 'on the spot', so to speak. Second, in principle it is possible that different members of the community use different compounds, but all compounds share some structural property, for example a specific word order. But in order to be able to identify the structure of compounds, we need to identify string of words as compounds in the first place, which takes us back to point zero. In order to avoid this inherent circularity and to get a point of entry into the system, we decided to look first at clear-cut cases of compounding, that is, compounds that are conventionalized and lexicalized. If these are identified, they may give us a clue to the structure of compounds in the language.

Conventionalization in form, then, is our first criterion. Yet even this seemingly straightforward criterion is not easy to apply. The degree of variability found in the ABSL community, described below, is such that there are hardly any cases where all or even most signers use precisely the same compound form. We therefore had to make do with partial uniformity across signers. Another possible criterion is whether signers retrieve these multi-word responses quickly and effortlessly, as they do with single word responses, or whether they construct the response while signing. Such a measure is, of course, subjective. However, when looking at a few dozen responses for each signer, such a distinction can be drawn in many cases. The criteria that we ended up using to identify compounds in our data are these: (a) they denote one concept; (b) they are uniform across at least some signers, (c) they share at least two components with some other signers; and (d) they are produced with ease and with a fluid movement, that is, without the hesitation which tends to characterize novel constructions in our tasks. Responses we were not sure about were not included in the study.

A picture naming task was administered on three different occasions, to three groups of participants (see Table 2 below). The pictures were of everyday objects found in the village, as well as fruits, vegetables and animals, all of which were familiar to the participants. The elicitation materials were different for each group. Group 1 had five participants: two sisters (in their late 40s) and three of their daughters (ages 20 and younger). They were shown 60 pictures. For 29 of the pictures we received compounds as responses. Group 2 consists of four second generation signers (in their 40s) and four third generation signers (in their teens and early twenties), three of whom are brothers. They were shown 66 pictures. We analyzed responses for 14 pictures as compounds. Group 3 consists of ten participants: three second generation signers, all siblings, and seven third generation signers. Of these, five are the children of one of the second generation signers, and two others are not related to that family. Responses to 8 of the 40 pictures they were asked to name were classified as compounds.[10] Three of group 1 signers and two of group 2 signers are included in group 3 as well. Since these tasks were administered in different occasions, we can check the individual consistency of these participants. Full details about the participants are found in the appendix.

Picture naming has the advantage of having no interference from another language, and no need to rely on knowledge of another language, and is therefore a good stimulus for monolingual ABSL signers. But it is restricted mainly to concrete objects. In order to get other types of lexical items, we asked a trilingual deaf signer

Table 2. the three groups participating in the picture naming task

Group 1	Group 2	Group 3
5 participants:	8 participants:	10 participants:
2 second generation signers	4 second generation signers	3 second generation signers
3 third generation signers	4 third generation signers	7 third generation signers
29 compounds	14 compounds	8 compounds

---

10. The number of multiple-word responses was much higher than the actual number of compounds analyzed. For example, in group 2 forty-five responses had more than one word in them, but only fourteen were identified as compounds according to our criteria. This high percentage of compounds in the vocabulary is characteristic of other sign languages developing in small insular communities. Washabaugh (1986;55) reports that in a study of 307 vocabulary items in Providence Island Sign Language, 40% of the signs were compounds. In ASL, in contrast, only 11% of the same vocabulary items were compounds.

(trilingual in ABSL, ISL and Hebrew) to translate a set of 218 Hebrew words into ABSL.[11] As in the picture naming task, quite a few of the signer's responses were multi-word forms. We regarded as compounds those responses that were signed with ease and fluidity, and were not preceded by hesitation. As in the previous task, responses that were unclear as to their compound status were excluded from the study.

c. How do compounds arise?

The criteria outlined in the previous section helped us establish that there are compounds in ABSL. After identifying as compounds some of the multiple-word constructions in the signers' responses, we were able to turn to investigate the three questions posed above. We start here with the question of how compounds arise in a language. Compounding expands vocabulary in the language by drawing from the existing lexicon, using combinations of two or three words to create distinctive new meaning. According to this view, compounding is a building process. When lacking a lexical item, a language user draws on two existing words which together convey the desired meaning. Under this scenario, three-word compounds seem to be more complex, since they are based on more building blocks.

However, there is another possible interpretation of the process by which compounds emerge, not by building but rather by carving. It is possible that signers start out with long unstructured strings of words, and, as these are used more often, they get reduced, finally ending as two- or three-word units. And indeed, this interpretation best fits what we find in ABSL. When signers are presented with a concept or an object that they do not have a word for, they produce many words that are semantically related to that concept.[12] For example, ABSL does not have a conventionalized lexical item for 'calendar', though calendars are used in the community, and the picture was of a calendar found in one of the participants' houses. In the picture naming task, when presented with a picture of a calendar, signers produced the following responses:[13]

(3) TIME+SEE+COUNT-ROWS+WRITE+TIME+CONTINUE+FLIP+SEE +COUNT-ROWS

(4) WRITE+ROW+MONTH+ROW+WRITE

---

11. The words in the list are not compounds in Hebrew, except for four words: cemetery (*beit- kvarot* 'house [of] graves'), factory (*beit-xaroshet* 'house [of] industry'), hospital (*beit-xolim* 'house [of the] sick') and school (*beit-sefer* 'house [of] books'). These are highly lexicalized compounds in Hebrew. Three of them were translated into ABSL as compounds, but different from the Hebrew compounds. One (*factory*) does not have an ABSL equivalent.

12. In a way, this is quite similar to the dvandva compounds described in Section 2.1, where a string of several basic category-level terms represents the superordinate term. In the case described here, properties of a term represent the term. In both cases, a term is expressed by using several subordinate terms. We thank Susan Goldin-Meadow for this point.

13. In these responses, we use the symbol + instead of ^, since we do not analyze them as compounds, as they are clearly non-uniform across signers.

(5) NUMBERS+ROW+MONTH+FLAT-ON-WALL+FLIP
(6) FLIP+WRITE+FLIP

The words in these responses relate to the function of a calendar (telling the time), its arrangement (rows), its internal form (written), its shape (rectangle), how it is being handled (by flipping pages). Responses vary greatly among signers, and they can also vary within a signer. The example in (6) is produced by the younger signer in that group (about 20 years old), and it consists only of two words, referring to its form and how it is being handled.

'Calendar' is an extreme example: there seems to be no conventionalization at all across these examples. Each signer recruits whatever lexical resources s/he can find in order to refer to this concept. Strings of words for other concepts are somewhat more conventionalized. In these cases, it seems that the signers have already narrowed down the number of words related to a concept. In 'stove/range top', there are four lexical items that signers draw on: COOK, TURN, WIDE-OBJECT, INSERT. However, signers vary as to how many and which items they select from this list, as the following examples show:

(7) TURN^COOK^WIDE-OBJECT
(8) TURN^FIRE^4^BURNER^ FIRE
(9) TURN^WIDE-OBJECT
(10) COOK^INSERT
(11) COOK^WIDE-OBJECT

At the other end of this continuum is a case where all signers use the same components in the same order. In our data we do not have any one compound that is signed uniformly by all signers in the study. But some signs are conventionalized within a family, like the sign KETTLE. There are different sign combinations meaning KETTLE, but two combinations (shown in Figure 1) are each consistently used by members of two different families (Sandler et al. in press).

We have described only three degrees of conventionalization here, but there are many intermediate cases. For example, in some cases all signers share one component, but differ on the others. Signers may share components but differ in the order of these components. The fact that so many of the responses in our data consist of more than two words may indicate that, at least in a new language, compounding may not be the result of putting two words together, but rather the result of narrowing down, of eliminating members of a long string of words until only two are left. Structure emerges when the types of words for describing an object are of similar function, and come in a particular order (e.g., a word describing the function, and a word describing the shape). We will describe these structural tendencies in Section 3.5.

 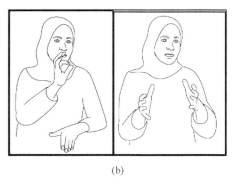

(a) (b)

Figure 1. Two different compounds meaning 'kettle':
a. TEA^POUR-from-handle as signed uniformly by all three members taped from one family. b. TEA^ROUND-OBJECT as signed uniformly by all five members taped from a different family

d. How do compounds get conventionalized?

The process described above demonstrates that we find a lot of variation along the long way towards conventionalization.[14] And indeed the variation we find in ABSL is quite overwhelming. In order to measure the degree of variation we found in the three picture naming tasks, we use two measures, developed in Israel (2009). One measure is the *mode*, the most common value (or the most common form) in a set.[15] In our case, the compound form used most frequently in a set of forms expressing the same notion is the mode. Since the three sets in our study are of different sizes, the mode is calculated as a proportion of the set size, rather than as an absolute value. So, for example, in group 1, four out of the five signers signed 'lemon' as SQUEEZE^ROUND-OBJECT. The mode for that item is therefore 80%. In group 2, four signers signed 'light bulb' as SCREW-IN^LIGHT. However, in this group there are eight signers, and therefore the mode value of that sign is only 50%. The higher the value of the mode, the more uniform the compound across that group of signers. The mean of the modes of all items per set represents the mode score of that set.

The mean mode values for the three sets are: groups 1 and 3 – 51.2%, group 2 – 28.5%. This means that on the average, in groups 1 and 3 about half of the signers produced the same compound form. In group 2 the number is even lower, less than a third of the signers in the group produced the same form. Groups 1 and 3 have more signers from the same family (or extended family) than group 2, which may explain

---

14. The variation in the ABSL community is not restricted to compounds. See Israel (2009) and Sandler et al. (in press) about variation in sign formation in ABSL.

15. Note that the mode does not have to constitute a majority in order to be the most common. If there are more than two choices, the mode can be less then half, so long as no other choice constitutes a greater fraction of the total.

their higher score. But nevertheless it is striking that even within the same family, compound productions are very variable. In some cases, the same person produced two different forms. One signer signed TURN^COOK in set 1 and COOK^INSERT in set 3 as a response for 'stove/range top'. Her sister signed COOK^TURN and TURN^WIDE-OBJECT for the same concept. Only two signs in group 1 responses got a score of 100%. In group 3 the highest score was 90%, and in group 2 only 50%.

The second measure used for measuring variation is the *number of variants* for each compound. This measure is independent of the mode. Take, for example, a hypothetical situation where, in a set of 10, the mode is 6. That is, six signers used the same form. The remaining four signers may also all use the same compound form, though different from that of the majority, resulting in two variants for that item. However, they may also use two, three or four different forms, resulting in three, four or five variants for that item. The higher the number of variants, the lower the uniformity of the form. As with the mode, the mean number of variants for each group was calculated as a proportion of the set size, because the sets are of different sizes. The mean value for number of variants in group 1 is 65% (3.26 out of a set of 5), of group 2 – 76% (6.1 out of a set of 8), and of group 3– 34% (3.4 out of 10). Combining the two measures together, we see that group 3 is the most uniform; next is group 1; and group 2 is the least uniform. But even in group 3, on average each sign has more than three variants, and only half of the signers use the same form.[16] The results are presented in Figure 2.

An interesting generational difference emerges in a few compounds: older signers use compounds, while younger signers produce a single word response. For describing a TV set, the four older signers in group 3 produced the compound MOVIE^WIDE-OBJECT whereas the four children signed only the first member, MOVIE. Similarly, in set 1, the two older signers produced a compound for 'closet' (CLOTHES^DOORS) and for 'dove' (PECK^WINGS). Their three daughters' responses were DOORS and WINGS.

---

16. It should be pointed out that some of the variants are more similar to each other than others. In some cases, two variants differ only in the order of elements (e.g. SCREW-IN^LIGHT vs. LIGHT^SCREW-IN 'light bulb'), whereas in others both the order and the lexical items themselves may be different (e.g., BRIDLE^RUN, RIDE^BRIDLE, MOUNT^BRIDLE^RIDE for 'horse'). The number-of-variant measure does not reflect these differences. Any two forms that are not identical were regarded as different variants.

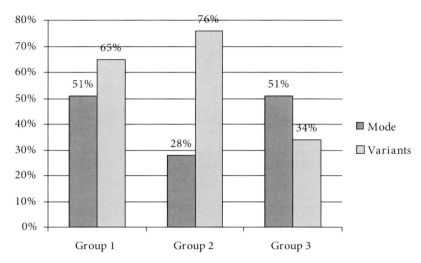

Figure 2. Degrees of conventionalization in ABSL compounds according to two measures: mean values for mode and number of variants in three ABSL groups

e. Conventionalization and the emergence of structure

As we have seen, the degree of variability in compound production in ABSL is very high, yet some compounds are more uniform than others. It is in these more conventionalized compounds that we find the emergence of properties that characterize compounds in more established sign language. We find evidence for two processes within these compounds: phonological reduction and increased structure.

Phonological reduction: Phonological reduction is at work in the three most uniform signs: TOMATO, EGG, and LEMON. It is manifested in three ways. First, some signers produce a smoother transitional movement between the two parts of both TOMATO and LEMON, as if the transitional movement – rotation of the hand – has become part of the form of the compound. This smoother movement usually goes together with a reduction of the movement of the first sign. The first member of TOMATO (a sign meaning 'squeeze') has a double movement, in which the fingers of the hand close to a fist. Five group 3 signers (one second generation and four third generation signers) reduce it to a single movement, which blends neatly with the transitional movement. The first member of LEMON has a different kind of movement, rubbing of the fingers against the thumb. In LEMON too, in the productions of four signers (all third generation signers), this movement is shorter and blends into the transitional movement. In these forms, then, the movements of the components are blended, and give the impression of a single movement in the entire compound.

Another type of phonological reduction appears in EGG – handshape assimilation (Sandler et al 2009). The compound is made up of CHICKEN^ SMALL-OVAL-OBJECT. CHICKEN is produced with the index finger in a curved shape and the hand

Figure 3. a. The standard form of the compound EGG: CHICKEN^ SMALL-OVAL-OBJECT. b. Handshape assimilation in EGG.

bending at the wrist twice, apparently motivated by the beak of a chicken pecking for food. The sign for SMALL-OVAL-OBJECT is produced with three spread, curved fingers, the palm oriented up. The basic compound is shown in Figure 3a. In one family, assimilation occurs. The first sign takes on the finger selection of the second, losing the 'curved beak' icon, so that the only difference between the first and second sign is the orientation of the hand: downwards for the first sign and upwards for the second (Figure 3b). Notice that both types of phonological process render the compound less iconic.

Increased structural regularity: The structure of compounds is usually expressed in terms of the linear order of the head and the modifier. In case of exocentric or coordinate compounds, structure can be defined only in linear terms (the order of the particular members of each compound), since there is no hierarchical relationship between the compound members (neither one is a head). We saw that in less conventionalized compounds in ABSL, signers often use multiple signs to describe an object. In case of more conventionalized compounds, these strings are reduced to two- or three-member units. Yet each compound can be conventionalized in a different way, resulting in different structures for different items. Is there any evidence for increase in structural regularity in any class of compounds? Can we talk about the structure of compounds in the language rather than the structure of a compound?

We found two structural tendencies emerging in the language. The first, which is stronger, has to do with compounds containing a Size and Shape Specifier (SASS). There is a tendency for the SASS member to be last. The other tendency is towards a modifier-head order in compounds containing a head and a modifier.

a. SASS compounds: In many cases, one of the signs used to refer to an object describes the size and shape of the object.[17] Some examples are: COLD^BIG-RECTANGLE 'refrigerator', DRINK-TEA^ROUNDED-OBJECT 'kettle', WATER^ROUNDED-OBJECT 'pitcher', CUCUMBER^LONG-THIN-OBJECT 'cucumber', PHOTO^FLAT-OBJECT 'photograph', CHICKEN^SMALL-OVAL-OBJECT 'egg', WRITE^LONG-THIN-OBJECT 'pencil', TV^RECTANGULAR-OBJECT 'remote control' (the last two are illustrated in Figure 4). We note that the SASSes

---

17. SASS signs are common in sign languages in general, though their form and distribution may vary from language to language.

do not tend to occur as independent words in the language, so that it is possible that we are looking at an early form of affixation in the language. However, we cannot construct criteria for distinguishing the two in this new language, and we refer to the complex forms with SASSes as compounds here. Compounds containing SASSes are very widespread in the language: they constitute 37% of the compounds in our data set. These compounds are the most uniform ones, and they also show a very strong structural tendency for the SASS to be the final member in the compound. This holds both within each signer (Figure 5) and across signers (Figure 6).

Figure 4. Two SASS compounds: a.WRITE^LONG-THIN-OBJECT 'pencil'. b. TV^RECTANGULAR-OBJECT 'remote control'.

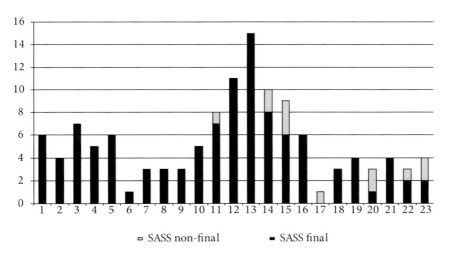

Figure 5. Structural tendency in SASS compounds: Number of SASS-final and SASS-non-final compounds in the production of each signer

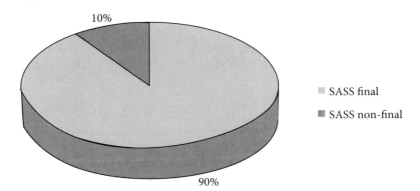

Figure 6. Percentage of SASS- final vs. SASS non-final compounds in our data

b. Head-modifier order: The other structural tendency is for a modifier-head order in endocentric compounds, as in PRAY^HOUSE 'mosque', SCREW-IN^LIGHT 'light-bulb', BABY^CLOTHES 'baby clothes', COFFEE^POT 'coffee pot'. These are less widespread in our data set (22%) than the SASS-type compounds, and the tendency is much less pronounced, for each individual (Figure 7) and in the entire set of data (Figure 8).

As Figures 7 and 8 show, the mod-head order occurs more often that head-modifier order, but the difference is not as striking as in the case of the SASS compounds. However, there is an interesting generalization even in this rather messy picture: the most uniform endocentric compounds, that is, those that received a high mode score, tend

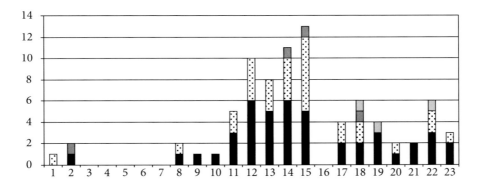

Figure 7. Structure of endocentric compounds in ABSL: Head-modifier order in the production of each signer

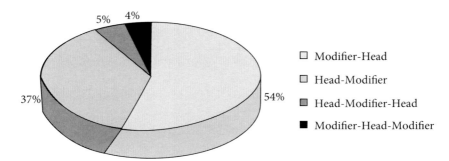

Figure 8. Percentage of different Head- modifier orders in our data

to exhibit a modifier-head order.[18] This finding can be interpreted in the following way: there is a high degree of variability, both within and across signers. But compounds that are agreed upon in the community, that is, the most conventionalized ones, tend to exhibit a particular structure. In a way, then, conventionalization within the community may arise before conventionalization in individual members of the community. These data and the interpretation we propose here are in support of Saussure's conception of language as a social construct.

Notice also that the order modifier-head is the reverse of the order found in phrases (Sandler et al. 2005). It therefore calls into question the assumption that compounds arise from the grammaticalization of phrases. The difference in word order in compounds (at least in those compounds that appear to be undergoing conventionalization) as opposed to phrases may indicate that today's morphology is not always yesterday's syntax, contra Givon (1971), but see Comrie 1980 for a different view.

In quite a few ABSL compounds, it is difficult to determine headedness. Some examples are: GUN^POLICE 'soldier', TAP-ON^STRONG 'iron', SWEAT^SUN 'summer'. This is, by no means, a peculiarity of ABSL. The examples in Table 1 and in Section 2.1 above show that many American Sign Language compounds are exocentric as well, and that therefore exocentricity is not necessarily a feature of compounds in a very young language.

Apart from the SASS and endocentric compounds, two other classes of compounds with consistent structure are found in our data. Both classes appear in the vocabulary elicited by translation from one of our consultants, but we have seen them used by other ABSL signers. Since these notions do not denote objects, they cannot be elicited in a picture naming task. One class denotes place names. In these compounds, one member is a pointing sign, which we gloss as THERE. Some examples are: PRAY^THERE 'Jerusalem', LONG-BEARD^THERE 'Lebanon', HEAD-MEDALLION^THERE 'Jordan', HEAD-SCARF^THERE 'Palestinian

---

18. There is one noticeable counter-example: the signs for 'grandmother' and 'grandfather' are MOTHER^OLD and FATHER^OLD respectively. This order is quite consistent across signers, and the fluidity of the transitional movement between the signs is evidence for its lexicalization.

Authority' and WIDE-HAT^THERE 'America'. These signs are characterized by a fluid transitional movement, and a consistent order: the pointing sign is final.

The second class of compounds consists of those whose first member is a pointing sign towards the head, eye or mouth: HEAD^GOOD 'smart', HEAD^'SO-SO' 'stupid', EYE^SOON 'wait', HEAD^OPPOSITE 'mistake', HEAD^WELL/PRECISELY 'understand'. Such compounds are found in many sign languages (see, e.g., Meir and Sandler 2008 for ISL, and Brennan 1990 for BSL). Pointing to a sense organ or a mental organ (i.e., to the head) seems to be a rich resource for word formation in gestural-visual languages, and ABSL is no exception.

3. Conclusion

All specific languages must arise through a process of conventionalization, of both structure and individual lexical items. In English, for example, N N compound structure is by far the most common and the most productive, and individual lexical items that follow that structure form many conventionalized compounds (*birdseed, earthwork*, etc.). French has conventionalized the V N compound structure and the individual lexical items that follow it (*ouvre-bouteilles, lave-vaiselle*). Neither language has many compounds of the type that is conventionalized in the other. We don't know exactly how these two languages arrived at the particular structures that they manifest (though each is also found in related languages and hence must have occurred in Germanic and Romance). As to individual lexicalized compounds, well *chaque mot a son histoire*.

The advantage of studying a new language is that we can see the process of conventionalization happening before our eyes. In ASL, for example, as noted above, Klima and Bellugi (1979) found that three-element dvandva compounds like CLARINET^PIANO^GUITAR 'musical instrument' were common enough to posit an N^N^N construction for the language. More recently, though, this construction has fallen out of favor, or at least become stigmatized. Thus, in a very short time frame, at least by most standards, one sign language has conventionalized a structure, one that is quite unusual because it has three parts rather than the usual two, and is losing it.

ABSL, which is younger than ASL, provides some evidence for the answer to a more general chicken-and-egg question: which comes first, the individual lexicalized compounds or the structural patterns? Overall, for compounds in ABSL, structure seems to be conventionalized faster, at least for some constructions (e.g., SASS and place compounds). Specifically, we see word order regularity before we see conventionalization of the individual lexical items that make up the compound. It may be that once a construction is conventionalized, it can serve as a tool or frame for creating new lexical items in a faster way, by adding lexical items into the slots. But this study shows that the construction itself is not there from the beginning. It has to be created and conventionalized as well. Furthermore the two compound constructions that we have found to be productive in ABSL, SASS compounds and place names, are far from what one might expect on universal grounds, either cognitive or grammatical. In fact, they are not even common in most other sign languages that have been studied. In the case of compounds, at least, it may be that structure simply happens.

Conventionalization goes hand in hand with other properties that characterize words rather than phrases – stable structure and more compact phonological form. In this, sign languages resemble spoken languages (as Klima and Bellugi have already shown) and ABSL compounding is indeed beginning to resemble compaction of the sort that has been identified in ASL by Klima and Bellugi and others. In older sign languages, however, the processes of compaction are already conventionalized and spread throughout the community. ABSL thus gives us the opportunity to see how a language might arrive at such constructions, how linguistic structure is carved from a much more diffuse "language blob".

Appendix

Information about participants

Participant	Group	age	Deaf/Hearing	Gender	languages
1	3	28	D	F	ABSL, ISL, [Hebrew]
2	3	22	D	M	ABSL, ISL, [Hebrew]
3 (=19)	3	23	D	M	ABSL, ISL, [Hebrew]
4	3	12	D	M	ABSL, [Arabic], some ISL signs
5 (=23)	3	late 40s	D	M	ABSL
6	3	6	D	F	ABSL, [Arabic], some ISL signs
7 (=11)	3	10	D	F	ABSL, [Arabic], some ISL signs
8	3	19	D	F	ABSL, ISL, [Hebrew]
9 (=12)	3	23	D	F	ABSL, ISL, [Hebrew]
10 (=14)	3	late 40s	D	F	ABSL
*11	1	7	D	F	ABSL, [Arabic], some ISL signs
*12	1	20	D	F	ABSL, ISL, [Hebrew]
13	1	17	H	F	ABSL, Arabic
*14	1	late 40s	D	F	ABSL
15	1	late 40s	D	F	ABSL
16	2	12	D	M	ABSL, Arabic, some Hebrew
17	2	16	H	M	ABSL, Arabic, Hebrew
18	2	17	D	M	ABSL, ISL, [Hebrew]
*19	2	19	D	M	ABSL, ISL, [Hebrew]
20	2	40s	H	M	ABSL, Arabic, Hebrew
21	2	40s	D	M	ABSL
22	2	40s	D	M	ABSL
*23	2	late 40s	D	M	ABSL

Three participants (7, 9, 10) participated in task 1 and task 3. These tasks were administered three years apart. Two participants (3, 5) participated in tasks 2 and 3, which were administered four years apart. The participants' ordinal number corresponds to the numbers in Figure 5 and 7.

Family relatedness:

Family A: Participants 1, 5, 10 and 15 are siblings. Participants 2, 6, 7, 8, and 9 are siblings and children of 10. Participant 13 is the child of 15.

Family B: Participants 3, 17 and 18 are siblings.

Family C: Participant 4 is the son of 22.

Family D: Participant 16 is the nephew of 21.

Family E: Participant 20

Language knowledge: Deaf signers have different degrees of limited knowledge (indicated by square brackets in the table) of the written form of Hebrew or Arabic, depending on their schooling.

Acknowledgements

We thank Douglas McKenney for his help in glossing and coding the ABSL compounds, and for his helpful comments. This work is supported by a grant from the National Institute on Deafness and other Communication Disorders (NIH R01 DC 6473–06). The pictures in Figures 1, 3 and 4 are copyright of the Sign Language Research Laboratory at the University of Haifa.

First language acquisition of compounds

With special emphasis on early
German child language

Wolfgang U. Dressler, Laura E. Lettner
and Katharina Korecky-Kröll
Department of Linguistics and Communication Research
of the Austrian Academy of Sciences

This chapter discusses early phases of first language acquisition of compounds in German based on longitudinal data of two Austrian children and compares these data to results on compound acquisition in other languages. The first compounds to emerge in German (simultaneously with the emergence of noun and verb inflection and of diminutives) were subordinate and endocentric two-member noun-noun compounds without linking elements. The first correct linking element which emerged later on is *-n* after word-final schwa of the first member. Order of emergence of compound patterns can be related to factors such as frequency, productivity, morphotactic and morphosemantic transparency. Left-headed and exocentric compounds had not yet emerged in our child speech corpora, and only one coordinate compound appeared.

1. Introduction

The acquisition of compounding has been investigated much less than the acquisition of inflection. In addition to two recent reviews (Nicoladis 2006; Berman 2009), there have been several studies on English (notably Clark et al. 1985, 1986; Nicoladis 2002), as well as on Swedish (Mellenius 1996, 1997), Hebrew (Berman & Clark 1989; Clark & Berman 1984, 1987; Berman 2009 § 4.4) and French (Nicoladis 2002, 2007).

The most comprehensive study is Berman (2009), which stresses, in addition to binarity, markedness, intonation and conventionality, the role of input, frequency, productivity, morphotactic and morphosemantic transparency as being crucially involved in the age, order and degree of complexity of emergence of compounds. Nicoladis (2006) also argues for the importance of productivity and frequency being a trigger in the usage of compounds (cf. also Clark 2003): in French, where compounds are not productive, we only find lexicalized ones until the age of 3;0; the first neologisms appearing only afterwards.

Little to no research has been done on other languages thus far, except German. Clahsen et al.'s (1996) experimental research results in the claim that the German linking elements (interfixes) -e, -er and -(e)n (as in Kind+er+garten) have to be considered as stored irregular plural suffixes, whereas the "regular" plural suffix -s (e.g. *Auto-s* 'car-s') cannot occur as a linking element in compounds (unless lexicalized, as in *Chip+s+fabrikant* 'chips producer'), according to level ordering in Lexical Phonology. The interfix -s, as in *König+s+hof* 'king's court' cannot be a plural suffix but derives historically from a productive genitive singular suffix. Moreover, in order to demonstrate the differences in acquisition between regular and irregular inflection, as well as between composition and inflection in German, the authors conducted two production experiments with 66 German children between 3 and 8 years of age. The majority of the children overgeneralized noun plurals with -s, less frequently than with -e, and least with -(e)n. Whenever children overgeneralized a specific plural marker, they did not use the same affix as the linking element within compounds, e.g. in PL. *Clown-en (< Clown-s) – Clown+fresser* 'clown eater', *Kabel-s (< zero plural Kabel* 'cable-s'), *Kabel+fresser).*

Following Clahsen et al. (1996), Bartke (1998) carried out additional experiments concerning plural suffixes and the same affixes within compounds with typically developing and SLI children. Typically developing children mostly omitted the "regular" -s-suffix within compounds correctly, but SLI children more often omitted other plural suffixes (the same ones that they preferably overgeneralized in plural elicitation tasks). Bartke interpreted these results as a misclassification of the regular default plural suffix by SLI children and as a proof of different processing levels for "regular" plural formation and compounding (cf. Clahsen et al. 1996).

In her MA thesis, Streith (1997) conducted both a plural formation test and a compound formation test with 30 Viennese children between 5;0 and 6;10. The children had to transform a complex noun phrase into a noun-noun compound. It was found that children preferred both the plural suffix and the interfix -(e)n, which is not compatible with Clahsen et al.'s (1996) and Bartke's (1998) claims.

Lettner's (2008) MA thesis was devoted to the description of the emergence and development of compounds and diminutives in one longitudinal corpus (Viennese girl Lena). Since its results have gone into this contribution, they are not reported in this introduction.

2. German compound formation

With rare exceptions which neither occur in early child speech (CS) nor in early child-directed speech (CDS), German compounds are right-headed, prototypically endocentric and subordinate, with a noun-noun structure (cf. Ortner & Müller-Bollhagen 1991; Becker 1992; Dressler et al. 2001).

Mere concatenation of two words is the default, but for noun-noun compounds it is only a weak default. Here pure concatenation competes with more or (mostly) less productive interfixation patterns (i.e. the insertion of or replacement by linking elements, cf. Dressler et al. 2001; Libben et al. 2002; Krott et al. 2007). The most productive interfixation rule inserts the interfix *-n* after a schwa-final first element, as in *Suppe+n+fleisch* 'soup meat'. Exceptions to this rule, e.g. *Kohle+papier* 'carbon paper', are very rare and are therefore marked, also in comparison to the larger family of *Kohle+n+X* compounds.

3. The data

We will briefly summarize the relevant findings in the literature, but base our presentation on the corpus of longitudinal naturalistic data of two Austrian children (Lettner 2008; Klampfer & Korecky-Kröll 2002), and compare these data to the diary data of one child observed by Franz Rainer (2008).

The two children discussed here are the girl Lena and the boy Jan who were both recorded in various everyday situations (e.g. playing, book reading, cooking) interacting with their mothers at their homes in Vienna. The ages examined are from 1 year and 3 months (hereafter abbreviated as 1;3) for Jan, and from 1;7 for Lena, until 3;0. We have at our disposal nearly 51 hours of recorded speech data for Jan and 67 hours for Lena. The data have been transcribed and coded using an adapted German version of CHILDES (cf. MacWhinney 2000) and were further analyzed in MS Office Excel 2007[1].

4. 3 phases of language acquisition

We divide early morphological development into 3 successive phases:
1. **Premorphology:** a rote-learning phase in which the child's speech production is limited to a restricted number of lexically stored inflectional forms. Extragrammatical morphological operations such as reduplicative onomatopoetics and truncations flourish.
2. **Protomorphology:** a phase in which the child starts to generalize over rote-learned forms, thereby detecting the morphological principle of (de)composing form and meaning word-internally. Thus the children begin to construct morphology creatively when coining their first analogical formations (cf. e.g. MacWhinney 1978; Dressler & Karpf 1995).

---

[1]. This study was supported by the Austrian Academy of Sciences and the Austrian Science Fund project P 17276-G03 "Noun development in a cross-linguistic perspective".

3. **Morphology Proper** (or **modularized morphology**): where (according to Dressler & Karpf 1995) children construct a sizeable number of morphological rules, create (non-innate) modules and submodules, and gradually acquire adult morphology, which already possesses all of its basic typological properties. At the beginning of this phase, the basic parts of adult morphology have already emerged, i.e. the core of morphology. We assume that before the age of approximately 3;0 children acquire this core morphology (cf. Ravid et al. 2008).

Whether new compounds are formed by analogy or via abstract schemas or rules (cf. Booij this volume) is a problem that has been recognized in first language acquisition studies since MacWhinney's (1978) thesis. For the case of productive patterns, we assume that, at least at the end of the protomorphological phase, a transition from analogy to schemas or rules takes place (cf. also Köpcke 1993).

5. Emergence of composition

In German, noun-noun (NN) composition[2] emerges at the beginning of the protomorphological phase, at the same time as noun inflection, diminutive formation and verb inflection. The criterion for pattern emergence we use is the appearance of miniparadigms, elaborated by Kilani-Schoch & Dressler (2002) for inflectional morphology. Whenever we find that three lemmas of the same word class, clearly distinct in morphotactic and morphosemantic properties, have emerged and recurred in spontaneous production in various contexts, we assume that the children have enough pattern variety in their uptake for detecting the morphological principle of (de)composing form and meaning word-internally. Adapted to compounding, this refers to the emergence of oppositions between compounds and their members.

Jan produces such oppositions at the onset of protomorphology, at 1;8: *Feuer+(wehr)+auto* 'fire(brigade)-car', *Müll+auto* 'garbage car', *Not+arzt+auto* 'emergency-doctor car', *Renn+auto* 'race car', *Polizei+auto* 'police car' with the simplex nouns *Auto* 'car', *Feuer* 'fire' and *Not+arzt* 'emergency doctor', the compound *Doppel+decker+bus* 'double-decker bus' and its constituent *Doppel+decker* 'biplane', as well as the compound *Segel+Schiff* 'sailing-boat' and its component *Schiff* 'boat'. One month later, at 1;9, Jan creates his first novel compound *Laster+wagen* < *Laster* & *Last+wagen* 'truck', another sign of productivity. This is the first attestation that a child has detected morphology simultaneously with verb and noun inflection, diminutive formation and compounding (cf. Klampfer & Korecky-Kröll 2002; Dressler et al. 2003).

The relatively late acquirer Lena reaches the phase of protomorphology two months later than Jan, at 1;10. At this age Lena produces the compound *Leni+omi*

---

2. We divide our analysis in the following 4 more important compound classes: Noun+Noun = NN, Verb+Noun= VN, Adjective + Noun= AN and Preposition+Noun = PN.

'Lenie-granny' and the simplex nouns *Lena*, hypocoristic *Leni* and *Oma* 'granny'. At 2;4 she produces *Käse+brot-e* 'cheese-breads', *Schokolade+n+brot-e* 'chocolate-breads' with their simplex nouns *Käse* 'cheese', *Schokolade* 'chocolate' and *Brot* 'bread'.

6. Amalgams

The acquisition of compound patterns by Lena during the protomorphological phase is confirmed by the fact that at 1;9, with few exceptions, she ceases to produce amalgams, such as *Reseikt* < *Kind+er+sekt* 'children sparkling wine' (1;9), *Medwa* < *Mineral+wasser* 'mineral water' (1;9), *Buli* < *Bild+er+buch* 'image book' (2;0), *Gudi* < *Klo+papier* 'toilet paper' (2;0), *Kosek* < *Kopf+hörer* 'headphones' (2;0), *Dassö* < *Tasche+ n+tuch* 'Handkerchief' (2;1), *Koffi/Koffe* < *Koch+löffel* 'cook spoon' (2;1), *Fon* < *Baby+fon* 'baby phone' (2;1), *Tis* < *T+shirt* (2;2, 2;3), and *Miketad* (2;8)/*Emiktad* (2;9) < *Musik+werk+statt*, 'music workshop', Lena's last one.

In Jan's data we also find such amalgams from 1;5 onwards, such as *Wonchta* < *Wohn+zimmer* 'living room' (1;5), *Bausne* < *Bau+stein-e* 'lit. construction stones' (1;5), *Fahta/Fahra* < *Fahr+rad* 'bicycle' (1;9); *Aubub/Abub/Aubus* < *Auto+bus* (1;6), *Ettnauto* < *Rettung+s+auto* 'emergency car' (1;8), *Liefwagn* < *Liefer+wagen* 'panel truck' (1;9); *Terad* < *Motor+rad* 'motor bike' (1;8), *Bamme* < *Bad+e+wanne* 'lit. bath tub" (1;8), *Nozt* < *Not+arzt* 'emergency doctor' (1;8), *Notztauto* < *Not+arzt+auto* 'emergency doctor car' (1;8), *Lufblon/Lofblon* < *Luft+ballon* 'air balloon' (1;9), *Sonnsternis* < *Sonne+n+finsternis* 'lit. sun eclipse' (1;10), *Retznauto* < *Rettung+s+auto* 'emergency car' (1;11, 2;0), *Dampfein* < *Dampf+eisen+bahn* 'vapor (metal) train' (1;11), *Klopier* < *Klo+papier* 'toilet paper' (2;2), etc. *Tosauger* < *Staub+sauger*, 'aspirator' is the last one in Jan's corpus, at 2;7.

Such amalgams indicate a lack of decomposability, and their progressive disappearance is evidence of the decomposability of compounds at around 2 years of age. Thus, at the same time that the device of compounding appears to be detected by our two children (cf. § 5), their production of amalgams, which stem from a preceding period, declines and soon almost totally disappears.

Table 1 displays the first occurrences of compounds of various categories (Catg.[3]) with interfixes (Intf.[4]) or without (0) in Jan's and Lena's corpora. Morphologically erroneous forms are marked by an asterisk (*). If a member of a compound occurs within the same month either as a simplex or as member of another compound, it is written in bold face.

---

3. Aside from the compound categories that have already been presented – NN, VN, AN and PN (cf. p.325 note 1) – we introduced the abbreviation "ag." for agentive compounds taking the agentive suffix -*er* and "rec." for recursive compounds.

4. Possible displayed interfixes of German are 0, -*(e)n*, -*e*, -*er* , -*s* and -*ens* (cf. p.337 Table 6).

7. Compound noun developments up to 3;0

Table 1. First emergent compound categories (including interfixes and errors) in Jan's and Lena's corpora

Age	Jan	Catg.	Intf.	Age	Lena	Catg.	Intf.
1;8	Auto+*bus*	NN	0	1;8	Huhu+*mama*	NN	0
	Segel+*schiff*	NN	0		Baby+*hannah*	NN	0
	Müll+*auto*	NN	0	1;9	Hand+*tuch*	NN	0
	Straße+n+*bahn*	NN	-n	2;1	*Lippe+*stift*	NN	*0
	Seife+n+*blase-n*	NN	-n		Back+*ofen*	VN	0
	Kind+er+*garten*	NN	-er		Koch+*löffel*	VN	0
	Doppel+decker+*bus*	rec.	0	2;2	*Kind+e+*kassette*	NN	*-e
	Hub+*schrauber*	ag.	0		Ober+*teil*	PN	0
	Fahr+*rad*	VN	0		Unter+*hose*	PN	0
	Renn+*auto*	VN	0		Bad+e+*hose*	VN	-e
	Sprech+*probe*	VN	0	2;3	*(Mine)ral+e+*wasser*	NN	*-e
1;9	Ente+n+*mama*	NN	-n		*Bild+*buch*	NN	*0
	Ente+n+*papa*	NN	-n	2;4	Rutsch+*auto*	VN	0
	Kind+er+*zimmer*	NN	-er		*(Schoko)lad+*brot-e*	NN	*0
	*Hase+*mama*	NN	*0	2;5	Kind+er+*mama*	NN	-er
	Staub+*sauger*	ag.	0		*Platte+*spieler*	ag.	*0
	Rasen+*mäher*	ag.	0	2;6	Kind+er+*garten*	NN	-er
	Renn+*fahrer*	VN	0		Geist+er+*mann*	NN	-er
1;10	*Sonne+*schirm*	NN	*0		Bild+er+*buch*	NN	-er
	*Last(+)er+*wagen*	NN	*-er		Kopf+*hörer*	ag.	0
	Doppel+decker+*zug*	rec.	0		*Bad+*zimmer*	VN	*0
	Fern+*seher*	ag.	0	2;7	Baby+husten+*saft*	rec.	0
	Unter+*hose*	PN	0		*Zähne+*weh*	NN	*-e
1;11	Abschied+s+*bussi*	NN	-s		*Gummi+s+*bärli(-s)*	NN	*-s
	Kind+er+*sitz*	NN	-er	2;8	Tanne+n+*baum*	NN	-en
	Feuer+wehr+*auto*	rec.	0		Tasche+n+*tuch*	NN	-en
	Bad+e+*wanne*	VN	-e		*Luft+e+*b(all)on*	NN	*-e
	Bad+e+*zimmer*	VN	-e	2;9	Geburt+s+tag+s+*fest*	rec.	-s
	Laut+*sprecher*	ag.	0		Münze+n+park+*platz*	rec.	-n/0
	Alt+*papier*	AN	0		Groß+*mutter*	AN	0
2;0	Rettung+s+*auto*	NN	-s		Hoch+*bett*	AN	0
	Liebling+s+*sache-n*	NN	-s	2;10	*Lauf+s+*lotti*	NN	*-s
	Blau+*licht*	AN	0	2;11	Vor+*zimmer*	PN	0
	Bunt+*stift*	AN	0		Nach+*mittag*	PN	0
2;1	Bild+er+*buch*	NN	-er	3;0	*Ameise+*buch*	NN	*0

Age	Jan	Catg.	Intf.	Age	Lena	Catg.	Intf.
	*Kassette+recorder	NN	*0				
2;2	Pferd+e+kutsche	NN	-e				
2;3	Hund+e+aa-s	NN	-e				
	Sonder+zug	PN	0				
2;4	Bank+e+sache-n	NN	*-e				
	Klapp+e+tür	VN	*-e				
	Vor+zimmer	PN	0				
2;9	*Zwerg+e+spiel	NN	*-e				

We consider a category to have emerged, when the mini-paradigm criterion (cf. § 5) is fulfilled, at least in a reduced form. That is, we find 3 compounds of the same category (including interfix categories), and least one member of each of these 3 compounds has occurred as a simplex or part of some other compound.

7.1 Transparent concatenative compounds

By age 3;0 the basic adult patterns have emerged to a large extent in Lena's and Jan's corpora:
In addition to NN-compounds (Jan from 1;8, Lena from 1;9), we find VN-compounds. For example, in Lena's corpus we find *Back+ofen* 'lit. cook-oven' (2;1), *Koch+löffel* 'lit. cook-spoon' (2;1), with the category emerging at 2;2. In Jan's corpus, we find *Renn+fahrer* 'lit. race-driver' (1;10), with the category emerging at 1;9.

AN-compounds appear only at the age of 2;9 in Lena's corpus (if at all as a category) and remain rare (e.g. *Groß+mutter* 'grandmother' and *Hoch+bett* 'lit. high-bed'). Jan, as an early talker, exhibits his first AN-compounds at 1;11 and 2;0, but without proof of the emergence of the category.

This difference in emergence between AN-compounds and NN- and VN-compounds is consistent with the greater importance of the word classes of nouns and verbs in contrast to that of adjectives. Note that simplex adjectives emerge at the same time as nouns and verbs, but in much smaller numbers. In both children, VN-compounding emerges one month later than NN-compounding, which supports the prototypicality of NN-compounds.

We also find compounds with the final agentive suffix *-er* (cf. Melloni & Bisetto this volume): at 2;5 Lena produces the erroneous form **Platte+spiel-er*, for *Platte+n+spiel-er* 'record player', and the category is established at 2;6. Jan, at 1;8 produces *Kugel+schreib-er* 'ball-point pen' and *Hub+schraub-er* 'helicopter' once (but later 9 times), and at 1;9 he produces *Staub+saug-er* 'dust cleaner', but without coocurrence of any compound member.

No left-headed or exocentric compounds emerge, and the only coordinate compound occurring is *Strumpf+hose* 'pantyhose' (Lena: 2;7, Jan: 2;5); This confirms the status of endocentric subordinate NN-compounds as prototypic compounds (cf. Dressler 2005, 2006).

Recursive compounds emerge in Lena's speech at 2;7, when she innovates *Baby+husten+saft* 'baby cough mixture' (alongside *Husten+saft* 'cough mixture'), and we see this again at 2;9. Jan's first example appears at 1;8, when he produces *Doppel+decker+bus* 'biplane bus'; further examples occur at 1;10 and 1;11.

7.2 Interfixed compounds

Productive interfixing with *-n* after schwa emerges at 2;7 in Lena's creative neologism *Ente+n+schule* 'duck school', followed at 2;8 by *Tasche+n+tuch* 'handkerchief' and *Tanne+n+baum* 'fir-tree'. Corresponding interfixations appear in Jan's corpus by 1;8: *Seife+n+blase-n* 'soap-bubbles' (established as a category at 1;9), followed, e.g., by *Orange+n+zuck-erl* 'orange bonbon' (2;4) and *Tasche+n+lampe* 'flash-light' (3;0).

Earlier, Lena produced many compounds lacking this productive interfix, e.g. at 2;1 and 2;3 **Lippe+stift* 'lip stick', at 2;5 **Platte+spieler* 'record-player' and at 3;0 **Ameise+buch* 'antbook'. Jan produced **Hase+mama* 'rabbit mummy' at 1;8 and **Ente+auto* 'duck-car' at 2;2. Thus, our two children appear to have a certain preference, during an early period of the protomorphological phase, for an output-oriented pattern of compounds whose first member ends in schwa (cf. § 20).

Erroneous homophonous patterns have also been produced via incorrect *-e-*interfixes by both children. Lena produced **Kinn+e+sette* for *Kind+er+kassette* 'child-cassette' (2;2), **(Mine)ral+e+wasser* 'mineral water' for *Mineral+wasser* (2;3), **Zähn+e+weh* for *Zahn+weh* 'tooth ache' (2;7), **Luft+e-bon-e* for *Luft+ballon-e* 'air balloons' (2;11). Jan produced **Bank+e+sache* 'bank thing' (2;4), **Zwerg+e+spiel* 'dwarf play' (2;9). Such incorrect forms cease to be produced after 3;0 (with one exception: Lena's **Luft+e+spiel-e* 'air plays', at 3;8), another manifestation of the beginning of core morphology. Other interfixes emerge later: a) *-s*-interfixation in Jan regularly at 2;0, but only rarely in Lena, b) *-er*-interfixation in Jan at 2;1, and in Lena at 2;6.

Similarly, Mellenius (1997: 75) claims that Swedish children have acquired productive compounding by 3 years of age. But only the more important parts of adult compounding emerge by the phase of core morphology, which is to say, the salient islands of morphology have emerged, and we tentatively propose the strong claim that these islands of compounding constitute the prototypes of adult grammar of compounds, which adults should also be able to process faster due to the importance of acquisition at an earlier age. (More in our conclusions: § 21).

8. Frequency distributions in Lena's and Jan's compound noun development 1;7 – 3;0

Table 2 shows the monthly development of Lena's compounds in lemmas and tokens. NN-compounds and VN-compounds start at the same very low level (about 2 lemmas and under 5 tokens), but develop very differently. From 2;3 onwards, NN-compounds multiply and have already reached a high level (of 18 lemmas and nearly 50 tokens) during the protomorphological phase (NB: the month 2;5 is an outlier). The percentage of NN-compounds among all compounds is even higher in her output (about 76%) than in her input (about 70%) (cf. Table 3), indicating a typical overgeneralization of the most productive pattern. In contrast, the percentage of VN-compounds hardly increases.

With the compounds divided into categories, we can see more clearly the peaks in the frequency of the use of compounds in the child's input and output. Since the mother's peaks follow Lena's peaks we have an example of fine-tuning, i.e. of mother's adaptation to child speech.

The frequency developments of the early talker Jan are similar, with the increases simply coming earlier, already at age 1;8 (cf. Tables 4 and 5).

Both language-internally and cross-linguistically, the early emergence of lexical and grammatical elements and of children's preferences heavily depend on input token and type frequency, and in the case of compounds, on the family size (cf. Krott & Nicoladis 2005; Krott et al. 2007, 2009).

Table 2. Frequencies of compound nouns in Lena's output 1;7 – 3;0

CN	NN		VN		AN		PN		Total	
Age	Le	To	Le	To	Le	To	Le	To	Le	To
1;7	–	–	–	–	–	–	–	–	–	–
1;8	2	2	–	–	–	–	–	–	2	2
1;9	2	8	–	–	–	–	–	–	2	8
1;10	1	1	–	–	–	–	–	–	1	1
1;11	1	2	–	–	–	–	–	–	1	2
2;0	2	3	–	–	–	–	–	–	2	3
2;1	1	1	3	5	–	–	–	–	4	6
2;2	2	5	1	1	–	–	2	3	5	9
2;3	3	11	–	–	–	–	2	4	5	15
2;4	10	16	1	1	–	–	1	1	12	18
2;5	2	2	–	–	–	–	–	–	2	2
2;6	17	20	4	9	–	–	1	1	22	30
2;7	11	18	1	1	–	–	–	–	12	19
2;8	10	19	1	3	–	–	2	4	13	26
2;9	18	47	7	17	2	2	–	–	27	66
2;10	18	29	4	4	–	–	–	–	22	33
2;11	8	14	6	6	–	–	3	5	17	25
3;0	19	35	2	3	2	2	–	–	23	40
Total	105	233	26	50	3	4	5	18	139	305
Total %	75,54	76,39	18,70	16,40	2,16	1,31	3,60	5,90	100	100

Table 3. Frequencies of compound nouns in Lena's input 1;7 – 3;0

CN	NN		VN		AN		PN		Total	
Age	Le	To	Le	To	Le	To	Le	To	Le	To
1;7	22	36	–	–	2	2	–	–	24	38
1;8	23	43	6	9	3	9	–	–	32	61
1;9	75	119	27	48	6	11	3	5	111	183
1;10	21	36	9	16	3	4	–	–	33	56
1;11	19	34	8	13	4	5	2	6	33	58
2;0	22	34	9	10	1	2	3	6	35	52
2;1	37	62	12	20	2	12	3	6	54	100
2;2	21	29	9	15	1	1	3	8	34	53
2;3	26	53	12	29	2	10	2	4	42	96
2;4	17	30	10	13	2	2	1	1	30	46
2;5	28	51	6	7	2	2	–	–	36	60
2;6	60	102	20	47	6	9	4	9	90	167
2;7	74	143	11	12	4	4	4	7	93	166
2;8	45	85	9	18	2	2	4	13	60	118
2;9	74	143	27	76	4	4	3	4	108	227
2;10	35	63	6	9	5	9	3	3	49	84
2;11	35	47	14	16	2	2	3	5	54	70
3;0	59	128	7	15	5	34	3	7	74	184
Total	442	1238	125	373	31	124	17	84	615	1819
Total %	71,87	68,06	20,33	20,50	5,04	6,82	2,76	4,62	100	100

Table 4. Frequencies of compound nouns in Jan's output 1;3 – 3;0

CN Age	NN Le	NN To	VN Le	VN To	AN Le	AN To	PN Le	PN To	Total Le	Total To
1;3	–	–	–	–	–	–	–	–	–	–
1;4	–	–	–	–	–	–	–	–	–	–
1;5	–	–	–	–	–	–	–	–	–	–
1;6	–	–	–	–	–	–	–	–	–	–
1;7	–	–	–	–	–	–	–	–	–	–
1;8	25	153	3	11	–	–	–	–	28	164
1;9	26	82	6	22	–	–	–	–	32	104
1;10	25	61	8	14	1	2	1	7	35	84
1;11	27	80	3	10	3	25	–	–	33	115
2;0	35	194	11	59	8	20	–	–	54	273
2;1	25	61	3	5	2	5	–	–	30	71
2;2	39	94	9	27	1	1	–	–	49	122
2;3	31	52	5	9	1	1	2	2	39	64
2;4	26	60	13	18	1	3	1	2	41	83
2;5	15	24	3	3	3	6	1	1	22	34
2;6	34	70	5	8	1	3	–	–	40	81
2;7	8	27	5	10	1	2	–	–	14	39
2;8	28	60	7	9	2	4	–	–	37	73
2;9	14	26	1	2	–	–	–	–	15	28
2;10	12	19	6	10	1	1	–	–	19	30
2;11	11	29	3	11	–	–	–	–	14	40
3;0	20	29	2	2	1	1	–	–	23	32
Total	217	1121	48	230	15	74	4	12	284	1437
Total %	76,41	78,01	16,90	16,01	5,28	5,15	1,41	0,84	100	100

Table 5. Frequencies of compound nouns in Jan's input 1;3 – 3;0

CN	NN		VN		AN		PN		Total	
Age	Le	To	Le	To	Le	To	Le	To	Le	To
1;3	17	43	10	15	–	–	–	–	27	58
1;4	7	11	1	1	–	–	1	3	9	15
1;5	6	10	2	4	–	–	–	–	8	14
1;6	6	13	4	10	–	–	1	1	11	24
1;7	9	18	4	6	1	3	–	–	14	27
1;8	81	335	15	33	4	6	3	3	103	377
1;9	72	261	21	71	4	4	2	2	99	338
1;10	77	186	13	35	6	7	1	7	97	235
1;11	69	193	15	27	8	43	3	5	95	268
2;0	64	256	19	88	7	19	2	2	92	365
2;1	33	62	8	9	4	5	2	4	47	80
2;2	46	108	19	49	3	6	1	3	69	166
2;3	54	113	13	25	3	4	2	5	72	147
2;4	66	130	26	70	6	12	5	8	103	220
2;5	76	114	14	18	3	21	9	17	102	170
2;6	56	127	16	29	3	4	2	2	77	162
2;7	56	89	19	36	3	11	2	2	80	138
2;8	57	104	15	33	2	4	4	9	78	150
2;9	33	61	6	8	2	8	1	4	42	81
2;10	64	111	18	37	4	6	2	4	88	158
2;11	44	75	8	11	4	4	–	–	56	90
3;0	49	89	5	11	4	11	4	9	62	120
Total	656	2509	144	626	42	178	32	90	874	3403
Total %	75,06	73,73	16,48	18,40	4,81	5,23	3,66	2,64	100	100

In Lena's output, 19% of all noun lemmas and 5% of all noun tokens are compounds; in her input, up to 35% of all noun lemmas are compounds, with an average of 11% for the tokens. For Jan, the percentages of compounds among nouns are even higher: 33% for the lemmas and 18% for the tokens in the output, and 41% for the lemmas and 19% for the tokens in the input.

9. Order of emergence

To what extent does frequency in the input predict the order of emergence in the output? Current acquisitionist assumptions (cf. Tomasello 2003; Krott et al. 2009) hold that the input frequency in the caregiver's child-directed speech predicts the order of emergence in the child's output. More precisely, input token frequency predicts the onset of rote learning of tokens of a pattern, and input type frequency predicts the chronological order of acquisition in the sense of productive use of patterns.

As shown in Tables 2 and 3, the frequency of compounds rises steadily both in types and tokens beginning at 2;3; that is, with the start of Lena's protomorphological phase, her mother fine-tunes Lena's production and offers the child more and more compounds when she notices that the child is already acquiring them. As expected, there are many more compounds in the input than in the children's output.

If we look at the input frequencies for Lena, we see that both type and token frequency of NN-compounds significantly outnumber (about 76%) the frequencies of VN-compounds (about 17%). As predicted, VN-compounds emerge in Lena's speech a half-year later (at 2;1) than NN-compounds (at 1;8). However, if we look at the input frequency of AN-compounds (2%) and PN-compounds (4%), then the emergence of PN-compounds one month after VN-compounds is at odds with the great difference between their frequencies in the input. Furthermore, AN-compounds are more frequent in the input than PN-compounds, but in the output the AN-compounds emerge only at 3;8, i.e., one and a half years later than PN-compounds.

Comparing these results with those of Jan, we see (Tables 4 and 5) that just as in Lena's input, the type and token frequencies of the NN-compounds in Jan's input greatly outnumber those of VN-compounds (74% to 17%) even though they indeed emerge at the same time (1;8) in Jan's output. PN- and AN-compounds emerge last after NN- and VN-compounds (at 1;10), whereas AN-compounds are not as late as in Lena's case.

Thus, input frequency is only a very rough predictor for determining the order of acquisition of nominal compounds.

10. Productivity

For this reason, many psycholinguists (Clark & Berman 1984; Clark 1993: 126–140; Mellenius 1996, 1997; Nicoladis 2006: 101–103) add the category of productivity to that of frequency. But how should productivity be measured? Here we will apply the criteria used in the processing study by Dressler et al. (2005; cf. Dressler & Ladányi 2000).

A productive compound pattern is one which is applied freely and unconsciously to new loan words. This is the case in German with several compound types, such as:
- Interfixless NN-compounds: *Laser+drucker* 'laser printer', *Haupt+computer* 'main computer;
- NN-compounds with the interfix *-n* after a first element ending in schwa: *Garage+n+besitzer* 'garage owner', *Coyote+n+fell* 'coyote hide'. Other interfixed compounds also fulfil this criterion.

Among further criteria, let us just mention compounding of abbreviations. This criterion is only fulfilled by German interfixless compounds, e.g. *KFZ-Versicherung* 'car insurance', *Lok+führer* 'engine-driver' from *Lokomotive* 'engine'. But since abbreviations rarely end in (always unstressed) schwa, this is not a sufficient argument against full productivity of *-n*-interfixed compounds.

Furthermore, full productivity can be graded according to the criterion of competition: morphological patterns which have no competing pattern in a given structural context are more productive than patterns which have to compete. This criterion is fulfilled for German NN-compounds only by the two cited types of interfixless compounds and compounds with *-n*-interfixation after schwa.

11. Emergence of interfixed compounds

In Lena's corpus, the most productive German compound type is interfixless NN-compounds, the weak default among NN-compounds, which emerges first (at 1;8) and is then overgeneralized.

The second-most productive type is NN-compounds with *-n*-interfix after schwa, which only emerges an entire year later, yet is still less productive. Other interfixed NN-compound types appear only exceptionally and emerge even later, as we see in Jan's corpus in the compounds with interfix *-er* at 2;5 and with *-s* at 2;7 (for *-e* emerging at 2;2 cf. § 7).

In addition, Streith's (1997) production and correction experiments with 5 and 6 year old Viennese children revealed comparable trends: *-n*-interfixed and interfixless NN-compounds fared much better than any other interfixed compounds. Similar results have been found in Swedish (cf. Mellenius 1996, 1997).

Our interfix analysis (cf. Table 6) presupposes that we do not agree with Clahsen's analysis (Clahsen et al. 1992, 1996; Clahsen 1999) of interfixed compounds. Clahsen analyzes interfixes as unproductive plural suffixes and bars the appearance of an *-s*-plural suffix within compounds since it is considered the regular, default suffix. As has been shown in several studies (Fuhrhop 1998; Laaha et al. 2006; Elsen 1991; Dressler 2005; Dressler et al. 2001; Libben et al. 2002), German interfixes are not plural suffixes, and the *-s*-plural suffix is neither the regular default plural suffix of German nor the only productive plural suffix.

Note that, consistent with our hypotheses, interfixes develop much later than plural suffixes, which emerge at the beginning of protomorphology and are well developed by the period of core morphology (including the unproductive *-er*-suffixes and umlaut), well ahead of homophonous interfixes (cf. § 7).

Table 6. Lena's and Jan's interfix distribution in Lemmas 1;7 – 4;0

	Lena	Lena %	Jan	Jan %
0	135	79,9	181	73
-(e)n	8	4,7	31	12,5
-e	11	6,5	15	6,0
-er	8	4,7	8	3,2
-s	4	2,4	10	4,0
-es	–	–	–	–
-ens	–	–	–	–
other	3	1,8	3	1,3
Total	169	100	248	100

12. Phrases vs. compounds

A specific problem in the study of early compounds lies in difficulties of differentiating between compounds and phrases, e.g. by means of stress. A frequent German example of an ambiguous juxtaposition of nouns (cf. Berman 2009, § 4.4; Ackema & Neeleman, Montermini this volume), especially with boys, is, at Jan's age of 1;8, *Papa Auto, Mama Auto,* which may be (a), the compounds *Papa+Auto, Mama+Auto* 'daddy-car, mummy-car' (normally absent in adult adult-directed speech) or may correspond to (b), the colloquial adult possessive noun phrases *dem Papa sein Auto, der Mama ihr Auto* 'lit. to the daddy his car, to the mummy her car', or (c), the equivalent Standard possessive genitive phrases *Papa+s Auto, Mama+s Auto,* or may even correspond to (d), the adult clause *Papa/Mama hat/gehört das Auto* '(to) daddy/mummy has/belongs the car' (more examples and analyses can be found in Vollmann & Bruyère 1995).

In adult German, intonation and compound stress (on the first element) vs. phrasal stress (normally on the second element) normally differentiate between phrases and compounds. In child speech, however, both prosody and context often underdetermine the choice between the two interpretations. For example, for several months Franz Rainer's child has produced what Rainer interprets to be compounds with two main stresses (Rainer § 2.1.1; for Dutch cf. Fikkert 2001: 77). In general, children appear to acquire compounds with their regular stress patterns but may require up to 12 years of age for full mastery of prosodic patterns (cf. Nicoladis 2006: 118; Vogel & Raimy 2002). In contrast, Mellenius (1997: 75) reports that Swedish compound stress is acquired with the first emerging compounds.

13. Morphotactic transparency

Many studies (cf. Slobin 1985; Aksu-Koç & Slobin 1985; Peters 1997; Dressler 2009: 144) have established the fact that young children prefer morphotactic (or phonological) transparency to morphotactic opacity to a much greater extent than adults.

This results in an earlier emergence and preferred usage of compounds with no interfixes or other stem changes of the first compound element. We have already mentioned the earlier emergence of, and preference for, German interfixless compounds, including overgeneralization of this most transparent pattern. This is confirmed by Franz Rainer's rich diary data of his daughter Carmen.

According to Mellenius (1997, 2004), Swedish children also acquire the opacifying deletion of the final thematic vowel of the first element (as in *fick+pengar* 'pocket money' from *ficka* 'pocket') very early, but the correct insertion of the interfix -*s* is acquired much later and mastered only around age 5. In Hebrew, too, where compounds are left-headed, morphotactically transparent compounds are acquired before those whose left head element is morphologically modified (cf. Clark & Berman 1984, 1987; Berman 2009 § 4.4).

14. Morphosemantic transparency

The universal preference for morphosemantic transparency reveals itself in young children's literal interpretation of partially opaque compounds. A recent example from Dressler's grandson Paul at 2;6:

(1) *Oma, du hast Taschengeld: Du hast Geld in der Tasche.*
    'Granny, you have pocket money: you have money in the pocket'

At 3;3 Jan produces a similar interpretation of the compound *Winter+zauber+tee* 'winter-do-magic-tea', the name for a certain kind of tea, when he firsts utters:

(2) *Ich mag den Winterzaubertee.*
    'I like the winter-do magic-tee'

A few lines later, he asks his mother:

(3) *Kamma damit den Winter herzaubern?*
    'Is it possible to bring the winter magically with it?'

Another example of such a semantic transparency comes from Jan at 3;6:

(4) *Ein Buntstift, der is(t) ein Stift der bunt is(t).*
    'A colored pencil, this is a pencil that is colored'.

Greek children's sensitivity to the degree of morphosemantic transparency has been experimentally ascertained by Stephany (1980, 1997: 204, 259; cf. Clark and Berman 1984) as well.

Compounds are more descriptive and thus more morphosemantically transparent than synonymous derivatives, as we see in the contrast between *dishwashing machine* vs. *dish-washer* (cf. Crocco Galèas & Dressler 1992). This explains why Clark & Hecht (1982; cf. Clark, Hecht & Mulford 1986) have come to the conclusion that English children acquire transparent compounds earlier than synonymous derivatives and even often replace conventional agent and instrument nouns with neologistic compounds, as in the example: *open man* and *open thing* for *open+er*. And thus they disambiguate the ambiguous agent and instrument noun *open-er*.

Although Romance languages are less rich in compounding than Germanic languages, examples of the replacement of derivational agent nouns by compounds also occur in Italian children (cf. Lo Duca 1990: 124–129, 154, 169–174). In spontaneous speech forms such as the following were observed: *taglia+capell-i* 'lit. hair-cutter' (6;2–6;6) for *parrucch+iere* 'hair-dresser' or *porta+posta* 'lit. mail carrier' (5;5) for *post+ino* or *porta+lettere* 'mailman'. Similar examples have occurred in naming tasks: *scopa+strad-e* 'lit. street sweeper' (3;11) for *spazz+ino* 'scavenger' or *scala+montagn-e* 'lit. mountain climber' (3;9) for *scala+tore* 'mountaineer'.

Thus, for reasons of greater morphosemantic transparency, young children appear to have a phase where they prefer compounds to more productive derivation, provided that their respective language has a sufficiently rich system of compounding (cf. Clark 1993: 148, 2003: 298 f.; Berman 2009). Note that interfixed compounds are also morphosemantically less transparent than interfixless ones, because the interfix does not contribute to the meaning of the compound.

15. Clark's principles of conventionality and contrast

The preference for morphosemantic transparency described above may conflict with conventional opaque meanings of single compounds.

According to Clark (2003: 282–284), young children inherently prefer conventional words, i.e. they "give priority to words that are already established in the lexicon". Thus they would only coin new words, including compounds, to fill gaps in their incomplete lexicon. But even acquiring the appropriate adult words is not enough for replacing their neologisms. Clark explains, "Before they give up a coinage, they must work out that the meaning of their own word [...] and of the adult word [...] are identical" (Clark 2003: 283). Moreover, she claims that children produce new words only if they think that their meaning is different from the meanings of the words they have already acquired – this is Clark's principle of contrast.

As we have also tried to show for the acquisition of diminutives (cf. Savickienė & Dressler 2007), Clark's strong version of her principle of conventionality and contrast extends the principle of synonymy blocking (cf. Rainer 1988) too far.

As far as the acquisition of compounds is concerned, Clark's view is challenged by variability in the child's lexicon at a given time. Examples from Jan's corpus are: *Zwerg+en+rad* 'dwarf wheel' (2;2), *Zwerg+rad* 'lit. dwarf wheel' (2;9), **Zwerg+e+spiel* 'dwarf play' (2;9), and from Lena's corpus **Luft+a+bon* and **Luft+e+bon* 'air balloon' (3;8) and *Reis+luft+ballon* 'rice air balloon' etc.

16. Morpheme order

Children appear to acquire the correct order of compound elements early on; that is to say, the head position is acquired early (cf. Clark et. al 1985; Berman & Clark 1989).

Reversal of order is extremely rare: there is no clear example in Lena's nor in Jan's corpus. Dressler's daughter Stasi once produced (at 2;6) *Berg+häf-erl* instead of the mountain name *Häf-erl+berg* lit. 'cup-diminutive-mountain'.

Rainer (2008: § 2.1.5) cites several examples of his daughter (only at 3;1–4;5) but classifies them as slips of the tongue, which is rather improbable, because such errors do not appear in the corpora of children's slips of the tongue (cf. Jaeger 2005).

This confirms the doubts of Nicoladis (2006: 11–114) about the correct interpretation of English spontaneous and experimental data which exhibit problems with the correct order of the English pattern OBJECT-VERB-*er* of synthetic compounds, as in erroneous *breaker-bottle* instead of *bottle-breaker*. Could this result from the influence of word order in sentences (Clark et al.1986)?

The very robustness of morpheme order in compounds from their emergence onwards is of doubtful relevance for linguistic theory. First, it is simply a sign of acquisition of compounds as wholes (at first without decomposition). Later in a language like German, which almost completely lacks left-headed compounds, we must ask why children would change their habit of producing right-headed compounds. There is not even much disturbing impact of syntactic word order in a language where possessive compounds and possessive phrases usually have the same word order (cf. § 12). Thus detailed studies of compound order and phrase order in typologically different languages would be important for the main topic of this volume.

17. Recursivity

Hauser, Chomsky and Fitch (2002) and Chomsky (2007) consider recursivity to be the most fundamental characteristic of the innate human language capacity. Lena's data show late emergence of recursive compounding at 2;7: *Baby+husten+saft* 'baby cough mixture'. At this age we even have an example of Lena's awareness of recursivity:

(5) Lena: *du machst *ein hust(e)nsaf(t).*
              'you're making a cough mixture'.
    Mother: **ein hust(e)nsaft fürs baby?*
              'a cough mixture for the baby?'
    Lena: mhm.
              mhm.
    Lena: *das heisst babyhustensaft.*
              'this is called baby cough mixture'.

Jan, as a precocious speaker, already has recursive compounds at 1;8: *Not+arzt+auto* 'emergency doctor car', in alternation with *Auto* 'car' and *Not+arzt* 'emergency doctor'. He also has a few phrasal compounds, e.g. *Gute+nacht+geschichte* 'good-night-story' (and *Dispy-gute-nacht-geschichte* 'Dispy-good-night-story') at 2;3 as well as *Goofy-und-Mickey-Buch* 'Goofy-and-Mickey-book' at 2;6.

Why does recursivity, an allegedly innate capacity, manifest itself in compounds in the case of Lena, only a full year after the emergence of two-member compounds?

One explanation is the general preference for binary constructions, which seems to account for the aforementioned constraint in early child morphology. This holds also for the acquisition of inflection in agglutinating languages in which many inflectional suffixes may be concatenated. But in early protomorphology, both Turkish and Hungarian children produce only inflectional forms with one suffix, i.e. strictly binary constructions.

A second answer may lie in the young child's difficulty in producing multisyllabic words. Consequently, young children produce truncated forms and amalgams, as we have seen before in § 6, cf. Elsen (1991) and Rainer (2008).

18. Typology

Children have been shown to be very sensitive to the typological characteristics of the language they acquire (cf. Slobin 1985; Berman 1986, 2009; Peters 1997; Devescovi et al. 2005; Laaha & Gillis 2007; Xanthos et al. 2008). The early emergence of morphological patterns appears to be best predicted by the amount of morphological richness in a given language. The wealth of productive inflectional morphology and its importance for the expression of syntactic functions (plus its role in competition with syntax) predicts early emergence of inflectional morphology, as we have been able to demonstrate in a comparison of nine languages (cf. Laaha & Gillis 2007; Xanthos et al. 2008).

Can this finding be extended to compounding? Presumably it can be, according to available evidence. Among the languages studied, the Germanic ones have the greatest wealth of nominal compounding, and compounding emerges earliest in these languages (cf. Clark 1993: 151–159). In Romance languages and in Hebrew, compounding is less rich and emerges later (between 3 and 4 years of age for Hebrew, cf. Clark & Berman 1984, 1987; Berman 2009: § 2, 3, 5.3). The same seems to hold for Slavic languages, according to the little evidence we have: e.g. the first 500 words of a young Czech child (Pačesová 1968) include only 5 compounds.

19. Innate universals?

Since in several linguistic models first language acquisition is regarded as a prime field of (external or substantive) evidence for basic theoretical linguistic claims, the question arises whether this contribution can give any evidence or allow any argumentation for or against the assumption of innate grammatical universals.

In § 17, we discussed the late emergence of recursivity in compounding. Yet its relatively late emergence does not undermine the assumption of an innate capacity of recursivity. But why should recursivity be a specific phenomenon of innate universal grammar? There is clearly recursivity in mathematics, yet this is a very different cognitive domain which occupies a very different location in the brain. And we see no reason why recursive calculation should be derived from linguistic recursivity. Moreover, should apes be incapable of performing recursive operations such as putting a small matrioshka into a larger matrioshka and this matrioshka into an even larger one? Furthermore, European starlings utilize recursivity; these songbirds are described as recognizing "acoustic patterns defined by a recursive, self-embedding, context-free grammar" (Gentner et al. 2006).

Another nativist position has been Pinker's (1984) assumption of a default-seeking mechanism. This could be supported by the fact that children start compounding with the (only weak) default of interfixless noun-noun compounds. However, Swedish children appear to start simultaneously with two types of compounds: simple concatenation of two nouns, as in German, and noun-noun compounds with deletion of the final stem vowel of the first element. Moreover, we see no reason why humans should be endowed with a default-seeking mechanism specific to grammar. Is it not in fact the case that we look for defaults in most types of human behavior?

Next, in inflectional morphology there is the hotly debated double route model, contrasting an innate rule capacity with storage (which allows just sporadic analogies, cf. Pinker 1984; Clahsen 1999). Clahsen, Sonnenstuhl and Blevins (2003) have extended this dual-mechanism model to derivational morphology; we suggest that one might want to extend this model to compounding. But there is nothing in sight which is similar to the division between strong and weak preterits in English, German and Dutch. Rather, what we find is a cline of productivity, which is incompatible with a strict dual mechanism model, similar to what we have shown for the acquisition of German plurals (Laaha et al. 2006).

Snyder (1995; cf. Sugisaki & Isobe 2000) has assumed an innate compounding parameter which is supposed to account for the contrast between languages with rich, productive, recursive compounding and languages with limited compounding and a correspondence in acquisition. However, in both, cross-linguistic distribution and in corresponding emergence, we find neither a clear-cut contrast between such two types of languages nor a corresponding clear-cut distinction in acquisition. Again, concatenation is not limited to grammar.

20. Natural morphology

In our own framework, Natural Morphology (cf. Dressler 1999; Kilani-Schoch & Dressler 2005), we look for universal preferences instead of strict universals, preferences which we derive from more general, extralinguistic preferences. In this context, we have found evidence in early child language for a greater importance of the following universal preferences than in adult target languages: preferences for morphosemantic and morphotactic transparency, for binarity, and for the figure-ground preference in terms of the early acquisition of the head vs. non-head distinction.

For acquisition, we subscribe to a constructivist framework, whereby children construct their grammar according to general predispositions and make generalizations based on their input (cf. Dressler & Karpf 1995). The strongest evidence for this self-organization model comes from acquisition paths which deviate from adult input, i.e. where the child engages in a "blind alley", from which he or she must quickly return. Our contribution includes one such case, in which both Viennese children, at an early phase, generalize having the first member of a compound end in a schwa (cf. § 7).

21. Conclusions

Our main findings concerning the theoretical relevance in the study of the acquisition of compounds can be summarized as follows. First, we have found a close parallelism between order of emergence and degree of prototypicality and markedness (cf. § 20): prototypical noun compounds, i.e. endocentric and subordinate binary and purely concatenative (i.e. interfixless) NN-compounds emerge first (cf. § 6, 7). The fact that left-headed compounds did not emerge cannot be taken as acquisitional support for the unmarkedness of right-headed compounds, because left-headed ones are unproductive and extremely rare in German. The order of emergence of other categories than nouns as first members follows the relative importance of word classes: verbs are more important than adjectives and even more so than other word classes that have not emerged as first elements in our corpora.

Interfixed compounds are morphosemantically and morphotactically more opaque than purely concatenative ones. They emerge later than the prototypical interfixless, i.e. purely concatenative compounds (cf. § 13, 14, 20). The by far most productive interfixation type (interfix -*n* after noun-final schwa) emerges first among interfixed compounds. Productivity seems to be a better predictor than frequency for the order of emergence (cf. § 9, 10). That recursive compounding starts late can be attributed to several factors and, thus, cannot discriminate between models that put high or low emphasis on the importance of recursivity (cf. § 17, 19). Morpheme order is very robust from the beginning, but, as for other aspects of our contribution, there is a need for thorough studies of compound acquisition in many more languages. Therefore, we want to extend our approach in a new subproject on compounding within our longitudinal *Crosslinguistic Project on Pre- and Protomorphology in Language Acquisition*.

Many more studies in more languages, particularly on age-of-acquisition effects, are also needed for testing our tentative claim, namely that by approximately the age of 3 years children have acquired core morphology, i.e., as far as compounds are concerned, the basic patterns of compounding are used by this age (cf. Dressler et al. 2001; Libben et al. 2002, and also § 7).

List of abbreviations

A	adjective
ABL	ablative case
ABS	absolutive case
Adv	adverb
AGT	grammatical agent
An.Gr.	Ancient Greek
AN-compound	Adjective+Noun compound
ATR	Advanced Tongue Root
Bul.	Bulgarian
Cat.	Catalan
CL	classifier
CAUS	causative
CM	Construction Morphology
Cm	compound marker
CN	compound noun
CompG	Composite Group
Conj	Conjunction
Cz.	Czech
Daff	derivational affix
DAT	dative
DEF	definite
dim	diminutive
DISTR	distributive
DU	dual
Dut.	Dutch
East A.	East Asian (languages)
Eng.	English
EMPH	emphatic
Endo	Endocentric
EP	European Portuguese
ERG	ergative
EXCL	exclusive

Exo	Exocentric
FACT	factual
FEM	feminine
FREQ	frequentative
Ft	foot
FUT	future
GEN	Genitive
Ger.	German
Germ.	Germanic (languages)
Gr.	Greek
HAB	habitual
I.E.	Indo-European
IMI	Part of imitative co-compound
IMP	imperative
INCL	inclusive
INDIC	indicative
Infl	Inflection
INTR	intransitive
ISV	Intervocalic-s Voicing
It.	Italian
Jap.	Japanese
LAM	Lesbian, Aivaliot, Moschonisiot
Lat.	Latin
LAT	lative
Le	lemma
LE	Linking Element
LIS	Lexicalized Interpretation Schema
LK	linker
LOC	locative case
MASC	masculine
N	noun
NEUT	neuter gender
NDVC	'non-affixal (de)verbal compound
NEG	negative
NLP	Natural Language Processing
NMZ	nominalizer
NN-compound	Noun+Noun compound
nom pref	nominal prefix
NOM	nominative

NP	Noun Phrase
NS	noun suffix
Num	Numeral
NV	Noun-Verb
OBL	oblique case
OPT	optative
P	preposition
PAT	grammatical patient
PL	plural
PN-compound	Preprosition+Noun compound
Pol.	Polish
POSS	Possessive
PP	Prepositional Phrase
Ppt	past participle
PPh	Phonological Phrase
PRF	perfective aspect
Pro	pronoun
PROG	progressive
PROP	proper
PRS	present
PRT	partitive
Prt	particle
PW	Phonological Word
PW^{max}	Maximal Phonological Word
Q	quantifier
R	relation
REAL	realis
REP	repetitive
REV	reversive
Rom.	Romance (languages)
Rus.	Russian
SEM	meaning of a linguistic unit
SG	singular
Slav.	Slavic (languages)
SMG	Standard Moden Greek
sN	semiword (noun)
sA	semiword (adjective)
Sp.	Spanish
ss	same subject

ST	stative
SUBORD	subordinative mode
Suf	suffix
To	token
Tot	total
TR	transitive
UBH	Unitary Base Hypothesis
UOH	Unitary Output Hypotheis
V	Verb
VN-Compound	Verb+Noun compound
VV dvandva compounds	Verb+Verb dvandva compound
VNC N	non-affixal (de)verbal compound
VP	Verb Phrase
X	variable for lexical category
Y	variable for lexical category
Y;M	year;month of child's age
Z	variable for lexical category

Master list of references

Antelme, Michel. 2004. "Khmer". Arnaud, ed. 2004.149–184.
Abakah, Emmanuel. 2006. "The Tonology of Compounds in Akan". *Linguistic Variation and Applied Linguistics* 17.1–34.
Abney, Stephen. 1987. *The English Noun Phrase in its Sentential Aspect*. MIT Ph.D. dissertation, Cambridge, Mass.
Ackema, Peter. 1999. *Issues in Morphosyntax*. Amsterdam & Philadelphia: John Benjamins.
Ackema, Peter. 2000. Review of Josefsson 1998. *Studies in Language* 24. 694–703.
Ackema, Peter, & Ad Neeleman. 2001. "Competition between Syntax and Morphology", *Optimality Theoretic Syntax* ed. by Geraldine Legendre, Jane Grimshaw & Sten Vikner, 29–60. Cambridge, Mass., MIT Press.
Ackema, Peter and Ad Neeleman. 2002. "Effects of Short-term Storage in Processing Rightward Movement". *Storage and Computation in the Language Faculty* ed. by Sieb Nooteboom, Fred Weerman and Frank Wijnen, 219–256. Dordrecht: Kluwer.
Ackema, Peter & Ad Neeleman. 2004. *Beyond Morphology: Interface conditions on word formation*. Oxford: Oxford University Press.
Ackema, Peter & Ad Neeleman. "The Role of Syntax and Morphology in Compounding". This volume.
Ackerman, Farrel & Adele Goldberg. 1996. "Constraints on Adjectival Past Participles". *Conceptual Structure, Discourse and Language* ed. by Adele E. Goldberg, 17–30. Stanford: CSLI.
Adams, Valerie. 1973. *An Introduction to Modern English Word-Formation*. London: Longman.
Adams, Valerie. 2001. *Complex Words in English*. Harlow: Pearson Education.
Aikhenvald, Alexandra Y. 2007. "Typological Distinctions in Word-formation". *Language Typology and Syntactic Description* ed. by Timothy Shopen, 2nd ed., vol. III, 1–65. Cambridge: Cambridge University Press.
Aksu-Koç, Ayhan & Dan I. Slobin. 1985. "The Acquisition of Turkish". *The Crosslinguistic Study of Language Acquisition* ed. by Dan I. Slobin, vol.I, 839–878. Hillsdale: Erlbaum.
Alcoba Rueda, Santiago. 1987. "Los parasintéticos: Costituyentes y estructura léxica". *Revista de la Sociedad Española de Lingüística* 17:2.245–68.
Alexiadou, Artemis. 1997. *Adverb Placement*, Amsterdam: John Benjamins.
Allen, Margaret Reece. 1978. *Morphological Investigations*. Ph.D. dissertation, University of Connecticut, Storrs, Ct.
Amha, Azeb. 2001. *The Maale Language*. Leiden: Research School of Asian, African, and Amerindian Studies. University of Leiden.
Amiot, Dany. 2005. "Between Compounding and Derivation: Elements of word formation corresponding to prepositions". Dressler, Kastovsky, Pfeiffer & Rainer, eds. 2005.183–195.
Amiot, Dany. 2008. *La composition dans une perspective typologique*. Arras: Artois Presses Université.
Amiot, Dany & Georgette Dal. 2007. "Integrating Neoclassical Combining Forms into a Lexeme-Based Morphology". *On-Line Proceedings of the Fifth Mediterranean Morphology*

Meeting ed. by Geert Booij, Luca Ducceschi, Bernard Fradin, Emiliano Guevara, Angela Ralli & Sergio Scalise, 323–336. Bologna: Università di Bologna.
Anderson, Steven. 1992. *A-morphous Morphology*. Cambridge: Cambridge University Press.
Anderson, Steven. & David W. Lightfoot. 2002. *The Language Organ: Linguistics as cognitive physiology*. Cambridge: Cambridge University Press.
Andrews, Sally, Brett Miller & Keith Rayner. 2004. "Eye Movements and Morphological Segmentation of Compound Words: There is a mouse in mousetrap". *European Journal of Cognitive Psychology* 16.285–311.
Andriotis, Nikolaos. 1960. *Simvoli sti Neoelliniki Sinthesi*. Vol. VII. Athens: National Library.
Arcodia, Giorgio Francesco, Nicola Grandi & Fabio Montermini. 2009. "Hierarchical NN Compounds in a Cross-Linguistic Perspective", *Italian Journal of Linguistics* 21.1. 11–33.
Arens, Yigal, John Granacki & Alice Parker. 1987. "Phrasal Analysis of Long Noun Sequences". *Proceedings of the 25th Annual Meeting of the Association for Computational Linguistics*, 59–64, Stanford, California. Stanford: Association for Computational Linguistics.
Arnaud, Pierre J. L. 2004. "Problématique du nom composé". Arnaud, ed. 2004. 329–353.
Arnaud, Pierre J.L., ed. 2004. *Le nom composé: Données sur seize langues*. Lyon: Presses Universitaires de Lyon.
Aronoff, Mark. 1976. *Word Formation in Generative Grammar*. Cambridge, Mass.: MIT Press.
Aronoff, Mark. 1994. *Morphology by Itself*. Cambridge, Mass.: MIT Press.
Aronoff, Mark. 2007. "In the Beginning Was the Word". *Language* 83:4. 803–830.
Aronoff, Mark, Irit Meir, Carol Padden & Wendy Sandler. 2004. "Morphological Universals and the Sign Language Type". *Yearbook of Morphology* 2004.19–39.
Aronoff, Mark, Irit Meir & Wendy Sandler. 2005. "The Paradox of Sign Language Morphology". *Language* 81:2.301–344.
Aronoff, Mark, Irit Meir, Carol Padden & Wendy Sandler. 2008. "The Roots of Linguistic Organization in a New Language". *Interaction Studies: A special issue on holophrasis vs. compositionality in the emergence of protolanguage* 9:1. 131–150.
Ascoop, Kirstin. 2005. "Affixoidhungrig? Skitbra! Status und Gebrauch von Affixoiden im Deutschen und Schwedischen". *Germanistische Mitteilungen* 65.17–28.
Ascoop, Kristin & Torsten Leuschner. 2006. Affixoidhungrig? Skitbra! Comparing affixoids in Swedish and German. *Sprachtypologie und Universalienforschung* 59. 241–252.
Asher, Robert E. & T. C. Kumari. 1997. *Malayalam*. London & New York: Routledge.
Awbery, Gwenllian Mair. 2004. "Welsh". Arnaud, ed. 2004.303–327.
Baayen, Harald. 1992. "Quantitative Aspects of Morphological Productivity". *Yearbook of Morphology* 1991. 109–149.
Baayen, Harald. 2001. *Word-Frequency Distributions*. Dordrecht: Kluwer.
Baayen, Harald. 2003. "Probabilistic Approaches to Morphology". *Probabilistic linguistics* ed. by Rens Bod, Jennifer Hay & Stefanie Jannedy, 229–287. Cambridge, Mass.: MIT Press.
Baayen, Harald. 2009. "Corpus Linguistics in Morphology: Morphological productivity". *Corpus Linguistics: An International handbook* ed. by Anke Lüdeling & Merja Kytö, vol. II, 899-919. Berlin/New York: Walter de Gruyter.
Baayen, Harald, Richard Piepenbrock & Leon Gulikers. 1995. *The CELEX Lexical Database* (CD-ROM). Linguistic Data Consortium, University of Pennsylvania, Philadelphia, PA.
Baayen, Harald & Antoinette Renouf. 1996. "Chronicling the Times: Productive lexical innovations in an English newspaper". *Language* 72.69–96.
Baayen, Harald, Ton Dijkstra & Robert Schreuder. 1997. "Singulars and Plural in Dutch: Evidence for a parallel dual route model". *Journal of Memory and Language* 36.94–117.

Baayen, Harald, Laurie Feldman & Robert Schreuder. 2006. "Morphological Influences on the Recognition of Monosyllabic Monomorphemic Words". *Journal of Memory and Language* 53.496–512.
Baayen, Harald, Lee Wurm & Joanna Aycock. 2007. "Lexical Dynamics for Low Frequency Complex Words. A Regression study across tasks and modalities". *The Mental Lexicon* 2.419–463.
Baker, Mark. 1988. *Incorporation: A theory of grammatical function changing*. Chicago: University of Chicago Press.
Baker, Mark. 1995. *The Polysynthesis Parameter*. Oxford: Oxford University Press.
Bakken, Kristin. 1998. *Leksikalisering av Sammensetninger*. Oslo: Universitetsforlaget.
Bakker, Peter, Norval Smith & Tonjes Veenstra. 1995. 'Saramaccan'. *Pidgins and Creoles* ed. by Jacques Arends, Pieter Muysken & Norval Smith. 165–178. Amsterdam & Philadelphia: John Benjamins, 165–178.
Baldwin, Timothy, Tanaka, Takaaki. 2004. "Translation by Machine of Complex Nominals: Getting it right". *Second ACL Workshop on Multiword Expressions: Integrating processing*, 24–31, Barcelona. Barcelona: Association for Computational Linguistics
Balota, David, Melvin Yap, Michael Cortese, Keith Hutchison, Brett Kessler, Bjorn Loftis, James Neely, Douglas Nelson, Greg Simpson & Rebecca Treiman. 2007. "The English Lexicon Project". *Behavior Research Methods* 39.445–459.
Barker, Chris. 1998. "Episodic *-ee* in English: A thematic role constraint on new word formation". *Language* 74.695–727.
Baroni, Marco, Silvia Bernardini, Federica Comastri, Lorenzo Piccioni, Alessandra Volpi, Guy Aston & Marco Mazzoleni. 2004. "Introducing the *la Repubblica* Corpus: A large, annotated, TEI(XML)-compliant corpus of newspaper Italian". *Proceedings of the Fourth International Conference on Language Resources and Evaluation* ed. by Maria T. Lino, Maria F. Xavier, Fátima Ferreira, Rute Costa & Raquel Silva, 1771-1774. Paris: ELRA.
Baroni, Marco, Emiliano Guevara, Vito Pirrelli. 2007. "NN Compounds in Italian: Modelling category induction and analogical extension". *Lingue e Linguaggio* 2.263–290.
Bartke, Susanne. 1998. *Experimentelle Studien zur Flexion und Wortbildung. Pluralmorphologie und lexikalische Komposition im unauffälligen Spracherwerb und im Dysgrammatismus*. Tübingen: Max Niemeyer Verlag.
Bauer, Laurie. 1978. *The Grammar of Nominal Compounding*. Odense: Odense University Press.
Bauer, Laurie. 1983. *English Word-formation*. Cambridge: Cambridge University Press.
Bauer, Laurie. 1990. "Beheading the Word". *Journal of Linguistics* 26.1–31.
Bauer, Laurie. 1998. "When Is a Sequence of Noun+Noun a Compound in English?". *English Language and Linguistics* 2.65–86.
Bauer, Laurie. 2001a. *Morphological Productivity*. Cambridge: Cambridge University Press.
Bauer, Laurie. 2001b. "Compounding". *Language Typology and Language Universals:An international handbook* ed. by Martin Haspelmath, Ekkehard König, Wulf Oesterreicher & Wolfgang Raible, 695–707. Berlin & New York: Mouton de Gruyter.
Bauer, Laurie. 2003. *Introducing Linguistic Morphology*. 2nd ed. Washington, D.C.: Georgetown University.
Bauer, Laurie. 2005. "The Borderline between Derivation and Compounding". Dressler, Kastovsky, Pfeiffer & Rainer, eds. 2005. 97–108.
Bauer, Laurie. 2006. "Compound". *Encyclopedia of Language and Linguistics* ed. by Keith Brown [et al.], vol II, 719–726. Oxford: Elsevier.

Bauer, Laurie. 2007. "Apparently Exocentric Attributives in English". Paper presented at the Second International Conference on the Linguistics of Contemporary English, Toulouse, July 2007.
Bauer, Laurie. 2008. "Dvandva". *Word Structure* 1.1–20.
Bauer, Laurie. 2009. "Typology of Compounds". Lieber & Štekauer, eds. 2009.343–356.
Bauer, Laurie. "The Typology of Exocentric Compounding". This volume.
Bauer, Laurie & Antoinette Renouf. 2001. "A Corpus-based Study of Compounding in English". *Journal of English Linguistics*. 29: 2.101–123.
Bauer, Winifred. 1993. *Maori*. London & New York: Routledge.
Beard, Robert. 1995. *Lexeme-Morpheme Base Morphology. A general theory of inflection and word formation*. Albany: New York Press.
Beard, Robert. 1998. "Derivation". *The Handbook of Morphology* ed. by Andrew Spencer & Arnold Zwicky, 44–65. Oxford: Blackwell.
Becker, Thomas. 1990. *Analogie und morphologische Theorie*. München: Wilhelm Fink.
Becker, Thomas. 1992. "Compounding in German". *Rivista di Linguistica* 4.5–36.
Becker, Thomas. 1994. "Back-Formation, Cross-Formation, and 'Bracketing Paradoxes'". *Yearbook of Morphology* 1993. 1–26.
Benczes, Réka. 2006. *Creative Compounding in English*. Amsterdam & Philadelphia: John Benjamins.
Berg, Thomas. 2007. "The Internal Structure of Four Noun Compounds in English and German". *Corpus Linguistics and Linguistic Theory* 2–2.197–231.
Berger, Adam, Stephen Della Pietra & Vincent Della Pietra. 1996. "A Maximum Entropy Approach to Natural Language Processing". *Computational Linguistics* 22:1.39–71.
Berger, Hermann. 1998. *Die Burushaski-Sprache von Hunza und Nager*. Wiesbaden: Otto Harrassowitz.
Berman, Ruth A. 1986. "The Acquisition of Morphology/Syntax: A crosslinguistic perspective". *Language Acquisition* ed. by Paul Fletcher & Michael Garman, 429–447. Cambridge: Cambridge University Press.
Berman, Ruth A. 2009. "Children's Acquisition of Compounds". *The Handbook of Compounding* ed. by Rochelle Lieber & Pavol Štekauer, 298–322. Oxford: Oxford University Press.
Berman, Ruth & Eve V. Clark. 1989. "Learning to Use Compounds for Contrast: Data from Hebrew". *First Language* 9.247–270.
Bernardini, Silvia, Marco Baroni & Stefan Evert. 2006. "A WaCky Introduction". *Wacky! Working Papers on the Web as Corpus* ed. by Marco Baroni & Silvia Bernardini, 9–40. Bologna: GEDIT.
Bertram, Raymond, Jukka Hyönä & Alexander Pollatsek. 2004. "Morphological Parsing and the Use of Segmentation Cues in Reading Finnish Compounds". *Journal of Memory and Language* 51.325–345.
Biber, Douglas & Victoria Clark. 2002. "Historical Shift in Modification Patterns with Complex Noun Phrase Structures: How long can you go without a verb?" *English Historical Syntax and Morphology* ed. by T. Fanego, J. Pérez-Guerra and M. J. López-Couso, 43–66. Amsterdam & Philadelphia: JohnBenjamins.
Bickerton, Derek. 1990. *Language and Species*. Chicago: University of Chicago Press.
Bisang, Walter. 1988. *Hmong Texte. Eine Auswahl mit Interlinearübersetzung aus Jean Mottin, Contes et légendes hmong blanc*. (Arbeiten des Seminars für Allgemeine Sprachwissenschaft der Universität Zürich, 8). Zürich.
Bisang, Walter. 1992. *Das Verb im Chinesischen, Hmong, Vietnamesischen, Thai und Khmer. Vergleichende Grammatik im Rahmen der Verbserialisierung, der Grammatikalisierung und der Attraktorpositionen*. Tübingen: Gunter Narr.

Bisetto, Antonietta. 1999. "Note sui composti VN dell'italiano". *Fonologia e morfologia dell'italiano e dei dialetti d'Italia. Atti del XXXI congresso della Società di Linguistica Italiana* ed. by Paola Benincà, Alberto Mioni & Laura Vanelli, 503–538. Roma: Bulzoni.
Bisetto, Antonietta. 2006. "The Italian Suffix *-tore*". *Lingue e Linguaggio* 5.261–280.
Bisetto, Antonietta & Sergio Scalise. 2005. "The Classification of Compounds". *Lingue e Linguaggio* 4.319–332.
Bisetto, Antonietta & Chiara Melloni. 2007. "Parasynthetic Compounding". Paper presented at the Sixth Mediterranean Morphology Meeting, Patras, Ithaca, Greece, 27–30. September 2007.
Bisetto, Antonietta & Sergio Scalise. 2007. "Selection is a Head Property". *Acta Linguistica Hungarica* 54:4. 361–380.
Bisetto, Antonietta & Chiara Melloni. 2008. "Parasynthetic Compounding". *Lingue e Linguaggio* 7:2.233–260.
Bloomfield, Leonard. 1935. *Language*. London: Allen & Unwin.
Boase-Beier, Jean. 1987. *Poetic Compounds*. Tübingen: Max Max Niemeyer.
Bok-Bennema, Reineke & Brigitte Kampers-Manhe. 2005. "Taking a Closer Look at Romance VN Compounds". *New Perspectives on Romance Linguistics. Morphology, Syntax, Semantics, and Pragmatics*, vol. I ed. by Chiyo Nishida & Jean-Pierre Y. Montreuil, 13–26. Amsterdam & Philadephia: John Benjamins.
Booij, Geert. 1977. *Dutch Morphology: A study of word formation in generative grammar*. Dordrecht: Foris.
Booij, Geert. 1985. Coordination Reduction in Complex Words: A case for prosodic phonology. *Advances in Non-linear Phonology* ed. by Harry van der Hulst & Norval Smith, 143–160. Dordrecht: Foris.
Booij, Geert. 1988, "The Relation between Inheritance and Argument Linking: Deverbal nouns in Dutch". *Morphology and Modularity* ed. by Martin Everaert *et al.*, 57–73. Dordrecht: Foris.
Booij, Geert. 1994. "Against Split Morphology". *Yearbook of Morphology* 1993. 27–50.
Booij, Geert. 1996. "Inherent versus Contextual Inflection and the Split Morphology Hypothesis". *Yearbook of Morphology* 1996. 1–16.
Booij, Geert. 1999. "The Role of the Prosodic Word in Phonotactic Generalizations". *Studies on the Phonological Word* ed. by Tracy Alan Hall & Ursula Kleinhenz, 47–72. Amsterdam & Philadelphia: John Benjamins.
Booij, Geert. 2002. *The Morphology of Dutch*. Oxford: Oxford University Press.
Booij, Geert. 2005a. "Compounding and Derivation: Evidence for construction morphology". Dressler, Kastovsky, Pfeiffer & Rainer, eds.2005.109–132.
Booij, Geert. 2005b. *The Grammar of Words: An introduction to linguistic morphology*. Oxford: Oxford University Press. [2007^2]
Booij, Geert. 2007. "Construction Morphology and the Lexicon". *Selected Proceedings of the 5th Décembrettes: Morphology in Toulouse* ed. by Fabio Montermini, Gilles Boyé, & Nabil Hathout, 34–44. Somerville, Mass: Cascadilla: Proceedings Project. www.lingref.com, document #1613.
Booij, Geert. 2008. "Recycling Morphology: Case endings as markers of Dutch constructions". Manuscript, Universiteit Leiden. [http://website.leidenuniv.nl/~booijge/pdf/Recycling%20morphology.pdf].
Booij, Geert. 2009a. "Lexical Integrity as a Formal Universal: A constructionist view". Scalise, Magni & Bisetto, eds. 2008.83–103.
Booij, Geert. 2009b. "Compounding and Construction Morphology". Lieber & Štekauer, eds. 2009.201–216.

Booij, Geert. "Compound Construction: Schemas or analogy? A construction morphology perspective". This volume.

Booij, Geert, Christian Lehmann & Joachim Mugdan, eds. 2000. *Morphology*. Berlin & New York: Walter de Gruyter.

Borer, Hagit. 1998. "On the Morphological Parallelism between Compounds and Constructs". *Yearbook of Morphology* 1998.45–66.

Borer, Hagit. 2005. *Structuring Sense. Vol. I: In name only*. Oxford: Oxford University Press.

Borthwick, Andrew, John Sterling, Eugene Agichtein, & Ralph Grishman. 1998. "Exploiting Diverse Knowledge Sources via Maximum Entropy in Named Entity Recognition". *Proceedings of the Sixth Workshop on Very Large Corpora, Montréal, Université de Montréal* ed. by Eugene Charniak, 152–160. Montréal: Association for Computational Linguistics.

Botha, Rudolf. 1981. "A Base Rule Theory of Afrikaans Synthetic Compounding". *The Scope of Lexical Rules* ed. by Michael Moortgat, Harry v.d. Hulst & Teun Hoekstra, 1–77. Dordrecht: Foris.

Botha, Rudolf. 1985. *Morphological Mechanisms*. Oxford: Pergamon.

Bourigault, Didier. 1993. "An Endogenous Corpus-Based Method for Structural Noun Phrase Disambiguation". *Proceedings of the 6th Meeting of the European Chapter of the Association for Computational Linguistics, Utrecht, Netherlands* 81–86. Utrecht: Association for Computational Linguistics.

Brennan, Mary. 1990. *Word Formation in British Sign Language*. Stockholm: University of Stockholm.

Brinton, Laurel J. & Elizabeth Closs Traugott. 2005. *Lexicalization and Language Change*. Cambridge: Cambridge University Press.

Bruce, Gösta, Claes-Christian Elert, Olle Engstrand & Pär Wretling. 1999. "Phonetics and Phonology of the Swedish Dialects – A project presentation and a database demonstrator". *Proceedings of the International Congress of Pho netics*. 321–324.

Burrow, Thomas. 1955. *The Sanskrit Language*. London: Faber & Faber.

Burzio, Luigi. 2005. "Sources of Paradigm Uniformity". *Paradigms in Phonological Theory* ed. by Laura J. Downing, T. Alan Hall & Renate Raffelsiefen, 65–106. Oxford: Oxford University Press.

Bybee, Joan. 1985. *Morphology*. Amsterdam & Philadelphia: John Benjamins.

Carlson, Barry. 1990. "Compounding and Lexical Affixation in Spokane". *Anthropological Linguistics* 32.69–82.

Carstairs-McCarthy, Andrew. 1992. *Current Morphology*. London: Routledge.

Ceccagno, Antonella & Sergio Scalise. 2006. "Classification, Structure and Headedness of Chinese Compounds". *Lingue e Linguaggio* 2.233–260.

Ceccagno, Antonella & Bianca Basciano. 2007. "Compound Headedness in Chinese: An analysis of neologisms". *Morphology* 17:2. 207–231.

Ceccagno, Antonella & Bianca Basciano. 2009. *Shuobuchulai – La formazione delle parole in cinese*. Bologna: Serendipità Società Cooperativa.

Ceccagno, Antonella & Bianca Basciano. 2009. "Sino-Tibetan: Mandarin Chinese". Lieber & Štekauer, eds. 2009.478–490.

Chomsky, Noam. 1981. *Lectures on Government and Binding*. Dordrecht: Foris.

Chomsky, Noam. 1995. *The Minimalist Program*. Cambridge, Mass.: MIT Press.

Chomsky, Noam. 2004. "Beyond Explanatory Adequacy". *Structures and Beyond. The cartography of syntactic structure* ed. by Adriana Belletti, 104–131. Oxford: Oxford University Press.

Chomsky, Noam. 2007. "Approaching UG from Below". *Interfaces + Recursion = Language?* ed. by U. Sauerland & H.-M. Gärtner, 1–19. Berlin & New York: Mouton de Gruyter.

Church, Kenneth W., Hanks Patrick. 1989. "Word Association Norms, Mutual Information and Lexicography". *Proceedings of the 27th Annual Meeting of the Association for Computational Linguistics*, Vancouver, University of British Columbia, 76–83. Vancouver, B.C,: Association for Computational Linguistics.

Cinque, Guglielmo. 1999. *Adverbs and Functional Heads*. Oxford: Oxford University Press.

Clahsen, Harald. 1999. "Lexical Entries and Rules of Language: A multidisciplinary study of German inflection". *Behavioral and Brain Sciences* 22.991–1013, 1046–1060.

Clahsen, Harald, Gary Marcus, Susanne Bartke & Richard Wiese. 1996. "Compounding and Inflection in German Child Language". *Yearbook of Morphology* 1996.115–142.

Clahsen, Harald, Ingrid Sonnenstuhl & James P. Blevins. 2003. "Derivational Morphology in the German Mental Lexicon: A dual mechanism approach". *Morphological Structure in Language Processing* ed. by R. Harald Baayen & Robert Schreuder, 125–155. Berlin & New York: Mouton de Gruyter.

Clahsen, Harald, Monika Rothweiler, Andreas Woest & Gary Marcus. 1992. "Regular and Irregular Inflection in the Acquisition of German Noun Plurals". *Cognition* 45.225–255.

Clark, Eve V. 1993. *The Lexicon in Acquisition*. Cambridge: Cambridge University Press.

Clark, Eve V. 2003. *First Language Acquisition*. Cambridge: Cambridge University Press.

Clark, Eve V. & Barbara F. Hecht. 1982. "Learning to Coin Agent and Instrument Nouns". *Cognition* 12.1–24.

Clark, Eve V. & Ruth A. Berman. 1984. "Structure and Use in the Acquisition of Word Formation". *Language* 60.547–590.

Clark, Eve V. & Ruth A. Berman. 1987. "Types of linguistic knowledge: Interpreting and producing compound nouns". *Journal of Child Language* 14.547–567.

Clark, Eve V., Susan A. Gelman & Nancy M. Lane. 1985. "Noun compounds and category structure in young children". *Child Development* 56.84–94.

Clark, Eve, Barbara Hecht & Randa Mulford. 1986. "Acquiring Complex Compounds: Affixes and word order in English". *Linguistics* 24.7–29.

Comrie, Bernard. 1980. "Morphology and Word Order Reconstruction: Problems and prospects". *Historical Morphology* (Trends in Linguistics, Studies and Monographs 17) ed. by Jacek Fisiak, 83–96. The Hague: Mouton.

Conrad, Robert J. & Kepas Wogiga. 1991. *An Outline of Bukiyip Grammar*. (Pacific Linguistics C 113.) Canberra: Australian National University.

Coolen, Riet, Henk J. Van Jaarsveld & Robert Schreuder. 1991. "The Interpretation of Isolated Novel Nominal Compounds". *Memory & Cognition* 19.341–352.

Corbin, Danielle. 1980. "Contradictions et inadéquations de l'analyse parasynthétique en morphologie dérivationnelle". *Théories linguistiques et traditions grammaticales* ed. by A. M. Dessaux-Berthonneau, 181–224. Lille: Presses Universitaires de Lille.

Corbin, Danielle. 1987. *Morphologie dérivationnelle et structuration du lexique*. Tübingen: Max Niemeyer.

Corbin, Danielle. 1992. "Hypothèses sur les frontières de la composition nominale". *Cahiers de grammaire* 17.26–55.

Costello, Fintan J. & Keane, Mark T. 1997. "Polysemy in Conceptual Combination: Testing the constraint theory of combination". *Nineteenth Annual Conference of the Cognitive Science Society* ed. by Michael G. Shafto and Pat Langley, 137–142. Hillsdale, N.J.: Lawrence Erlbaum.

Coulson, Seana. 2001. *Semantic Leaps: Frame-shifting and conceptual blending in meaning construction*. Cambridge: Cambridge University Press.

Creissels, Denis. 2004. "Bambara". Arnaud, ed. 2004.21–46.

Crocco Galèas, Grazia & Wolfgang U. Dressler. 1992. "Trasparenza morfotattica e morfosemantica dei composti nominali più produttivi dell'italiano d'oggi". *Linee di tendenza dell'italiano contemporaneo". Atti del XXV congresso della Società di Linguistica Italiana*, ed. by Bruno Moretti, Dario Petrini & Sandro Bianconi. 9–24. Roma: Bulzoni.

Culicover, Peter W., Nowak Andrzej. 2003. *Dynamical Grammar.* Oxford: Oxford University Press.

Daelemans, Walter. 2002. "A Comparison of Analogical Modeling of Language to Memory-based Language Processing". *Analogical modeling* ed. by Royal Skousen, Deryle Lonsdale & Dilworth B. Parkinson, 157–179. Amsterdam & Philadelphia: John Benjamins.

Dalton-Puffer, Christiane & Ingo Plag. 2000. Category-wise, Some Compound-type Morphemes Seem to be Rather Suffix-like: On the status of *-ful, -type,* and *-wise* in present-day English. *Folia Linguistica* 34.225–244.

Darmesteter, Arsène. 1877. *De la création actuelle de mots nouveaux dans la langue française et des lois qui la régissent.* Paris: Vieweg.

Dasgupta, Sajib, Naira Khan, Asif I. Sarkar, Dewan S. H. Pavel & Mumit Khan. 2005. "Morphological Analysis of Inflectional Compound Words in Bangla". *Proceedings of the 8th International Conference on Computer and Information Technology* (ICCIT), Dhaka, Bangladesh. Dhaka: Islamic University of Technology.

De Jong, Nivja, Robert Schreuder & Harald Baayen. 2000. "The Morphological Family Size Effect and Morphology". *Language and Cognitive Processes* 15.329–365.

De Jong, Nivja, Laurie B. Feldman, Robert Schreuder, Matther Pastizzo, & R. Harald Baayen. 2002. "The Processing and Representation of Dutch and English Compounds: Peripheral morphological and central orthographic effects". *Brain and Language* 81:1–3.555–567.

De Mauro, Tullio. 1999. *Grande dizionario italiano dell'uso.* Torino: UTET.

Delfitto, Denis & Chiara Melloni. 2009. "Compounds Don't Come Easy", *Lingue e Linguaggio* 7.75–104.

Devescovi, Antonella, Maria Cristina Caselli, Daniela Marchione, Patrizio Pasqualetti, Judy Reilly & Elizabeth Bates. 2005. "A Crosslinguistic Study of the Relationship between Grammar and Lexical Development". *Journal of Child Language* 32.759–786.

Di Sciullo, Anna Maria. 2005. *Asymmetrical Morphology.* Cambridge, Mass.: MIT Press.

Di Sciullo, Anna Maria. 2009. "Why are Compounds a Part of Human Language? A view from asymmetry theory". Lieber & Štekauer, eds. 2009.145–177.

Di Sciullo, Anna Maria & Edwin Williams. 1987. *On the Definition of Word.* Cambridge, Mass.: MIT Press.

Di Sciullo, Anna-Maria & Angela Ralli. 1999. "Theta-Role Saturation in Greek Compounds". In Artemis Alexiadou, Geoffrey Horrocks & Melita Stavrou eds. *Studies of Modern Greek Generative Syntax,* 185–200. Dordrecht: Kluwer.

Dik, Simon. 1968. *Coordination: Its implication for the theory of general linguistics.* Amsterdam: North-Holland.

Dimela, Eleonora. 2005. *I prothimatopoiisi stin Kritiki dialecto. I periptosi ton sin-, sjo-, so-.* M.A. Thesis. University of Athens.

Dimmendaal, Gerrit Jan. 1983. *The Turkanta Language.* Dordrecht & Cinnaminson, N.J.: Foris.

Dixon, Robert M.W. & Alexandra Y. Aikhenvald. 2002. "Word: A typological framework". *Word. A Cross-Linguistic Typology* ed. by Robert M.W. Dixon & Alexandra Y. Aikhenvald, 1–41. Cambridge: Cambridge University Press.

Don, Jan. 2009. "IE, Germanic: Dutch". Lieber & Štekauer, eds. 2009.370–385.

Don, Jan, Mieke Trommelen & Wim Zonneveld. 2000. "Conversion and Category Indeterminacy. *Morphology. An International Handbook on Inflection and Word Formation.* Vol.I, ed.by Geert Booij, Christian Lehman and Joachim Mugdan in colloboration with Wolfgang Kesselheim and Stavros Skopeteas, 943–952. Berlin/New York: Walter de Gruyter.

Donabédian, Anaïd. 2004. "Arménien". Arnaud, ed. 2004.3–20.

Donalies, Elke. 2004. *Grammatik des Deutschen im europäischen Vergleich: Kombinatorische Begriffsbildung*, vol. I, *Substantivkomposition*. Mannheim: Institut für deutsche Sprache.

Doronin, Vladimir. 1993. *Kočkodikeś – Pakśa narmuń*. Saransk: Mordovskoj kńižnoj izdateľstvaś.

Downing, Pamela. 1977. "On the Creation and Use of English Compounds". *Language* 53.810–42.

Dowty, David. 1991. "Thematic Proto-roles and Argument Selection". *Language* 67.547–619.

Drachman, Gabriel & Angeliki Malikouti-Drachman. 1999. "Greek Word Accent". *Word Prosodic Systems in the Languages of Europe* ed. by Harry van der Hulst, 897–945. Berlin & New York: Mouton de Gruyter.

Dressler, Wolfgang U. 1999. "What is natural in Natural Morphology?" *Travaux du Cercle Linguistique de Prague* 3.135–144.

Dressler, Wolfgang U. 2005. "Towards a Natural Morphology of Compounding". *Linguistica* XLV.29–40.

Dressler, Wolfgang U. 2006. "Compound Types". *The Representation and Processing of Compound Words* ed. by Gary Libben & Gonia Jarema, 23–44. Oxford: Oxford University Press.

Dressler, Wolfgang U. 2009. "Approche typologique de l'acquisition de la langue première". *Apprentissage des Langues* ed. by Michèle Kail, Michel Fayol & Maya Hickmann, 137–149. Paris: CNRS Éditions.

Dressler, Wolfgang U. & Annemarie Karpf. 1995. "The Theoretical Relevance of Pre- and Protomorphology in Language Acquisition". *Yearbook of Morphology* 1994.99–122.

Dressler, Wolfgang U. & Anna M. Thornton. 1991. "Doppie basi e binarismo nella morfologia italiana". *Rivista di Linguistica* 3:1.3–22.

Dressler, Wolfgang U., Marianne Kilani-Schoch & Sabine Klampfer. 2003. "How does a child detect morphology? Evidence from production." *Morphological structure in language processing* ed. by R. Harald Baayen & Robert Schreuder, 391425. Berlin: Mouton de Gruyter.

Dressler, Wolfgang U. & Mária Ladányi. 2000. "Productivity in Word Formation: A morphological approach". *Acta Linguistica Hungarica* 47.103–144.

Dressler, Wolfgang U., Gary Libben, Jacqueline Stark, Christiane Pons & Gonia Jarema. 2001. "The Processing of Interfixed German Compounds". *Yearbook of Morphology* 2001.185–220.

Dressler, Wolfgang U., Dieter Kastovsky, Oskar E. Pfeiffer & Franz Rainer, eds. 2005. *Morphology and Its Demarcations*. Amsterdam & Philadelphia: John Benjamins.

Dressler, Wolfgang U., Gary Libben, Gonia Jarema, Jacqueline Stark & Christiane Pons. 2005. "Produttività nel processamento di composti: Esempi tedeschi con e senza interfissi". Grossmann & Thornton, eds. 2005.153–162.

Dryer, Matthew. 1992. "The Greenbergian Word Order Correlations". *Language* 68.81–138.

Durie, Mark. 1997. "Grammatical Structures in Verb Serialization". *Complex Predicates* Alsina, Alex & Bresnan, Joan & Sells, Peter eds. 1997. CSLI Lecture Notes 64. 289–354. Stanford: Center for the Study of Language and Information.

Duroiselle, Charles. 1997. *Practical Grammar of the Pali Language*. Tullera: Buddha Dharma Education Association.

Elsen, Hilke. 1991. *Erstspracherwerb. Der Erwerb des deutschen Lautsystems*. Wiesbaden: Deutscher Universitätsverlag.

Embick, David & Rolf Noyer. 2001. "Movement Operations after Syntax". *Linguistic Inquiry* 32.555–595.

Embick, David & Alec Marantz. 2008. "Architecture and Blocking". *Linguistic Inquiry* 39:1.1–53.
Emmorey, Karen, ed. 2003. *Perspectives on Classifiers in Sign Languages*. Mahwah, New Jersey: Lawrence Erlbaum Associates.
Emonds, Joseph. 2000. *Lexicon and Grammar: The English syntacticon*. Berlin & New York: Mouton de Gruyter.
Emonds, Joseph. 2009. "Universal Default Right Headedness and how Stress Determines Word Order". *Lingue e Linguaggio* 1.55–24.
Erben, Johannes. 2006. *Einführung in die deutsche Wortbildungslehre*. V ed., Berlin: Schmidt.
Estes, Zachary. 2003. "A Tale of Two Similarities: Comparison and integration in conceptual combination". *Cognitive Science* 27.911–921.
Estes, Zachary & Lara L. Jones. 2006. "Priming via Relational Similarity: A COPPER HORSE is faster when seen through a GLASS EYE". *Journal of Memory and Language* 55.89–101.
Evans, Nicholas D. 1995. *A Grammar of Kayardild*. Berlin & New York: Mouton de Gruyter.
Evers, Arnold. 1975. *The Transformational Cycle in Dutch and German*. Ph.D. dissertation, Utrecht University.
Evert, Stefan & Marco Baroni. 2007. "ZipfR: Word frequency distributions in R". *Proceedings of the 45th Annual Meeting of the Association for Computational Linguistics: Posters and demonstrations session* ed. by Annie Zaenen & Antal van den Bosch, 904–911. East Stroudsburg, Penn.: ACL.
Fabb, Nigel. 1984. *Syntactic Affixation*. MIT Ph.D. dissertation, Cambridge, Mass.
Fabb, Nigel. 1998. "Compounding". *The Handbook of Morphology* ed. by Andrew Spencer & Arnold M. Zwicky, 66–83. Oxford: Blackwell.
Fanselow, Gisbert. 1985. "What is a Possible Complex Word?" *Studies in German Grammar* ed. by Toman Jindřich, 289–318. Dordrecht: Foris.
Feldman, Laurie, Patrick O'Connor & Fermín Moscoso del Prado Martín. 2009. "Early Morphological Processing is Morpho-semantic and not Simply Morpho-orthographic: An exception to form-then-meaning accounts of word recognition". *Psychonomic Bulletin and Review* 16:4.684–715.
Ferrari-Bridgers, Franca. 2005. "Italian [VN] Compound Nouns: A case for a syntactic approach to word formation". *Romance Languages and Linguistic Theory 2003* ed. by Twan Geerts, Ivo van Ginneken & Haike Jacobs, 63–80. Amsterdam & Philadelphia: John Benjamins.
Ferrari-Bridgers, Franca. 2005/a. *A Syntactic Analysis of the Nominal Systems of Italian and Luganda. How nouns can be formed in the syntax*. Ph.D. dissertation, New York University.
Fikkert, Paula. 2001. "Compounds Triggering Prosodic Development". *Approaches to Bootstrapping. Phonological, Lexical, Syntactic and Neurophysiological Aspects of Early Language Acquisition* ed. by Jürgen Weissenborn & Barbara Höhle, Vol. II, 59–86. Amsterdam: John Benjamins.
Finin, Timothy Wilking. 1980. *The Semantic Interpretation of Compound Nominals*. Ph.D. dissertation, University of Illinois, Urbana-Champaign.
Fleischer, Wolfgang. 1969. *Wortbildung der Deutschen Gegenwartssprache*. Leipzig: EB Bibliographisches Institut.
Fradin, Bernard. 2000. "Combining Forms, Blends and Related Phenomena". *Extragrammatical and Marginal Morphology* ed. by Anna M. Thornton & Ursula Doleschal, 11–59. München: Lincom Europa.
Fradin, Bernard. 2003. *Nouvelles approches en morphologie*. Paris: Presses Universitaires de France.
Fradin, Bernard. 2005. "On a Semantically Grounded Difference between Derivation and Compounding". Dressler, Kastovsky, Pfeiffer & Rainer, eds. 2005.161–182.

Fradin, Bernard. 2009. "IE: Romance, French". Lieber & Štekauer, eds. 2009.417–435.
Francis, W. Nelson & Henry Kučera. 1982. *Frequency Analysis of English Usage: Lexicon and grammar.* Boston: Houghton Mifflin.
Friberg, Karin. 2007. "Decomposing Swedish Compounds Using Memory-Based Learning". *Proceedings of the 16th Nordic Conference of Computational Linguistics NODALIDA-*2007 ed. by Joakim Nivre, Heiki-Jaan Kaalep, Kadri Muischnek and Mare Koit, 224–230. Tartu: University of Tartu.
Frost, Ram, Jonathan Grainger & Kathleen Rastle. 2005. "Current Issues in Morphological Processing: An introduction". *Language and Cognitive Processes* 20.1–5.
Fuhrhop, Nanna. 1996. "Fugenelemente". *Deutsch – typologisch* ed. by Ewald Lang & Gisela Zifonun, 525–550. Berlin/New York: Walter de Gruyter.
Fuhrhop, Nanna. 1998. *Grenzfälle morphologischer Einheiten.* Tübingen: Stauffenburg.
Fusellier-Souza, Ivani. 2006. "Emergence and Development of Signed Languages: From diachronic ontogenesis to diachronic phylogenesis". *Sign Language Studies* 7:1.30–56.
Gaeta, Livio. 2006. "Lexical Integrity as a Constructional Strategy". *Lingue e Linguaggio* 5.67–82.
Gaeta, Livio. 2008. "Constituent Order in Compounds and Syntax: Typology and Diachrony". *Morphology* 18.117–141.
Gaeta, Livio. "Synthetic Compounds: With special reference to German". This volume.
Gaeta, Livio & Davide Ricca. 2003. "Frequency and Productivity in Italian Derivation: A comparison between corpus-based and lexicographical data". *Italian Journal of Linguistics* 15:1. 63–98.
Gaeta, Livio & Davide Ricca. 2006. "Productivity in Italian Word Formation: A variable-corpus approach". *Linguistics* 44:1.57–89.
Gaeta, Livio & Davide Ricca. 2009. "*Composita solvantur*: Compounds as lexical units or morphological objects?". *Italian Journal of Linguistics* 21:1. 35–70.
Gagné, Christina L. 2001. "Relation and Lexical Priming During the Interpretation of Noun-Noun Combinations". *Journal of Experimental Psychology: Learning, memory, and cognition* 27.236–54.
Gagné, Christina L. 2002. "Lexical and Relational Influences on the Processing of Novel Compounds". *Brain and Language* 81.723–735.
Gagné, Christina L. 2009. "Psycholinguistic Perspectives". Lieber & Štekauer, eds. 2009.255–271.
Gagné, Christina L. & Gregory L. Murphy. 1996. "Influence of Discourse Context on Feature Availability in Conceptual Combination". *Discourse Processes* 22.79–101.
Gagné, Christina L., Shoben, Edward J. 1997. "Influence of Thematic Relations on the Comprehension of Modifier-Noun Compounds". *Journal of Experimental Psychology: Learning, memory and cognition* 23:1.71–87.
Gagné, Christina L. & Thomas L. Spalding. 2004. "Effect of Relation Availability on the Interpretation and Access of Familiar Noun-Noun Compounds". *Brain and Language* 90.478–486.
Gagné, Christina L. Thomas L. Spalding & Hongbo Ji. 2005. "Re-Examining Evidence for the Use of Independent Relational Representations During Conceptual Combination". *Journal of Memory and Language* 53.445–455.
Gagné, Christina L. & Thomas L. Spalding. 2006. "Relation Availability Was Not Confounded with Familiarity or Plausibility". *Journal of Experimental Psychology: Learning, memory, and cognition* 32.1431–1437; discussion 1438–1442.
Gagné, Christina L. Thomas L. Spalding, Lauren Figueredo & Allison Mullaly. 2009. " Does Snowman Prime Plastic Snow? The effect of position in accessing relational information during conceptual combination". *The Mental Lexicon* 4.41–76.

Gagné, Christina & Thomas Spalding. 2009. "Constituent Integration During the Processing of Compound Words: Does it involve the use of relational structures?" *Journal of Memory and Language* 60:1.20–35.

Gagné, Christina L. & Thomas L. Spalding. "Relational Competition during Compound Interpretation". This volume.

Garefalakis, Nikolaos. 2002. *Lexiko Idiomatismon Kritikis Dialectou (Perioxi Sitias)*. Sitia: Ekdoseis Dimou Sitias.

Gather, Andreas. 2001. *Romanische Verb-Nomen-Komposita: Wortbildung zwischen Lexikon, Morphologie und Syntax*. Tübingen: Gunter Narr.

Gay, Linda, William B. Croft. 1990. "Interpreting Nominal Compounds for Information Retrieval". *Information Processing and Management* 26:1.21–38.

Gentner, Timothy Q., Kimberley M. Fenn, Daniel Margoliash & Howard C. Nusbaum. 2006. "Recursive Syntactic Pattern Learning by Songbirds". *Nature* 440.1204–1207.

Gerdts, Donna B. 1998. "Incorporation". *TheHandbook of Morphology* ed. by Andrew Spencer & Arnold Zwicky, 84–104. Oxford: Blackwell.

Giraudo, Hélène & Jonathan Grainger. 2001. "Priming Complex Words: Evidence for supralexical representation of morphology". *Psychonomic Bulletin and Review* 8.127–131.

Goddard, Cliff. 2005. *The Languages of East and South-East Asia: An introduction*. Oxford: Oxford University Press.

Goldberg, Adele & Farrel Ackerman. 2001. "The Pragmatics of Obligatory Adjuncts". *Language* 77.798–814.

Good, Jeff. 2004. "Tone and Accent in Saramaccan: Charting a deep split in the phonology of a language". *Lingua* 114.575–619.

Gouesse, Marie-Josèphe. 2004. "Hongrois". Arnaud, ed. 2004.131–148.

Graczyk, Randolph. 2007. *A Grammar of Crow – Apsáalooke Aliláau*. Lincoln: University of Nebraska Press.

Grandi, Nicola & Anna Pompei. Forthcoming. "Per una tipologia dei composti del greco". *La morfologia del greco tra tipologia e diacronia* ed. by Ignazio Putzu, Giulio Paulis, Gianfranco Nieddu & Pierluigi Cuzzolin. Milano: Franco Angeli.

Greenberg, Joseph H. 1963. "Some Universals of Grammar with Particular Reference to the Order of Meaningful Elements". *Universals of Language* ed. by Joseph H. Greenberg, 73–113. Cambridge, Mass.: MIT Press.

Grimm, Jacob. 1826. *Deutsche Grammatik*. Göttingen: Günther.

Grossmann, Maria & Anna M. Thornton, eds. 2005 *La formazione delle parole. Atti del XXXVII congresso della Società di Linguistica Italiana*. Roma: Bulzoni.

Grossmann, Maria & Franz Rainer. 2009. "Italian Adjective-Adjective Compounds: Between morphology and syntax". *Italian Journal of Linguistics* 21:1. 71–96.

Guevara, Emiliano & Sergio Scalise. 2004. "V-Compounding in Dutch and Italian". *Cuadernos de Lingüística del Instituto Universitario Ortega y Gasset* 11.1–29.

Guevara, Emiliano & Sergio Scalise. 2008. "Searching for Universals in Compounding". Scalise, Magni, Bisetto, eds. 2008.101–128.

Haiman, John. 1983. "Iconic and Economic Motivation". *Language* 59.781–819.

Haiman, John. 1985. *Natural Syntax*. Cambridge: Cambridge University Press.

Halle, Morris, & Alec Marantz. 1993. "Distributed Morphology and the Pieces of Inflection". *The View from Building 20* ed. by Kenneth Hale & Samuel J. Keyser, 111–176. Cambridge, Mass.: MIT Press.

Harley, Heidi. 2009. "Compounding in Distributed Morphology". Lieber & Štekauer, eds. 2009.129–144.
Harley, Heidi & Rolf Noyer. 1999. "Distributed Morphology". *Glot International* 4:4.3–9.
Harrell, Frank. 2001. *Regression Modeling Strategies*. Berlin: Springer.
Harris, James. 1991. "The Exponence of Gender in Spanish". *Linguistic Inquiry* 22.27–62.
Haspelmath, Martin. 1993. *A Grammar of Lezgian*. Berlin & New York: Mouton de Gruyter.
Haspelmath, Martin. 2001. "The European Linguistic Area: Standard Average European". *Language Typology and Language Universals* ed. by Martin Haspelmath, Ekkehard König, Wulf Oesterreicher & Wolfang Raible, 1492–1510. Berlin/New York: Walter de Gruyter.
Haspelmath, Martin. 2002. *Understanding Morphology*. London: Arnold.
Haspelmath, Martin. 2004a. "Coordinating Constructions: An overview". *Coordinating Construction* ed. by Martin Haspelmath, 3–39. Amsterdam & Philadelphia: Jon Benjamins.
Haspelmath, Martin. 2004b. "Does Linguistic Explanation Presuppose Linguistic Description?" *Studies in Language* 28:3.554–579.
Haspelmath, Martin. 2007. "Coordination". *Language Typology and Syntactic Description. Volume II: Complex construction* ed. by Timothy Shopen, 1–51. Cambridge: Cambridge University Press.
Hathout, Nabil & Fabio Montermini, eds. 2007. *Morphologie à Toulouse. Actes du Colloque International de Morphologie 4e Décembrettes*. München: Lincom Europa.
Hatzidakis, George. 1905–1907. *Meseonika ke Nea Ellinika*. Athens: Sakellariou.
Hauser, Marc D., Noam Chomsky & William T. Fitch. 2002. "The Faculty of Language: What is it, who has it, and how did it evolve?" *Science* 298.1569–1579.
Hayes, Bruce. 1989 [1984]. The Prosodic Hierarchy in Meter. *Rhythm and Meter* ed. by Paul Kiparsky & Gilbert Youmans, 201–260. Orlando, Florida: Academic Press.
Henderson, John. 2002. The Word in Eastern/Central Arrernte. *Word* I ed. by R. M.W. W. Dixon & Alexandra Y. Aikenvald, 100–124. Cambridge: Cambridge University Press.
Hinds, John. 1986. *Japanese*. London: Croom Helm.
Hohenhaus, Peter. 2005. "Lexicalization and Institutionalization". Štekauer & Lieber, eds. 2005.353–373.
Hoijer, Harry. 1946. "Chiricahua Apache". *Linguistic Structures of Native America* ed. by Harry Hoijer, 55–84. New York: Viking Fund.
Holmer, Arthur J. 1996. *A Parametric Grammar of Seediq*. Lund: Lund University Press.
Holmes, Philip & Ian Hinchliffe. 1994. *Swedish: A comprehensive grammar*. London: Routledge.
Hualde, Jóse Ignacio. 2003. "Compounds". *A Grammar of Basque* ed. by Jóse Ignacio Hualde & Jon Ortiz de Urbina, 351–362. Berlin & New York: Mouton de Gruyter
Huang, James. 1984. "Phrase Structure, Lexical Integrity and Chinese Compounds". *Journal of the Chinese Language Teacher's Association* 2.53–78.
Huddleston, Rodney & Geoffrey Pullum. 2005. *The Cambridge Grammar of the English Language*. Cambridge: Cambridge University Press.
Hulst, Harry van der, ed. 1999. *Word Prosodic Systems in the Languages of Europe*. Berlin & New York: Mouton de Gruyter.
Hüning, Matthias. 1999. *Woordensmederij: De geschiedenis van het suffix -erij*. Ph.D. dissertation, Universiteit Leiden. Den Haag: Holland Academic Graphics.
Hüning, Matthias. 2000. "Monica en andere gates. Het ontstaan van een morfologisch procédé." *Nederlandse Taalkunde* 5.121–132.

Hyönä, Jukka, Raymond Bertram & Alexander Pollatsek. 2004. "Are Long Compound Words Identified Serially via their Constituents? Evidence from an eye-movement contingent display change study". *Memory & Cognition* 32.523–532.

Iacobini, Claudio. 2004a. "Parasintesi". *La formazione delle parole in italiano* ed. by Maria Grossmann & Franz Rainer, 165–188. Tübingen: Max Niemeyer.

Iacobini, Claudio. 2004b. "Composizione con elementi neoclassici". *La formazione delle parole in italiano* ed. by Maria Grossman & Franz Rainer, 69–96. Tübingen: Max Niemeyer.

Idomeneas, Marios. 2006. *Kritiko Glossari*. Athens: Academy of Athens.

Inkelas, Sharon & Cheryl Zoll. 2005. *Reduplication. Doubling in morphology*. Cambridge: Cambridge University Press.

Israel, Assaf. 2009. *Sublexical Variation in Three Sign Languages*. MA thesis. University of Haifa.

Itô, Junko & Armin Mester. 2006. "Weak Layering and Word Binarity". *A New Century of Phonology and Phonological Theory. A festschrift for professor Shosuke Haraguchi on the occasion of his sixtieth birthday* ed. by Takeru Honma, Masao Okazaki, Toshiyuki Tabata & Shinichi Tanaka. Tokyo: Kaitakusa. 26–65.

Jackendoff, Ray. 1997. *The Architecture of the Language Faculty*. Cambridge, Mass.: MIT Press.

Jackendoff, Ray. 2002. *Foundations of Language*. Oxford: Oxford University Press.

Jackendoff, Ray. 2009, "Compounding in the Parallel Architecture and Conceptual Semantics". Lieber & Štekauer, eds. 2009.105–128.

Jackendoff, Ray & Stephen Pinker. 2005. "The Nature of the Language Faculty and its Implications for the Evolution of Language". (Reply to Fitch, Hauser, and Chomsky). *Cognition* 97.211–225.

Jacobson, Steven. 1984. *Yup'ik Eskimo Dictionary*. Fairbanks: University of Alaska, Alaska Native Language Center.

Jacquemin, Christian. 2001. *Spotting and Discovering Terms through NLP*, Cambridge, Mass.: MIT Press.

Jaeger, Jeri J. 2005. *Kid's Slips: What young children's slips of the tongue reveal about language development*. Mahwah, N. J.: Lawrence Erlbaum.

Jespersen, Otto. 1924. *The Philosophy of Grammar*. New York: Barnes & Noble.

Jespersen, Otto. 1943. *A Modern English Grammar on Historical Principles*. Part VI, Morphology. London: George Allen & Unwin.

Ji, Hongbo & Christina L. Gagné. 2008. "Lexical and Relational Influences on the Processing of Chinese Modifier-Noun Compounds". *The Mental Lexicon* 2.387–417.

Johnston, Trevor, & Adam Schembri. 1999. "On Defining Lexeme in a Signed Language". *Sign Language & Linguistics* 2:2.115–85.

Joseph, Brian D. 2003. "Morphologization from Syntax". *Handbook of Historical Linguistics* ed. by Brian D. Joseph & Richard Janda, 472–492. Oxford: Blackwell.

Josefsson, Gunlög. 1998. *Minimal Words in a Minimal Syntax*. Amsterdam: John Benjamins.

Kabak, Barış & Irene Vogel. 2001. "The Phonological Word and Stress Assignment in Turkish". *Phonology* 18.315–360.

Kageyama, Taro. 1982. "Word Formation in Japanese". *Lingua* 57.215–258.

Kageyama, Taro. 2008. "Semantic Effects of Left-hand Elements on Right-hand Head Structure". *The 136th Linguistic Society of Japan Handbook. Linguistic Society of Japan.* 68–73.

Kageyama, Tarō. 2009. "Isolate: Japanese". Lieber & Štekauer, eds. 2009.512–526.

Kastovsky, Dieter. 2005. "Conversion and/or Zero". *Approaches to Conversion/Zero Derivation* ed. by Laurie Bauer & Salvador Valera, 31–50. Münster: Waxmann.

Katamba, Francis. 1993. *Morphology*, London: Macmillan.

Kay, Paul & Karl E. Zimmer. 1976. "On the Semantics of Compounds and Genitives in English". *Proceedings of the Sixth California Linguistics Association*. San Diego: San Diego State University. 29–35.

Kayne, Richard. 1994. *The Antisymmetry of Syntax*. Cambridge, Mass.: MIT Press

Kennedy, Graeme, ed. 2002. *A Concise Dictionary of New Zealand Sign Language*, Wellington New Zealand: Bridget Williams Books.

Keuleers, Emmanuel & Walter Daelemans. 2007. Memory-based Learning Models of Inflectional Morphology: A methodological case study. *Lingue e Linguaggio* 6.151–174.

Keuleers, Emmanuel, Dominiek Sandra, Walter Daelemans, Steven Gillis, G. Durieux, G. & E. Martens. 2007. "Dutch Plural Inflection: The exception that proves the analogy". *Cognitive Psychology* 54.283–318.

Kiefer, Ferenc. 2001 "Productivity and Compounding". *Naturally! Linguistic Studies in Honour of Wolfgang Ulrich Dressler* ed. by Chris Schaner-Wolles, John Rennison, & Friedrich Neubarth, 225–231.Torino: Rosenberg and Sellier.

Kilani-Schoch, M. & Wolfgang U. Dressler. 2002. "The Emergence of Inflectional Paradigms in Two French Corpora: An illustration of general problems of pre- and protomorphology". *Pre- and Protomorphology: Early phases of morphological development in nouns and verbs* ed. by Maria D.Voeikova & Wolfgang U. Dressler, 45–59. Münich: Lincom Europa.

Kilani-Schoch, Marianne & Wolfgang U. Dressler. 2005. *Morphologie naturelle et flexion du verbe français*. Tübingen: Gunter Narr.

Killingley, Siew-Yue & Dermot Killingley. 1995. *Sanskrit*. München & Newcastle: Lincom Europa.

Kimball, Geoffrey David. 1985. *A Descriptive Grammar of Koasati*. Ph.D. dissertation, Tulane University.

Kiparsky, Paul. 1982. "Lexical Morphology and Phonology". *Linguistics in the Morning Calm* ed. by The Linguistic Society of Korea, 3–91. Seoul: Hanshin.

Kisch, Shifra. 2004. "Negotiating deafness in a Bedouin community". *Genetics, Disability and Deafness* ed. by J. V. Van Cleve, 148–173. Washington, D.C.: Gallaudet University Press.

Kisch, Shifra. 2008. "Deaf Discourse: The social construction of deafness in a Bedouin community". *Medical Anthropology* 27: 3.283–313.

Klampfer, Sabine & Katharina Korecky-Kröll. 2002. "Nouns and Verbs at the Transition from Pre- to Protomorphology: A longitudinal case study on Austrian German". *Pre- and Protomorphology: Early phases of morphological development in nouns and verbs* ed. by Maria D. Voeikova & Wolfgang U. Dressler, 61–74. Münich: Lincom Europa.

Klima, Edward S. & Ursula Bellugi. 1979. *The Signs of Language*. Cambridge, Mass.: Harvard University Press.

Koehn, Philipp & Kevin Knight. 2003. "Empirical Methods for Compound Splitting". *Proceedings of the Ttenth Cconference on European Chapter of the Association for Computational Linguistics*, Budapest, 187–193 Budapest: Association for Computational Linguistics.

Komatsu, Lloyd K. 1992. "Recent Views of Conceptual Structure". *Psychological Bulletin* 112. 500–526.

Kornfeld, Laura Malena. 2009. "IE, Romance: Spanish". Lieber & Štekauer, eds. 2009.436–452.

Koskenniemi, Kimmo. 1983. *Two-level Morphology. A general computational model for word-form recognition and production*. Department of General Linguistics: University of Helsinki.

Koutita-Kaimaki, Mirto & Asimakis Fliatouras. 2001. "Blends in Greek Dialects. A morphosemantic analysis". *Proceedings of the First International Conference of Modern Greek Dialects and Linguistic Theory* ed. by Angela Ralli, Brian D. Joseph & Mark Janse, 117–130. Patras: University of Patras.

Köpcke, Klaus-Michael. 1993. *Schemata bei der Pluralbildung im Deutschen: Versuch einer kognitiven Morphologie*. Tübingen: Gunter Narr.
Krott, Andrea. 2001. *Analogy in Morphology: The selection of linking elements in Dutch compounds*. Nijmegen: Max Planck Institut für Psycholinguistik.
Krott, Andrea, Harald Baayen & Robert Schreuder. 2001. "Analogy in Morphology: Modeling the choice of linking morphemes in Dutch". *Linguistics* 39.51–93.
Krott, Andrea & Elena Nicoladis. 2005. "Large Constituent Families Help Children Parse Compounds". *Journal of Child Language* 32.139–158.
Krott, Andrea, Robert Schreuder, R. Harald Baayen & Wolfgang U. Dressler. 2007. "Analogical Effects on Linking Elements in German Compound Words". *Language and Cognitive Processes* 22.25–57.
Krott, Andrea, Christina L. Gagné & Elena Nicoladis. 2009. "How the Parts Relate to the Whole: Frequency effects on children's interpretations of novel compounds". *Journal of Child Language* 36.85–112.
Kruisinga, E. 1932. *A Handbook of Present-Day English*. V edition. Groningen: Noordhoff.
Ksanthinakis, Antonios. 1996. *To Glossiko Idioma tis Ditikis Kritis. Leksilogio me Ermineftika kai Etimologika Scholia*. Chania: Dimotiki Politistiki Epixeirisi Chanion.
Kubozono, Haruo. 2002. "Mora and Syllable". *The Handbook of Japanese Linguistics* ed. by Natsuko Tsujimura, 31–61. Oxford: Blackwell.
Kuperman, Victor, Raymond Bertram & Harald Baayen. 2008. "Morphological Dynamics in Compound Processing". *Language and Cognitive Processes* 23.1089–1132.
Kuperman, Victor, Robert Schreuder, Raymond Bertram & Harald Baayen. 2009a. "Processing Trade-Offs in the Reading of Dutch Derived Words". Manuscript, Stanford University.
Kuperman, Victor, Robert Schreuder, Raymond Bertram & Harald Baayen. 2009b. "Reading Polymorphemic Dutch Compounds: Towards a multiple route model of lexical processing". *Journal of Experimental Psychology: Human perception and performance* 35.876–895.
Kurisu, Kazutaka. 2000. "Richness of the Base and Root-Fusion in Sino-Japanese". *Journal of East Asian Linguistics* 9.147–185.
Laaha, Sabine, Dorit Ravid, Katharina Korecky-Kröll, Gregor Laaha & Wolfgang U. Dressler. 2006. "Early Noun Plurals in German: Regularity, productivity or default?" *Journal of Child Language* 33.271–302.
Laaha, Sabine & Steven Gillis, eds. 2007. *Typological perspectives on the acquisition of noun and verb morphology. Antwerp Papers in Linguistics 112*. Antwerp: Antwerp University.
Lakoff, George & Mark Johnson. 1980. *Metaphors We Live By*. Chicago: University of Chicago Press.
Lambrecht, Knud. 1984. "Formulaicity, Frame Semantics and Pragmatics in German Binomial Expressions". *Language* 60:4.753–796.
Lane, Harlane, Richard Pillard & Mary French. 2000. "Origins of the American Deaf-world: Assimilating and differentiating societies and their relation to genetic patterning". *Sign Language Studies* 1:1.17–44.
Langacker, Ronald. 1991. *Foundations of Cognitive Grammar. Vol. II: Descriptive Applications*. Stanford California: Stanford University Press.
Lapointe, Stephen. 1981. "A Lexical Analysis of the English Auxiliary System". *Lexical Grammar* ed. by Teun Hoekstra, Harry van der Hulst & Michael Moortgat, 215–254. Dordrecht: Foris.
Lapointe, Steven. 1980. *A Theory of Grammatical Agreement*. MIT Ph.D. dissertation, Cambridge, Mass.
Lauer, Mark. 1995. *Designing Statistical Language Learners: Experiments on noun compounds*. Ph.D. dissertation, Macquarie University.

Lees, Robert. 1960. *The Grammar of English Nominalizations*. Bloomington: Indiana University
Leonard, Rosemary. 1984. *The Interpretation of English Noun Sequences on the Computer*. Amsterdam: North Holland.
Lettner, Laura E. 2008. *Der Erwerb von Nominalkomposition und Diminutivbildung durch ein Wiener Kind. Eine longitudinale Fallstudie von 1;7 bis 4;3*. MA thesis, University of Vienna.
Leuschner, Torsten, & Nancy Decroos. 2008. "Wortbildung zwischen System und Norm. Affixoïden im Deutschen und im Niederländischen". *Sprachwissenschaft* 33.1–34.
Levelt, Willem J. M. 1989. *Speaking: From intention to articulation*. Cambridge, Mass.: MIT Press.
Levi, Judith. 1978. *The Syntax and Semantics of Complex Nominals*. New York: Academic Press.
Lewy, Ernst. 1911. *Zur finno-ugrischen Wort- und Satzverbindung*. Göttingen: Vandenhoeck.
Li, Charles N. 1971. *Semantics and the Structure of Compounds in Chinese*. Ph.D. dissertation, University of California, Berkley.
Li, Charles N. & Sandra A. Thompson. 1981. *Mandarin Chinese*. Berkeley: University of California Press.
Li, Yafei. 2005. *X° A Theory of the Morphology-Syntax Interface*. Cambridge, Mass.: MIT Press.
Libben, Gary. 2006. "Why Study Compound Processing?" *The Representation and Processing of Compound Words* ed. by Gary Libben & Gonia Jarema, VII-XI Oxford: Oxford University Press.
Libben, Gary, Gonia Jarema, Wolfgang U. Dressler, Jacqueline Stark & Christiane Pons. 2002. "Triangulating the Effects of Interfixation in the Processing of German compounds". *Folia Linguistica* 36.23–43.
Libben, Gary & Gonja Jarema, eds. 2006. *The Representation and Processing of Compound Words*. Oxford: Oxford University Press.
Libben, Gary, Monika Boniecki, Marlier Martha, Karin Mittermann, Katharina Korecky-Kröl & Wolfgang U. Dressler. 2009. "Interfixation in German compounds: What factors govern acceptability judgements?" *Italian Journal of Linguistics* 21.1. 149–180
Liberman, Mark & Richard Sproat 1992. "The Stress and Structure of Modified Noun Phrases in English". *Lexical Matters* ed. by Ivan Sag & Anna Szabolcsi, CSLI Lecture Notes 24,131–81. Chicago: University of Chicago Press.
Liddell, Scott K. & Robert E. Johnson. 1986. "American Sign Language Compound Formation Processes, Lexicalization and Phonological Remnants". *Natural Language and Linguistic Theory* 8.445–513.
Lieber, Rochelle. 1981. *On the Organization of the Lexicon*. Bloomington, Ind.: Indiana University Linguistics Club. [MIT Ph.D. dissertation, Cambridge, Mass., 1980].
Lieber, Rochelle. 1983. "Argument Linking and Compounding in English". *Linguistic Inquiry* 14.251–286.
Lieber, Rochelle. 1992. *Deconstructing Morphology: Word formation in syntactic theory*. Chicago: University of Chicago Press.
Lieber, Rochelle. 2003. "Compound Interpretation: Lexical semantics not syntax". *Topics in Morphology. Selected Papers from the Third Mediterranean Morphology Meeting* ed. by Geert Booij, Janet DeCesaris, Angela Ralli & Sergio Scalise, 241–254. Barcelona: Publications of Institut Universitari de Linguistica Aplicada, Universitat Pompeu Fabra.
Lieber, Rochelle. 2004. *Morphology and Lexical Semantics*. Cambridge: Cambridge University Press.
Lieber, Rochelle. 2006. "The Category of Roots and the Roots of Categories: What we learn from selection in derivation". *Morphology* 16.247–272.
Lieber, Rochelle. 2009a. "A Lexical Semantic Approach to Compounding". Lieber & Štekauer, eds. 2009.78–104
Lieber, Rochelle. 2009b. "IE, Germanic: English". Lieber & Štekauer, eds. 2009.357–369.

Lieber, Rochelle. Forthcoming. "Towards an OT Morphosemantics: The case of *-hood, -dom,* and *-ship*". To appear in *Linguistische Berichte*.
Lieber, Rochelle."On the Lexical Semantics of Compounds". This volume.
Lieber, Rochelle & Sergio Scalise. 2006. "The Lexical Integrity Hypothesis in a New Theoretical Universe". *Lingue e Linguaggio* 1.7–32
Lieber Rochelle & Pavol Štekauer eds. 2009. *The Oxford Handbook of Compounding*. Oxford: Oxford University Press.
Lieber, Rochelle & Pavol Štekauer. 2009. "Introduction: Status and definition of compounding". Lieber & Štekauer, eds. 2009.3–18.
Lo Duca, Maria Giuseppa. 1990. *Creatività e regole: Studio sull'acquisizione della morfologia derivativa dell'italiano*. Bologna: Il Mulino.
Lombardi Vallauri, Edoardo. 2005. "When Are Phrases 'Compounds'? The case of Japanese". *La formazione delle parole*. Grossmann & Thornton, eds. 2005.309–334.
Lyons, John. 1977. *Semantics*. Cambridge: Cambridge University Press.
MacWhinney, Brian 1978. *The acquisition of Morphophonology*. Chicago: Chicago University Press.
MacWhinney, Brian 2000. *The CHILDES Project: Tools for analyzing talk. Vol. 1: Transcription format and programs*. Mahwah, N. J.: Lawrence Erlbaum.
MacWhinney, Brian. 2004. "A Unified Model of Language Acquisition". *Handbook of Bilingualism: Psycholinguistic approaches* ed. by Judith F. Kroll & Annette M. B. De Groot, 49–67. Oxford: Oxford University Press.
Maguire, Phil, Barry Devereux, Fintan Costello & Arthur Cater. 2007. "A Reanalysis of the CARIN Theory of Conceptual Combination". *Journal of Experimental Psychology: Learning, memory and cognition* 33. 811–821.
Maiden, Martin & Cecilia Robustelli. 2000. *A Reference Grammar of Modern Italian*. London: Arnold.
Maina, S.J. 1987. "Principles Adopted for the Enrichment of Kiswahili Language". *New Language Planning Newsletter* 2:2.1–3
Maling, Joan. 2001. "Dative: The Heterogeneity of the Mapping among Morphological Case, Grammatical Functions, and Thematic Roles". *Lingua* 111.419–464.
Malkiel, Yakov. 1978. Derivational Categories. *Universals of Human Language. Volume III: Word structure* ed. by Joseph H. Greenberg, 125–149. Stanford California: Stanford University Press.
Marchand, Hans. 1960. *The Categories and Types of Present-day English Word-formation. A synchronic-diachronic approach*. Wiesbaden: Otto Harrassowitz. (Second edition 1969, Münich, Beck).
Marchand, Hans. 1967. "Expansion, Transposition and Derivation". *La Linguistique* 1.3–26.
Marcus, Mitchell. 1980. *A Theory of Syntactic Recognition for Natural Language*. Cambridge, Mass.: MIT Press.
Martinet, André. 1979. *Grammaire Fonctionelle du Français*. Paris: Didier.
Masini, Francesca. 2006. "Binomial Constructions: Inheritance, specification and subregularities". *Lingue e Linguaggio* 5.207–232.
Matthews, Peter H. 1974. *Morphology* Cambridge: Cambridge University Press.
McCawley, James D. 1974. "Prelexical Syntax". *Semantic Syntax* ed. by Pieter A. M. Seuren. 29–43. London: Oxford University.
McClelland James L. & Karalyn Patterson. 2002. "Rules and Connections in Past Tense Inflections: What does the evidence rule out". *Trends in Cognitive Science* 6.465–472.
McDonald, David B. 1982. *Understanding Noun Compounds*. Ph.D. dissertation, Carnegie-Mellon University, Pittsburgh, PA.
McIntyre, Joseph. 2006. *Hausa Verbal Compounds*. Ph.D. dissertation, University of Leiden.

McWhorter, John. 1998. "Identifying the Creole Prototype: Vindicating a typological class". *Language* 74.788–818.
Meier, Richard, Kearsey Cormier & David Quinto-Pozos, eds. 2002. *Modality and Structure in Signed and Spoken Languages*. Cambridge: Cambridge University Press.
Meir, Irit, Carol Padden, Mark Aronoff & Wendy Sandler. 2007. "Body as Subject". *Journal of Linguistics* 43.531–563.
Meir, Irit & Wendy Sandler. 2008. *A Language in Space: The story of Israeli sign language*. New York: Lawrence Erlbaum Associates.
Meir, Irit, Wendy Sandler, Carol Padden & Mark Aronoff. In press. "Emerging Sign Languages". Oxford Handbook of Deaf Studies ed. by Marc Marschark & Patricia Spencer, (Language and Education 2). Oxford: Oxford University Press.
Melissaropoulou, Dimitra & Angela Ralli. 2008. "Headedness in Diminutive Formation: Evidence from modern Greek and its dialectal variation". *Acta Linguistica Hungarica* 55.183–204.
Mellenius, Ingmarie. 1996. "Children's Comprehension of Swedish Nominal Compounds". *Children's Language* ed. by Carolyn E. Johnson & John H.V. Gilbert, 167–182. Mahwah, N.J.: Lawrence Erlbaum.
Mellenius, Ingmarie. 1997. *The Acquisition of Nominal Compounding in Swedish*. Lund: Lund University Press.
Mellenius, Ingmarie 2004. "Word formation." *The Acquisition of Swedish Grammar* ed. by Günlög Josefsson, Christa Platzak & Gisela Håkansson, 75–93. Amsterdam: Benjamins.
Melloni, Chiara & Antonietta Bisetto. "Parasynthetic compounds: Data and Theory". This volume.
Meyer, Ralf. 1993. *Compound Comprehension in Isolation and in Context: The contribution of conceptual and discourse knowledge to the comprehension of German novel noun-noun compounds*. Tübingen: Max Niemeyer.
Mithun, Marianne. 1997. "Lexical Affixes and Morphological Typology". *Essays on Language Function and Language Type* ed. by John Haiman, Joan Bybee, & Sandra Thompson, 357–372. Amsterdam & Philadelphia: John Benjamins.
Mithun, Marianne. 1998a. "The Sequencing of Grammaticization Effects". *Historical Linguistics 1997* ed. by Monica Schmidt, Jennifer Austin, & Dieter Stein 291–314. Amsterdam & Philadelphia: John Benjamins.
Mithun, Marianne. 1998b. "Yup'ik Roots and Affixes". *Languages of the North Pacific Rim* 4 ed. by Osahito Miyaoka & Minoru Oshima 63–76. Kyoto, Japan: Kyoto University Graduate School of Letters.
Mithun, Marianne. 1999. *The Languages of Native North America*. Cambridge: Cambridge University Press.
Mithun, Marianne. 2009b. Mohawk. *The Oxford Handbook of Compounding*. Lieber & Štekauer, eds. 2009.564–588.
Mithun, Marianne. "Constraints on Compounds and Incorporation". This volume.
Mohanan, Karuvannur Puthanveettil. 1986. *The Theory of Lexical Phonology*. Dordrecht: Reidel.
Molinsky, Steven. 1973. *Patterns of Ellipsis in Russian Compound Noun Formation*. Mouton: The Hague.
Mondini, Sara, Gonia Jarema, Claudio Luzzatti, Cristina Burani & Carlo Semenza. 2002. "Why is 'Red Cross' Different from 'Yellow cross'? A neuropsychological study of noun-adjective agreement with Italian compounds". *Brain and Language* 81.621–634.
Montermini, Fabio. 2006. "A New Look on Word-Internal Anaphora on the Basis of Italian Data". *Lingue e linguaggio* 5.127–148.

Montermini, Fabio. 2008a. "La composition en italien dans un cadre de morphologie lexématique". Amiot, ed. 2008.161–187.
Montermini, Fabio. 2008b. *Il lato sinistro della morfologia. La prefissazione in italiano e nelle lingue del mondo.* Milano: FrancoAngeli.
Montermini, Fabio. "Units in compounding". This volume.
Mühlhäusler, Peter. 1979. *Growth and Structure of the Lexicon of New Guinea Pidgin.* Canberra: Australian National University.
Mühlhäusler, Peter. 2004. "Tok Pisin". Arnaud, ed. 2004.249–267.
Namer, Fiammetta. 2007. "Composition néoclassique: Est-on dans l'"hétéromorphosémie'?" Hathout & Montermini 2007. 187–206.
Naumann, Bernd & Petra M. Vogel. 2000. "Derivation". *Morphology 2000*.929–942.
Neeleman, Ad & Hans van de Koot. 2006. "On Syntactic and Phonological Representations". *Lingua* 116.1524–1552.
Neijt, Anneke & Robert Schreuder. 2007. "Rhythm versus Analogy – Prosodic Form Variation in Dutch Compounds". *Language and Speech* 50.533–566.
Neijt, Anneke, Loes Krebbers and Paula Fikkert. 2002. "Rythm and Semantics in the Selection of Linking Elements". *Linguistics in the Netherlands 2002* ed. by Hans Broekhuis and Paula Fikkert, 117–127. Amsterdam: John Benjamins.
Nespor Marina. 1999. "Stress Domains". van der Hulst. 1999.117–159.
Nespor, Marina & Irene Vogel. 1986. *Prosodic Phonology.* Dordrecht: Foris.
Nespor, Marina & Angela Ralli. 1996. "Morphology-Phonology Interface: Phonological domains in Greek compounds". *The Linguistic Review* 13.357–382.
Newton, Brian. 1972. *The Generative Interpretation of a Dialect. A study of modern Greek phonology.* Cambridge: Cambridge University Press.
Nguyễn, Đình Hoà. 1965 "Parallel Constructions in Vietnamese". *Lingua* 15.125–139.
Nicoladis, Elena. 2002. "What's the Difference Between 'toilet paper' and 'paper toilet'? French-English bilingual children's crosslinguistic transfer in compound nouns". *Journal of Child Language* 29.843–863.
Nicoladis, Elena. 2006. "Preschool Children's Acquisition of Compounds". *The Representation and Processing of Compound Words* ed. by Gonia Jarema & Gary Libben, 96–124. Oxford: Oxford University Press.
Nicoladis, Elena. 2007. "Acquisition of Deverbal Compounds by French-speaking Preschoolers". *The Mental Lexicon* 2.1.79–102.
Noonan, Michael. 2003. "Chantyal". *The Sino-Tibetan Languages* ed. by Graham Thurgood & Randy J. LaPolla, 315–335. London & New York: Routledge.
Noyer, Rolf. 1993. "Optimal Words: Towards a declarative theory of word formation", Manuscript, Princeton University.
Ó Séaghdha, Diarmuid. 2008. *Learning Compound Noun Semantics.* Ph.D. dissertation, University of Cambridge.
Olowsky, Knut. 2002. "What is a Word in Dagbani?" *Word* ed. by R. M.W. Dixon & AlexandraY. Aikenvald, 205–226. Cambridge: Cambridge University Press.
Olsen, Susan. 2000. "Copulative Compounds. A closer look at the interface between morphology and syntax". *Yearbook of Morphology* 2000.279–320.
Ortner, Lorelies & Elgin Müller-Bollhagen eds. 1991. *Deutsche Wortbildung: Substantivkomposita.* Berlin & New York: Mouton de Gruyter.
Oshita, Hiroyuki. 1995. "Compounds: A view from suffixation and A-structure alteration". *Yearbook of Morphology* 1995.179–205.

Ourn, Noeurng & John Haiman. 2000. "Symmetrical Compounds in Khmer". *Studies in Language* 24.483–514.
Pačesová, Jaroslava. 1968. *The Development of Vocabulary in the Child*. Brno: Universita Purkyně.
Packard, Jerome. 2000. *The Morphology of Chinese. A linguistic and cognitive approach*. Cambridge: Cambridge University Press.
Padrosa Trias, Susanna. 2007. Catalan Verbal Compounds and the Syntax-Morphology Competition. *Proceedings of Incontro di Grammatica Generativa* ed. by Antonietta Bisetto & Francesco E. Barbieri, 63–85. http://amsacta.cib.unibo.it/2397/1/PROCEEDINGS_IGG33.pdf.
Pandharipande, Rajeshwari V. 1997. *Marathi*. London: Routledge.
Park, Seong-Bae, Jeong-Ho Chang & Byoung-Tak Zang. 2004. "Korean Compound Noun Decomposition Using Syllabic Information Only". *Computational Linguistics and Intelligent Text Processing* ed. by Alexander Gelbukh, 146–157. Berlin/Heidelberg: Springer.
Paul, Hermann. 1920. *Deutsche Grammatik*. Vol. V: *Wortbildungslehre*. Halle/Saale: Max Niemeyer.
Perry, Robert. 2007. "Persian Morphology". *Morphologies of Asia and Africa* ed. by Alan S. Kaye. Winona Lake: Eisenbrauns.
Peters, Ann M. 1997. "Language Typology, Prosody, and the Acquisition of Grammatical Morphemes". *The Crosslinguistic Study of Language Acquisition* ed. by Dan I. Slobin, vol.V, 136–197. Mahwah: Erlbaum.
Pinker, Steven. 1984. *Language Learnability and Language Development*. Cambridge: Harvard University Press.
Pinker, Steven & Michael Ullman. 2002. "The Past and Future of the Past Tense". *Trends in Cognitive Science*, 6.456–463.
Pinker, Steven & Ray Jackendoff. 2005. "The Nature of the Language Faculty and its Implications for the Evolution of Language". *Cognition* 97.211–225.
Pirrelli, Vito. 2002. "Per un superamento della dicotomia lessico-grammatica. Aspetti di composizionalità 'debole' nel linguaggio", *La lessicografia bilingue tra presente e avvenire* ed. by Elena Ferrario & Virginia Pulcini, 187–203.Vercelli: Edizioni Mercurio.
Pirrelli, Vito & Emiliano Guevara. Forthcoming. "Understanding NN Compounds" *Atti Società di Linguistica Italiana 2008*, Pisa.
Plag, Ingo. 1999. *Morphological Productivity. Structural constraints in English derivation*. Berlin & New York: Mouton de Gruyter.
Plag, Ingo. 2003. *Word-Formation in English*. Cambridge: Cambridge University Press.
Plag, Ingo. 2006a. "Morphology in Pidgins and Creoles". *The Encyclopedia of Language and Linguistics* ed. by Keith Brown, 305–308. Oxford: Elsevier.
Plag, Ingo. 2006b. "The Variability of Compound Stress in English: Structural, semantic, and analogical factors". *English Language and Linguistics* 10.143–172.
Plag, Ingo, Gero Kunter, Sabine Lappe & Maria Braun. 2008. "The Role of Semantics, Argument Structure, and Lexicalization in Compound Stress Assignment in English". *Language* 84.760–94.
Pollatsek, Alexander & Keith Rayner. 1982. "Eye Movement Control in Reading: The role of word boundaries". *Journal of Experimental Psychology: Human Perception and Performance* 8. 817–33.
Pollatsek, Alexander, Jukka Hyönä & Raymond Bertram. 2000. "The Role of Morphological Constituents in Reading Finnish Compound Words". *Journal of Experimental Psychology: Human, Perception and Performance* 26.820–833.

Pollock, Jean-Yves. 1989. "Verb Movement, Universal Grammar and the Structure of IP". *Linguistic Inquiry* 20.365–424.
Primus, Beatrice. 1999. *Case and Thematic Roles*. Tübingen: Max Niemeyer.
Probal, Dasgusta, Alan Ford & Rajendra Singh. 2000. *After Etymology: Towards a substantivist linguistics*. München: Lincom Europa.
Pustejovsky, James, Sabine Bergler & Peter Anick. 1993. "Lexical Semantic Techniques for Corpus Analysis". *Computational Linguistics* 19:2.331–358.
Quirk, Randolph, Sidney Greenbaum, Geoffrey Leech & Jan Svartvik. 1985. *A Comprehensive Grammar of the English Language*. London & New York: Longman.
Rabel, Lili. 1961. *Khasi, a Language of Assam*. Baton Rouge: Louisiana State University.
Raffray, Claudine N. Martin J. Pickering & Holly P. Branigan. 2007. "Priming the Interpretation of Noun-Noun Combinations". *Journal of Memory and Language* 57.380–395.
Rainer, Franz. 1988. "Towards a Theory of Blocking: The case of Italian and German quality nouns". *Yearbook of Morphology* 1988.155–185.
Rainer, Franz. 1993. *Spanische Wortbildungslehre*. Tübingen: Max Niemeyer.
Rainer, Franz. 2005. "Constraints on Productivity". Štekauer & Lieber, eds. 2005.335–352.
Rainer, Franz. 2008. *Carmens Erwerb der deutschen Wortbildung*. Manuscript, submitted to Verlag der Österreichischen Akademie der Wissenschaften.
Ralli, Angela. 1988. *Eléments de la morphologie du grec moderne: La structure du verbe*. Ph.D. Dissertation, Université de Montréal.
Ralli, Angela. 1992. "Compounds in Modern Greek". *Rivista di Linguistica* 4.143–174.
Ralli, Angela. 2004. "Stem-based vs. Word-based Morphological Configurations: The case of modern Greek preverbs". *Lingue e Linguaggio* 2.241–275.
Ralli, Angela. 2007a. *I sinthesi lekseon: mia diaglosiki morfologiki prosengisi*. Athens: Patakis.
Ralli, Angela. 2007b. "Compound Marking in a Cross-Linguistic Approach". *Morphologie à Toulouse. Actes du Colloque International de Morphologie 4e Décembrettes* ed. by Nabil Hathout & Fabio Montermini, 207–220. München: Lincom Europa.
Ralli, Angela. 2008a. "Composés déverbaux grecs à 'radicaux liés'". Amiot, ed. 2008,189–210.
Ralli, Angela. 2008b. "Compound Markers and Parametric Variation". *Language Typology and Universals (STUF)* 61: 19–38.
Ralli, Angela. 2009a. "I.E. Hellenic: Modern Greek". Lieber & Štekauer, eds. 2009.453–463.
Ralli, Angela. "Compounding versus Derivation". This volume.
Ralli, Angela. In preparation. *Greek Compounds*. Berlin: Springer.
Ralli, Angela. 2009b. "Morphology meets Dialectology: Insights from modern Greek dialects". *Morphology* 19: 87–105. (2009, Special issue *Morphology meets Dialectology*).
Ralli, Angela. 2009c. "Greek [V V] Dvandva Compounds: A linguistic innovation in the history of Indo-European languages". *Word Structure* 2.48–68.
Ralli, Angela & Athanasios Karasimos. 2009. "The Role of Constraints in Compound Formation: The case of bare-stem constraint". *Lingue e Linguaggio* 8.53–74
Ralli, Angela & Eleonora Dimela. To appear. "On the Borderline between Prefixation and Compounding: The *sa-adverbs* in the dialectal varieties of Lesbos, Kydonies (Aivali) and Moschonisia". *Proceedings of the III International Conference of Modern Greek Dialects and Linguistic Theory* ed. by Mark Janse, Brian D. Joseph, Pavlos Pavlou & Angela Ralli. Nicosia: Kykkos publications.
Ramat, Paolo. 2001. "Degrammaticalization or Transcategorization?" In *Naturally! Linguistic Studies in Honour of Wolfgang Ulrich Dressler Presented on the Occasion of his 60th Birthday*

ed. by Chris Schaner-Wolles, John Rennison & Friedrich Neubarth, 393–401. Torino: Rosenberg & Sellier.

Ratnaparkhi, Adwait. 1998. *Maximum Entropy Models for Natural Language Ambiguity Resolution*. Ph.D. dissertation, University of Pennsylvania

Ravid, Dorit, Wolfgang U. Dressler, Bracha Nir-Sagiv, Katharina Korecky-Kröll, Agnita Souman, Katja Rehfeldt, Sabine Laaha, Johannes Bertl, Hans Basbøll, Hans & Steven Gillis. 2008. "Core Morphology in Child Directed Speech: Crosslinguistic corpus analyses of noun plurals". *Corpora in language acquisition research: finding structure in data* ed. by Heike Behrens, 25–60. Amsterdam: John Benjamins.

Resnik, Philip. 1993. *Selection and Information: A class-based approach to lexical relationships*. Ph.D. dissertation, University of Pennsylvania, Philadelphia, PA.

Ricca, Davide. 2005. "Al limite tra sintassi e morfologia: i composti aggettivali V-N nell'italiano contemporaneo". Grossmann & Thornton, eds. 2005.465–486.

Ricca, Davide. "Corpus Data and Theoretical implications: With Special Reference to Italian V-N Compounds". This volume.

Rice, Keren. 2009. "Athapaskan: Slave". Lieber & Štekauer, eds. 2009.542–563.

Rivet, Anne. 1999. "Rektionskomposita und Inkorporationstheorie". *Linguistische Berichte* 179. 307–342.

Rizzi, Luigi. 1997. "The Fine Structure of the Left Periphery". *Elements of Grammar* ed. by Liliane Haegeman, 281–337. Dordrecht: Kluwer.

Roeper, Thomas. 1999. "Leftward Movement in Morphology". *MIT Working Papers in Linguistics* 34.35–66.

Roeper, Thomas & Muffy Siegel. 1978. "A Lexical Transformation for Verbal Compounds". *Linguistic Inquiry* 9.199–260.

Rogers, Timothy T. & McClelland James L. 2004. *Semantic Cognition: A parallel distributed approach*. Cambridge, Mass.: MIT Press.

Rosen, Sara Thomas. 1989. "Two Types of Noun Incorporation: A lexical analysis". *Language* 65.294–317.

Rumelhart David E., McClelland James L. & the PDP Research Group. 1987. *Parallel Distributed Processing. Foundations*. Cambridge, Mass.: MIT Press.

Rushdie, Salman. 1981 / 1995. *Midnight's Children*. London: Vintage.

Ryder, Mary Ellen. 1994. *Ordered Chaos: The interpretation of English noun-noun compounds*. Berkeley: University of California Press.

Sabatini, Francesco & Vincenzo Coletti. 1997. *DISC – Dizionario Italiano Sabatini Coletti. Edizione in CD-Rom*. Florence: Giusti.

Sadock, Jerrold. 1991. *Autolexical Syntax*. Chicago: University of Chicago Press.

Sahlgren, Magnus. 2006. *The Word Space Model*. Ph.D. dissertation, Stockholm University.

Sandler, Wendy. 1989. *Phonological Representation of the Sign: Linearity and nonlinearity in American sign language*. Dordrecht: Foris.

Sandler, Wendy. 1993a. "A Sonority Cycle in American Sign Language". *Phonology* 10.243–279.

Sandler, Wendy. 1993b. "Linearization of Phonological Tiers in American Sign Language". *Phonetics and phonology. Vol. III: Current issues in ASL phonology* ed. by G. Coulter, 103–129. San Diego, Calif.: Academic Press.

Sandler, Wendy, Irit Meir, Carol Padden, & Mark Aronoff. 2005. "The Emergence of Grammar: Systematic structure in a new language". *Proceedings of the National Academy of Sciences* 102: 7.2661–2665

Sandler, Wendy & Diane Lillo-Martin. 2006. *Sign Language and Linguistic Universals*. Cambridge: Cambridge University Press.
Sandler, Wendy, Mark Aronoff, Irit Meir & Carol Padden. In press. "The Gradual Emergence of Phonological Form in a New Language". *Natural Language and Linguistic Theory*.
Sandra, Dominiek. 1994. "The Morphology of the Mental Lexicon: Internal word structure viewed from a psycholinguistic perspective". *Language and Cognitive Processes* 9.227–269.
Sapir, Edward. 1921. *Language: An Introduction to the study of speech*. New York: Harcourt, Brace.
Saunders, Ross & Philip W. Davis. 1975. "Bella Coola Lexical Suffixes." *Anthropological Linguistics* 17.154–189.
Savickienė, Ineta & Wolfgang U. Dressler, eds. 2007. *The Acquisition of Diminutives. A crosslinguistic perspective*. Amsterdam: John Benjamins.
Scalise, Sergio. 1984. *Generative Morphology*. Dordrecht: Foris.
Scalise, Sergio. 1992. "Compounding in Italian". *Rivista di Linguistica* 4.175–199.
Scalise, Sergio. 1994. *Morfologia*. Bologna: Il Mulino.
Scalise, Sergio, Antonietta Bisetto & Emiliano Guevara. 2005. "Selection in Compounding and Derivation". Dressler, Kastovsky, Pfeiffer & Rainer, eds. 2005.133–150.
Scalise, Sergio & Emiliano Guevara. 2006. "Exocentric Compounding in a Typological Framework". *Lingue e linguaggio* 2.185–206.
Scalise, Sergio, Elisabetta Magni & Antonietta Bisetto, eds. 2008. *Universals of Language Today*. Berlin: Springer.
Scalise, Sergio & Antonietta Bisetto. 2009. "The Classification of Compounds". Lieber & Štekauer, eds. 2009.49–82.
Scalise, Sergio, Antonio Fábregas & Francesca Forza. 2009. "Exocentricity in Compounding". *Gengo Kenkyu. Journal of the Linguistic Society of Japan* 135.49–83.
Scalise, Sergio & Antonio Fábregas. "Head in Compounding". This volume.
Schaub, Willi. 1985. *Babungo*. London: Croom Helm.
Schlücker Barbara & Matthias Hüning. 2009. "Compounds and Phrases: A functional comparison between German A+N compounds and corresponding phrases". *Italian Journal of Linguistics* 21:1. 209-234.
Schmidt, Günter Dieterich. 1987. "Das Affixoid: Zur Notwendigkeit und Brauchbarkeit eines beliebten Zwischenbegriffs der Wortbildung". *Deutsche Lehnwortbildung* ed. by Hoppe Gabriele, 53–101. Tübingen: Gunter Narr.
Schreuder, Rob & Harald R. Harald. 1997. "How Complex Simplex Words can be". *Journal of Memory and Language* 37.118–139.
Seidenberg, M. S., M. C. MacDonald. 1999. "A Probabilistic Constraints Approach to Language Acquisition and Processing". *Cognitive Science* 23:4.569–588.
Selkirk, Elisabeth. 1982. *The Syntax of Words*. Cambridge, Mass.: MIT Press.
Serrano Dolader, David. 1995. *Las formaciones parasintéticas en español*. Madrid: Arco Libros.
Shoben, Edward. 1991. "Predicating and Nonpredicating Combinations". *The Psychology of Word Meanings* ed. by Paula J. Schwanenflugal, 117–135. Hillsdale, NJ: Erlbaum.
Siebert, Susann. 1999. *Wortbildung und Grammatik. Syntaktische Restriktionen in der Struktur komplexer Wörter*. Tübingen: Max Niemeyer.
Simon, Horst & Heike Wiese, eds. 2009. *Expecting the Unexpected: Exceptions in grammar*. Trends Linguistics: Studies and Monographs Series. Amsterdam: Mouton de Gruyter.
Slobin, Dan I. 1985. "Crosslinguistic Evidence for the Language-making Capacity". *The Crosslinguistic Study of Language Acquisition* ed. by Dan I. Slobin, vol. II, 1157–1256. Hillsdale: Erlbaum.

Smadja, Frank. 1993. "Retrieving Collocations from Text: Xtract". *Computational Linguistics* 19:1.143–177.
Snyder, William. 1995. *Language Acquisition and Language Variation: The role of morphology*. MIT Ph.D. dissertation, Cambridge, Mass.
Søgaard, Anders. 2004. "Compounding Theories and Linguistic Diversity". *Linguistic Diversity and Linguistic Theories* ed. by Zygmunt Frajzyngier, Adam Hodges & David S. Rood, 319–337. Amsterdam & Philadelphia: John Benjamins.
Sohn, Ho-min. 1994. *Korean*. London & New York: Routledge.
Sohn, Ho-min. 1999. *The Korean Language*. Cambrige: Cambridge University Press.
Spalding, Thomas L. & Christina L. Gagné. 2007. "Semantic Property Activation During the Interpretation of Combined Concepts". *The Mental Lexicon* 2.25–47.
Spalding, Thomas L. & Christina L. Gagné. 2008. "CARIN Theory Reanalysis Reanalyzed: A comment on Maguire, Devereux, Costello, & Cater (2007)". *Journal of Experimental Psychology: Learning, memory, and cognition* 34.1573–1578.
Spencer, Andrew. 1991. *Morphological Theory: An introduction to word structure in generative grammar*. Oxford: Blackwell.
Springer, Ken & Gregory L. Murphy. 1992. "Feature Availability in Conceptual Combination". *Psychological Science* 3.111–117.
Sproat, Richard. 1985. *On Deriving the Lexicon*. MIT Ph.D. dissertation, Cambridge, Mass.
Sproat, Richard. 1986. "The Projection Principle and the Syntax of Synthetic Compounds". *Proceedings of the 16th Annual meeting of the North East Linguistics Society*, 462–475.
Sproat, Richard. 1988. "Bracketing Paradoxes, Cliticization and Other Topics: The mapping between syntactic and phonological structure". *Morphology and Modularity* ed. by Martin Everaert, Arnold Evers, Riny Huybregts & Mieke Trommelen, 339–360. Dordrecht: Foris.
Sproat, Richard. 1994. "English Noun-Phrase Accent Prediction for Text-to-Speech". *Computer Speech and Language* 8.79–94.
Štekauer, Pavol. 2005a. *Meaning Predictability in Word Formation: Novel, context-free naming units*. Amsterdam & Philadelphia: John Benjamins.
Štekauer, Pavol. 2005b. "Compounding and Affixation. Any difference?" Dressler, Kastovsky, Pfeiffer & Rainer, eds. 2005.151–159.
Štekauer, Pavol. 2006. "On the Meaning Predictability of Novel Context-Free Converted Naming Units". *Linguistics* 44.489–539.
Štekauer, Pavol. 2009. "Meaning Predictability of Novel Context-Free Compounds". Lieber & Štekauer, eds. 2009.272–298.
Štekauer, Pavol & Rochelle Lieber, eds. 2006. *Handbook of Word-Formation*. (= *Studies in Natural Language and Linguistic Theory*, vol. 64. Berlin: Springer.
Štekauer, Pavol, Salvador Valera & Lívia Körtvélyessy. 2008. "Universals, Tendencies and Typology in Word-Formation. A cross-linguistic study". Manuscript, Josef Šafárik University.
Stephany, Ursula. 1980. "Zur psychischen Realität der Dimension der Deskriptivität". *Wege zur Universalienforschung. Sprachwissenschaftliche Beiträge zum 60. Geburtstag von Hansjakob Seiler* ed. by Gunter Brettschneider & Christian Lehmann, 549–555. Tübingen: Gunter Narr.
Stephany, Ursula. 1997. "The Acquisition of Greek". *The Crosslinguistic Study of Language Acquisition* ed. by Dan I. Slobin, vol. IV, 183–333. Mahwah: Erlbaum.
Stephenson, Edward. 1969. "*Frying Pan* versus *Frypan*: A trend in English compounds?" *American Speech* 44.299–302.
Storms, Gert & Edward J. Wisniewski. 2005. "Does the Order of Head Noun and Modifier Explain Response Times in Conceptual Combination?" *Memory & Cognition* 33.852–61.

Streith, Margarete. 1997. *Fugenbildungen im Erstspracherwerb*. MA thesis, University of Vienna.
Stump, Gregory T. 2001. *Inflectional Morphology. A theory of paradigm structure*. Cambridge: Cambridge University Press.
Sugisaki, Koji & Miwa Isobe. 2000. "Resultatives Result from the Compounding Parameter: On the Acquisitional Correlation between Resultatives and N-N Compounds in Japanese". *Proceedings of the 19th West Coast Conference on Formal Linguistics* ed. by Roger Billerey and Brook D. Lillehaugen, 493–506. Somerville: Cascadilla Press.
Sulkala, Helena & Merja Karjalainen. 1992. *Finnish*. London & New York: Routledge.
Sutton-Spence, Rachel & Bencie Woll. 1999. *The linguistics of British Sign Language*. Cambridge: Cambridge University Press.
Szigeti, Imre. 2002. *Nominalisierungen und Argumentvererbung im Deutschen und Ungarischen*. Tübingen: Max Niemeyer.
Szymanek, Bogdan. 1993. *Introduction to Morphological Analysis*. Warszawa: Wyd. Naukowe PWN: [00/ET 310 S999]
Szymanek, Bogdan. 2005. "Remarks to Polish Compounding". *CompoNet*, available at http://componet.sslmit.unibo.it/.
Taft, Marcus. 2003. "Morphological Representation as a Correlation Between Form and Meaning". *Reading Complex Words: Cross-language studies* ed. by Egbert M. H. Assink & Dominiek Sandra, 113–137. Amsterdam: Kluwer Academic.
Taft, Marcus & Kenneth Forster. 1976. "Lexical Storage and Retrieval of Polymorphemic and Polysyllabic Words". *Journal of Verbal Learning and Verbal Behavior* 15.607–620.
Taylor, John R. 2002. *Cognitive grammar*. Oxford: Oxford University Press.
Ten Hacken, Pius. 2000. "Derivation and Compounding". *Morphology* 2000. 349–359.
Thompson, Laurence C. 1987. *A Vietnamese Reference Grammar*. Honolulu: University of Hawai'i Press.
Thornton, Anna M. 2005. *Morfologia*. Roma: Carocci.
Thornton, Anna M. 2007. "Phénomènes de réduction en italien". *Des sons et des sens. Données et modèles en phonologie et en morphologie* ed. by Elizabeth Delais-Roussarie et Laurence Labrune, 241–268. Paris: Hermès Lavoisier.
Timušev, Dmitri A., ed.1971. *Obrazcy komi-zyrjanskoj reči*. Syktyvkar: Akademija Nauk SSSR.
Tollemache, Federigo. 1945. *Le parole composte nella lingua italiana*. Roma: Rores.
Tomasello, Michael. 2003. *Constructing a Language: A Usage-Based Theory of Language Acquisition*. Cambridge: Harvard University Press.
Townsend, Charles E. 1980. *Russian Word Formation*. Columbus, Ohio: Slavica Publishers.
Trillos Amaya, Maria. 1999. *Damana*. München & Newcastle: Lincom Europa.
Tuggy, David. 2007. "Schematicity". *The Oxford Handbook of Cognitive Linguistics* ed. by Dirk Geeraerts & Hubert Cuyckens, 82–116. Oxford: Oxford University Press.
van den Heuvel, Wilco. 2006. *Biak. Description of an Austronesian language of Papua*. Utrecht: LOT.
Vanderwende, Lucy. 1994. "Algorithm for Automatic Interpretation of Noun Sequences". *Proceedings of the 15th conference on Computational linguistics, Kyoto, Japan*, 782–788. Kyoto: Association for Computational Linguistics.
Varela, Soledad. 1990a. *Fundamentos de morfología*. Madrid: Sintesis.
Varela, Soledad. 1990b. "Composición nominal y estructura temática". *Revista española de lingüística* 20.55–81.
Veenstra, Tonjes. 2006. "Modeling Creole Genesis: Headedness in morphology". *Structure and Variation in Language Contact* ed. by Ana Deumert & Stephanie Durrleman (eds.) *Structure and Variation in Language Contact*. 61–83.Amsterdam & Philadelphia: John Benjamins.

Vermeerbergen, Myriam, Lorraine Leeson & Onno Crasborn. 2007. *Simultaneity in Signed Languages: Form and function*. Amsterdam & Philadelphia: John Benjamins.

Vigário, Marina. 2003. *The Prosodic Word in European Portuguese*. Berlin & New York: Mouton de Gruyter.

Vigário, Marina. 2008. "Prosodic Structure between the Prosodic Word and the Phonological Phrase: Recursive nodes or an independent domain?" Manuscript, University of Lisbon.

Villoing, Florence. 2009. "Les mots composés VN". *Aperçus de morphologie du français* ed. by Bernard Fradin, Françoise Kerleroux & Marc Plénat, 175–197. Saint-Denis: Presses Universitaires de Vincennes.

Vogel, Irene. 2008. "Universals of Prosodic Structure". Scalise, Magni & Bisetto, eds. 2008.59–82

Vogel, Irene. 2009. "The Status of the Clitic Group". *Phonological Domains: Universals and deviations* ed. by Janet Grijzenhout & Bariş Kabak, 15–46. Berlin & New York: Mouton de Gruyter.

Vogel, Irene & Donna Jo Napoli. 1995. "The Verbal Component in Italian Compounds". *Contemporary Research in Romance Linguistics: Papers from the 22nd linguistics symposium on Romance languages* ed. by Jon Amastae, Grant Goodall, Mario Montalbetti & Marianne Phinney, 367–381. Amsterdam & Philadelphia: John Benjamins.

Vogel, Irene & Eric Raimy. 2002. "The Acquisition of Compound vs. Phrasal Stress: The role of prosodic constituents". *Journal of Child Language* 29.225–250.

Vollmann, Ralf & Sabine Bruyère. 1995. "Über den Erwerb mentaler Operationen am Beispiel der Possession: eine Korpusanalyse". *Grazer Linguistische Studien* 43.117–131.

Wälchli, Bernhard. 2005. *Co-compounds and Natural Coordination*. Oxford: Oxford University Press.

Wälchli, Bernhard. 2007a. "Lexical Classes: A functional approach to 'word formation'". *New Challenges in Typology: Broadening the horizons and redefining the foundations* ed. by Matti Miestamo & Bernhard Wälchli. 153–175. Berlin & New York: Mouton de Gruyter.

Wälchli, Bernhard. 2007b. "Ko-Komposita (im Vergleich mit Parallelismus und Reduplikation)." *Wiederholung, Parallelismus, Reduplikation. Strategien der multiplen Strukturanwendung* ed. by Andreas Ammann & Aina Urdze (Diversitas Linguarum 16). 81–107. Bochum: Norbert Brockmeyer.

Wälchli, Bernhard. 2009. "Data Reduction Typology and the Bimodal Distribution Bias". *Linguistic Typology* 13.77–94.

Warren, Beatrice. 1978. *Semantic Patterns of Noun-Noun Compounds*. Gothenburg Studies in English 41, Göteborg: Acta Universtatis Gothoburgensis.

Westermann, Gert & Kim Plunkett. 2007. "Connectionist Models of Inflection Processing". *Psycho-computational Issues in Morphology Processing and Learning* ed. by V. Pirrelli, *Lingue e Linguaggio* 2.291–311.

Whitney, William. 1889. *Sanskrit Grammar*. Leipzig: Breitkopf & Härtel.

Wiese, Richard. 1996. *The Phonology of German*. Oxford: Clarendon Press.

Williams, Edwin. 1981. "On the Notions 'Lexically Related' and 'Head of a Word'". *Linguistic Inquiry* 12.245–274.

Williams, Edwin. 1981. "Argument Structure and Morphology". *Linguistic Review* 1.81–114.

Williams, Edwin. 2007. "Dumping Lexicalism". *The Oxford handbook of Linguistic Interfaces* ed. by Charles Reiss & Gillian Ramchand, 353–381. Oxford: Oxford University Press.

Wilmanns, Wilhelm. 1896. *Deutsche Grammatik*. Abt. 2. Strassburg: Karl J. Trübner.

Wisniewski, Edward J. 1996. "Construal and Similarity in Conceptual Combination". *Journal of Memory and Language* 35:3.434–453.

Wisniewski, Edward J. 1997. "When Concepts Combine". *Psychonomic Bulletin & Review* 4. 167–183.

Wood, Simon. 2006. *Generalized Additive Models*. New York: Chapman & Hall/CRC.

Wurzel, Wolfgang U. 1996. "Morphologischer Strukturwandel: Typologische Entwicklungen im Deutschen". *Deutsch – typologisch* ed. by Ewald Lang & Gisela Zifonun, 492–524. Berlin/New York: Walter de Gruyter.

Wurzel Wolfgang U. 1998. "On the Development of Incorporating Structures in German". *Historical Linguistics 1995* ed. by Richard M. Hogg & Linda van Bergen, vol. II, 331–344. Amsterdam & Philadelphia: John Benjamins.

Xanthos, Aris, Sabine Laaha, Steven Gillis, Ursula Stephany, Ayhan Aksu-Koç, Anastasia Christofidou, Natalia Gagarina, Gordana Hrzica, Nihan Ketrez, Marianne Kilani-Schoch, Katharina Korecky-Kröll, Melita Kovačević, Klaus Laalo, Marijan Palmović, Barbara Pfeiler, Maria D. Voeikova & Wolfgang U. Dressler. 2008. "On the Role of Morphological Richness in the Early Development of Noun and Verb Inflection". Manuscript, Université de Lausanne.

Yip, Moira. 1978. "The Integrity of Lexical Nodes", Unpublished MIT manuscript.

Zemskaja, Elena. 1992. *Slovoobrazovanie kak dejatel'nost'*. Moskva: Nauka.

Zeshan, Ulrike. 2000. *Sign language in Indo-Pakistan: A description of a signed language*. Amsterdam & Philadelphia: John Benjamins.

Zuffi, Stefano. 1981. "The Nominal Composition in Italian. Topics in generative morphology". *Journal of Italian linguistics* 6:2.1–54.

Zwicky, Arnold. 1985. "Heads". *Journal of Linguistics* 21.1–29.

Language index

A
Aivaliot 69, 346
Akan 148
Apache 170
Arapesh 179
Armenian 81, 192, 195, 196
Arrerernte 146
Auslan 304

B
Babungo 171
Bambara 84
Basque 192, 194, 196
Bella Coola 101
Biak 101
Bulgarian 116, 345
Burmese 184
Burushaski 174

C
Catalan 84, 116, 345
Central Alaskan Yup'ik 13, 37, 38, 40
Chantyal 173
Chinantec 180
Chinese (see Mandarin Chinese)
Corfiot 69, 72
Cretan 69–72
Crow 130, 146, 305
Czech 206, 210, 342, 345

D
Dagbani 15, 147
Damana 171, 172
Danish 81, 267
Dutch 15, 17, 24, 88, 89, 93–98, 103–106, 116, 147–149, 153, 157–160, 192, 204–207, 257, 258, 262, 265, 267, 270, 337, 342, 345

E
English 5, 15, 17, 23, 25, 29, 31–35, 42, 45, 59, 61, 82, 87, 94, 95, 102, 103, 106, 107, 111, 116, 119, 120, 123, 127–131, 140, 141, 146–150, 152, 153, 155, 156, 158–160, 167–170, 172, 173, 177, 183, 185, 187, 190, 192, 193, 195, 196, 200–202, 216, 219, 225, 257, 258, 260, 263–265, 267, 270, 273, 274, 279, 280, 287, 292, 300, 303, 305, 309, 320, 323, 339, 340, 342, 345
    American English 120, 131, 141, 183
    Indian English 120, 183, 192
Erźa 179, 180

F
Fijian 15, 146, 158
Finnish 90, 116, 170, 268
French 81, 82, 87, 103, 116, 119, 140, 170, 179, 187, 192, 193, 209, 220, 305, 308, 309, 320, 323

G
Georgian 146
German 16, 17, 59, 81, 95, 98, 116, 161, 162, 173, 192, 206, 219–222, 224, 225, 233, 234, 267, 273, 275, 323–327, 335–338, 340, 342, 343, 346
Greek 5, 10, 14, 57, 59–73, 81, 89, 95, 116, 119, 180, 193, 195, 196, 216, 220, 235, 339, 345–347
    Ancient Greek 59, 61, 63, 195, 216, 345
    Modern Greek 14, 57, 59, 60, 63, 70, 71, 73, 95, 116, 180, 193, 195, 196

H
Hausa 15, 147, 148
Hebrew 305, 308, 311, 321–323, 338, 342

Hellenistic koine 60
Hmong 180, 184
Hungarian 116, 146, 147, 193, 341

I
Indonesian 299
Iroquoian 38
Italian 2, 6, 9, 15, 16, 82, 84, 86, 88, 90, 91, 94, 99, 100, 110, 114, 116, 119, 121–123, 146, 151, 156, 171, 174, 187–189, 191–193, 199, 200, 206, 212–214, 216, 217, 219, 237–240, 242, 244–246, 248, 251–254, 272–274, 282, 283, 285, 339, 346

J
Japanese 39, 82, 100, 102, 116, 118, 124, 171, 184, 185, 194, 197, 274, 305, 346
Jarawara 146

K
Kapampangan 13, 14, 37–39, 41–45, 48, 50–55
Karen 180
Kayardild 174
Khalkha Mongolian 184
Khasi 180, 181
Khmer 172, 173, 184, 185, 188, 193
Koasati 170
Komi 179
Korean 116, 171, 173, 184, 185, 275

L
Lahu 184
Latin 10, 59, 103, 116, 119, 214, 216, 220, 305, 346
Lesbian 69, 346
Lezgian 173, 174

M
Maale 99
Malayalam 194
Maltese 192

Mandarin Chinese 9, 82, 100, 101, 116-118, 123, 155, 158, 172, 177, 178, 183-186, 193, 195, 196, 274, 299, 305
Maori 100
Marathi 147, 194, 196
Mari 178
Mixe 180
Mohawk 13, 14, 37, 38, 40, 42–47, 49–56, 62, 101
Mongolian (see Khalkha Mongolian)
Moschonisiot 69, 346
Muinane 84

N
Natchez 170

O
Old Uyghur 173

P
Pāli 194, 196
Peloponnesian 69, 72
Persian 81
Polish 116, 123, 210, 245, 347
Portuguese 15, 34, 89, 116, 151, 152, 157, 161, 345

R
Russian 81, 84, 116, 146, 187, 192, 208, 210–212, 214, 347

S
Salishan 101
Sanskrit 100, 169, 173, 177, 178, 305, 306
Saramaccan 13, 21, 33–35
Seediq 174
Sign language VII, 13, 17, 178, 301–307, 310, 315, 319, 320, 322
  Al-Sayyid Bedouin Sign language 17, 301, 302, 304, 307
  American Sign language 17, 178, 301, 303, 304, 319
  Australian Sign language
  British Sign language 304
  Indo-Pakistani Sign language 304
  Israeli Sign language 303, 304
  New Zeeland Sign language
Slave 101
Spanish 100, 102, 112, 114, 116, 119, 121–123, 140, 178, 193, 249, 254, 348
Spokane 101, 102

Standard Average European 16, 177, 178, 187
Swahili 172
Swedish 24, 30–32, 95, 98, 116, 148, 275, 323, 330, 336–338, 342

T
Thai 184
Tibetan 184, 186
Tok Pisin 120, 179, 192
Turkana 170, 172, 174
Turkish 9, 116, 146, 153, 341
Tuva 184

V
Vietnamese 100, 123, 172, 179, 182, 184, 185, 305

W
Wakashan 101
Welsh 85
White Hmong 184

Y
Yimas 146
Yup'ik 13, 14, 37, 38, 40–44, 46, 47, 49–56, 101

Subject index

A
abstractness, degree of 95, 106, 107
affixoid 58, 60, 69, 96, 103
allomorphy 5, 93, 104-105, 201, 240, 245
amalgams 327, 341
analogy 78, 89, 93, 106, 251, 284, 326
argument structure 38, 42, 44, 55, 100, 113, 202, 219, 223, 225-227, 229, 231
assimilation 82, 142, 304, 315, 316

B
backderivation 224, 231
backformation 26
bare-stem constraint 64-66, 68
binarity 323, 343
Binary Branching Hypothesis 202
binomial interpolation 241, 242
binomial(s) 4, 181, 186, 191
bisyllabic (verb)bases 244, 245, 246, 254
bracketing paradox 201, 206, 214, 215, 216, 223, 231

C
category changing affix 59, 201, 203, 208, 209, 217
child speech 324, 331, 337
child-directed speech 324, 335
class type 180, 182, 183
cline 72, 103, 342
competition between syntax and morphology 24, 29, 203, 217
compound, compounding
adjectival (V-N) 61, 98, 238-9, 246, 248-250, 252-254
Adjective-Noun 209, 327-335
agentive 327
appositional 172, 179
atypical 157, 160
attributive 7, 92, 100, 117, 140, 185, 188, 191, 193, 195-196, 282, 283
bahuvrihi 68, 169, 170, 207-210, 217
co-compound 16, 120-122, 124, 125, 172, 173, 177-178, 1190, 192-197
coordinate 7, 9, 16, 92, 97, 117, 120, 121, 124, 125, 135, 140, 172, 173, 177, 178, 179, 185-197, 206, 305, 306, 316, 323, 329
deictic 288
dvandva 61, 65, 121, 124, 172, 177, 178, 180, 183, 305, 306, 311, 320
endocentric 9, 10, 14, 18, 41, 42, 54, 91, 125, 130, 140, 141, 167, 172, 173, 174, 187, 190, 191, 216, 287, 288, 304, 305, 318, 319, 323, 325, 329, 343
exocentric 1, 6, 8-10, 15, 18, 68, 99, 109, 120-125, 130, 140, 141, 167, 168-175, 186, 190, 191, 200, 207, 213, 215, 216, 237, 305, 316, 319, 323, 329
hyperonymic 177 FF.
hyponymic 16, 41, 53, 111, 120, 167, 173, 177-178, 186-188, 190-197
interfixed 330, 335, 336, 339, 344
karmadhāraya 193, 196
left branching 153, 276, 277, 278
lexicalized 80, 84-86, 145, 149, 163, 183, 237, 247, 252, 253, 280, 284, 291, 303, 304, 309, 311, 320, 324
metaphorical 169, 173-174
metonymical 121
neoclassical 7, 59, 61, 82-83, 119, 155, 156
nominal 61, 67, 68, 105, 118, 123, 173, 188, 197, 201, 208, 211, 216, 224, 225, 231, 238, 239, 246, 248-250, 335, 341
non affixal (de)verbal 15, 127, 128, 129-136, 138-141
novel 282, 288, 290-291, 309, 326
Noun-Noun 42, 101, 105, 107, 178, 184, 196, 263, 271-285, 287, 291, 323-326, 327-335, 342, 343
Noun-Verb 24-26, 28, 32, 33
parasynthetic 16, 199-217
particle-verb 30-32, 35, 104-105
phrasal 7, 80, 86, 341,
place name 319, 320
preposition-noun 213, 214, 326, 327-335
possessive 340
recursive 327, 330, 341, 343, 344
relational 185, 252, 282, 283
right branching 154, 276, 277
root 5, 10, 21, 24, 26, 28-32, 35, 82, 87, 89, 92, 127, 128, 130, 135, 140, 203, 204, 208, 209, 211, 212, 214
SASS 316-320
sequential 303, 307
simultaneous 301, 303, 306
subordinate 7, 8, 18, 117, 120, 140-141, 177-179, 183, 188, 191, 206, 323, 325, 329, 343
synthetic 15, 16, 21, 23-30, 32-35, 41, 54, 61, 69, 99, 127-132, 135-141, 169, 170, 171, 199-205, 208, 212, 216, 217, 219-222, 225, 226, 227, 228, 229, 230, 231-235, 280, 340
transpositional 169, 171, 172
Verb-Noun 237-254, 326, 328-335

Verb-Noun Phrase 86, 90, 253
Verb-Verb 9, 11, 12, 23, 61, 65, 171, 181, 184, 197
compound classification 7, 13, 92, 116, 129, 140, 173, 179, 250, 279, 280, 285
compound development 328-331
compound elicitation 308
compound identification 273-276
compound interpretation 3, 7, 15, 17, 26, 42, 85, 107, 127-132, 135-141, 171, 173, 185, 188, 189, 194, 195, 213, 270, 272-274, 276, 278-282, 284, 285, 287, 288, 290-297, 338
compound(ing) marker 62, 63, 64, 66, 67, 68, 89, 115, 181, 196, 206
compound parsing 272-274, 276, 278
compound-specific stress rule 62, 63
compound splitting 275
compound stress 5, 6, 15, 50, 51, 62, 63, 66, 84, 106, 107, 146, 148, 149, 150-157, 159, 270, 271, 274, 309, 337
compounding and derivation 5, 13, 14, 57-73, 95, 101-104
Composite Group 145, 152, 153, 163
compositional semantics 54, 55, 204, 208, 209, 216
compositionality (week/strong) 3, 284
concept combination 272, 278
conceptual information 295
conceptual knowledge 288, 294, 296, 297, 300
confix 59
conflation 204, 205, 207, 232, 234, 235
constraint
  asymmetrical 282
  bare-stem 63-66, 68
  blocking 66-68
  grammatical 279
  head movement 22
  Lexical Integrity 14, 37, 48, 50 , 54, 55
  morphological 60, 238

non-redundancy 207
No-phrase 14, 37, 38, 45, 50, 55
paradigmatic 285
phonological 119, 238, 244
phonotactic 146
pragmatic 189, 205, 206
syntactic 243
construction morphology 4, 14, 16, 58, 78, 93, 100, 199, 200, 204, 213, 219, 232, 235
constructional idiom 96, 99, 100, 102, 103, 107, 204, 205
conventionalization 17, 53, 301, 308, 309, 312, 313, 315, 319-321
conversion 57, 67, 68, 124, 128-130, 132-134, 139, 207, 240, 248, 249
coordination 7, 16, 65, 97, 142, 172, 177-179, 181-186, 188-197, 250, 252, 295, 297
  accidental 179, 190, 191
  adversative 188, 197
  conjunctive 7, 185, 187-190, 192, 195
  disjunctive 185, 186, 188
  loose 190
  hyperonymic 177-178, 185, 188, 190-192, 195-197
  hyponymic 186 FF.
  natural 179, 181-183, 185, 190, 191, 194, 196
  tight 190
creolisation 33

D
derivation 13, 14, 30, 32, 35, 40, 46, 52, 57-69, 72, 73, 77, 85, 86, 95, 101, 131, 143, 200, 201, 204, 206, 207, 221, 223-225, 231, 239, 240, 242, 243, 244, 245, 339
derivational affix 61, 63, 64, 66, 95, 103, 130, 206-209, 211-213, 215, 216, 240, 242, 243
derivational suffix 16, 60, 62, 64, 65, 67, 101, 103, 199, 200, 202, 207, 208, 210, 212, 215, 239, 241
derived stem 43, 54
diachrony 15, 68, 93, 182
dialect 14, 57, 60, 65, 69-73, 148, 187, 308
diminutive formation 66, 323, 324, 326

Distributed Morphology 4, 15, 24, 125, 134

E
emergence of compounds 284, 323, 324, 334, 335, 341, 342, 343, 344
entrenchment 232-235, 238, 242, 249, 284
event/ive nouns 133, 240, 241, 242, 250
exocentricity 1, 8-10, 15, 109, 120, 123, 167, 174, 319
expansion 59
extrinsic order 66, 68

F
family size 17, 95, 257-259, 262, 263, 264, 265, 268, 269, 331
features 113
  categorial 123-124
  morphological 122-123
  semantic 120-122
frequency 8-10, 17, 32, 51, 52, 131, 182-184, 192, 232-234, 238-243, 249-250, 257-260, 262, 264, 265, 267-270, 272, 275, 278, 284, 289, 290, 297, 298, 323, 330-335, 344
frequency spectrum 242, 250

G
gapping 97, 161-163
grammar-lexicon divide 284
grammaticalization 72, 103, 301, 308, 319

H
hapax(es) 180, 237, 238-247, 250-254
head 2, 5-10, 14, 15, 16, 17, 21-24, 30, 31, 34, 35, 41, 42, 45, 56, 59, 70, 80, 89, 91, 92, 98-101, 106, 107, 109-125, 130, 133, 135, 138-140, 149, 157, 167, 169, 170, 172-174, 181, 189, 193, 201-204, 209, 213-215, 217, 219-223, 225, 227, 231, 248, 252, 257-260, 262-265, 267-271, 273, 277-283, 289-291, 293-299, 304, 305, 308, 316, 318-320, 338, 340, 343
  categorial 113, 116, 124, 125, 189
  morphological 8, 124, 125

movement 21-23, 47, 222
multiple 109, 120
semantic 113, 116, 121-125, 189, 213
headedness 1, 8, 15, 30, 93, 95, 99, 109, 114, 117, 119, 121, 125, 172, 204, 214, 305, 319, 324, 340, 343
hierarchical lexicon 95, 98, 99, 107
hyponymy 120, 167, 173

I
idiom 4, 25, 96, 99, 100, 102, 103, 107, 122, 204, 205, 232
inalienable possession 210
incorporation 4, 13, 22, 37-40, 42, 44, 45, 51-53, 55, 56, 180, 221-224, 227, 230, 231, 235
inflection 1, 6, 18, 23, 62, 64, 84, 89, 112, 172, 180, 181, 207, 224, 323, 324, 326, 341
 in compounding
 inflection class 68, 91, 92, 124, 125, 133, 245
inflectional ending 59, 62-64
inheritance 25, 33, 202, 222, 223, 225, 226, 228
input frequency 323, 335
institutionalization 53, 54
instrument 41, 123, 130, 212, 238, 241, 242, 250, 251, 339 123
intensifying function 69, 70, 72
interfix 270, 324-325, 327-330, 335-340, 342-344
IS A Condition 111

L
language acquisition ix, 13, 17, 272, 323, 325, 326
lexeme 5, 6, 15, 58, 59, 69, 71, 72, 77, 78, 80-82, 85-92, 95, 96, 97, 102-107, 119, 179, 184, 186, 200, 203, 206, 208, 211, 215, 216, 239, 252
lexical affix 101, 102
lexical blocking 232, 234
lexical category 1, 6, 10, 29, 41, 79, 95, 97, 110-112, 124, 125, 191, 222, 305
lexical decision 17, 257-260, 262 - 265, 267, 268, 270, 291, 292
Lexical Integrity Hypothesis 14, 37, 38, 48, 55

lexicalization 16, 53, 54, 99, 103, 114, 149, 237, 238, 245, 253, 254, 308, 319
Lexicalized Interpretation Schema 282
lexical similarity 281
linker 39, 40, 44, 45, 48, 51, 55, 56
linking element 5, 6, 18, 62, 88, 24, 62, 70, 88, 96, 98, 102, 106, 107, 115, 116, 117, 120, 145, 149, 163, 206, 207, 223, 224, 323-325
locations 41, 130, 213, 238, 250, 278, 296, 302, 304, 306

M
mapping principle 29-32, 35, 159
metonymy 10, 121, 122, 125, 174, 185
modality 38, 301-303
mode 17, 313-315
Morbo Comp Corpus/Project 8, 15, 116, 117, 125, 129, 131
morpheme order 340, 344
morphological information 112, 125, 295
morphological merger 203, 205, 209, 213, 216, 217
morphological module 4, 21
morphological richness 341
morphological role 293
morphological schema 101, 102 106
morphological word 84, 85
morphologization 72
morphology
 core 326, 330, 336, 344
 modularized 326
 premorphology 325, 344
 protomorphology 325, 326, 336, 341, 344
morphology-syntax competition 203, 207, 209, 217, 341

N
naming force 254
natural language processing 272
Natural Morphology 343, 344
neologism 52, 54, 70, 324, 330, 339
new formation 54, 251
new language 302, 307, 309, 312, 317, 320
nominalization 29-34, 124, 134

No Phrase Constraint (see constraint)
noun incorporation 13, 22, 37, 38, 42, 51-53, 55, 56

O
object-oriented 128-130, 132, 135, 138, 139, 141-144
P
parasynthesis 199-201, 204, 206, 212, 219
parsing 268, 272-276, 278, 279, 285
particle verbs 30-32, 35, 104, 105
pause 50, 51, 55
percolation 111-114, 120
permanent lexicon 58
phonological attrition 71
phonological law 71
Phonological Phrase 145, 149-152, 163
phonological reduction 315
phonological rules 81, 89, 146, 147
Phonological Word 15, 32, 83, 145, 146, 150, 152, 159, 163, 180, 195
phrasal derivation 31, 32, 35
phrasal stress 148, 150, 152-155
phrases vs. compounds 337
polysemy 103, 238
prefixation 59, 61, 72, 91, 115
prefixoid 72, 96, 97, 102
prepositional-object oriented 132, 139, 144
priming 290, 292-296, 299
Principle of Coindexation 133, 135, 137, 138
probabilistic knowledge 285
productivity 18, 51-55, 71, 103, 128, 188, 191, 192, 202, 205, 217, 234, 240-243, 246, 250, 251, 262, 271, 282, 284, 306, 323, 326, 335, 336, 342, 344
prosodic structure 15, 150, 160, 161
pseudo-affix 58

Q
quantifier 46, 169

R

recursion/recursivity 145, 149-152, 151, 157-159, 161, 163, 271-272, 276, 327, 330, 340-343, 344
relation availability 17, 287, 288, 290-293, 296, 299
relational adjectives 214, 242, 250-253
relational information 289, 293, 294, 298-299
relational interpretation 297-299
relational similarity 281, 282
relational structure 288-289, 294
relisting 132, 133
restrictions 29, 59, 72, 137, 162, 177, 197, 204, 208, 223, 226-227, 229, 237, 238, 243-247, 296, 299
  categorial 72
  phonological 237, 244-245
  morphological 237, 245-246
  selectional 226, 247
  syntactic 243
Right Hand Head Rule 8, 99, 115

S

Scalise-Bisetto classification 7, 140
selectional features 112
selectional restriction 226, 247
semantic concentration 98
semantic-encyclopedic information 295, 297
semantic role 42, 43 226-229, 231
semi-affix 58, 103
semi-word 10, 58
Separation Hypothesis 29, 224
sign language vii,13, 17, 301-308, 310, 315-322
skeleton 132-134, 136-139
Sprachbund 184, 192

split morphology 224
stem 5, 6, 15, 16, 23, 38, 40, 41, 43, 45, 46, 47, 51-57, 58FN2, 59, 60, 62-69, 78, 80-82, 87, 88, 96, 104, 119, 123, 155-158, 199, 200, 205, 206, 207, 209, 211, 212, 216, 217, 240FN4, 245, 246, 338, 342
stratum 61, 185
stress 5, 6, 15, 24FN 5, 37, 50, 51, 61FN7-63, 66, 70FN22, 84, 106, 107, 146, 148-157, 159, 161-163, 225FN4, 270, 271, 274FN2, 309, 337
subject-oriented 99, 127, 129-132, 135-139, 141, 144
sublexical reference 48, 50
subschemas 14, 93, 100-105
suffix 9, 16, 28, 30, 33, 40, 41, 51, 54, 62, 65, 67, 68, 86, 87, 102, 103, 123, 136, 147, 156-158, 161, 170, 199-203, 205-216, 240, 241, 262, 324, 327, 329, 336, 341
suffixoid 58
syntactic function 24, 226, 227, 229, 341
syntactic merger 28, 203, 204, 209, 216, 217
syntactic module 24
synthesis 204, 208, 216, 219-221

T

thematic vowel 63, 338
theta-role saturation 67
token frequency 17, 232-234, 240, 241, 249, 257, 269, 330-335
tokenization 274
tone 15, 33, 37, 84, 146, 148, 163, 180
transparency 18, 83, 222, 270, 323, 338, 339, 343
  government transparency corollary 222

morphosemantic 18, 323, 338, 339, 343
morphotactic 323, 338, 343
semantic 55, 270, 338
transposition 59, 171-173
type frequency 330-335
typology 12, 13, 15, 85, 167, 168, 174, 178, 182, 184, 302, 341

U

Unitary Output Hypothesis 237, 238, 248, 249, 251, 254
universals 342-343
Universal Grammar 157, 163, 342

V

variability 309, 315, 319, 340
vocabulary growth curve 241

W

weak compositionality 284
word 4-6, 50-51, 78, 83 ff., 150
word-based morphology 77, 78, 82, 86, 87, 89, 92
word formation 14, 16, 50, 53, 55, 57, 58, 59, 60, 61, 69, 93-95, 101, 106, 153, 168, 184, 201, 202, 204, 205, 212, 219-221, 224, 228, 232, 234, 235, 237, 240, 248, 254, 272, 301, 302, 306, 307, 320
word form 82, 87, 179
word order 34, 182, 233, 319, 320, 340
word order (of head and modifier) 318-319
word-syntax 203

Z

zero affixation 57, 133, 134
zero derivation 35
zero morph 170

CURRENT ISSUES IN LINGUISTIC THEORY

E. F. K. Koerner, Editor

Zentrum für Allgemeine Sprachwissenschaft, Typologie
und Universalienforschung, Berlin
efk.koerner@rz.hu-berlin.de

Current Issues in Linguistic Theory (CILT) is a theory-oriented series which welcomes contributions from scholars who have significant proposals to make towards the advancement of our understanding of language, its structure, functioning and development. CILT has been established in order to provide a forum for the presentation and discussion of linguistic opinions of scholars who do not necessarily accept the prevailing mode of thought in linguistic science. It offers an outlet for meaningful contributions to the current linguistic debate, and furnishes the diversity of opinion which a healthy discipline must have. A complete list of titles in this series can be found on the publishers' website, *www.benjamins.com*

312 **OPERSTEIN, Natalie:** Consonant Structure and Prevocalization. 2010. x, 234 pp.
311 **SCALISE, Sergio and Irene VOGEL (eds.):** Cross-Disciplinary Issues in Compounding. viii, 382 pp. Expected April 2010
310 **RAINER, Franz, Wolfgang U. DRESSLER, Dieter KASTOVSKY and Hans Christian LUSCHÜTZKY (eds.):** Variation and Change in Morphology. Selected papers from the 13th International Morphology Meeting, Vienna, February 2008. With the assistance of Elisabeth Peters. 2010. vii, 249 pp.
309 **NICOLOV, Nicolas, Galia ANGELOVA and Ruslan MITKOV (eds.):** Recent Advances in Natural Language Processing V. Selected papers from RANLP 2007. 2009. x, 338 pp.
308 **DUFRESNE, Monique, Fernande DUPUIS and Etleva VOCAJ (eds.):** Historical Linguistics 2007. Selected papers from the 18th International Conference on Historical Linguistics, Montreal, 6–11 August 2007. 2009. x, 311 pp.
307 **CALABRESE, Andrea and W. Leo WETZELS (eds.):** Loan Phonology. 2009. vii, 273 pp.
306 **VIGÁRIO, Marina, Sónia FROTA and M. João FREITAS (eds.):** Phonetics and Phonology. Interactions and interrelations. 2009. vi, 290 pp.
305 **BUBENIK, Vit, John HEWSON and Sarah ROSE (eds.):** Grammatical Change in Indo-European Languages. Papers presented at the workshop on Indo-European Linguistics at the XVIIIth International Conference on Historical Linguistics, Montreal, 2007. 2009. xx, 262 pp.
304 **MASULLO, Pascual José, Erin O'ROURKE and Chia-Hui HUANG (eds.):** Romance Linguistics 2007. Selected papers from the 37th Linguistic Symposium on Romance Languages (LSRL), Pittsburgh, 15–18 March 2007. 2009. vii, 361 pp.
303 **TORCK, Danièle and W. Leo WETZELS (eds.):** Romance Languages and Linguistic Theory 2006. Selected papers from 'Going Romance', Amsterdam, 7–9 December 2006. 2009. viii, 262 pp.
302 **FERRARESI, Gisella and Maria GOLDBACH (eds.):** Principles of Syntactic Reconstruction. 2008. xvii, 219 pp.
301 **PARKINSON, Dilworth B. (ed.):** Perspectives on Arabic Linguistics. Papers from the annual symposium on Arabic linguistics. Volume XXI: Provo, Utah, March 2007. 2008. x, 206 pp.
300 **VAJDA, Edward J. (ed.):** Subordination and Coordination Strategies in North Asian Languages. 2008. xii, 218 pp.
299 **GONZÁLEZ-DÍAZ, Victorina:** English Adjective Comparison. A historical perspective. 2008. xix, 252 pp.
298 **BOWERN, Claire, Bethwyn EVANS and Luisa MICELI (eds.):** Morphology and Language History. In honour of Harold Koch. 2008. x, 364 pp.
297 **DOSSENA, Marina, Richard DURY and Maurizio GOTTI (eds.):** English Historical Linguistics 2006. Selected papers from the fourteenth International Conference on English Historical Linguistics (ICEHL 14), Bergamo, 21–25 August 2006. Volume III: Geo-Historical Variation in English. 2008. xiii, 197 pp.
296 **DURY, Richard, Maurizio GOTTI and Marina DOSSENA (eds.):** English Historical Linguistics 2006. Selected papers from the fourteenth International Conference on English Historical Linguistics (ICEHL 14), Bergamo, 21–25 August 2006. Volume II: Lexical and Semantic Change. 2008. xiii, 264 pp.
295 **GOTTI, Maurizio, Marina DOSSENA and Richard DURY (eds.):** English Historical Linguistics 2006. Selected papers from the fourteenth International Conference on English Historical Linguistics (ICEHL 14), Bergamo, 21–25 August 2006. Volume I: Syntax and Morphology. 2008. xiv, 259 pp.
294 **FRELLESVIG, Bjarke and John WHITMAN (eds.):** Proto-Japanese. Issues and Prospects. 2008. vii, 229 pp.
293 **DETGES, Ulrich and Richard WALTEREIT (eds.):** The Paradox of Grammatical Change. Perspectives from Romance. 2008. vi, 252 pp.

292 NICOLOV, Nicolas, Kalina BONTCHEVA, Galia ANGELOVA and Ruslan MITKOV (eds.): Recent Advances in Natural Language Processing IV. Selected papers from RANLP 2005. 2007. xii, 307 pp.
291 BAAUW, Sergio, Frank DRIJKONINGEN and Manuela PINTO (eds.): Romance Languages and Linguistic Theory 2005. Selected papers from 'Going Romance', Utrecht, 8–10 December 2005. 2007. viii, 338 pp.
290 MUGHAZY, Mustafa A. (ed.): Perspectives on Arabic Linguistics. Papers from the annual symposium on Arabic linguistics. Volume XX: Kalamazoo, Michigan, March 2006. 2007. xii, 247 pp.
289 BENMAMOUN, Elabbas (ed.): Perspectives on Arabic Linguistics. Papers from the annual symposium on Arabic Linguistics. Volume XIX: Urbana, Illinois, April 2005. 2007. xiv, 304 pp.
288 TOIVONEN, Ida and Diane NELSON (eds.): Saami Linguistics. 2007. viii, 321 pp.
287 CAMACHO, José, Nydia FLORES-FERRÁN, Liliana SÁNCHEZ, Viviane DÉPREZ and María José CABRERA (eds.): Romance Linguistics 2006. Selected papers from the 36th Linguistic Symposium on Romance Languages (LSRL), New Brunswick, March-April 2006. 2007. viii, 340 pp.
286 WEIJER, Jeroen van de and Erik Jan van der TORRE (eds.): Voicing in Dutch. (De)voicing – phonology, phonetics, and psycholinguistics. 2007. x, 186 pp.
285 SACKMANN, Robin (ed.): Explorations in Integrational Linguistics. Four essays on German, French, and Guaraní. 2008. ix, 239 pp.
284 SALMONS, Joseph C. and Shannon DUBENION-SMITH (eds.): Historical Linguistics 2005. Selected papers from the 17th International Conference on Historical Linguistics, Madison, Wisconsin, 31 July - 5 August 2005. 2007. viii, 413 pp.
283 LENKER, Ursula and Anneli MEURMAN-SOLIN (eds.): Connectives in the History of English. 2007. viii, 318 pp.
282 PRIETO, Pilar, Joan MASCARÓ and Maria-Josep SOLÉ (eds.): Segmental and prosodic issues in Romance phonology. 2007. xvi, 262 pp.
281 VERMEERBERGEN, Myriam, Lorraine LEESON and O.A. CRASBORN (eds.): Simultaneity in Signed Languages. Form and function. 2007. viii, 360 pp. (incl. CD-Rom).
280 HEWSON, John and Vit BUBENIK: From Case to Adposition. The development of configurational syntax in Indo-European languages. 2006. xxx, 420 pp.
279 NEDERGAARD THOMSEN, Ole (ed.): Competing Models of Linguistic Change. Evolution and beyond. 2006. vi, 344 pp.
278 DOETJES, Jenny and Paz GONZÁLEZ (eds.): Romance Languages and Linguistic Theory 2004. Selected papers from 'Going Romance', Leiden, 9–11 December 2004. 2006. viii, 320 pp.
277 HELASVUO, Marja-Liisa and Lyle CAMPBELL (eds.): Grammar from the Human Perspective. Case, space and person in Finnish. 2006. x, 280 pp.
276 MONTREUIL, Jean-Pierre Y. (ed.): New Perspectives on Romance Linguistics. Vol. II: Phonetics, Phonology and Dialectology. Selected papers from the 35th Linguistic Symposium on Romance Languages (LSRL), Austin, Texas, February 2005. 2006. x, 213 pp.
275 NISHIDA, Chiyo and Jean-Pierre Y. MONTREUIL (eds.): New Perspectives on Romance Linguistics. Vol. I: Morphology, Syntax, Semantics, and Pragmatics. Selected papers from the 35th Linguistic Symposium on Romance Languages (LSRL), Austin, Texas, February 2005. 2006. xiv, 288 pp.
274 GESS, Randall S. and Deborah ARTEAGA (eds.): Historical Romance Linguistics. Retrospective and perspectives. 2006. viii, 393 pp.
273 FILPPULA, Markku, Juhani KLEMOLA, Marjatta PALANDER and Esa PENTTILÄ (eds.): Dialects Across Borders. Selected papers from the 11th International Conference on Methods in Dialectology (Methods XI), Joensuu, August 2002. 2005. xii, 291 pp.
272 GESS, Randall S. and Edward J. RUBIN (eds.): Theoretical and Experimental Approaches to Romance Linguistics. Selected papers from the 34th Linguistic Symposium on Romance Languages (LSRL), Salt Lake City, March 2004. 2005. viii, 367 pp.
271 BRANNER, David Prager (ed.): The Chinese Rime Tables. Linguistic philosophy and historical-comparative phonology. 2006. viii, 358 pp.
270 GEERTS, Twan, Ivo van GINNEKEN and Haike JACOBS (eds.): Romance Languages and Linguistic Theory 2003. Selected papers from 'Going Romance' 2003, Nijmegen, 20–22 November. 2005. viii, 369 pp.
269 HARGUS, Sharon and Keren RICE (eds.): Athabaskan Prosody. 2005. xii, 432 pp.
268 CRAVENS, Thomas D. (ed.): Variation and Reconstruction. 2006. viii, 223 pp.
267 ALHAWARY, Mohammad T. and Elabbas BENMAMOUN (eds.): Perspectives on Arabic Linguistics. Papers from the annual symposium on Arabic linguistics. Volume XVII–XVIII: Alexandria, 2003 and Norman, Oklahoma 2004. 2005. xvi, 315 pp.
266 BOUDELAA, Sami (ed.): Perspectives on Arabic Linguistics. Papers from the annual symposium on Arabic linguistics. Volume XVI: , Cambridge, March 2002. 2006. xii, 181 pp.